Jady, dear Fri
    Its Fun
how God continues to interweave
things in Koinonia. Remembering K-27
with you and rejoicing in the Lord
this K-62 weekend.

                    Love,
                    Teresa Kinley
                    K-62 Musician

EAGLES' WINGS

EAGLES' WINGS

Daily Devotional Meditations for a Whole Year.

Edited by ALAN CAIRNS

AMBASSADOR

Belfast Northern Ireland Greenville South Carolina

Ambassador Publications
a division of
Ambassador Productions Ltd.
Providence House
16 Hillview Avenue,
Belfast, BT5 6JR
Northern Ireland

Emerald House
1 Chick Springs Road, Suite 203
Greenville,
South Carolina 29609, USA
www.emeraldhouse.com

ISBN 0 907927 73 4

Cover photo by Thomas D. Mangelsen/Images of Nature

PREFACE

The wide acceptance of our first book of daily devotional Bible readings, *Footprints of Faith,* encourages me to hope that this new production will be equally welcomed by God's people.

Eagles' Wings provides a brief meditation on a text of Scripture for each day of the year. At the end of each reading there is a noteworthy saying from a writer or preacher that will afford further food for thought. To complete the usefulness of the book we have printed the much-loved Calendar of Daily Bible Readings, first published by Robert Murray McCheyne.

Here then is a book to keep by your side throughout the year. Prayerfully used, it will lead you to wait upon the Lord and *mount up with wings as eagles* into the spiritual heights of fellowship with God. At least, that is the prayerful desire of all of us who have had a part in producing it.

I owe a deep debt of gratitude to our writers, who took time out of their busy schedules to produce the meditations that will, I trust, be beneficial to all who read them. To my wife, Joan, for her typing of the manuscripts, to Mary Christopher for her invaluable editorial assistance, and to Stephen Christopher for designing the book and preparing it for printing, I am also sincerely grateful. Many hands have touched the publication of this work. Most important, I trust it will have the touch of the hand of God. May He be pleased to use it for His own glory and for the good of His people to a greater extent than we have ever imagined.

Alan Cairns, Editor
September, 1991

Soaring Saints

They shall mount up with wings as eagles.

ISAIAH 40:31

Andrew Murray tells the story of how, on a visit to Switzerland, he saw an eagle that reminded him of many of God's people. It was a "splendid bird, but it was chained to a rock. It had some twenty or thirty feet of chain attached to its legs, and to an iron bolt in the rock. There was the king of birds, meant to soar into heaven, chained down to earth."

God means His people to soar. He has given them the wings of faith to mount up into the heavenlies to enjoy the blessings of His grace in Christ. No eagle can be content to dwell on earth. No Christian can be content to be held in his experience to a life of bondage or spiritual frustration.

How have we entered this new year? Have we come into it on eagles' wings? Or are we chained to earth by fleshly lusts or worldly pursuits? Whatever holds us back from soaring to the actual enjoyment of our blessings in Christ must be confessed as sin and repudiated. We must mount up and live above the world and sin.

This is not to be misunderstood as some sort of perfectionism. Even eagles are not always on the wing. And sometimes their wings are not as strong as at other times. They are still eagles, but they need to renew their strength. Every Christian knows from personal experience the spiritual parallel of this. That is why we must "wait upon the Lord." It is the lack of waiting prayerfully and submissively on the Lord that most chains us to earth. Let us mark this first day of the year by waiting upon the Lord. Let us give Him the time that we have all too often stolen and used in selfish pursuits. Let us do this not merely today, but every day. We will find that our God keeps His Word. He will give us new strength. He will energize our faith. He will cut the chains of earth, and we will soar into the realms of vital godliness on eagles' wings.

—A. C.

Every child of God is born with eagle wings.
God means you to live a heavenly life.
ANDREW MURRAY

Time and Eternity

My days are swifter than a weaver's shuttle.

JOB 7:6

Life is swift and short. Even if we live to what is generally called "a ripe old age," it is "soon cut off, and we fly away" (Psa. 90:10). The Scriptures compare our life to "a vapour, that . . . vanisheth away" (James 4:14), to "a watch in the night," and to "a tale that is told" (Psa. 90: 4, 9).

Thus our time on earth is precious. For our souls it is the valley of decision, the vestibule to eternity. Only in this life do sinners have the opportunity to repent and receive Christ. Only in this life can Christians stand for God, spread the gospel, and lay up treasure in heaven. That is why Paul urges us to redeem the time (Eph. 5:16) and exhorts us to holiness: "The night is far spent, the day is at hand: let us therefore cast off the works of darkness" (Rom. 13:12).

Soon we will all be in a world where time will be no more. Someone has described eternity as being like God winding up a giant clock and setting the pendulum in motion. As it swings from side to side, its solemn ticking seems to say, "For ever and ever, for ever and ever, for ever and ever." For every soul who grasps the brief opportunity life affords to get right with God by faith in Christ, eternity holds the prospect of glory *for ever and ever.* For every unbelieving, impenitent sinner it holds the prospect of woe *for ever and ever.*

At the beginning of another year, when our minds naturally turn to the passage of time and to our prospects for the future, let us think long and hard on these things. We now have time and opportunity to embrace the gospel and then to spread it. But it is a fleeting opportunity. Let us grasp it in the light of eternity.

—S. B. C.

Let the year be given to God in its every moment!
G. CAMPBELL MORGAN

Strong in Faith

He staggered not at the promise of God through unbelief;
but was strong in faith, giving glory to God. ROMANS 4:20

Faith is ever engaged in a war. There are enemies which daily oppose this grace in a Christian's life. Now the two greatest enemies with which our faith must contend are *feelings* and *human reasoning.* Indulging in either of these is dangerous for the believer. They will attack the very vitals of our hope and confidence in the Lord. Is it not true that when the Lord tests your faith with respect to some promise, your feelings tell you that His Word *will not* be fulfilled to you? And does not your human reasoning tell you that the promise *cannot* be fulfilled?

But consider Abraham. Paul said, "He staggered not at the promise." It literally reads, "He was not in strife with himself." In other words, there was no battle going on in Abraham's heart as to whether or not God would fulfil His promise of a son. Furthermore, we read that "he considered not his own body now dead" (v. 19). Again, human reasoning told him that this promise could not be fulfilled to a man ninety-nine years old. But this man "against hope believed in hope" (v. 18).

The question is, how did he do it? The answer is found in verse 21. You see, Abraham was "fully persuaded that, what he had promised, he was able also to perform." In other words, Abraham looked to the character of God. He knew that the God who made such a promise was no liar, and that He had the power to fulfil His Word.

Tell me, dear child of God, how fares your faith? Do you feel the Lord's Word will not hold good for you? Have you reasoned yourself into a dungeon of depression? Then look away from yourself. Look to Him who cannot lie and hence must fulfil His own Word by the sheer arm of omnipotence!

—J. W.

Where reason cannot wade there faith may swim.
THOMAS WATSON

Perfect Cleansing in the Blood

It is the blood that maketh an atonement for the soul.
LEVITICUS 17:11

Bible doctrines often have a key book, chapter, and verse in the Bible. For example, justification is expounded in Romans, explained in Galatians 3, and epitomized in Galatians 3:11. Leviticus is undoubtedly the key book on the blood sacrifice, having over eighty references to it, and Exodus 12, the great Passover section, is the key chapter. The key verse on the blood atonement is Leviticus 17:11.

This emphasis on the blood has caused many to attack Leviticus and deride the blood sacrifice, using the term "slaughterhouse religion." But whether proud, sinful man likes it or not, the blood sacrifice is God's way, and the only way for sinful man to be reconciled to God. The multitude of Old Testament sacrifices, detailed in Leviticus and elsewhere, are but signposts to the "one sacrifice for sins for ever" (Heb. 10:12) offered by our great High Priest, Jesus Christ.

Look anywhere in the Bible and you are immediately confronted with the awful fact of the sinfulness of man. The dark thread of his iniquity is everywhere to be seen, even in the lives of the holiest of men and women. "All have sinned" and "There is none righteous" are the dread pronouncements of God's Word (Rom. 3). Thankfully, running parallel to this dark thread of man's sin is the crimson thread of God's redemption. The Bible is crying out, "There is a way back to God from the paths of sin." That way is the way of the cross.

The apostle John declares, "The blood of Jesus Christ his Son cleanseth us from all sin" (I John 1:7). How many sins does the blood atone for? The answer is *all* sin. Upon confession of our sins, that same blood cleanses from *all* unrighteousness. From how much unrighteousness? *All* unrighteousness. Christian, do not let the devil rob you today of assurance of sins forgiven. There is perfect, present cleansing in the blood of Christ.

—F. McC.

The Lord Jesus took our place that we might have His peace; He took our sin that we might have His salvation.
ANONYMOUS

The Plea of Love

O Israel, return unto the Lord thy God.   HOSEA 14:1

The famous nineteenth-century Baptist preacher, C. H. Spurgeon, said that throughout the book of Hosea there is thunder, sometimes a low rumbling, sometimes peal on peal. We would expect the book to close with a fearful declaration of judgment on impenitent Israel, but, surprisingly, it is the voice of pleading that we hear in the last chapter. It is hard for God to watch people that He has loved and favoured go on in their rebellion and be ruined. And it is hard for God to watch us, whom He has created, going astray to our own shame and loss. To stop Israel (and us) from going further away, God pleads most tenderly, "O Israel, return unto the Lord thy God."

Sometimes we become so taken up with the thought of the impending doom of the ungodly that we forget that God is longsuffering and has no pleasure in the death of the wicked. The American evangelist D. L. Moody once allowed a young preacher called Henry Moorhouse to preach for him while he was away. When Moody returned, he asked his wife how young Moorhouse was doing. She said that people liked him because he told them that God loved them. Moody was upset and felt that Henry Moorhouse was wrong. But when he heard him for himself his attitude changed, and D. L. Moody's preaching was never the same again.

How precious it is to think that God cares so much for creatures who have sinfully wandered away from Him! God even tells us what we are to say when we come back. We must say, "Take away all iniquity, and receive us graciously" (v. 2). And God promises that if we return in that spirit, He will heal our backsliding and love us freely.

If you want to discover how much God loves you, read the fourteenth chapter of Hosea.

—G. F.

The God of heaven is slow to anger, and is
especially loth to abandon a people to utter ruin
that have been in special relation to Him.
MATTHEW HENRY

A Pleasure To Please

For I do always those things that please him.

JOHN 8:29

This statement could be uttered only by God's unique and perfect Son. The life of Christ was in absolute harmony with the will of the Father. Twice the Gospels record that the Father spoke directly from heaven, stating, "This is my beloved Son, in whom I am well pleased."

In Matthew 3:17 the Father was well pleased with His Son's *obedience*. This particular commendation came after His baptism, to which our Lord submitted in order to fulfil all righteousness. As our Saviour, Christ kept every command in our place. In doing so He earned a perfect righteousness for us and splendidly pleased our heavenly Father. Christians are called to be like Christ and therefore to be "doers of the word, and not hearers only" (James 1:22). While saints will never achieve perfection in this life, true sons of God will yearn to please their heavenly Father in all they do.

At Christ's transfiguration in Matthew 17:5 the Father spoke of His good pleasure in His Son's *speech*. The Father commanded the disciples, "Hear ye him." Christ's speech, just as His life, was ever directing men toward the Father. The Son came into the world to reveal the Father (John 1:18). Every sermon and every conversation revealed the only true God. The Christian, too, is to show forth his heavenly Father in word and deed. It is an honour when your speech and life "betray" that you are a son of God (Matt. 26:73).

What horrible regrets you will have at the close of life's journey if you do not use your days of opportunity to please the God of your salvation. Therefore, as a willing disciple of Christ, begin today to do those things which will delight your Father which is in heaven.

—I. G.

We are born subjects, and to obey God is perfect liberty.
SENECA

Directives for Public Worship

For God is in heaven, and thou upon earth.

ECCLESIASTES 5:2

Whether at home, work, or church, God is the absolute King of our lives. The more we realize this fact, the more we can truly enjoy the life that God has given. We can have no true contentment or peace in the ebb and flow of life apart from faith in the sovereign Lord. But sometimes, indeed often, in the vicissitudes of life we fail to keep things in the proper perspective. The failure to remember and acknowledge God's absolute sovereignty makes us careless even in the place of worship. God's being in heaven and our being on earth declares His exalted position over all our affairs. In Ecclesiastes 5 the Preacher gives some imperatives for worship that will help us keep things in the proper perspective and direct us to the spiritual worship that God demands.

When we enter into the place of worship, we should use self-restraint. The thought of being in God's presence should cause a holy hush to come over our souls. "The Lord is in his holy temple: let all the earth keep silence before him" (Hab. 2:20). As Moses removed his shoes before the burning bush, so should we keep our feet as we enter the house of God. We should also come to worship in submission, being ready to hear. We should expect to hear a word from the Lord, remembering that the purpose of hearing is that we might obey. Hearkening to God's Word is better than any ritual (I Sam. 15:22). We should also come to worship in sincerity. We must not be like fools who irreverently, ignorantly, and heartlessly go through the outward forms of worship. The Lord Jesus said, "They that worship him must worship him in spirit and in truth" (John 4:24). Anything less is not only wrong worship, it is an attack on the sovereign greatness of our God.

—M. P. V. B.

Posture in worship is too often imposture.
THOMAS WATSON

A Divine Division

And I will put a division between my people and thy people.
EXODUS 8:23

Division is a forbidden word in our society. The world does not want to hear about things that divide one man from another. There is a preoccupation today with the things that unite men, the things that dispel conflict and separation. This spirit has passed over into the religious world. And yet the principle of division is a very real part of the Christian experience, a principle we ignore at our peril, a principle here set down by God Himself.

The division between those who are of Christ and those who are yet children of the world goes back to eternity. There the Father chose and covenanted a people unto Christ. Ours is not to understand the mechanics of His choice or the motives underlying it, but to accept it. In each succeeding age, Christ and His seed have stood apart, separated from all mankind.

By the cross, that division is reinforced: we are crucified to the world and the world to us. The cross, in a sense, stands guard between the church and the world which crucified her Lord. The division ought to be worked out in our daily lives. There is a difference between believers and worldlings. We must see to it that we are separated unto God in our outward walk and behaviour. The Holy Spirit, as He works in us to conform us to Christ, will bring about a division in our hearts, the inner life. Our tasks, our desires, our hopes and aspirations—these will become different. There will be a growing away from the world, and in all of our affairs we shall begin to know the reality of going forth "unto him without the camp" (Heb. 13:13).

—T. N.

Better a holy discord than a profane concord.
THOMAS ADAMS

The Hearing Ear

The hearing ear, and the seeing eye,
the Lord hath made even both of them.

PROVERBS 20:12

How marvellous is the faculty of hearing! Within each ear there is
a space not much larger than a hazelnut. This space is crammed
with enough electrical circuits to provide a telephone service for a
good-sized city. The auditory nerve leading to the brain is only the
diameter of a pencil lead yet contains more than thirty thousand
circuits. How sensitive is the eardrum, a tough, tightly stretched
membrane less than half an inch across! The faintest vibration,
causing a minute displacement of perhaps only a millionth of a
centimeter, is wonderfully transformed into intelligible sound. All
this is testimony indeed to the creative handiwork of God!

The natural man has no ear for spiritual things. It is the work
of divine grace to unstop the ears of the spiritually deaf. The ears
of Christ's sheep have been opened. "My sheep hear my voice"
(John 10:27). Yea more, "they know his voice" (v. 4). He has called
them by name. Remember Mary, lingering in the garden? Just one
word fell from the Saviour's lips: *Mary.* She cried out, "Rabboni."
She knew His voice! "The sheep, though the most simple creature,
is superior to all animals in this, that he soon hears his shepherd's
voice, and will follow no other" (Martin Luther). The Lord speaks
to us through the Scriptures of truth. As John Burgon said, "The
Bible is none other than the voice of Him that sitteth on the
throne." In the secret place, ever seek the better part, to sit at
Jesus' feet and hear His Word. Go to the sanctuary prayerfully.
"Speak, Lord; for thy servant heareth" (I Sam. 3:9). Be ready to
hear (Eccles. 5:1). There is much attendance without attention,
much hearing without hearkening. It should be our greatest joy to
truly hear the voice of our Beloved.

—M. P.

Take heed of drowsiness in hearing.
THOMAS WATSON

9

Steadfastness

Stand fast in the Lord.

PHILIPPIANS 4:1

It is a remarkable fact that at several crucial junctures in Paul's letters, the practical outcome of the Christian's warfare against the world and Satan is defined as a matter of "standing." In the final chapter of Ephesians, for instance, Paul exhorts the Christian soldier not so much to advance into battle, but to "stand." He writes, "Take unto you the whole armour of God, that ye may be able to withstand in the evil day, and having done all, to stand (Eph. 6:13-14).

If we were writing the passage and using Paul's military imagery, we would most likely speak of invasion, marching, or conquest. But Paul does not do that. Instead he correctly speaks of standing. The implication of the command is that the Captain of our salvation, the Lord Jesus Christ, has already done or is now doing the conquering. We have to hold the ground He has conquered for us. It is on the basis of the great conquests of Christ on behalf of His people when He died and rose again that the Christian warrior must stand.

Christians everywhere are called to steadfastness. The world around is changing its fashions of thought and conduct, but the child of God must stand fast. The enemy is constantly changing his methods of attack upon us, but clothed with the whole armour of God, we are to remain standing. Our heart may melt with fear, but we can say with the psalmist, "What time I am afraid, I will trust in thee" (Psa. 56:3).

We began our Christian life by trusting the Saviour's finished work; so, come what may, we must not and will not draw back. We intend by God's grace to remain steadfast, proving that we are indeed true disciples. The Lord Himself who stands fast and does not forsake His saints has promised to preserve us and at last to clothe us in white raiment as victors who have overcome.

—D. C.

**Religion is not a matter of fits,
starts and stops, but an everyday affair.**
DAVID LIVINGSTONE

The Sin of Doing Nothing

Be sure your sin will find you out.

NUMBERS 32:23

The sin that Moses warns against in these words is the sin of doing nothing. Reuben and Gad wished to remain on the east of Jordan while their brethren went to war on the other side. There are many Reubenites and Gadites still with us—people who have no heart for the battle against the Lord's enemies, though they are quite happy to enjoy the benefits that others fight hard to win. The land that these two tribes desired was territory "which the Lord smote before the congregation of Israel" (v. 4). Now these men wished to take possession of it, but they did not want to fight themselves.

What base ingratitude such a spirit displays! Our gospel liberties can be traced back through a history of imprisonment, torture, exile, loneliness, martyrdom, and much more. Such was the lot of those who suffered that we might have the faith today. How ungrateful we are to them if we do not now contend for that faith.

Furthermore, this sin is a discouragement to those who are currently engaged in the conflict. In not putting your neck to the work, you are committing the sin of discouraging others who are endeavouring to serve God.

Then again, it is a sin that divides the Lord's army. Many of the rifts in congregations stem from the behaviour of those who are mere idlers, "working not at all, . . . busybodies" (II Thess. 3:11).

This sin will "find you out." It will come home to you if you fail to lend all your strength to the work of God. Regret, a troubled conscience, shame before the Lord—these are just a few of the ways in which this sin will find you out. May God stir our hearts and help us flee from it.

—J. G.

An idle life and a holy heart is a contradiction.
THOMAS BROOKS

The Security of Saints

Say ye to the righteous, that it shall be well with him:
for they shall eat the fruit of their doings.

ISAIAH 3:10

Discouragement is a major weapon in Satan's arsenal to oppose God's people and check their progress. Perhaps today finds you downhearted and feeling that your life and service have been in vain. You appear to labour to no effect; you seem to pray without obtaining an answer. Here is a word from God for you: "Say ye to the righteous, that it shall be well with him: for they shall eat the fruit of their doings."

It is well with God's people. Let us rejoice today in that. Our guilt is gone. We are declared righteous, not because of our good works, but because of the righteousness of Christ imparted to us. We are fully accepted by God. We are united to Christ. Nothing can ever sever us from Him. He keeps us. He subdues our iniquities. He rises for our defence against every foe. He hears our prayer. He meets our needs. These are objective truths, not mere wishful thoughts. When our circumstances appear to contradict these statements, let us trust in God. If sin is robbing us of the enjoyment of them, let us bring it to the blood and find restored fellowship with our Father in Christ (I John 1:7-9).

It will be well with God's people. Our future is even brighter than our present. Soon we shall see the King in His beauty. Soon the very presence of sin will be removed from us. Soon all the pleasures of the Father's house will be ours. Then shall we "eat the fruit" of our doings. The devils tempts us to believe that it is vain to serve the Lord. He confuses us by pointing to the prosperity of the wicked. Let us not judge too quickly. Look at the final scene. Our reward is sure. We do not serve Christ in vain. We have the best of both worlds: salvation now and heaven to follow.

—A. C.

If it be sweet to be growing corn of the Lord here,
how much better to be gathered into His barn.
ROBERT MURRAY MCCHEYNE

A Spiritual House

Ye also, as lively stones, are built up a spiritual house.

I PETER 2:5

The church of Christ is looked upon not only as a growing body, as in verse 2, but also as a growing house. Every safe house must rest upon a sure and steadfast foundation. There is only one foundation: "Behold, I lay in Sion a chief corner stone, elect, precious" (v. 6). Isaiah calls this corner stone "a sure foundation" (Isa. 28:16). This foundation is Jesus Christ. On this rock alone the true spiritual house of God is built—that house that will withstand storms and floods and cannot and will not fall. On that sure foundation Christ has promised to build His church, and the gates of hell shall not prevail against it.

The corner stone and the foundation shape, direct, and fashion the house that is built upon them. The stones laid on this foundation follow its line and direction. Every believer built on Christ is conformed to the image of his foundation, which is Jesus Christ. They follow His line and direction.

The stones of this house are living stones (v. 5). Once they lay in the dark quarry of nature, but God the Holy Spirit dug them out and quickened them for their appointed place in the house of God. This spiritual house is, as Paul puts it, a "building fitly framed together [growing] unto an holy temple in the Lord" (Eph. 2:21). No other building will stand the test of the judgment day. Everything built by man will collapse (Heb. 12:26, 27). Let us therefore make sure that we are truly built upon Christ and not upon some movable foundation.

—R. J. B.

**Christ's true church is built of
living stones, not of dead wood.**
ALEXANDER SIMPSON

13

Jehovah Shammah

The Lord is there.

EZEKIEL 48:35

In the Hebrew text *The Lord is there* is *Jehovah Shammah,* a title that provides an inspiring conclusion to the book of Ezekiel. What a blessing if in the last thing we write, we impart something of the Saviour's name. Such a desire prompted Charles Wesley to say, "Happy, if with my latest breath I may but gasp His name."

The last stroke of the prophet's pen produces the name that makes heaven what it is. To be called *Jehovah Shammah* is the honour of the city of the Great King. There are all too many places of which it must be said that the Lord is not there. But this title explains the difference between a heaven on earth and a hell on earth. "Where Jesus is, 'tis heaven there."

This wonderful name eases the burden of grief and fear for the believer in the evil day. It holds out the kind of promise that comforted and fortified the heart of David: "Yea, though I walk through the valley of the shadow of death, I will fear no evil: for thou art with me" (Psa. 23:4). The Lord will be there when the battle is done, as He was before the battle began.

Jehovah Shammah inspires confidence in the exercise of prayer. How blessed is the hallowed hour of worship when the Lord Jesus stands among us, His presence powerfully manifest and His name glorified. Then likewise, at His table, or when witnessing, our experience is altogether transformed by His being there. Here, too, is the promise of rich reward in the searching of Scripture. The Lord is there on every page. All the divine names seem comprehended in this marvellous title.

Jehovah Shammah is the name to delight us in the hour of His coming. He will be there—in the air—in the midst of His people—on the summit of Olivet—in the brightness of His glory. Yes, praise the Lord, we will all be there with Him in that great and glorious day.

—J. D.

Do we reckon the presence of the Lord to be
the greatest of blessings? Very much depends
upon our answer to this question.

C. H. SPURGEON

Soulwinning

He which converteth the sinner from the error
of his way shall save a soul from death.

JAMES 5:20

"Salvation is of the Lord" (Jon. 2:9). He alone can quicken a dead soul and forgive his sins. But He uses human instruments in bringing the gospel of salvation to sinners. He gives His people the privilege of being soulwinners—those whose ministry is used by the Holy Spirit to convert the lost to Christ. John the Baptist was one such soulwinner (Luke 1:15-16). Paul was another whom the Lord sent to sinners "to open their eyes, and to turn [or, convert] them from darkness to light, and from the power of Satan unto God" (Acts 26:18). Now James tells us that this privilege is not limited to an elite in the church but is extended to all God's people. It is a work for every Christian to do.

It is an important work. It deals with the great issues of eternity. It saves souls from death and hell. Beside this work all other earthly endeavours pale into insignificance. No doubt it is good to feed and clothe men, to educate and employ them. But what are these things in the light of eternity? What good have we done if we leave men to perish in their sins?

Let us not be sidetracked. We may save a fortune, but we cannot take it with us to heaven. Would we not be better to spend our fortune—and our very selves—to save souls? We can and will take the souls we win to heaven with us. Let us then give ourselves from this day on to the work of winning souls for Christ.

—A. C.

**No man can be a Christian who is
unconcerned for the salvation of others.**
RICHARD HALDANE

Possessing Our Possessions

The children of Israel went every man unto his inheritance to possess the land.

JUDGES 2:6

What a rich land of blessing the Lord has given to His people! "The Lord thy God bringeth thee into a good land ... thou shalt not lack any thing in it" (Deut. 8:7, 9). Paul's New Testament description of this wonderful provision of grace is found in Ephesians 1:3: "Blessed be the God and Father of our Lord Jesus Christ, who hath blessed us with all spiritual blessings in heavenly places in Christ." Peter affirms that God's "divine power hath given unto us all things that pertain unto life and godliness" (II Pet. 1:3).

Our Father has not saved us to leave us without anything that is necessary to true spirituality and godliness. He has given us His Spirit, whose specific task is to make us know "the things that are freely given to us of God" (I Cor. 2:12). It is inexcusable, then, for us to live in ignorance of our spiritual inheritance or to fail to enjoy it to the full. This spiritual fulness is the great reality of New Testament Christianity. "Ye are complete in him" (Col. 2:10). That is, "Ye are in Him, made full." All the fulness of God dwells in Christ. We are in Christ. Therefore we are filled with all the fulness of God. "In Christ" is never the place of spiritual impoverishment.

Christians need to learn what they have and are by virtue of their union with Christ. They need to know the glorious truth of free justification and the imputed righteousness of Christ. That is the basis of a life of peace and power, a life of victory over sin, and a life of liberty to serve the Lord in love, free from guilt motivation and manipulation.

Are you possessing your possessions? Cry for the ministry of the Spirit to teach you what is yours in Christ and to lead you into the enjoyment of it by faith.

—A. C.

He that has Christ has all things, and he that has not Christ has nothing.
MARTIN LUTHER

The Lord's Twin Gifts

The Lord will give grace and glory.

PSALM 84:11

God's gifts are given to us as freely as the air we breathe, and two of His gifts are grace and glory. Spurgeon comments: "The little conjunction 'and' in this verse is a diamond rivet binding the present with the future; grace and glory always go together. God has married them and no one can divorce them. The Lord will never deny a soul glory to whom He has freely given to live upon His grace."

When the father of Dr. Harry Ironside lay dying, the descending sheet which Peter saw in a vision was dominant in his mind. Over and over he mumbled, "A great sheet and wild beasts and—and—and—" Seemingly he could not recall the next words and would start over and over again. A friend whispered, "John, it says 'creeping things.'" "Oh, yes, that's how I got in! Just a poor, good-for-nothing creeping thing! But I got in—saved by grace!"

The second blessing of the promise is that of glory. The grace that has saved us will one day present us perfect in a glorified state to be with Christ forever. Thomas Brooks, the Puritan, wrote, "Under the name of 'grace' all spiritual good is wrapped up; and under the name of 'glory' all eternal good is wrapped up; and under the last clause 'no good thing will he withhold' is wrapped up all temporal good: all put together speaks our God to be an all sufficient portion."

Truly we can sing today with confidence and thanksgiving:

> *'Tis Jesus the First and the Last*
> *Whose Spirit shall guide us safe home:*
> *We'll praise Him for all that is past,*
> *And trust Him for all that's to come.*
>
> —S. B.

Grace is young glory.
ALEXANDER PEDEN

17

The Race of Faith

So run, that ye may obtain.

I CORINTHIANS 9:24

Paul learned his preaching style from One he never heard in the flesh, the Lord Jesus. The Lord constantly used earthly illustrations to convey divine truth, with the effect of powerfully focussing the hearer's attention and aiding his retention. Paul likewise used ordinary things to carry great spiritual truths, and on several occasions used even the sporting arena to present some practical truth to his hearers.

In the illustration before us he likens the Christian life to a race. Elsewhere he presents Jesus as the starting line and the finishing point, and encourages his listeners to lay aside every weight so that they may finish their course with joy. Here he gives further guidance as to how the race should be run.

In an earthly race there may be many competitors, but only one winner. Often athletes, while they would like to win, are content just to place well. In other words, they have not really put their all into the task of winning. Paul warns the Christian to serve Christ with such dedication that the "Well done" from the Saviour's lips is his primary objective.

The one who will thus succeed must be "temperate in all things" (v. 25). All his energies will be brought into subjection to the one great aim of serving and exalting Christ. He will not run the race uncertainly. He will start well, and his eye will be on the finish line. People will know he is an out-and-out Christian. He will finish well.

In the battle for truth he will not be "as one that beateth the air" (v. 26)—all action but with little forward movement. The true athlete has an economy and efficiency of movement so that all his power is channelled towards winning the race. May God help us not to spin our wheels and beat the air, producing lots of noise and action but at the end of the day achieving little for the Lord.

—F. McC.

If you fall, don't give up—*get up!*
ANONYMOUS

Caught in Our Own Ambush

They lay wait for their own blood; they lurk privily for their own lives.
PROVERBS 1:18

Despite the fact that many adolescents hold views to the contrary, fathers do know more than their sons on the general affairs of life. Solomon demonstrates a knowledge of the enticements that the young will invariably encounter from the wicked of this world. He is even able to quote them (v. 11). The language of temptation does not alter with the years. Neither does the Christian's response. "Walk not thou . . . with them" (v. 15). David, Solomon's father, had issued the same advice a generation before in the opening lyrics of his psalter: "Blessed is the man that walketh not in the counsel of the ungodly, nor standeth in the way of sinners, nor sitteth in the seat of the scornful" (Psa. 1:1).

Such counsel is not based upon Christian ethics alone, though that is sufficient reason for us to avoid sin. No! Solomon's plea to his son was also based on the practical consideration that sin brings its own judgment. In words that may well be paraphrased by the familiar declaration, "They will come to a bad end," Solomon declared, "They lay wait for their own blood; they lurk privily for their own lives." There is no more risky life than that of the man or woman who lives in defiance of God. It has been rightly observed that such persons "shall not live out half their days" (Psa. 55:23). Sin is a time bomb ticking away. Those who embrace it have no way of knowing when it will destroy them. Paul urged Timothy, "Flee . . . youthful lusts." Be assured, sin shall destroy those who do not keep their distance. "Sin, when it is finished, bringeth forth death" (James 1:15). Let the prayer of Jabez be ever in our hearts: "Keep me from evil, that it may not grieve me!" (I Chron. 4:10).

—I. F.

O Lord, help us to hear the serpent's
rattle before we feel its fangs.
T. DeWitt Talmage

The Paradise of God

To him that overcometh will I give to eat of the tree of life,
which is in the midst of the paradise of God.

REVELATION 2:7

Paradise refers to a garden. The paradise of God is the garden of God. The expression very obviously is intended to carry our minds back to the book of Genesis and the garden of Eden. In Genesis paradise was lost in Adam. In Revelation it is regained in Christ. In Genesis the cherubim barred the way to the tree of life because of sin. In Revelation the Lord opens up the way to the tree of life through the righteousness of Christ.

To Christians struggling with the problems of life and the disappointments that meet us on every hand, what sweeter promise can there be than the assurance of a place in the garden of God? Be strong! Face the challenges of this life by faith in Christ. Do not compromise your testimony or try to come to terms with the world. Faith in Christ means victory over the world (I John 4:4), and overcomers have an assured place in the garden of God, the Eden above.

What a place that will be! Christ has regained for us all that Adam lost, and He has delivered us from the very possibility of ever losing paradise again. For all His people the garden of God will be first and foremost a place of life. There the tree of life blooms forever. There is no down side to life in paradise. There the light of life casts no shadows. In God's eternal Eden we will live in peace, in purity, and in perfect joy, for there we will live in uninterrupted fellowship with Him. Christ and His people will never be separated, and there will be nothing to mar their everlasting enjoyment of each other.

We have only two questions to answer: Will I be there? And, am I living now amid the darkness of earth in the light of heaven? To be able to answer those questions aright is the essence of true salvation.

—A. C.

Heaven will pay for any loss we may suffer to gain it;
but nothing can pay for the loss of heaven.
RICHARD BAXTER

The Pearl of Psalms

The Lord is my shepherd.

PSALM 23:1

No psalm is more familiar or precious to saints than the twenty-third. It has blessed and comforted God's people since David first sang it on the Judaean hills. In trial or in prosperity, its message is timeless and universal for the trusting saint. It speaks to us of God's providential care and His gracious provision for us in and through the Lord Jesus Christ.

That the Lord is our Shepherd reminds us that we are His possession and that He will provide for us, protect us, and guide us. *He provides rest for the weary.* In His order, rest precedes activity. Since the place of rest is the place of God's presence, this order is essential. Only as we enjoy these habitations of peace and waters of rest can we negotiate the daily course of life with spiritual success. *He renews us.* When we are weak, He strengthens. When we are sinful, He sanctifies. When we are sorrowful, He satisfies. *He guides us.* There is no risk of losing our way, because He leads along straight, clearly marked tracks. By His Word and by His providence, He makes the way clear. *He protects us.* Sometimes those straight paths lead through deep, dark valleys. But even here our pace is steady, because His presence keeps danger away from us and us away from danger. *He secures our peace.* As our gracious host, He invites us to a victory celebration. Even though the enemy may surround us, He guarantees our safety and turns seeming defeat to triumph. *He shows us friendship.* His benevolent loyalty is constantly hunting and pursuing us. To be overtaken by this swift pursuer is to experience the joy of unceasing fellowship in the presence of the Lord.

—M. P. V. B.

**Our Shepherd goes before us and His sheep-dogs—
goodness and mercy—come behind us, so that
we need fear no attack from any direction.**
ALEXANDER SIMPSON

Full, Free Justification

THE LORD OUR RIGHTEOUSNESS.

JEREMIAH 23:6

There is a world of peace and joy for the Christian who has learned this truth. Here is the very heart of the gospel. What Christ has done and the relationship He sustains to His people in the sight of God are the true essence of the good news. We are too prone to be moved away from the objective work of Christ to some subjective experience of our own as the basis of our hope. We must resist this tendency, for it is fatal to all true Christian experience. Consider the blessedness of knowing that the Lord is our righteousness.

Here is the ground of our salvation. The Lord Jesus Christ has fulfilled the law of God, both by obeying its precept and by paying its penalty. God imputes Christ's righteousness to us, giving us a perfect pardon and a legal title to heaven. The ground of that righteousness is not in anything we have done before or after conversion, but in the perfect obedience of Christ. He gives us a righteousness as full and complete as if we had fulfilled the whole law.

Here, then, we also have a true basis of assurance of salvation. Is Christ our righteousness? Then He is also our acceptance. Can God reject the righteousness of His Son? No more can He reject any soul to whom He has imputed that righteousness. How much better off would saints struggling with doubt be if they were directed away from trying to analyse the quality of their decision in coming to Christ and looked instead to His full and perfect righteousness on their behalf.

God accepts no accusation of the devil against a justified soul (Rom. 8:33-34). Neither should we. Do not allow the enemy to disturb your peace by flashbacks to sin that has been put under the blood. Do not be fooled into thinking that you need to do some sort of penance to regain God's favour. The Lord is our righteousness. That sets us free from the bondage of penance and installs us in the liberty to serve God as sons. Our service does not enhance our standing; it expresses it.

—A. C.

It is vain to accuse those whom God acquits; you need not fear an accuser, not because innocent, but because justified.
THOMAS MANTON

The New Covenant

Behold, . . . I will make a new covenant.　　**HEBREWS 8:8**

It is important to remember that when Paul speaks of the "new covenant" he does not refer to something altogether new and unheard of. The Old Testament is replete with references to this same covenant, a covenant of grace initially declared when man fell and thereafter progressively revealed and administered under the various types and shadows of the old economy. With the coming of Christ Himself there was a fulfilment of all those prefigurations, and the covenant was set forth in its full-orbed meaning.

Christ is the Mediator of the new covenant. His blood is the blood of that everlasting covenant. His death is the executing of that covenant, "for where a testament is, there must also of necessity be the death of the testator" (Heb. 9:16). By His sacrifice Christ has secured for His people all the blessings that were promised from all eternity in that covenant. Consequently, when we read the terms of this covenant, we find the Lord Himself declaring what He does for His people. He *regenerates* them, for He puts His laws into their hearts and writes them in their minds (10:16). These terms speak of regeneration. God graciously quickens sinners, drawing them to Himself and giving them a new heart, a heart to obey Him and love Him. Furthermore, He *remits* their sin: "I will be merciful" (8:12). The word *merciful* means "propitious," indicating that God's wrath has been appeased. Christ has satisfied the just demands of God concerning our unrighteousness, the wrong done to God the sovereign and righteous Judge; concerning our sins, referring to our missing the mark of glorifying God; and concerning our iniquities, that is, our lawlessness, the setting up of our own will against God's. So complete is the satisfaction that Christ has rendered, that God remembers all these evils no more. Thus He *receives* those for whom the satisfaction is made. He is to them a God and they are to Him a people. Are you one of His people?

—J. G.

**The covenant is a rocky foundation
to build on for life or for death.**
C. H. SPURGEON

23

Unsinkable Saints

Underneath are the everlasting arms.

DEUTERONOMY 33:27

When the great liner *Titanic* set sail on her maiden voyage, her makers hailed her as unsinkable. How wrong they were! Today she lies at the bottom of the ocean, a tragic reminder that the best efforts of man are frail and feeble. The only vessels that cannot sink are those that are held afloat by the gracious power of God.

The same is true of those human vessels that are launched from birth on to the storm-tossed ocean of life. Their desired destination is the port of heaven, but millions never arrive. As we sail on we see all around us the wreckages of countless vessels. Some, like the *Titanic*, sailed boldly forth, confident in their own unsinkability. Their confidence was only misplaced brashness that led them to shipwreck. But among all those shipwrecks there is not one true believer in Christ. Saints are unsinkable, for undergirding every one of them are the arms of the eternal God. Our frail barque cannot break asunder, even in the most terrible tempests of life.

Perhaps you feel threatened today. You feel a storm is brewing. You fear that some great wave of trouble will overflow your soul. Then grasp this truth: saints are unsinkable. True, we may have to battle wind and rain and tide. We may ship some water. Our faith will be put to the test. But we will not sink. We will make it safely to our destination, for the everlasting arms undergird our vessel.

Let us then sail on with confidence. Let us navigate by the chart and compass of Scripture even when they lead us into heavy weather. Nothing can break our souls unless it first break our God. The most furious storm can only drive us into the security of His everlasting arms.

—A. C.

Never did a believer in Jesus die or drown in his voyage to heaven.
ROBERT TRAILL

Testimony

They took knowledge of them, that they had been with Jesus.
ACTS 4:13

The enemies of Christ had listened to and observed the apostles and had reached a conclusion concerning them: "they had been with Jesus." Beloved, the world is always watching us—scrutinizing every word, measuring every act and attitude—and it is not slow to mark our inconsistencies and failures. We are epistles "read of all men" (II Cor. 3:2). What a sobering thought! "Man looketh on the outward appearance"—true, and like it or not, he judges Christianity by what he sees in us. What does he see? That which causes him to criticize and condemn? Or that which compels him to say, "The Lord hath done great things for them" (Psa. 126:2)?

Depend upon it, the ungodly know when we have been with Jesus. Spending time with Him leaves its mark upon us. Moses had upon his countenance the evidence that he had been in the presence of God (Exod. 34:29-30). Let us ever look to Him, feed upon Him, and draw from the fulness that is in Him, and the result will be that as the branch in the vine (John 15), we will bear fruit to Christ's glory. "Let your light so shine before men, that they may see your good works, and glorify your Father which is in heaven" (Matt. 5:16).

> *Take time to be holy, the world rushes on;*
> *Much time spend in secret with Jesus alone.*
> *By looking to Jesus, like Him thou shalt be;*
> *Thy friends in thy conduct His likeness shall see.*

—D. F.

**A Christian's life should be nothing
but a visible representation of Christ.**
THOMAS BROOKS

Separated unto God

All the days of his separation he is holy unto the Lord.
NUMBERS 6:8

The book of Numbers treats the subject of resignation to the Lord's will—something that involves, of course, abandonment of self-will. There are many examples in Numbers of those who made shipwreck because they would not renounce the carnal will.

To instil this spirit of consecration in the Israelites, the Lord revealed the law of the Nazarite through Moses. The title *Nazarite* means "separated," and every aspect of the vow of the Nazarite was designed to teach that the believer is to be a separated person. Like the Nazarite, while he lives among people, he is not to be like them. "*In* the world but not *of* the world" is a principle that never changes.

The Nazarite's consecration demanded that the Lord have first place in his life. When a loved one died, he was not to touch the body lest he "make himself unclean," for "the consecration of his God" was "upon his head" (v. 7). Christ Himself shows the meaning of this in Luke 14:26, where He teaches that the believer must love Him more than the dearest on earth. Even the savour of death was not to be upon the Nazarite. If he suddenly and unavoidably touched the dead, he had to be cleansed. The believer is to be one in whom the life of God is seen. There should be nothing of the stench of the world about us, but rather the fragrance of the risen Christ.

The Nazarite's vow of separation governed his diet and his appearance. He was not permitted to consume anything pertaining to the vine or to shave his head. Surely there is a hint here of abstaining from fleshly appetites, as well as of showing Christ by outward behaviour and appearance. Let us constantly put on the Lord Jesus and "make not provision for the flesh, to fulfil the lusts thereof" (Rom. 13:14), but through the Spirit mortify the deeds of the body. As Christ was, so may we be "separate from sinners" (Heb. 7:26).

—J. G.

For all the world forsake not Christ,
but all the world forsake for Christ.
ANONYMOUS

Living Above Fear

Fear not, neither be discouraged. DEUTERONOMY 1:21

Nothing more effectively hinders our spiritual usefulness than fear and discouragement. As long as we live above these we can withstand every furious assault of the world and of the devil. When we are fearful—it matters little whether it is a fear of man, or of suffering, or of death—and our hearts are downcast, we are easily overcome.

Are you living under the clouds of fear and discouragement? What is it that you fear? Why are you discouraged? Do you feel forsaken by God? Are you labouring under some great grief? Is your soul cast down because of some failure or sin? Are you paralysed by the fear of man? The causes of fear and discouragement are myriad. The cure is the same in every case.

David speaks of that cure in Psalms 42 and 43. "Hope thou in God" is his remedy. The solution to our problems with fear and discouragement is in the Lord. This is what Moses was teaching the Israelites in Deuteronomy chapter 1, and it is what the Holy Spirit is teaching us today.

The Lord, Jehovah, is our God (Deut. 1:21); so why need we fear any mere man—or, indeed, any power of hell? As our God, the Lord is faithful to all His covenant promises. He has purchased us for Himself; He has pardoned us; He has made a full and rich provision for our every need. He assures us of His presence. He is with us in every path of life, however dark or difficult it may be. He will uphold us in every trial and will make us triumph over every foe. And despite the devil's whisper that we will ultimately perish, He guarantees our safe arrival in glory. We have a great and all-sufficient Saviour. He cannot and will not fail us. Hope in Him. Victory over fear will never be ours through some psychological trick. It can be ours only as we submerge ourselves in His great love for us, for "perfect love casteth out fear" (I John 4:18). Let us then come out of the darkness of dread and discouragement and encourage our souls in the Lord.

—A. C.

Let none but the servants of sin be the slaves of fear.
JOHN FLAVEL

Power To Forgive

Forgiving one another, even as God for Christ's sake hath forgiven you.
EPHESIANS 4:32

One of our standards of holiness ought to be to treat others as God has treated us in Christ. Paul applies this truth to the area of forgiveness. How often do we find ourselves becoming bitter because of the way another believer has treated us? When we lose sight of God's forgiveness of our sins, forgiving even a brother in Christ becomes an impossible task. We ought to forgive in the same way God has forgiven us.

Our forgiveness ought to be mixed with kindness. "Be ye kind one to another." History records the brutal treatment of a pope who made a king stand barefoot in the snow for three days in order to be forgiven. If God forgives us freely by His grace, how can we be mean to those who seek forgiveness from us?

Our forgiveness is also to be with tenderness of heart. "Be ye ... tenderhearted" is Paul's admonition. David's great affection for the wayward Absalom (II Sam. 18:5, 33) falls infinitely short of that great compassion which God has demonstrated to us through Christ. But does our affection for penitent brethren not fall far short of David's? How shall we deal with our hard hearts? There is but one way. Feeling the warmth of God's compassion to us will melt our hearts toward others.

Above all, when we view that great debt we owed God freely removed for Christ's sake, our forgiving of others seems a light thing. Our Lord tells of a king's condemnation of the greatly forgiven servant who would not forgive another (Matt. 18:21-35). Could it be that the day of judgment will reveal what many of God's children already suspect, that those who cannot forgive others have themselves never been forgiven by God?
—M. W. A.

**He that demands mercy, and shows none,
ruins the bridge over which he himself is to pass.**
THOMAS ADAMS

Good Medicine

A merry heart doeth good like a medicine.

PROVERBS 17:22

A Christian lady was always so bright and cheerful that everyone wondered at her joyous spirit. "But, sister," said a friend, "you must have some clouds in your life." "Clouds?" she replied. "Why, of course. If there were no clouds, where would the showers of blessing come from?"

There is no joy like the joy of the Christian. It is one of the fruits of the Holy Spirit. It is a joy in believing; it is a rejoicing in the Lord. Thus the child of God can rejoice always. The best of this world's joy is but for a season, but that of the Christian is a joy that remains (John 15:11). It is a joy of which only sin can rob him. Hence David cried, "Restore unto me the joy of thy salvation" (Psa. 51:12). It is a joy far above all common joy. It is a "joy unspeakable and full of glory" (I Pet. 1:8). Human language is inadequate to describe it. Truly, the joy of the Lord is our strength (Neh. 8:10). Through despondency of spirit the disciples failed to watch and pray with our Lord in the garden. Yet the same men, strengthened by the joy of the Lord, "departed from the presence of the council, rejoicing that they were counted worthy to suffer shame for his name" (Acts 5:41). It was for the joy set before our Lord Jesus that the great Servant of Jehovah endured the cross, despising the shame.

Christian, here is the best of all medicines: "Rejoice evermore" (I Thess. 5:16). One day we shall hear the blessed invitation, "Enter thou into the joy of thy Lord." "Here joy begins to enter into us, there we shall enter into joy.... What joy shall the soul have, when it bathes itself forever in the pure and pleasant fountain of God's love? ... If a cluster of grapes here be so sweet, what will the full vintage be? How should all this set us a-longing for that place where sorrow cannot live, and joy cannot die" (Thomas Watson).

—M. P.

Keep company with the more cheerful sort of the godly; there is no mirth like the mirth of believers.
RICHARD BAXTER

Sanctifying the Lord in Our Lives

The heathen shall know that I am the Lord, . . .
when I shall be sanctified in you before their eyes.

EZEKIEL 36:23

The child of God is to wear the name of the Lord like a garment. This name is upon him everywhere he goes. He will want to honour God's name by his conduct and be careful not to drag that name in the gutter. Thus the Christian is said, in the language of Scripture, to sanctify His Saviour's great name. The unconverted will look upon the spiritual dress of the Christian, to see the name of God and to see Christ there. The Christian in this way becomes the Bible for an ungodly society. God is to be sanctified in His people, and the people are to sanctify the Lord.

Now the Christian knows about sanctification, but this verse speaks of something different. Some who have heard of sanctification have never heard of *God* being sanctified. The Scripture requires all of us to see to it that God is sanctified in our lives. Remember, sanctification in the Bible does not mean sinlessness. It means "being set apart for a holy use."

For God to be sanctified means that His personal presence is so in and upon His people that they are separated, made notable and distinguished by what He has done for them and through them. God's name sets the believer apart from the rest of men. He wears that name like a garment, and the child of God must keep his garments clean in a world of defilement. He is to treat God as he treats His name. He will therefore honour Him, hold Him in awe, declare Him abroad, and glorify Him as the great God of heaven.

—J. D.

Holiness in us is the copy or transcript
of the holiness that is in Christ.
PHILIP HENRY

Burdened for Others

I . . . tell you even weeping.

PHILIPPIANS 3:18

The essence of true religion is to love God with our whole being and our neighbour as ourselves. Paul states that to love our neighbour as ourselves fulfils the whole law (Gal. 5:14).

In Romans 10:1 the great apostle tells us what his heart's desire was. It was to see his kinsmen saved by the grace of God. In the previous chapter he said, "I have great heaviness and continual sorrow in my heart. For I could wish that myself were accursed from Christ for my brethren, my kinsmen according to the flesh" (Rom. 9:2, 3). Paul's heart ached with sorrow and a loving desire. He sorrowed at the prospect of his kinsmen going to hell, and he passionately longed that they might turn to Christ and be saved.

Here in Philippians Paul weeps as he warns against following the examples of seducers and evil teachers (Phil. 3:18-19). Many who profess Christ's name in reality "are the enemies of the cross of Christ," for though they claim a saving interest in Christ, their sinful and idolatrous lives are a flagrant denial of the true faith. Paul does not mince his words when it comes to defending the purity of the gospel. He is perfectly right to denounce false teachers whose religion will take souls to hell rather than heaven.

Like his Master, the Lord Jesus, who wept over Jerusalem (Matt. 23:37), Paul longed to see people saved and nurtured in the truth. Such should be the heart desire of all Christians. Are you burdened for others?

—D. C.

He who has no experience of the love of Christ for others very likely has no saving knowledge of the love of Christ at all.
ALEXANDER SIMPSON

Revive Us Again

Wilt thou not revive us again: that thy people may rejoice in thee?
PSALM 85:6

Psalm 85 is a prayer of David for revival. What God had done in past days inspired him to look forward in faith and prayer that God would do it again. In verse 6 we have three great principles of revival.

Notice first of all the *source* of revival. David recognized the truth of the sovereignty of God in revival; only God can send revival. It is not something that the church works up, but something that the Lord sends down. Isaiah prayed, "Oh that thou wouldest rend the heavens, that thou wouldest come down, that the mountains might flow down at thy presence" (Isa. 64:1).

David also speaks of the *subject* of revival. "Wilt thou not revive us again?" The emphasis needs to be placed upon *us*. The Lord's people are the subjects of revival. Every one of us needs the breath of the Holy Ghost to quicken us and revive us in our service for the Master.

Finally, we have the *song* of revival. One of the fruits of true revival is that of song and spiritual rejoicing. When revival comes, God's people come back to the fountain of joy, the Lord Himself, and they begin to rejoice in who He is and what He has done for them. Let us pray that we may expect such revival days both in our lives and in our land.

—S. B.

**When God is about to do a great work,
He pours out a spirit of supplication.**
JONATHAN EDWARDS

The Fear and Favour of God

But the midwives feared God.

EXODUS 1:17

Fear. It is a negative word, a word that conveys the sense of that dark emotion which floods our lives from time to time, and a word that elicits our sympathy for those who are ensnared by it. "The fear of God"—that is another matter altogether! Here is not the slavish dread of a mistreated servant for a wicked master, but the reverential awe of a child for its beloved father. The man or woman who lives in the fear of God will form the habit of referring every issue to Him. What is His will? What will please Him? What will honour Him?

No doubt such questions, or the like, would have crossed the minds of these Hebrew midwives. They had to take a decision. The command of the king was clear enough, but to follow his direction would surely offend the Lord. I am convinced that this fact made the decision relatively straightforward: God must not be grieved, and so the midwives "did not as the king of Egypt commanded them." A God-fearing attitude may well mean that we refuse to do what the world expects of us. We shall be constrained to say, as did Nehemiah, "So did not I, because of the fear of God" (Neh. 5:15).

It could not have been easy for the midwives to take such a stand, but they did not lose by it. "Therefore God dealt well with the midwives" (Exod. 1:20). We cannot promise that temporal prosperity will always be the result of such resolution, but he who is motivated by the fear of God will surely enjoy the favour of God.

—T. N.

We fear men so much, because we fear God so little.
WILLIAM GURNALL

Effective Praying

The effectual fervent prayer of a righteous man availeth much.

JAMES 5:16

Elijah was the prophet of fire. The amazing incident on Mount Carmel, when he called down fire on the carcass of the sacrificial bullock, stands out in everyone's memory as the greatest event in his momentous career. Yet when James was inspired to summarize Elijah's great ministry, he did not mention his calling down fire. Rather, he went much deeper and reached to the real secret of Elijah's greatness, his prayer life.

We tend to be dazzled by the spectacular. At times what the Lord does is spectacular, and we should be impressed. But too often in our love of the spectacular we neglect the most important thing of all—our communion with the Lord. We admit we need what Elijah had—his power, his knowledge of God, his lionlike boldness, his childlike faith, and his epoch-making results. But to enjoy any of these we need to experience Elijah's praying. That is why James used the prophet as an example of the principle in today's text.

The great encouragement of this verse is that God answers prayer for ordinary people. Elijah was a man of natural passions. He was not a superman. He was "a man subject to like passions as we are" (v. 17). He could be explosive, emotional, exuberant, or exhausted just as we can. "And he prayed earnestly" (v. 17). Literally, "he prayed in his prayer." God always honours that kind of praying. When we become earnest in prayer—when we stop *playing* and start *praying*—we will discover that "Elijah's God still lives today and answers still by fire," as the old hymn puts it. Let us, like Elijah, put our passion into praying. Then and only then will we become powerful in the service of the Lord.

—A. C.

Prayer can do anything that God can do.
E. M. BOUNDS

Making Up for Lost Time

I will restore to you the years that the locust hath eaten.

JOEL 2:25

Joel tells us that the Jews had lost time, and that this time lost had run into years. The thought of lost time is a depressing one, and yet we all have to admit that we have lost years from our allotted span through our failure to live for God and obey His voice. When Naomi returned to Bethlehem after ten wasted years in the country of Moab, the full extent of her loss seemed to stare her in the face. She felt that *Marah,* which means "bitter," would be a more appropriate name for her than *Naomi,* which means "pleasant." If you are feeling depressed by thinking about how many years you have lost, God has a cheering thought here to scatter the gloom: "I will restore to you the years that the locust hath eaten."

Maybe you are saying as you read this, "Impossible! When time is lost, it can't be recovered; it is water under the bridge, gone forever." That is true, but what God does is to compensate for the time lost through our carelessness and waywardness. When Naomi returned to Bethlehem, she must have been expecting to spend her last days as a poor, broken old woman. But she brought back her daughter-in-law Ruth, a saved young woman. Ruth married Boaz, who was a man of wealth and influence in Bethlehem. When Boaz and Ruth's son was born, the women of the district celebrated with Naomi and told her the child would be a restorer of her life and a nourisher of her old age.

When Naomi returned, God compensated her for the years she had lost. He can do the very same for you and me. Hallelujah!

—G. F.

You cannot have back your time, but there is a
strange and wonderful way in which God can
give back to you the wasted blessings.
C. H. SPURGEON

United or Untied?

That there be no divisions among you.

I CORINTHIANS 1:10

"Behold, how good and how pleasant it is for brethren to dwell together in unity!" (Psa. 133:1). The unity of the saints is a precious gift. This oneness is spoken of as "the unity of the Spirit" (Eph. 4:3), and therefore it is the work of the Holy Spirit to bind in Christ the members of His blood-washed church.

There is another force abroad, a demonic spirit that tries to destroy the essential unity of believers. That alien power was already at work in the Corinthian church, hence Paul's strong appeal to be united in Christ and without division.

In local churches, like Corinth, there is the danger that Christians will divide over *personalities,* not understanding that God can call a James and a John, sons of thunder, and also call a Barnabas, a son of consolation. They split over *prominence,* given to one and not to another, not realizing that God gives differing gifts to each child.

Others divide over *performance* and grumble because someone else seems to be doing better than they are. They forget God's words to Cain: "If thou doest well, shalt thou not be accepted?" *Prophetical* interpretations can divide. The study of eschatology is difficult, and many an interpretation is speculative. It seems unwise to divide because someone else's speculation does not match yours. Still others squabble over *political* issues. But human policies are fallible. It is the Scripture that is the infallible Word of God.

Paul exhorted the Corinthians to "speak the same thing," to have "the same mind," and to pursue a united witness for Christ. The word *united* becomes *untied* when the personal pronoun *I* is displaced. Let us think less of the *I* today, and more of *Him.*

—F. McC.

It is a fearful thing to make a rent and a hole in
Christ's mystical body because there is a spot in it.
SAMUEL RUTHERFORD

Arrows of Death

Their quiver is as an open sepulchre. JEREMIAH 5:16

This is the Lord's description of the armies of Babylon that were soon to assault Jerusalem. The rain of deadly arrows from the archers prompted this graphic description. Many a mortal wound would they inflict; many a grave would they fill. Theirs were arrows of death.

The Babylonians are not alone in loosing this frightening battery upon ill-defended souls. We expect such fire-power from a belligerent army, but there are people who in a spiritual sense wreak the same havoc, often while pretending great friendship or spirituality.

Are not the words of a backbiter arrows of death? If you assassinate a man's character, are you any the less a murderer? This is why the Scriptures call the man who hates his brother a murderer (I John 3:15). Despite this strong condemnation, many a church resembles a battlefield over which the salvoes of poisoned words, vicious recriminations, and other forms of verbal abuse constantly fly. Let us each learn to govern his tongue. Gossip, unjust criticism, whispering campaigns, and slander may appear to be harmless—they always do to the perpetrator. The truth is, they are not harmless. If you are guilty of any of these, remember, your behaviour is deadly.

James says that the tongue engaged in such wickedness "is set on fire of hell" (James 3:6). How much worse is it when we facilely proceed from such diabolical activity to the praise of God! Rightly does James protest, "My brethren, these things ought not so to be" (v. 10). Let us recognize the evil of shooting arrows of death from our mouths and cry for the sanctifying, cleansing coal from heaven's altar to set our lips on fire in a better cause (Isa. 6:6-7). With a tongue set aflame by the Lord we will proclaim His Word to a dying world. Then our words will be arrows of conviction and messages of mercy.

—A. C.

A sharp tongue is the only edged tool
that grows keener with constant use.
WASHINGTON IRVING

Hearing the Shepherd

Why hear ye him?

JOHN 10:20

The worldling asks, "Why this Bible at your kitchen table and at your bedside? Why attend a church that is all preaching and prayer with nothing to entertain?" These are real questions from the lips of worldlings, but the Christian can answer them a thousand times over!

Hearing Christ's voice is the mark of true sheep. Our Lord says, "My sheep hear my voice" (John 10:27). All who claim to be Christ's redeemed sheep have heard His voice humbling them and calling them to sit at His feet in the enjoyment of pardon from all sin. Do you see that sheep darting from the flock, seeking its own way in rebellion to the Shepherd's voice? That is a lost sheep, but Christ's sheep hear His voice and follow Him.

Their shepherd speaks *words of truth.* Many hirelings are clamouring for your ears, but Christ alone speaks savingly to your soul. He tells you, "I am the good shepherd: the good shepherd giveth his life for the sheep" (v. 11). No other supposed saviour speaks words of truth and life as our beloved Redeemer in His death.

This good Shepherd also speaks *words of love and mercy.* Go to one of Christ's sheep, Mary Magdalene, out of whom went seven devils, and ask her, "Why hear ye him?" With flowing tears she will tell the story of her Saviour's multiplied mercies. His words of pardon were music to her ears and the song of her soul. The Master's voice inspires His hearing sheep to listen with the fullest assurance to the Shepherd of their souls and to turn a deaf ear to the criticism of the world.

—I. G.

Only once did God choose a completely sinless preacher.
ALEXANDER WHYTE

On the Lord's Side

Blessed are all they that put their trust in him.

PSALM 2:12

Although Christ is precious to those who know Him as Lord and Saviour, He is not precious to all. We cannot but be sickened when we see the blatant disregard shown to our Lord on every hand. He is mocked by arrogant sinners, and His authority is ignored by virtually all. If sinful man had his way, every vestige of true Christianity and every thought of Christ would be set aside. Admittedly, there are times when it seems that sinful man is getting his way. It sometimes appears that wickedness has usurped the throne of God Himself. But faith knows that things are not always what they appear to be. Psalm 2 gives a sight of reality. It shows us both heaven and earth and assures us that heaven rules. It shows us our precious Christ, who is the Lord of every man's destiny. It shows that in the spiritual arena, "it's not over until it's over." And it shows that when it is over, we had best be on the Lord's side.

In the face of rebellious opposition by every race and social class, God sits with eternal authority on His throne, where He does whatsoever He desires. His laughing at man's rebellious folly would be comical if the issues at stake were not so grave. What utter folly to reject and spurn the Lord! Overriding man's silly efforts to throw off divine rule, God declares that Christ is enthroned and gives Him universal authority. One way or another, every man must submit to the authority of Messiah. Eternal destiny is linked to the Son. Those who reject Him perish, but blessed are those who trust. Therefore, be smart, be instructed, serve Him with fear, rejoice with trembling, and above all kiss the Son, embracing Him in love and faith.

—M. P. V. B.

There is nothing got by scuffling with God.
WILLIAM GURNALL

Honourable Mention

Salute Tryphena and Tryphosa, who labour in the Lord.
ROMANS 16:12

Who were they? Indeed, who were the vast majority of the long list of names in Romans 16 to whom Paul sends his greetings? We would wonder what profit there is to be gained by the consideration of these verses. If we look a little more closely, we will see that there is a valuable lesson to be learned from this passage of seemingly disjointed salutations.

Let us remember first that these were people to whom Paul wanted especially to give his regards. Somewhere, somehow, their lives had crossed his. Probably they had been won to Christ through Paul's ministry and had repaid the apostle by helping him through very difficult times. Paul loved them because they were the Lord's people, but he felt especially indebted to them and wanted to be remembered to them because of their service.

There is no mention of their gifts, money, or winning personalities—just their labour. These were just common, ordinary people who served the Lord in whatever way they could. And for that, they are forever immortalized in God's Word.

Somehow we have got it all backwards. It seems that too often the wealthy, or the intelligent, or the gifted get most of the recognition in many churches. I do not know who these people in this passage were, but God wants us to remember them for their work in His vineyard. You see, what is vital to the work of God is the common, ordinary labourer. Too many Christians feel useless to God because they do not have many talents or much money or a winning personality. But what God wants is *you!*

It was their labours that put these people in Paul's heart and prayers. Now tell me, if you were living then, would he have remembered you? Would your name be found among these servants of God? If not, why not? Oh, let nothing keep you back from throwing your all into God's work.

—J. W.

Oh, then be ashamed, Christians, that worldlings are
more studious and industrious to make sure of pebbles,
than you are to make sure of pearls.
THOMAS BROOKS

The Power of Prayer

They that wait upon the Lord shall renew their strength.

ISAIAH 40:31

Every great expenditure of energy tends to produce an opposite reaction. Elijah discovered this truth when he succumbed to fatigue and depression after his marvellous victory on Mount Carmel. It happens to us all. Even the strongest of men grow weary. Is that your present experience? Are you so spiritually, emotionally, and mentally worn out that you do not have the energy to study, pray, or serve as you know you ought? If so, do not despair, for the Lord has a word for you. It is a word of encouragement and instruction as to how to have your strength renewed.

The secret of renewing your strength is to wait upon the Lord. Wait. That means you must take time in the Lord's presence. It means you must be patient. David said, "I waited patiently for the Lord; and he inclined unto me, and heard my cry" (Psa. 40:1). You should wait submissively and expectantly, pleading the promise of God. And, of course, you should wait restfully. Here is one of the great secrets of renewing spiritual strength or recovering emotional balance: rest in the Lord. Rest in His atoning work at Calvary. Rest in His enduring love. Rest in His precious promises. "In returning and rest shall ye be saved; in quietness and in confidence shall be your strength" (Isa. 30:15).

The Lord can renew your strength. He can revive your soul and make you a faithful and useful servant of His Son. It all starts in the place of prayer. Weariness will flee as you wait upon the Lord.

—A. C.

When you have submitted yourself completely and trusted entirely . . . you shall renew your strength.
C. H. SPURGEON

The Rigours and Rewards
of True Holiness

Then shalt thou understand the fear of the Lord,
and find the knowledge of God.

PROVERBS 2:5

The earnest Christian soul is advancing toward the "city which hath foundations, whose builder and maker is God" (Heb. 11:10). God does not lightly use the terms of battle and toil when describing the endeavours required by those engaged in this pilgrimage. The plastic smiles and the tinfoil graces of modern "Christianity" are far removed from the reality of serving God in an "untoward [or, perverse] generation" (Acts 2:40). The appropriation of grace requires us to "receive," "hide," "incline," "apply," "cry after," "lift up the voice," "seek," and "search" (Prov. 5:1-4). Here is the flurry of activity that marks the truly saved. Such activity is the proof of true grace residing within the heart. We are not inclined by nature toward such pursuits. Before conversion we ran after the iniquities of this world. But grace changed that. Like a newborn lamb instinctively seeking its mother's milk for nourishment, so the soul born again by the power of God's Holy Spirit and washed in the Saviour's blood seeks nourishment from God's ordained means of grace. The chief of these are the Bible, prayer, and the fellowship of fellow believers.

What a full-time business being a Christian is! But what gains there are from it! There is preservation from the "evil man" (v. 12) and deliverance from the "strange woman" (v. 16), metaphors for the sins of the world and the flesh. The treasures of this world bring ultimate sorrow and misery—not fit reward for the efforts required to obtain them. On the other hand, labouring for the treasures of heaven brings no sorrow in its wake. In bending our backs in such labours, we find rest and reap a harvest in time and a harvest in eternity. Gods pays double wages. In time, our ways are guarded, for God "preserveth the way of his saints" (v. 8). In eternity, He will embrace and welcome us into heaven with eternal glory.

—I. F.

There is nothing but heaven worth setting our hearts upon.
RICHARD BAXTER

Suffering for Christ

For unto you it is given in the
behalf of Christ . . . to suffer for his sake.

PHILIPPIANS 1:29

Every Christian is expected to experience his share of suffering for the truth. He should not shrink from it nor take the easy road out by compromising. Dear child of God, are you prepared to endure affliction for the sake of Christ, or are you looking for the line of least resistance?

We recall that the children of Ephraim, fully armed and carrying bows, turned back in the day of battle because they were not prepared to take their share of suffering along with their brethren (Psa. 78:9). How many are like Obadiah, who moved in secret to protect the prophets of the Lord, yet publicly associated with Ahab, an avowed enemy of the Lord! He was not prepared to take his share of suffering alongside Elijah (I Kings 18). How many there are today who are prepared to believe in Christ but are not prepared to suffer for Him!

In contrast, we think of Moses, who chose rather to suffer affliction with the people of God because he esteemed "the reproach of Christ greater riches than the treasures in Egypt" (Heb. 11:25, 26), and of Epaphroditus, who laboured in the gospel until "he was nigh unto death" (Phil. 2:30). The Philippians had witnessed Paul's persecution in their own city and had seen his steadfastness in the Lord (Acts 16:19-40). All these and others were prepared to suffer for the cause of Christ. Which company would you be found in?

Trusting Christ does not mean an end to the conflict. The Bible says, "Yea, and all that will live godly in Christ Jesus shall suffer persecution" (II Tim. 3:12). Remember, it is for His sake. He suffered for us. The very least we can do to show our love to Him is to be willing to suffer for Him.

—D. C.

It is and should be the care of a Christian
not to suffer for sin, nor sin in suffering.
VAVASOR POWELL

A Message from God

I have a message from God unto thee.

JUDGES 3:20

The world's first gospel telephone service commenced years ago in New York. A preacher was confined to bed by illness when one day the telephone rang. When he answered, the caller said, "Sorry, wrong number." "No," replied the preacher spontaneously, "you have not reached a wrong number. I have a message from God for you." And he proceeded to give the caller the message of the gospel. From that beginning grew a ministry that has reached countless thousands in different parts of the world.

I have a message from God for you. We Christians should never forget that we are Christ's witnesses. We have the message the world needs. We often waste our time and effort speaking about earthly, inconsequential things, but rarely do we give out our message from God.

Our message is a message of God's judgment upon sin. That was Ehud's message to Eglon. We cannot expect that it will be popular. This sin-crazed world does not want to hear that God disapproves of its wickedness. There are many churches and preachers who are all too willing to change the Biblical message to agree with modern ungodliness. But the servant of Christ cannot do that. Our message from God can never be anything but one of God's judgment on sin.

Without that we can never bring a message of hope to the sinner. Our message from God is that God in love has sent His Son to be the propitiation for—the sacrifice to appease God's wrath against—our sins (Rom. 3:25). There is power in the blood of Jesus Christ to reconcile the guiltiest sinner to God, and thus our message to all sinners is "Repent ye, and believe the gospel" (Mark 1:15). By faith in Christ, without any merit or works of their own, guilty sinners are pardoned, justified, and made new creatures in Christ. What a message! Surely it is worth telling.

—A. C.

I preached as never sure to preach again,
And as a dying man to dying men.
RICHARD BAXTER

44

Be Prepared

If the iron be blunt, and he do not whet the edge, then must he put to more strength: but wisdom is profitable to direct.

ECCLESIASTES 10:10

Sharpening axes is mainly the concern of lumberjacks, but in analogy it speaks to all of us regardless of the work God has given us to do. The lesson is on the surface and obvious: there is an advantage in being prepared for any task. Labour is unavoidable. Although the sorrow and sweat of labour are part of sin's curse, the fact of labour is God's gift. Rather than focussing on the curse, we should recognize it as God's gift, use it, and enjoy it. "Whatsoever thy hand findeth to do, do it with thy might" (Eccles. 9:10). God has put an axe in our hands, and we should learn to use it for His glory.

Every job requires tools of some sort. The more efficient we are in using them, the better we can perform our task. A dull axe will eventually do the job, but it requires more effort and results in a ragged cut. It is wise to prepare for the job by making sure our tools are in good working condition.

Being prepared is good advice for everyday life, and it applies to spiritual work as well. Regardless of our calling, we have the common tools of Scripture and prayer for the work of the ministry. We prepare for service by knowing as much as we can about God's Word and by seeking the Lord in prayer for the necessary measure of His Spirit to complete the task. It is foolish to attempt spiritual work without spiritual tools. Let us give ourselves, therefore, to diligence not only in the actual demonstrations of service, but in the necessary time of preparation in the tool shed of meditation, prayer, and Bible study.

—M. P. V. B.

The price of mastery in any field is thorough preparation.
ANONYMOUS

Strangers in the Earth

Peter, an apostle of Jesus Christ, to the strangers scattered throughout Pontus, Galatia, Cappadocia, Asia, and Bithynia.

I PETER 1:1

Peter first addresses these people to whom he writes by inspiration as "strangers." It is a suitable title for the believing church, though of course we should be neither strangers to one another in the church nor strangers to God and the courts of His presence. Peter addresses the believers as strangers from a different point of view. In different places throughout his epistle he defines what he means by this particular manner of address.

In I Peter 2:11 he speaks about some things to which a Christian should be a stranger—"fleshly lusts, which war against the soul." Notice the tender language of the apostle. He implores the believers in love as strangers and pilgrims to abstain from these things. In the first sin it was a desiring, a fleshly lust, that constituted the fall in the heart of Eve (Gen. 3:6). Let us be strangers to such things by identifying through faith with the victory of Christ's death and resurrection.

In I Peter 4:4 he introduces some people who think the Christian strange. They think it strange that these believers no longer run with the world. They see a change in their lives that is inexplicable to them. Can the ungodly see that mysterious change in your life, a change that is wrought by the divine operation of the Holy Spirit? Does the peculiarity of holiness mark you as a stranger in the world?

Finally, in I Peter 4:12, he underlines some things that the Christian should not think strange—the fiery tests and affliction to which we are appointed in this world. These are only the tools in the loving hand of the Master Potter by which He conforms us more and more to the image of His Son. They are His means of making us feel that we are strangers on the earth and of separating us more and more unto Himself.

—R. J. B.

The pressures of life are the hands of the Potter.
ANONYMOUS

Numbered Because Ransomed

Take ye the sum of all the congregation.

NUMBERS 1:2

The title of the book of Numbers is taken from the Septuagint and refers to one of the outstanding events recorded in the book, the numbering of the people. At both the beginning and the end of the book, the sum of the congregation of Israel is given.

The emphasis on the numbering of the people conveys various lessons to us, one of them being that "the Lord knoweth them that are his" (II Tim. 2:19). He is aware of each one in His family. The company of the redeemed no man can number, but the Lord has a register of the entire host. Their names are "written in the book of life of the Lamb" (Rev. 13:8). Notice that this count taken in the opening chapter of Numbers was in accordance with specific conditions which the Lord had earlier revealed to Moses. Exodus 30:12 shows that no one could be numbered among God's people unless he first paid "a ransom for his soul." It is only the ransomed who make up the true congregation of the Lord.

Observe that the ransom price was fixed by the Lord: "half a shekel after the shekel of the sanctuary" (Exod. 30:13). The Lord Himself has set the standard for inclusion among the host who are marching to Zion, and He will accept no other. Christ's blood is that ransom price. It alone meets the divine requirements. We must neither add to nor take from the gospel, just as the Israelites were not to give more or less than that half shekel. If you are yet unsaved, you must learn that you can never be counted among the redeemed until you make "his soul an offering for sin" (Isa. 53:10). Christ poured out His soul unto death. He gave His life a ransom for many, the life being His own precious blood, since "the life of the flesh is in the blood" (Lev. 17:11). That is a sufficient payment for sin. Rest in it alone; nothing else will do.

—J. G.

Christ was numbered among sinners that sinners might be numbered among saints.
ALEXANDER SIMPSON

Effective Evangelism

They were pricked in their heart.　　ACTS 2:37

The breaking of the hearts of the Jews who assembled to hear Peter's sermon at Pentecost was as much a miracle as the gift of tongues. Those who listened to the apostle's words had but recently demonstrated their determination to hold to their self-righteousness and had callously demanded the death of the Son of God. Now there was conviction, conversion, confession of Christ, continuance in faith, and consecration to God. How did it come about? What preceded this pricking of hearts is most instructive.

There was clearly the exercise of prayer. Comparing Acts 1:4 with Acts 2:1 reveals that the church had assembled to wait on God in prayer. It was this supplication with earnestness and expectancy that brought blessing upon the church and made such an impact on the hearts of the unconverted. Do we desire the same blessing? Then let us pray!

For those who thus waited, there was then the experience of power (2:4). When they ministered, it was in the "demonstration of the Spirit and of power" (I Cor. 2:4). Without prayer before God, we are without power before men. This power is promised to those who pray (Luke 11:13). As Spurgeon once said, "One bright blessing which . . . prayer brings . . . is . . . an anointing from the Holy One."

Then there was the exaltation of a Person. Peter's message was full of Christ—His person, passion, power, and pardon— nothing more and nothing less. It was this Christ-centred preaching by Philip that God mightily owned and blessed in Samaria (Acts 8:5-8), and Paul's determination to preach "Christ crucified" (I Cor. 1:23) resulted in notorious characters being transformed in rebirth. Nothing can break the heart like the sight of the crucified Saviour. "They shall look upon me whom they have pierced, and they shall mourn" (Zech. 12:10). Let us pray for grace to present Christ to lost souls with the power and demonstration of the Holy Spirit. Only then can our evangelism be effective.

—D. F.

Some like to live within the sound of church or chapel bell;
I'd rather run a rescue shop within a yard of hell.
WILLIAM BOOTH

___

48

The Seeing Eye

The hearing ear, and the seeing eye, the Lord
hath made even both of them.   PROVERBS 20:12

The eye is most exquisitely and delicately constructed. This little organ has tens of millions of electrical connections and can handle one and a half million simultaneous messages. The retina alone, covering less than a square inch, contains 137 million light-sensitive receptor cells. The tiny muscles of the eye, milligram for milligram, are among the body's strongest. On average, they move about one hundred thousand times daily, bringing objects into sharp focus. A similar exercising of the leg muscles would entail a fifty-mile walk. Truly, we are fearfully and wonderfully made.

Oh, how precious is the gift of sight! It is pre-eminently the learning sense. We absorb an estimated 80 percent of all our knowledge by means of sight. Christian, guard the eye-gate. Resolve with the psalmist, "I will set no wicked thing before mine eyes" (Psa. 101:3).

How much more precious is spiritual sight! The natural man is spiritually blind. The Christian once was darkness, but now is light in the Lord. "One thing I know, that, whereas I was blind, now I see" (John 9:25). These are the words of a man blind from birth. He was ushered into a new world—the world of sight with all its attendant sensations. His experience strikes a chord in every redeemed heart.

Yet "he who sees most needs to have his eyes enlightened, for how little as yet of the glory of God have any of us beheld!" (C. H. Spurgeon). Oh, that increasingly "the Father of glory, may give unto you the spirit of wisdom and revelation in the knowledge of him: the eyes of your understanding being enlightened; that ye may know what is the hope of his calling, and what the riches of the glory of his inheritance in the saints, and what is the exceeding greatness of his power to us-ward who believe" (Eph. 1:17-19).

—M. P.

God's mind is revealed in Scripture, but we can see
nothing without the spectacles of the Holy Ghost.
THOMAS MANTON

49

Accepted in the Beloved

He hath made us accepted in the beloved. EPHESIANS 1:6

Paul knew what it was to be rejected by men. Even in Ephesus after a very fruitful ministry, the townspeople wanted to be rid of him (Acts 19:23-41). Yet Paul could face man's rejection knowing that the God who created him now also accepted him. To a world in which multitudes are labouring to obtain a favourable position before God, Paul boldly declares that he is accepted. The word *accepted* has the idea of one whom God has highly favoured (Luke 1:28). Indeed, the word comes from the same Greek root as the word for "grace." Our acceptance is not based on our merit, but is freely bestowed by God. What a range of spiritual and emotional problems this glorious truth deals with! While the world's psychologists vainly seek to bolster the ego of fallen men with talk of self-worth and self-esteem, the gospel points us to God's acceptance of us in Christ. If we have His favour, why should we ever fear the wrath or hatred of men or devils?

Notice that it is God Himself who makes us accepted. There is no room for human error, for our Father who is perfect (Matt. 5:48) guarantees our standing. Thus we have assurance that the work is complete. Our acceptance is not something we are still longing and waiting for: "He hath made us accepted." Let us then by faith rejoice that the work has already been completed.

The question is, how could a holy God ever accept a vile, wretched sinner? The answer is found in the Beloved. We are united to the One whom God loved before the foundation of the world (John 17:24) and whom He called His "beloved Son" (Matt. 3:17; 17:5). The beloved Son has atoned for all our sins (Heb. 1:3) and provided for us His perfect righteousness (Phil. 3:9). Yea, we are now "complete in him" (Col. 2:10). Keeping this great truth of acceptance before us, we, like Paul, can face a hostile world with confidence.

—M. W. A.

We are hateful in ourselves as sinners,
but accepted in Christ as sons.
MATTHEW POOLE

50

Home Safety

When thou buildest a new house, then thou shalt make a
battlement for thy roof, that thou bring not blood
upon thine house, if any man fall from thence.

DEUTERONOMY 22:8

The Jews built their homes with flat roofs to which there was
access from inside the building. The roof was therefore a place of
potential danger, for it would have been possible for a child, or
even an adult, to fall to his death. To ensure the safety of any who
might be on the roof, the Lord commanded His people to build a
battlement for the roof of every new house. The principle is clear:
God's people are responsible to do all in their power to ensure the
safety of all in their home.

This duty falls most heavily on Christian fathers. They have
a particular responsibility to build their home according to a safe
plan. Father, protect your family, especially your children, from
the dangers that can so easily befall them. We are told that most
accidents occur in the home. Spiritually, it is all too true that it is
in the home that children are exposed to the very things that
threaten their souls. Have not many fathers allowed their homes
to be a catchment pool for the filth of Hollywood? Have they not
failed to erect a defence against the constant stream of filth and
violence that emanates from their television sets, their video
recorders, and their music centres? How many Christian fathers
have lost their children to the world and the devil because they
built no protection against these insidious evils inside their
own homes! The best battlements are the Word of God, read
and obeyed; a warm, loving family worship of Christ; earnest
prayer; and a home regulated by the gospel of grace. Have you
built your battlement?

—A. C.

If you would train your children rightly, train them in the
way they should go and not in the way they would.

J. C. RYLE

51

The Privilege of Fellowship with God

Truly our fellowship is with the Father.

I JOHN 1:3

It is important that we think right about having fellowship with God. When communion with our gracious Lord becomes merely a duty, we have lost sight of one of the highest privileges known to man. The chief end of man is to glorify God and enjoy Him forever. Adam prior to the fall experienced unbroken fellowship with his Maker. Every thought of his heart was well pleasing to God. But when sin entered the world, everything changed. Adam was driven from his Creator's presence and stripped of the rich privilege of fellowship with God.

Let us never lightly esteem the glory that is ours in coming with boldness to the throne of grace. It took the very blood of Jesus Christ, God's only begotten Son, to restore us to this forfeited privilege. Do we realize that fellowship with our Creator and Redeemer is the reward of Christ's suffering? So may we cherish and glory in the cross of God's dear Son and continually apprehend it as our basis for fellowship with our Father in heaven. What was lost by the actions of the first Adam has been restored through the work of the last Adam.

Not only are Christ's sufferings the ground of our fellowship with God, but also the substance of communing with Him. The Lamb has brought us back to a privileged position of walking with God. So may we seek to follow the mind of God as we set our hearts on His beloved Son. Our holy God will not have fellowship with those who walk in darkness; therefore let us walk in the light of God's eternal love that delivered over Jesus Christ to pay the necessary punishment of sin in order that we should praise His holy name in heaven rather than gnash our teeth at Him for all eternity in hell.

—R. J. W.

Access to God lies open to none but His pure worshippers.
JOHN CALVIN

The Marks of the Christian

Parteth the hoof . . . and cheweth the cud. LEVITICUS 11:3

What are the distinguishing marks of the Christian? Sikhs and religious Jews are recognized by their dress; Moslems, by their use of "Peace be upon him" when speaking of Mohammed. But how does one recognize a Christian? This verse gives a hint of the answer.

The Lord put a difference between the clean and the unclean animals. The clean animal was recognized by two marks: it parted the hoof, and it chewed the cud. In other words, the distinguishing marks concerned the foot and the mouth.

The Christian likewise should be instantly distinguished in society by his holy *talk* and his holy *walk*. Paul encouraged the Colossians to let their "speech be alway with grace, seasoned with salt" (Col. 4:6). The Christian's conversation should always be seasoned with the salt of grace. He should be God's salt shaker, helping to season the language of the community.

The clean animal chewed the cud, suggesting to us that the believer is to digest and meditate on the Word of God as his daily food. With this Word in his heart, he will have holy conversation on his lips.

The clean animal parted the hoof. It had a peculiar walk; it was different from other animals. At one time the Christian walked according to the course of this world. Now, transformed by God's grace, he is to walk in love, circumspectly, as a child of light.

Be warned that the Christian must pass *both* tests. To have only the *talk* is hypocrisy. To have the *walk* without the testimony is self-righteousness. Some people can talk like a saint, but inconsistent actions damage their testimony. Worse is the Christian with "foot-and-mouth disease"—neither his lips nor his life is holy.

The believer who talks and walks right may not be the most popular fellow according to the world, but he will be blessed of God. Will you talk and walk for the Lord Jesus Christ today?

—F. McC.

**The secret of holiness is heart
occupation with Christ Himself.**
HARRY A. IRONSIDE

The Blessing of Bible Reading

Blessed is he that readeth, and they that hear the words of this prophecy, and keep those things which are written therein.

REVELATION 1:3

Seven times in the book of Revelation the Lord pronounces a blessing upon His people. Amid all the upheavals with which the book deals, this truth stands as an impregnable rock: God's people are a blessed people. Four of the seven blessings refer to their life of obedience (1:3; 16:15; 22:7, 14). The other three blessings refer to their death (14:13), resurrection (20:6), and participation in the marriage supper of the Lamb (19:9). How extensive is the blessing of salvation! We are now blessed in life, whatever opposition and affliction we suffer; we will be blessed in death; we will be blessed by being raised among the saints in the first resurrection; we will enjoy heaven forever. Let us face the world today as a people blessed indeed. Particularly let us lay hold of the first blessing. It is in three parts.

First, there is the blessing of *reading* the Bible. The reference is primarily to the public reading of the Revelation, but the blessing could be pronounced on reading this book only because it is true Scripture. The public reading of God's Word is a blessed and important part of the church's worship. It is also the fundamental part of each Christian's worship. We would be happier and more useful Christians if we gave ourselves to the constant reading of God's Word.

Second, there is the blessing of *hearing* the Bible. Hearing is equivalent to accepting and applying the message of the Bible to our daily lives and circumstances.

Finally, there is the blessing of *obeying* the Bible, "keeping" what it says. To keep is to remember and ponder so as to obey (cf. Luke 2:19).

The gateway to all the other blessings a Christian enjoys is Scripture. Read it, hear it, obey it, and experience for yourself the blessing pronounced by the Lord. Neglect it and you will find that nothing can really please or satisfy a saint who slights the Scriptures.

—A. C.

Whatever keeps me from my Bible is my enemy, however harmless it may appear to me.
A. W. TOZER

Ripe for Harvest

Thou shalt come to thy grave in a full age, like as a shock of corn cometh in in his season.

JOB 5:26

In these words there is a beautiful picture of the death of a Christian, the passing from this scene of time of one who is in a right relationship with God. The absolute certainty of the limitations placed upon our earthly span is plainly announced: "Thou shalt come to thy grave." It is wise to consider our latter end and to prepare for it. The Bible likens the departure of a believer from this world to a shock of corn ready for harvest, fully ripened and developed. Every child of God is ready for the reaper.

Our text does not say that every Christian comes to the grave in *old* age. It declares that they come to the tomb in *full* age. Not all Christians live to old age; nevertheless, every one who walks with God lives to a full age. They remain until their work is done, their race is won, and their course is finished. A young couple were called of the Lord to serve Him in the jungles of Brazil. They trained and prepared themselves for the task. Eventually the way was opened for them to depart. Upon arriving in Brazil by ship, they had to commence another long journey up the Amazon River. The young woman took ill and died on the boat. Her distraught husband had to bury her alongside the bank of the river, near a heathen village. When news of her death reached her loved ones back in Northern Ireland, many were speechless with shock and dismay. Today, near where her body is buried, through her husband's witness and testimony carried out amidst sorrow and adversity, a thriving Christian church operates in the village. Nevertheless, the strangest of all these events was the dead missionary's last letter home, written as she journeyed up the Amazon. After signing her name, she put John 17:4. The verse reads, "I have glorified thee on the earth: I have finished the work which thou gavest me to do." She had reached her full age. She was ready to go home.

—S. B. C.

We are immortal till our work is done.
GEORGE WHITEFIELD

Restored to Usefulness

*A bruised reed shall he not break, and
the smoking flax shall he not quench.*

ISAIAH 42:3

The reed and the flax, or wick, are descriptions of what God's people ought to be. The word translated "reed" signifies the *stalk* of wheat (Gen. 41:5, 22), from which we may deduce that we are to grow and produce fruit. It also signifies the *branches* of the candlestick in the tabernacle (Exod. 25:32), indicating that we are to be Christ's witnesses. It also signifies the *arm bone* between the shoulder and the elbow (Job 31:22), teaching us that we are to be the Lord's strong instruments to execute His will and to do His work. The reed was used in ancient times as a walking-cane. Christians are to be dependable in bearing the weight of trust placed in them by God and man. One kind of reed was used to produce sweet calamus for the holy anointing oil (Exod. 30:23). We are to have the holy fragrance of Christ about us. At times the reed was used in musical instruments to produce sounds of beauty and praise. There should be no sweeter sound on earth than a believer's praise.

The flax is the wick of a lamp or torch. It is meant to burn brightly and dispel the surrounding darkness with its light. It reminds us that Christians are "the light of the world" (Matt. 5:14).

All this tells us what we ought to be. But bruised reeds and smoking flax only add noxious fumes to the darkness. Humanly speaking they are useless and hopeless—but not to Christ. If you have fallen into spiritual defeat and have lost your usefulness, there is grace for you. The Saviour can repair the broken reed. He can restore brightness to the smoking flax. He will not discard you. Remember, even if your brethren have given you up, the Lord has not.

—A. C.

**God does not love us because we are valuable,
but we are valuable because God loves us.**
MARTIN LUTHER

Ministering Spirits

*Ministering spirits, sent forth to minister for
them who shall be heirs of salvation.* **HEBREWS 1:14**

The ministry of the angels of God is an integral part of His scheme
of redemption. There is abundant proof of this throughout all
Scripture, but nowhere more so than in connection with the life of
Christ the Redeemer. Angels announced His birth and warned
Joseph to flee with the young child. They ministered to Christ at
His temptation and in Gethsemane. They heralded His resurrection and accompanied Him at His ascension, as they will also do
at His return. Not surprisingly then, they minister to the heirs of
salvation whom Christ has redeemed.

One very striking fact emerges as we study their service for
God's people—the tremendous interest they have in the salvation
of sinners. Angels are holy, sinless beings, but creatures nonetheless and therefore not omniscient. Consequently, as they behold
God's redemptive dealings with sinful men, their knowledge increases. Paul says to the Ephesians, "Unto the principalities and
powers in heavenly places [will] be known by [or through] the
church the manifold wisdom of God" (Eph. 3:10). Peter also, in
referring to the things of Christ in our salvation, says, "Which
things the angels desire to look into" (I Pet. 1:12). Our salvation
arouses the deep interest of the angels of God. What a matter for
wonder it must be for them that God passed by their colleagues
who sinned, leaving them to the eternal consequences of their sin,
and yet He chose to save men, much lower creatures. The expression *to look into* speaks of someone stooping down to get a closer
view. How amazing it is that the angels who have spent their
entire existence in the presence of God, eternally happy and forever secure, should desire to look into the salvation of wretches
such as we are!

—J. G.

The angels are *ministering* spirits;
they are not *governing* spirits.
JOHN BROWN

Today and Tomorrow

Boast not thyself of to morrow; for
thou knowest not what a day may bring forth.

PROVERBS 27:1

All such boasting is evil. It is arrogant; it is presumptuous. "Go to now, ye that say, To day or to morrow we will go into such a city, and continue there a year, and buy and sell, and get gain" (James 4:13). How certain all is to these traders! They calculate on the future with unhesitating confidence. They plan as if everything were at their disposal. They pride themselves in certain gain. It is the language of folly. We know not what a day may bring forth. They plan for a whole year, when they cannot see even one day ahead. How frail is our hold on this world! Shall they go to such a city? What if health and strength flee? Can no accident befall them? Shall they buy and sell and get gain? Do prices never fluctuate? Do markets never collapse? Above all, they have no thought of God or His providence. As Thomas à Kempis said, "Man proposes, but God disposes." Saint of God, never be guilty of making your plans without God. Be careful to commit your ways to Him who is Lord of all. "In all thy ways acknowledge him, and he shall direct thy paths" (Prov. 3:6). Consciously recognize and bow in lowliest submission to divine providence. "For that ye ought to say, If the Lord will, we shall live, and do this, or that" (James 4:15).

Thomas Fuller was convicted about the practice of placing the words *God willing* in parentheses, as if they were not essential to the sentence. "Hereafter," he said, "I will write these words freely and fairly without any enclosure about them. Let critics censure it for bad grammar, I am sure it is good divinity." In similar spirit, the child of God ought to live each day as if it were his last. Opportunities missed today may be lost forever. Christian, this day, "whatsoever thy hand findeth to do, do it with thy might" (Eccles. 9:10).

—M. P.

One today is worth two tomorrows.
WILLIAM SECKER

The School of Affliction

Behold, I take away from thee the desire of thine eyes with a stroke.
EZEKIEL 24:16

Ezekiel's wife had died. No family is immune from sorrow and loss. Death comes to the best of God's servants. Ezekiel was the true disciple in sorrow. He bowed to God's benevolent will, learning submission by the things he suffered. Devotion does not offer indemnity. There are no exceptions when it comes to admission into the school of affliction. Everyone must enrol there. The Lord "scourgeth every son whom he receiveth" (Heb. 12:6).

God will sometimes take away from His saints that which He has given. He may see fit to remove from us some of our earthly comforts. He may take away our health in measure. Eyesight becomes impaired, or pain and affliction are constant companions. Inevitably a loved one is taken. God does not lightly afflict His people. There is a good purpose to it all. Suffering teaches the Christian many things: he must trust his God as much in the cloud as in the sunshine; God is the giver of all we possess; all things are given us on loan; no gift is greater than the Giver; God is to be glorified in everything, even in our grief; no child of God can really suffer loss, for heaven will bring blessed rest and everlasting compensation.

Death brought Ezekiel to a better understanding of the great heart of God. He knew God had forbidden him to make a show of mourning for his wife. That the servant must not drop a tear reminds us of a better hope. We sorrow not as those outside of Christ (I Thess. 4:13).

The prophet's wife did not die as one alone upon the earth. Her death coincided with the beginnings of darkest tragedy in Israel, the loss of many lives, the loss of the temple—felt in heaven as the loss of one's beloved. Yet there was a blessing. Ezekiel's family grief opened his own mouth, giving him an answer from God and a message of abiding comfort to the broken-hearted.

—J. D.

Grace grows best in the winter.
SAMUEL RUTHERFORD

Growth in Grace

The righteous shall flourish like the palm tree.

PSALM 92:12

The palm tree is God's Old Testament picture from the world of nature of the Christian. Everything about it gives us some insight into growth in grace. Let us consider together some of the unique features of the palm tree that have valuable lessons for us today.

The palm tree exists because of its God-given ability to find water. It has a tap root that can seek out water or hidden springs under the desert sands. Water, in the symbolic language of Scripture, is a type of the Holy Spirit. Christ Himself said, "He that believeth on me, as the scripture hath said, out of his belly shall flow rivers of living water" (John 7:38). The Christian can live only as he is born of the Spirit and filled by the Spirit day by day.

The palm tree, by divine design, was made to grow straight and upward. The Christian is called to live a life of uprightness and holiness. Ananias was told by the Lord that he would find the newly converted Saul of Tarsus in the "street which is called Straight" (Acts 9:11). Let us live to "shew that the Lord is upright" (Psa. 92:15).

The palm tree brings forth fruit in old age (v. 14). Authorities inform us that the palm tree produces its best fruit at from thirty to one hundred years of age. It was at thirty years of age that the Lord Jesus began His public ministry. There should be in the Christian life with the passing of years not only "fruit," "more fruit," and "much fruit" (John 15:2-5), but also, as with the palm tree, there should be flourishing fruitfulness that glorifies our Lord.

—S. B.

> Spiritual growth consists most in the growth
> of the root, which is out of sight.
> MATTHEW HENRY

Good News for Old Age

Even to your old age I am he; and even to hoar hairs will I carry you.
ISAIAH 46:4

Growing old is a shock to most people. That may be why so many men and women of maturing years use the skill of the beautician to cover the hoar hairs! A leading neurologist once said, "Retirement can be the severest shock that the human organism can sustain." He was right, for the declining years of life are in many cases fraught with worry and fear—and too often bring abandonment. Is there any more heart-rending sight than old men and women shut away in some institution, forgotten by family and friends? The older we grow, the less use the world has for us. I know that some years ago researchers claimed on the basis of the histories of four hundred famous men that 66 percent of the world's greatest work has been done by men past sixty. That encourages us that we can be useful and productive whatever our age, but it does not affect the fear of weakness and loneliness that grows with the passing of our youth.

The Lord has a word of comfort for all who are in the aging process—and, of course, that means us all without exception. He is the same; He never ages. His love is the same; it never lessens. His sustaining grace is the same; it never weakens. Others may forget us, but the Lord will not. He promises that He will support us and carry us. No trial will overwhelm us. No waves of trouble will drown our hope. He will be with us through life. He will be there when we are dying to carry us over Jordan. He will never leave us, but will bring us safe to glory. Whatever your age or condition, Christian, rejoice that the Lord is with you.

—A. C.

The hoary head is a crown of glory if found in the way of righteousness. It is a fool's cap if found in any other way.
W. B. KNIGHT

God's Great Power

That ye may know . . . the exceeding greatness
of his power to us-ward who believe.

EPHESIANS 1:18-19

God displays His omnipotence in both the work of creation and the work of redemption. In Ephesians 1:19-20 Paul records three ways God's power is seen in redemption. He speaks of that mighty power God used in the resurrection of Christ (v. 20). Man could only stand impotently at the grave of Christ and weep. Yet God with His mighty power laid hold of the dead body of Christ and raised it to life.

God also demonstrates His power when He regenerates the heart. We were dead in sin, but God quickened us together with Christ (2:5). Therefore, Paul attributes our believing "to the working of his mighty power" (1:19). The same power that raised Christ also gave life to us. With the hymn writer we confess:

> *To chase the shades of death away,*
> *And bid the sinner live!*
> *A beam of heaven, a vital ray,*
> *'Tis Thine alone to give.*

Then in our text we read about God using His power to revive the saint. The deadness of our hearts or of the hearts of those around us is no match for "the exceeding greatness of his power." Whether it is the overcoming of sin or the converting of the sinner, Paul wants us to know that divine omnipotence is available to the believer who will by faith lay hold of God for it. Let us then take God at His Word. How can we live impotent lives when such power is freely offered to us? Why should we be timid or doubtful in our witness when we represent the Almighty? Let us today boldly storm the strongholds of sin, expecting them to yield to "the exceeding greatness of his power."

—M. W. A.

One Almighty is more than all mighties.
WILLIAM GURNALL

Flies and Folly

*Dead flies cause the ointment of the apothecary to
send forth a stinking savour: so doth a little folly him
that is in reputation for wisdom and honour.*

ECCLESIASTES 10:1

Good perfume is expensive; it contains special ingredients and
requires special preparation. Hopefully, it spreads a pleasant
fragrance. What requires such effort and expense to make can be
easily spoiled and rendered useless. Whereas modern technology
helps assure the purity of the concoction, ancient chemists had
to be vigilant in efforts to prevent contamination. So sensitive
was the ancient brew that stray flies falling into the vat would
spoil the perfume. Ounce for ounce the flies were nothing in the
large vats, but their presence was strong enough to ruin the
batch. The perfume would lose its fragrance and thus its value.

Solomon, the Preacher, warns that our lives are like that
vat of precious perfume. A good testimony has an aroma that
flows from our lives just as sweet perfume. To have a good
name, reputation, or testimony requires consistent effort and
virtue. It takes a lifetime to make a good testimony; it takes only
a careless moment to ruin it. Folly or sin in the life of a believer
has the same "stinking" power as the fly in the ointment. A little
can destroy a lot. As Christians we are ambassadors of Christ.
It is vitally important that we represent Him well. The adage
that our lives are the only Bible some people read is sadly true;
yet it is a wonderful privilege for us to show the world the
power of the gospel and beauty of Christ. Let us seek to have
a testimony that speaks truly of Christ and cherish it as precious. Let us be careful to walk worthy of what Christ has made
us and prayerfully guard against the sins, even the "little" sins,
that nullify the value of our witness.

—M. P. V. B.

A Christian's life should be nothing but
a visible representation of Christ.
THOMAS BROOKS

Untied Tongues

Now therefore go, and I will be with thy mouth,
and teach thee what thou shalt say.

EXODUS 4:12

"Silent Christians"—there can be no doubt that the modern church is hindered in its witness by many believers who are just that. It is amazing to consider the great numbers who seem to have an opinion to voice on any subject save that which really matters— the power of Christ in saving their souls. "Be ready always to give an answer to every man that asketh you a reason of the hope that is in you with meekness and fear" (I Pet. 3:15). How pertinent is the counsel of Peter! And yet how seldom is his exhortation heeded!

If we analyse the reasons for this reticence, we will find that fear is often the major cause. The believer does not really lack confidence in the power of the message, but he has no confidence in his own ability to express that message. Moses gives vent to what many of us have felt at one time or another: "I am not eloquent . . . : I am slow of speech, and of a slow tongue" (Exod. 4:10). One can sense the divine forbearance and yet frustration in the reply from heaven: "Who hath made man's mouth? . . . have not I the Lord?" (v. 11). The God who creates the faculty of speech is the God who promises to give utterance in its employment: "I will be with thy mouth, and teach thee what thou shalt say." The wonderful thing is that the promise holds good! Knowing this, let us ask the Lord to give us some opportunity to speak for Him today, and let us trust in Him to provide the words and the wisdom.

—T. N.

If we did indeed look upon them as within a step of hell,
it would effectually untie our tongues.
RICHARD BAXTER

Joyful Thanksgiving

Always in every prayer of mine for you all making request with joy.
PHILIPPIANS 1:4

Is it not remarkable that Paul was thinking of others and not of himself as he awaited his trial in Rome? His mind went back to the believers in Philippi, and every remembrance of them brought joy to his heart. He warmly acknowledged their earnest participation in the work of "the gospel from the first day until now" (v. 5).

As he recollected the early days of his mission to Philippi, Paul thanked God continually for every member of the church. Among the first converts were Lydia and her household, the slave girl who had been demon possessed, and the burly Roman jailer who had fastened Paul's feet in the stocks (Acts 16:14-24). The apostle refused to dwell upon the scars incurred from the beatings he had received then. Rather, the very mention of those things brought joy to Paul, because it was through his suffering that the jailer and his family found Christ (vv. 25-34). How then could he exclude this man from his prayer of thanksgiving and joy? It is evident that Paul was far more sensitive to the mercies of God than to the antagonisms of men. "I would ye should understand, brethren, that the things which happened unto me have fallen out rather unto the furtherance of the gospel . . . and I therein do rejoice" (Phil. 1:12, 18).

The apostle's thanksgiving is couched in intimate terms: "I have you in my heart . . . I long after you all in the bowels of Jesus Christ" (vv. 7, 8). He had a fond recollection of his fellowship with the church at Philippi. It may be worth asking, Am I the kind of Christian that others remember with joy and thanksgiving to God?
—D. C.

Our lives should be such as men may safely copy.
C. H. SPURGEON

The Upper and the Nether Springs

Caleb gave her the upper springs and the nether springs.

JUDGES 1:15

Our Father always gives with a bountiful hand. We come like Caleb's daughter, requesting a blessing, and He gives us a double portion, "the upper springs and the nether springs."

There are upper springs and there are lower springs in the Christian life. We need both, and the Lord gives both. His grace is sufficient for every need and flows freely to us in every situation.

His upper springs may be taken to speak of the spiritual blessings in heavenly places that He gives us in Christ (Eph. 1:3). What rich springs of grace are the blessings Paul goes on to list in Ephesians chapter 1—election, predestination, adoption, acceptance in the beloved, redemption through the blood of Christ, the revelation of God's will, the sealing of the Holy Spirit, our eternal inheritance, and a place in the body of which Christ is the exalted Head. These spiritual blessings are the wells, or springs, of salvation, and we should learn to do what Isaiah speaks of: "With joy shall ye draw water out of the wells of salvation" (Isa. 12:3).

The lower springs may be taken to speak either of the special grace the Lord gives to us in those times when we are passing through some valley experience, or of His provision for our earthly needs. There are lower springs that meet the needs of the body as well as upper springs that meet the needs of the soul. There is grace to enable us to live in the joy of the Lord in this present world as well as grace to bring us safely to the Celestial City. There is no valley so deep, no suffering so great, and no affliction so trying but that God's grace can make our experience of it fruitful and beneficial.

O Christian, look up. Cry for a blessing. The river of God is full of water (Psa. 65:9). There are springs of divine help and favour for every believer in every situation.

—A. C.

Christ has springs of living water to turn our wilderness
into an Eden of fellowship and fruitfulness.
ALEXANDER SIMPSON

Acquitted by God

*Thou knowest that I am not wicked; and there
is none that can deliver out of thine hand.*

JOB 10:7

Job, the godly Old Testament believer, was under attack from
the powers of darkness. Satan had been permitted to deprive
him of property, family, and even his health and strength. His
friends thought he was a hypocrite, under deserved punishment
from God. In his woe and anguish Job turned to God, pleading
to know what exactly was happening to him. In the midst of his
supplications he uttered, under the inspiration of the Holy
Spirit, the words of today's text.

The word *wicked* is a legal term connected with justice and
judgment. Job confidently asserted that he did not stand condemned before God. In this he was absolutely correct. Nowhere in
the opening chapters of this book does God reject him. In fact, He
openly praises him. Thus this tried and tested servant of God
proclaimed a majestic and glorious Biblical truth, a doctrine that
is the core and essence of the gospel of our Lord Jesus Christ. That
truth is this: when a sinner comes to the Saviour for redemption,
his sins in a legal and just manner are put away and blotted out
to the satisfaction of God Himself, and he stands before Him
uncondemned (John 5:24).

Finally, Job's words append a solemn warning to this blessed
doctrine: "There is none that can deliver out of thine hand." One
day all must stand before Him. All must give an account before the
One who is all wise, all holy, all powerful. There is no escaping or
evading that day for which all other days were made. May we, like
Job, be ready, so that when we meet Him, our justification will
blossom into a wondrous glorification.

—S. B. C.

**Christ's righteousness, pleaded in the court of justice,
is our full and final discharge.**
ANONYMOUS

The Man God Uses

And Peter, fastening his eyes upon him with John, said, Look on us.

ACTS 3:4

All that the believer is and has belongs to the Lord. P?ul underlined this in I Corinthians 6:19-20: "Ye are not your own. . . . Ye are bought with a price." God wants our hearts (Prov. 23:26). He wants every faculty we possess (Rom. 12:1-2). He wants them to be used in His service and for His glory. In the story of the healing of the lame man at the Beautiful gate Peter exemplifies those whose every faculty is yielded to and used by the Lord.

Consider how he heard the cry of a needy soul. He did not pass by like the Levite and priest in the parable of the good Samaritan (Luke 10), but was evidently so affected by this pathetic appeal that he stopped in his course and turned aside to help. In doing so he was following the example of the Lord Himself who, above the din of the crowd that surrounded Him, heard the voice of blind Bartimaeus begging for mercy. Are our ears tuned to hear the cry of perishing sinners?

Then, too, Peter extended his hands towards him and lifted him up (Acts 3:7). Are we not also obliged, as the people of God, not only to hear, but to help—to be of practical assistance, to actually work, giving of time and energy in seeking to win lost souls to Christ? Let us labour as well as listen, and may our hands be active in obedience to the Lord's command, "Son, go work to day in my vineyard" (Matt. 21:28).

But why were the apostle's hands active and his hearing attentive? Surely because his heart was affected by the plight of this man. The concern, tenderness, and love that Peter had seen in his Lord were now graces produced by the Spirit of God in his own heart. May the Lord help us to listen for, labour for, and love lost souls for His glory!

—D. F.

You do not love the Lord at all unless
you love the souls of others.
C. H. Spurgeon

Constant Consultation

In all thy ways acknowledge him, and he shall direct thy paths.
PROVERBS 3:6

In the ordering of his affairs, the believer works in coalition with God. It was not always so. Since mankind's fall in Adam, sinful man acts in submission to a will controlled by sin. "Ye were the servants [or, slaves] of sin" (Rom. 6:20). Those who have come to Christ have, by the power of God, been renewed in their will. The Christian is set free from the power of sin. "Being then made free from sin, ye became the servants of righteousness" (Rom. 6:18).

Now the true child of God, as he plans and executes his "ways," freely and frequently consults with God. Regeneration has made him free from the dominion of sin. He now has a will that desires submission to God. Such submission requires an acknowledging of Christ as Lord over all our ways. The decisions of life will be ours, but the directions will be His. Consultation in all matters is therefore necessary.

The means of consultation are the Word of God and prayer. By the diligent use of both means, we are guided by the Holy Spirit according to the mind of Christ. As we earnestly seek the mind of God in prayer and in the study of His Word, we acknowledge His wisdom and His power and His abiding concern for the well-being of His people, even in the smallest matters of life. Those who ask for direction in all their ways are promised it. "He shall direct [or, keep straight] thy paths." Very often the main roads of life are straightforward, like the highways and motorways we travel. It is on the paths that we can get lost. The guidance given by God does not consist of vague generalities. No! "The steps [that is, each stride] of a good man are ordered [or, made sure] by the Lord" (Psa. 37:23).

—I. F.

The Lord does not shine upon us,
except when we take His Word as our light.
JOHN CALVIN

Satan Silenced!

They overcame him by the blood of the Lamb,
and by the word of their testimony. **REVELATION 12:11**

Have you ever felt your way in prayer or in witnessing blocked by some persistent accusation of the devil? Have you ever known an inward turmoil as some unseen enemy strikes despair into your heart and arouses your conscience to tell you that you can never get through to God, or you have no right to speak on His behalf to men? Who among us has not had this experience? The resurrection of past sins and the reiteration of present unworthiness are potent weapons in the devil's arsenal. However, there is a way of victory. He can be effectively silenced. Our text shows how.

First, we must learn that Satan's arguments and accusations are silenced by the blood of Christ. That is the objective ground of our victory. The blood has covered our sins from the sight of God and has purchased our entire acceptance with God. We are justified by Christ's blood (Rom. 5:9). There is no better way to silence Satan than to plead the blood of Christ.

Second, we must use the Word. "The word of their testimony" means the Word of God to which they bear testimony. The argument of Scripture has power to silence and subdue every accusation of Satan. Let us learn to preach the truth of God's Word to our own souls. Testify to its truth and personally stand upon it. It will give victory over Satan.

Finally, this victory is ours in every conceivable circumstance. Even the martyrs are reckoned to have enjoyed it in the loss of their lives. Since the *blood* gives us victory, we recognize that death is not defeat. Thus we hold loosely to life and the things of time, abandoning ourselves to God and His will. The devil can do nothing to hurt people like that, people who live by faith in the power of the blood of Christ and the Word of God.

—A. C.

Though the restless foe accuses, sins recounting like a flood;
Every charge our God refuses—Christ has answered with
His blood.
AUTHOR UNKNOWN

Murmuring

Yea, they despised the pleasant land, they believed not his word: but murmured in their tents, and hearkened not unto the voice of the Lord.
PSALM 106:24-25

The children of Israel were a nation of murmurers. Numbers, which contains the record of their wilderness journeys, could be called "The Book of Murmurings." The Israelites could always find something to grumble about. God names the sin of murmuring as one of the reasons for His judgment upon them in the wilderness. Paul says, "Neither murmur ye, as some of them also murmured, and were destroyed of the destroyer" (I Cor. 10:10). When will we realize that murmuring is a sin that not only displeases God and often discourages God's servants, but can also divide or destroy the work of God?

Sir Winston Churchill used to tell the story of a family that went on a picnic. During the afternoon their five-year-old son fell into the lake. None of the adults could swim. At great personal risk, a stranger who was passing by plunged into the water fully clothed and managed to save the life of the drowning child and present him safe and sound to his mother. Instead of expressing her gratitude for saving her son's life, she complained to the hero, "Where is Johnny's cap?" She had found something to complain about even in her gratitude.

To those who use the tongue to murmur and complain, Paul wrote, "Do all things without murmurings" (Phil. 2:14). A Swedish proverb says, "Those who wish to sing always find a song."

—S. B.

It is better to be mute than to murmur.
THOMAS BROOKS

71

Chosen of God

Elect according to the foreknowledge of God the Father.
I PETER 1:2

Peter first describes the relationship of the church earthward. They are *strangers scattered*. Then he describes their relationship Godward. They are *elect*—chosen. They are strangers to the world, but they are the children of God, known of God. Peter gives these people reason to magnify and praise God right at the beginning of this letter as he reminds them of the matchless grace of God in His sovereign and unconditional choice of them. In the presence of such a mystery, we can only humbly bow at His feet and thank Him that He should, according to the good pleasure of His will, choose even such unclean worms as we are.

Notice how the Trinity is involved in the salvation of our souls. First there is the basis in election. This is attributed to God the Father, to His foreknowledge—that is, His fore-ordination and His fore-love. Next there is the birth in regeneration. This is a direct operation of God the Holy Spirit, resulting in a new creature and a miraculous change. Then there is the blood in redemption. This is the work of God the Son in His once offering up of Himself a sacrifice to satisfy divine justice.

How wonderful is the plan and purpose of God's love in salvation! Let us bow our heads in contemplation of divine grace and lift up our redeemed hearts in worship to Father, Son, and Holy Ghost, the one God, equal in power and glory. —R. J. B.

God never repents of His electing love.
THOMAS WATSON

A Grateful Surrender

Behold, I have brought the firstfruits of the land,
which thou, O Lord, hast given me.

DEUTERONOMY 26:10

There are two deeply significant actions recorded in Deuteronomy 26, each accompanied by a very important speech made by the Israelites to the Lord. The first action was the presentation of the basket of firstfruits (v. 2). The accompanying speech (vv. 5-10) emphasized what the Lord had done for His people in bringing them out of Egypt into Canaan. The second action was the observance of the third year as the year of tithing, when the people gave to meet the needs of the Levites, the strangers, the fatherless, and the widows. The accompanying speech (vv. 13-15) stressed what God's people had done for the Lord.

The spiritual lessons are clear. We are debtors to the grace of God. All we are and have are His gifts to us. Thus we are to acknowledge our debt of gratitude to the Lord and hold loosely to the things of the world. We are to take all the Lord has given us—health, wealth, learning, skill—and dedicate it all to Him, especially to meet the needs of His servants and of the poor. We are not to abuse any worldly possessions to indulge the lusts of the flesh. We must not forget the Lord. Rather, in thankfulness, we should give back to Him the required portion of what He has so bountifully provided for us.

We should learn two vital principles. First, we can surrender ourselves and our possessions to the Lord only as we are overcome with a sense of our deep indebtedness to His saving grace. Let us but obtain a glimpse of the greatness of God's grace to us, and no sacrifice will appear too great for us to make for Him. Second, surrender to the Lord is with a view to rendering such service as will meet the needs of those around us. If our consecration to God does not produce concern for souls, it is bogus. Let us then ponder the Lord's great grace to us and set out to express our gratitude by spreading His provision to those who need it most.

—A. C.

Where God becomes a donor man becomes a debtor.
WILLIAM SECKER

A Good Night's Sleep

I will both lay me down in peace, and sleep.

PSALM 4:8

Catastrophes, disappointments, and vexations easily destroy peace of mind and buoyancy of spirit. How often we allow these apparent troubles to rob us of joy in the day and rest at night. It was precisely such experiences that revealed David's finest traits. It was true for him, as it should be for us, that adversity increases the sense of dependence on God. Psalm 4, David's bedtime prayer, reveals his secret of joy and peace that nothing could destroy. It is a secret worth knowing.

Peace comes as we remember what God has done for us in the past. David begins his prayer by addressing the God who had helped him before and then appealing to Him for fresh help (v. 1). Although he had been maligned by people and surrounded by trouble, God had vindicated him and opened up the way of escape. Past help from the Lord fuels the desire for new help. Remembering the Lord's past faithfulness leads to the assurance of His continuing care and concern. God has set apart His people to Himself (v. 3). No matter what trouble suggests to our hearts, we are His special treasure, the pupil of His eye. That is the reality that circumstances cannot change. The word *godly* designates those who are the objects of God's covenant love and loyalty. What a comfort to know that God has by covenant obligated Himself to us! No experience of adversity can compete with this unchanging truth. Making it the meditation of our hearts as we prepare for sleep (v. 4) displaces the worry that robs us of rest. The secret to a good night's sleep is rest in the Lord.

—M. P. V. B.

**Peace is the smile of God reflected
in the soul of the believer.**
WILLIAM HENDRIKSEN

Conceited Christians

Ye are puffed up.

I CORINTHIANS 5:2

One of the most obnoxious of human traits is pride, and yet it must be acknowledged that everybody to a greater or lesser degree suffers from it. Even the humble, cringing "Uriah Heeps" can be proud of their humility. Nobody, but nobody, likes a snob!

Christianity is a faith that begets humility. Recognizing the sovereignty of God and the poverty of man, the Christian should be of all men the most humble. Sadly, many Christians seem to glory more in themselves than in the cross of Christ.

Paul wrote his first Corinthian epistle to correct the errors of the church in Corinth. There was division, confusion, and carnality. Especially there was conceit. The Corinthian believers were puffed up like a balloon and filled with an inflated view of their own importance. The apostle draws the sharp cutting edge of the sword of the Spirit, the Word of God, and repeatedly punctures their pride.

A key expression of his is *Know ye not?* In other words, "You who know so much, do you not know even the simplest of Bible truths?" He reminds them that the wisdom of men is foolishness with God, that not many mighty are called, that salvation is all of the Lord. He deflates their ego with some piercing questions: "Who maketh thee to differ from another? and what hast thou that thou didst not receive? now if thou didst receive it, why dost thou glory, as if thou hadst not received it?" (4:7).

An inflated ego may be fine for the worldling travelling the sinful roads of this present proud world, but it is not the way God would have us travel to heaven. A humble, God-fearing Christian will find worldly ways rough going, but he will find the road to glory smooth as he is borne along by the wind of God, resting only on the merits of Christ. "God forbid that I should glory, save in the cross of our Lord Jesus Christ" (Gal. 6:14).

—F. McC.

Spiritual pride is the last resort of the tempter,
and whoever is enabled by divine grace to foil him
at this point, will foil him at all points.
WILLIAM G. T. SHEDD

Sitting Still or Still Sitting

Why do we sit still?

JEREMIAH 8:14

Solomon said that God "made every thing beautiful in his time" (Eccles. 3:11). There are times when it is a beautiful thing to sit still. "Be still, and know that I am God" (Psa. 46:10). There is nothing more beautiful or blessed than resting in our God and His full provision in Christ. Perhaps today you need to be reminded to sit still, to give up the frenzied care and worry that distract you. It is difficult to await the Lord's time to reveal His purpose in our sufferings and through our service, but wait we must. We dare not rush ahead of the Lord. Remember, "they that wait upon the Lord shall renew their strength" (Isa. 40:31). Why do we sit still? The reason is simple yet profound: our God is worthy of being trusted. He keeps in perfect peace those whose minds are stayed on Him (Isa. 26:3).

There are other times when to sit still is shameful. This is what Jeremiah had in mind. Are you unsaved? Why do you sit still in your sins, under the wrath of God? "Escape for thy life" (Gen. 19:17). Sit no longer in your lost state, but flee to Christ without delay. Are you a Christian who seems to be making no progress in spiritual things? Are you sitting still in your knowledge of Scripture and in your experience of prayer and fellowship with God? Are you one of those Christians who seem unmoved at the need of a lost world? Do you sit still while people all around you are perishing? Have you any real personal involvement in spreading the gospel? The Scripture admonishes us to redeem the opportunity (Eph. 5:16). So Jeremiah's question demands an answer: "Why do we sit still?" Why are you idle when there is work to do in the Lord's vineyard (Matt. 20:6)? Whether the reason is coldness of heart, or being too busy with other things, or timidity, we need to confess it and forsake it today. This is not a time to do nothing for God (John 9:4). Let us be up and doing.

—A. C.

Men think not of living holier, till they can live no longer.
WILLIAM SECKER

The Three Appearances of Christ

Christ . . . entered . . . into heaven . . . to appear in the presence of God for us: . . . once in the end of the world hath he appeared to put away sin. . . . Unto them that look for him shall he appear the second time without sin unto salvation.

HEBREWS 9:24-28

These three appearances of Christ vary as to time and location, but they are inseparably linked together as the successive stages of His high-priestly ministry. They set forth the character, continuity, and consummation of His priestly work.

When Christ came the first time it was for the specific purpose of putting away sin. To put away means "to disannul," or "to abrogate," or "to annihilate." The atoning sacrifice of Christ removes completely from His people the guilt and the penalty of their sins. It was a full and final atonement. But Christ's priestly ministry did not end with His crosswork. He has entered into heaven "to appear in the presence of God." At the throne of grace He intercedes "not for the world, but for them . . . given" to Him, whose sins He put away (John 17:9). Furthermore, for those same people, He will "appear the second time without sin unto salvation." Just as Aaron made the offering at the altar, entered the holiest of all, and then returned to the waiting people, so also will Christ come forth to consummate the salvation of His people. Then the redemption of their bodies will take place, and they will be changed.

Do you have this hope? Are you looking for Him? Wait on, for soon you will hear the joyful sound. Just as Israel heard the tinkling of the bells on Aaron's robe, signalling His emergence from the tabernacle, so also will the saints hear the sound of the trumpet, the shout of triumph, and the voice of the archangel, and so shall they "ever be with the Lord" (I Thess. 4:17).

—J. G.

Christ died; Christ arose; Christ intercedes; Christ is coming again. These four pillars support the whole temple of gospel truth.
ALEXANDER SIMPSON

Faithful unto Death

Though Noah, Daniel, and Job, were in it, as I live, saith the Lord
God, they shall deliver neither son nor daughter; they shall
but deliver their own souls by their righteousness.

EZEKIEL 14:20

This verse teaches that God has special instruments. These are notably righteous men, men of prayer. Spiritual power and holiness of life go hand in hand. Uncleanness of life is the enemy of power with God. We must never get away from the timeless counsel, "Be ye clean, that bear the vessels of the Lord" (Isa. 52:11).

Further, the blessing is with God and not in the greatest of men. In the communication quoted above, McCheyne tellingly made the point, "It is not great talents God blesses so much as great likeness to Jesus." We have made so much of the talent, and sometimes of the instrument, that the Lord has not received the glory. Yet it is His will that no flesh should glory in His presence.

The saints of Biblical times have the honour of antiquity, but men cannot actively extend their influence beyond their own lifetime. Even the mooted intercession from the two now dead, as Ezekiel writes, has no special merit in heaven.

The words of our text encouraged Ezekiel. A man of God in his fainting fits is likely to be assailed with the thought that God's special instruments could have done more had they been in his situation. "What more could I have done with God's vineyard?" he might have asked. The prophet faced exceedingly discouraging setbacks as he prayed and laboured. Then he discovered that were it possible for Noah, Daniel, and Job to come and dwell in the city, conditions there would be no more hopeful on that account.

Other fields might have been more fruitful for Ezekiel, but God had put him in the place where he laboured to stand as a faithful watchman. Stay where God has put you. Be there as long as God wants you to remain.

—J. D.

I feel like a man who has no money in his pocket, but is
allowed to draw for all he wants upon one infinitely rich:
I am, therefore, at once both a beggar and a rich man.
JOHN NEWTON

A Word of Warning

Now if any man have not the Spirit of Christ, he is none of his.
ROMANS 8:9

Sobering and striking words! Sobering because they deal with that relationship with Christ that determines our eternal destiny. Striking because of their appearance in this eighth chapter of Romans, a chapter devoted to assuring God's people of their standing in Christ. Why in the midst of such a comforting chapter does Paul introduce such a disconcerting statement? Because there will always be people who would take the comfort of this passage without first having taken the Christ of this passage. It is a word of warning to professing Christians.

"If any man . . ." It matters not your pedigree. You may come from a long line of godly people, but unless you possess the Spirit of Christ, you are none of His. Nor does a mere profession of faith make you God's child. Paul here speaks of *possessing* Christ's Spirit, not a *profession* of such. Walking an aisle, being baptized, or shedding tears has never saved a soul from hell. Once more, if any man, regardless of the persuasion of others, has not the Holy Spirit, he is lost. Do not go out into eternity resting on your reputation with others!

When a sinner is born again, he receives the life of Christ, a life that makes him a "new creature." And what are the evidences of the indwelling Spirit? Paul tells us that "as many as are led by the Spirit of God, they are the sons of God" (v. 14). But led where? First, led to Christ. Your desires and interest will be turned from the world to the Saviour. You will be led to pray. Christ's own have received "the Spirit of adoption, whereby we cry, Abba, Father" (v. 15). Last, you will be led into obedience to Christ. Those who possess the Spirit "do mortify the deeds of the body" (v. 13) because Christ's Spirit will gradually change them into His likeness.

Have you the Spirit of Christ? What a dreadful thing it would be to be none of His. Rest not until you have cast away all dependence upon self and cast your soul upon Christ.

—J. W.

Ah, if I am none of His, whose am I?
C. H. SPURGEON

The Day of Small Things

For who hath despised the day of small things?

ZECHARIAH 4:10

It is very easy to judge the worth of a work by its size. The idea that "big is beautiful" has become rooted in our thinking. The small corner store gives way to the supermarket or hypermarket, and men work on bigger and grander projects than ever before.

A. W. Pink once commented on this verse, suggesting that in the history of the church there are times of "small things," when there is a temptation to disparage the work of God because of its smallness.

The consciousness of size and numbers can easily prove a snare to churches and Christians. We should remember the line of the children's hymn that speaks of "you in your small corner, and I in mine" and realize that it may not be God's will for us to occupy a prominent position in the work of God.

In any case, there is plenty of work to do in our "small corner." When I was young I often heard the saying, "Take care of the pennies, and the pounds will look after themselves." If you and I would only apply that thought to the work of God, if we would take care of the small things and do them conscientiously, we would pave the way for greater usefulness and richer blessings.

We should never forget that God delights to use weak and insignificant things to bring glory to His own name. He chose to feed the multitude with just five loaves and two fish, He gave David victory over Goliath with a sling and a stone, and He gave Samson a great triumph over the Philistines with the jawbone of an ass. "Little is much when God is in it."

—G. F.

It is usually God's way to begin His great works with a day of small things.

C. H. SPURGEON

Sins Forgiven and Forgotten

*I, even I, am he that blotteth out thy transgressions
for mine own sake, and will not remember thy sins.*

ISAIAH 43:25

The great revival preacher H. Grattan Guinness preached from
this text one of the most memorable of all his messages. Indeed,
since he preached it and published it, preachers around the
world have repeated it as the best statement of the gospel from
this verse that they know. Guinness preached on *Sins Forgiven
and Forgotten,* in the course of which he made the following
points about free grace.

First, *it blots out our transgressions from God's Book.* The Lord
records all the words, thoughts, and actions of men. What a solemn thought! Who among us could ever face his past without
shame and condemnation? What a day will the judgment day be
when the books are opened! Do you fear it? Would you escape it?
Then it must be by divine pardon. Only God can forgive sins, and
He does blot out all the sins of all who trust in the atoning blood
of Christ. For believers the record is clear.

Second, *it blots out our transgressions with God's hand.* The
very hand that recorded our sins blots them out. The hand of Him
whom our sins offended erases all notice of them. The hand we so
long rejected when it was stretched forth to us in mercy removes
every trace of every sin through the blood of Jesus Christ.

Third, *it blots out our transgressions from God's memory.* "I
will not remember thy sins." Sometimes we have great difficulty
forgetting our past. It rises up to haunt us. But the Lord has
both forgiven and forgotten all our sins. Let us rest in that.
There is no sweeter truth this side of heaven.

—A. C.

The cross is the cost of my forgiveness.
ANONYMOUS

Christ the Rock

Speak ye unto the rock.

NUMBERS 20:8

Many years before the events surrounding today's text, the Lord told Moses to smite the rock to provide water for the people. Now, at Kadesh, He adds to the gospel type by instructing Moses to speak to the rock to obtain the precious supply. He was making the way of salvation very clear. Christ the Rock would be smitten once for all. His one great sacrifice would purchase eternal redemption for His people. The wound once given would open an inexhaustible fountain of blessing to meet the need of all who rest in Him. Thus no further stroke is needed or allowed. Rather, the thirsty sinner needs only to speak to the Rock, and he will find all that his soul needs in that constantly flowing river of the water of life.

The initial smiting of the rock was inflicted by Moses, the law-giver, the representative of the justice of God. The message is clear: when justice is satisfied, there will be no withholding of mercy. Since Christ has satisfied the justice of God by His suffering, His Father will unstintingly pour forth His merciful remedy for the parched souls of men. God will not, yea, cannot now withhold the blessings of the covenant. He is eternally satisfied and infinitely delighted with the travail of Christ's crosswork, and out of justice as much as mercy will bestow upon His people all that Christ won for them.

What error there is on this point! Rome, with its dogma of the Mass, would smite Christ again and again. Blasphemy, insult, and distrust are constantly being heaped upon Christ by those religions which would crucify Him afresh. Ignorance shrouds the souls of countless multitudes who are blinded by such religions to the sufficiency of Christ's finished work. Have you been in such ignorance, unwittingly smiting the Rock? Forsake that wicked way and those unrighteous thoughts. Speak to the Rock today, and He will have mercy upon you and will abundantly pardon.

—J. G.

Christ ... did not make a token payment
which God accepts in place of the whole.
Our debts are not cancelled; they are liquidated.
JOHN MURRAY

Blindness Banished
by the Light of the World

One thing I know, that, whereas I was blind, now I see.

JOHN 9:25

Robbery is the devil's art. Satan and his children ever seek to steal away the faith of God's children. While the Christian will be unable to explain every aspect of the operation of God's saving grace, his new spiritual light will make him resolute in his faith. The public may be totally sceptical of the scientist's claims before the experiment, but who will refute his findings when the results are clear for all to see? Many who could never hope to comprehend the intricate steps of the experimental process may nonetheless feel the benefits of the visible results and derive great comfort from them in daily life.

Reformed theologians agree that regeneration is executed by the direct operation of the Holy Spirit upon the human heart. It is the influence of one of the trinitarian Persons upon a human person. This definition rules out and sweeps away any instrumentality, whether it be preacher, priest, or church rite. Regeneration is the immediate act of God.

This divine act plants spiritual life into a dead soul. God savingly enlightens the mind naturally darkened by sin. This is the only answer to man's awful blindness. At the fall of man his eyes were put out, but in the miracle of the new birth God in grace restores his spiritual eyesight.

Theologians may be unable to explain this doctrine fully, but the ungodly cannot dismiss it on that account because hosts of God's people can testify from experience, "Whereas I was blind, now I see." The laws of electricity are above the minds of many who daily flip the electrical switch for light. When the world would rob the Christian of his faith in Christ, he may not have enough theological knowledge to answer every question, but of the enlightening power of the gospel he is certain. Who can argue against the light?

—I. G.

> One man with a glowing experience of God
> is worth a library full of arguments.
> VANCE HAVNER

The Field of the Slothful

And, lo, it was all grown over with thorns, and nettles had covered
the face thereof, and the stone wall thereof was broken down.
PROVERBS 24:31

Come, let us take a walk with Solomon. Let us with him pass
by the field of the slothful. As we gaze over the broken stone
wall, may we too receive instruction from this parable of nature.
The slothful man might have enriched himself by his field and
vineyard. It was a precious possession. It was fertile soil, as the
abundance of those thorns and nettles plainly proves. Where
they could so flourish, better things could be produced. The rain
watered the soil. It felt the warmth of the sun. Why this waste
of productive ground? This garden was neglected. It had not
been cultivated; it had not been weeded. Those thorns and
nettles bore testimony to that.

Ah, ruinous neglect! How insidious neglect is! How much is
lost by it! If we neglect the garden of our soul, it will not be left
empty. The rank weeds of sin will certainly grow up there with
their noxious fruit. We see in our text the sure result of being
slothful in the things of God. What unsightliness is here! What
waste is here! What dearth and devastation! There could have
been a field ripe with golden grain and choice vines loaded with
clusters of refreshing fruit. The soul of the Christian should be like
a well-watered garden—flourishing, fragrant, and fruitful.

Christian, be diligent in spiritual husbandry. Break up your
fallow ground. Sow to yourself in righteousness. Cultivate the
fruits of the Spirit. Build up the wall of godly habits. "Add to your
faith virtue; and to virtue knowledge; and to knowledge temperance; and to temperance patience; and to patience godliness; and
to godliness brotherly kindness; and to brotherly kindness charity.
For if these things be in you, and abound, they make you that ye
shall neither be barren nor unfruitful in the knowledge of our Lord
Jesus Christ" (II Pet. 1:5-8). Go and work today in your vineyard.
—M. P.

Deny sloth not only continuance, but countenance.
THOMAS ADAMS

The Blessed Hope

Behold, he cometh with clouds.

REVELATION 1:7

According to the apostle Paul, the blessed hope of the church is the return in glory of our great God and Saviour Jesus Christ (Titus 2:13). The passage of time has not dimmed that expectation. Jesus is coming again. That is the constant promise of Scripture.

Christ's coming is to be personal, physical, and actual. The promise cannot be spiritualized or idealized. It has not yet been fulfilled but remains before God's people as the fixed point toward which all the Bible's prophecies of the end time are irresistibly moving. Satan and sinners may mock this truth. They may sneer, "Where is the promise of his coming?" (II Pet. 3:4), but they cannot alter the glorious truth that Jesus is coming again. God's prophetic programme that leads to that glorious appearing is right on track and on time.

The Scripture uses this truth to stimulate us to be holy. It is impossible to hold this hope before us without living pure and holy lives (I John 3:3). The blessed hope is not indulgence in wild prophetic fancies that put the brain in a fever and lower the temperature of spiritual life. It is intensely practical and leads us to live in such a way that we will not be ashamed before Christ at His coming.

The promise of the Lord's return also brings comfort amid our sufferings and afflictions. It directs a bright beam from glory into the darkness of bereavement (I Thess. 4:13-18). It gives us strength to face death and overcome its terror (I Cor. 15:52-58). It assures us that these bodies in which we have so much limitation and trouble will soon be made like the glorious body of our Saviour. No more sickness, no more suffering, no more sadness, no more sin— this is the glorious expectation of the people of God. With John we eagerly cry, "Even so, come, Lord Jesus" (Rev. 22:20).

—A. C.

If I do not gaze with rapture on Christ in meditation
and prayer I deceive myself if I profess to be eager
to see Him coming again.
ALEXANDER SIMPSON

God's Witnesses

Go to Nineveh, that great city, and cry against it.

JONAH 1:2

No one likes to be the bearer of bad news. I well remember the time when a motor mechanic, stroking his beard in agitation, announced to me that the car which I had bought at a bargain price and of which I was so proud had a "dud" engine.

The prophet Jonah was sent to preach judgment against the city of Nineveh. The ancient city of Nineveh was the capital of Assyria. It was a vast city of great wealth. Its walls were 100 feet high and so wide that they could carry three chariots abreast. The population of Nineveh may have run into millions, for we are told in the book of Jonah that it contained 120,000 infants. Sadly, the city of Nineveh was notorious for its wickedness. It was noted for its lack of the fear of God and its cruel and immoral practices.

It was no easy task for Jonah to go to mighty Nineveh and cry against it. No doubt the thought of martyrdom must have entered his mind when God first spoke to him about going to the city. No one would willingly choose martyrdom. Archbishop Cranmer was so terrified at the prospect of being burnt at the stake that he at first recanted and denied the very truths that he loved dearly.

It is not easy for us to be faithful to our unsaved friends and tell them that if they are not saved they will be lost in hell, but that is what God requires of us. Just as Jonah had to be true to God and tell the Ninevites of coming judgment, so you and I have a duty to be true to God when speaking to our unsaved friends. May the Lord make our faithful witness fruitful in bringing the lost to Christ.

—G. F.

Truth must be spoken, however it be taken.
JOHN TRAPP

Counting Our Blessings

Every good gift and every perfect gift is from above,
and cometh down from the Father of lights, with whom
is no variableness, neither shadow of turning.

JAMES 1:17

The Lord gives His children only what is good for them. He never tempts them to sin. He works in them and upon them to keep them from sin and to lift them out of sin when they fall into it. Some early Christians needed to be reminded of these truths, for they tended to blame the Lord for the enticements to sin with which their trials were attended. The holiness and the goodness of God make such an idea monstrous.

Let us not make the mistake of those early believers. We would greatly lighten the burden of our afflictions if we ceased complaining and blaming the Lord and began to meditate upon His manifold mercies. He "daily loadeth us with benefits" (Psa. 68:19). The evidences of His goodness are all around us. He is the Creator, the "Father of lights" who made the heavenly bodies from which we derive our light, our heat, and even our entire environment. We should never forget that what we all too easily pass off as the facts of nature are in reality God's gracious gifts to us.

The Lord is not only our Creator. He is our Saviour, for He has regenerated us unto eternal life (James 1:18). His benefits in creation are great, but His gifts of saving grace are even greater.

Better still, the Lord is immutable in His kindness toward us. With Him is no variableness or shadow of turning. The lights in the heavens will cease to shine, but our Creator and Saviour will never cease to love us and bless us.

Have you been blaming God when you should have been blessing Him? Count your blessings. You really will be surprised at what the Lord has done.

—A. C.

God's giving deserves our thanksgiving.
ANONYMOUS

87

Christ Our Advocate

*Open thy mouth for the dumb in the cause of all such as are
appointed to destruction. Open thy mouth, judge righteously,
and plead the cause of the poor and needy.*

PROVERBS 31:8-9

In the opening three chapters of Romans, Paul lays the foundation
for his exposition of the gospel of God's grace, the dark background
against which he will set forth all the glory of the redemption
that is in Christ Jesus. Paul, as prosecuting counsel, has ar-
raigned man before the bar of God. He has exhaustively and
conclusively proved that all have sinned, that all have broken
God's law, that the whole world is guilty before God and under
His divine wrath. Have the prisoners anything to say? No, their
mouths are stopped; they stand speechless, condemned at the
bar of God's law (Rom. 3:19).

O happy day when we saw ourselves there, as guilty and hell-
deserving sinners! We were dumb. No more inventing a thousand
excuses for sin. No more parading forth our own supposed goodness. No more trusting in ourselves. We were unable to plead our
own cause. Our trust was placed in the advocacy of Him who is
King of Kings. "We have an advocate with the Father, Jesus Christ
the righteous" (I John 2:1). He appears in the presence of God for
us. He undertakes our cause and pleads the infinite virtue of His
sacrificial work. There is no more excellent or comprehensive
definition of our Saviour's high-priestly ministry in courts above
than that of Dr. T. Ridgley: "Christ maketh intercession, by His
appearing in our nature, continually before the Father in heaven,
in the merit of His obedience and sacrifice on earth, declaring
His will to have it applied to all believers, answering all accusations against them, procuring for them quiet of conscience,
notwithstanding daily failure, access with boldness to the throne
of grace, and acceptance of their persons and sacrifices."

Child of God, ever be looking unto Jesus, the Author and
Finisher of your faith.

—M. P.

We owe our standing in grace every moment,
to His sitting in heaven and interceding every moment.
THOMAS GOODWIN

A Godly Seed

By faith Jacob, when he was a dying, blessed both the sons of Joseph.
HEBREWS 11:21

Dying is a serious business, but with what utter lack of interest in self did the patriarchs die. This reference to Jacob "a dying" stands in a triad of verses dealing with the passing of three of the patriarchs—Jacob himself; his father, Isaac; and his son Joseph. How blessed to read of grandfathers, sons, and grandsons all dying in victory. Notice that though each man was both great and rich, in his dying moments his thoughts were of more important things. So many men when they approach death are concerned with financial matters, but they never give any thought to their spiritual well-being. These men of God had a greater concern than the earthly inheritance they were passing to their sons. Their chief concern was that their offspring would inherit the blessing of God.

They were all concerned about the future of their children and of the church of God. Isaac blessed his sons, Jacob blessed his grandsons, and Joseph spoke of generations not yet born. Parent—grandparent—are you praying for the children at your knees? These men prayed for and blessed their offspring because they were aware that the continued existence and witness of the church involves a godly seed. Spiritual carelessness, especially negligence and apathy in parents, has always resulted in the declension of the church and the work of God.

It should be noted that these men realized that they must relinquish the future of the church to the rising generations. How diligently therefore did they teach, train, and instruct those who succeeded them. Being faithful to God includes not only our own personal service, but also the matter of ensuring that there will be a progeny of "like precious faith" (II Pet. 1:1) to carry on God's work. Let us attend to these things, that we might be comforted in death by the knowledge that there are those who will be true to God in time to come.

—J. G.

**Holy families must be the chief preservers
of the interest of religion in the world.**
RICHARD BAXTER

89

A Difficult but Delightful Book

And the Lord called unto Moses.

LEVITICUS 1:1

Each January many Christians resolve to read the Bible from beginning to end. When they get to the difficult book of Leviticus, some give up, and others quickly scan through the book or bypass it altogether, to their great loss. If you are using the calendar of daily Bible reading printed at the back of this book, you are just about to launch into Leviticus. Do not be intimidated. You should study it carefully, for many reasons:

The significance of its writer. Moses was not insignificant. He was the greatest of Old Testament men. He should be listened to.

The sovereignty of its Author. Moses wrote, but God authored Leviticus. It has more of God's direct words than any other book.

The shortness of its focus. Genesis covers 2500 years, Exodus 360 years, but Leviticus about 30 days. The Lord directs our attention from wide-angle to close-up views of these important truths.

The system of its teaching. God speaks sometimes plainly and simply. At other times He uses parables and illustrations. In Leviticus He often employs symbolic or typical teaching. The Old Testament "shadows" give depth to the clear New Testament revelation of Christ.

The solemnity of its message. The key to Leviticus is not hard to find. Look for the words *holiness* and *atonement*, and you will see how sinful man can be made "at one" with the holy God.

The statements on the blood. Leviticus is hated by the modernist mostly because of its emphasis on the blood sacrifice. The key verse is "It is the blood that maketh an atonement for the soul" (17:11).

The Saviour that is presented. Jesus Christ is found on every page of Leviticus. Keep the above in mind as you start to read. Pray before you read that God will reveal Christ in the book. Leviticus then will not be drudgery, but a genuine delight.

—F. McC.

As we go to the cradle only in order to find the baby,
so we go to the Scriptures only to find Christ.
MARTIN LUTHER

Divine Visitation

Thou hast visited me in the night.

PSALM 17:3

The handmaid Hagar made a profound statement when she was approached by the Angel of the Lord in the wilderness: "Thou God seest me." The all-seeing eye of God is something no one can escape. This truth alone ought to encourage us to right living before the Lord. But God is more than just the casual observer of man's affairs. He is the divine, thorough inspector who investigates and examines every man. He deals with men according to what He knows their hearts to be. This is a warning to those whose hearts are not right, for God's investigation incites His wrath. It is a comfort to those who are right, for nothing about them or their circumstance escapes God's caring gaze. It should be an incentive to us all to so live as to cause no offence to our Lord: "Thou hast proved mine heart; thou hast visited me in the night; thou hast tried me, and shalt find nothing; I am purposed that my mouth shall not transgress."

Apart from the motivation to purity that God's visitation ought to provide, the fact that He enters into our affairs is an amazing thought. Compared to God's greatness and the magnificent vastness of His creation, we are insignificant, frail, impotent, and mortal. Yet our God has not forgotten us. He remembers us, thinks about us, and observing us attentively enters into fellowship with us. Although He is holy and separate from all sin and everything ordinary, He is near to us. Nothing about us—our needs, our desires, our actions, our thoughts—is trivial to God. We should be constantly conscious of the reality of God's seeing us. God's involvement is never neutral; so let us live that we do not displease Him.

—M. P. V. B.

As a Christian is never out of the reach of God's hand, so he is never out of the view of God's eye.
THOMAS BROOKS

Eyes Front!

*Let thine eyes look right on, and let
thine eyelids look straight before thee.*

PROVERBS 4:25

The devil is a master of distraction. In working his wiles upon men he finds an easy prey. How little it takes to distract the eye or the mind from the task at hand. I heard of a motorway pile-up that was caused when one driver was distracted by a buzzing insect in the car with him! It takes far less to distract us from the duties of our high calling in Christ. The consequences of distraction are also far more serious than a multiple crash on a highway.

It was looking at the forbidden fruit that distracted Eve and, in turn, Adam from the path of obedience. What eternal tragedy resulted from that disobedient movement of the eye!

Our eye is like the needle of a compass. It tells us the direction our hearts are inclined. It always points toward the magnetic north of our desires. Lot's wife turned and looked back toward Sodom. Her eye pointed the way of her heart. She was drawn back toward the evils of that city.

Keeping our eyes looking right on requires us to keep our hearts fixed on Christ. When the eye of our soul is faithfully engaged in "looking unto Jesus the author and finisher of our faith" (Heb. 12:2), then we have time for none of the devil's sideshows. Often we have to walk in the midst of Vanity Fair. The temptation to turn aside and contemplate its offers is very strong. The voices of the tempters are very persuasive. Then is the time to remember the prize that is set before you. Then is also the time to recall that we are walking a very narrow path. Therefore, we must "walk circumspectly," or accurately, as the Greek means (Eph. 5:15). Foolish distraction will cause us many a fall and many an injury. Christian, keep your eyes on Christ.

—I. F.

**The more we are "looking unto Jesus" the easier
it will be to "lay aside every weight."**
A. W. Pink

Preferred Students

If any man will do his will, he shall know of the doctrine.
JOHN 7:17

Doctrine is the meat and marrow of Christian living. Poor and sickly is the soul who has little or no doctrine. The Lord Jesus lived by doctrine and proclaimed it to each of His hearers.

As the servant of the Father in the covenant of grace, Christ came to deliver all the counsel of heaven to hungry souls. Among those who heard Him were many who refused this wisdom from above. Some of them had a certain curiosity about Christ's words, but were void of a heart to obey the truth. The Lord stresses that the seeker of truth must possess a genuine desire to use what He teaches him. He does not teach men spiritual truth merely to puff up their intellects. The fundamental condition for obtaining spiritual knowledge is a genuine heart desire to carry out the revealed will of God in our lives.

Those who are carnally minded prostitute what knowledge they receive to their own shame. They are as Judas, having many insights into the ways of the Lord, but using them only to betray Him all the more wickedly. Such false disciples condemn themselves to remaining in the dark concerning spiritual things.

William Burgon remarked, "It is a favourite maxim of the present day, that increased knowledge will bring with it growth in godliness. Scripture at all events entirely reverses the process. The way to know of the doctrine whether it be of God is to do his will." Jesus said, "I am the light of the world: he that followeth me . . . shall have the light of life" (John 8:12).

Walk in the truth, and you shall know the doctrine in demonstration and in power.

—I. G.

Other books were given for our information. The Bible was given for our transformation.
WALTER KNIGHT

The Pleasure of God

It pleased God.

I CORINTHIANS 1:21

Some people and religions present God as some sort of divine tyrant whose anger is never appeased. Nothing could be further from the truth. The God of the Bible is just, but He is also loving, merciful, and longsuffering. And He can be pleased.

Today's text speaks of the pleasure of the Lord. A close examination of Scripture will reveal that His pleasure rests in His Son, our Lord Jesus Christ. He is pleased with the *person* of Christ. He could say, "This is my beloved Son, in whom I am well pleased" (Matt. 3:17).

The heavenly Father is pleased with the *plenitude* of Christ, for Paul reminds us that "it pleased the Father that in him should all fulness dwell" (Col. 1:19). He is pleased with the *purity* of Christ because the sinless Jesus, like no earthly son, was able to say, "I do always those things that please him" (John 8:29).

We see the amazing love of God to sinners when we realize that God is pleased with the *passion* of Christ. Isaiah records that "it pleased the Lord to bruise him" (Isa. 53:10). Remember, He was bruised for our sins. God is also pleased with the *people* of Christ, for Samuel records that "it hath pleased the Lord to make you his people" (I Sam. 12:22). So the pleasure of God is wrapped up in the person of His dear Son. We can never please God if still in our sins, for they that are "in the flesh cannot please God" (Rom. 8:8). But when we come to Christ, confess our sins, and receive Him as our Saviour, then God is well pleased. When we exalt Christ, we please the Father.

Our text reminds us that God is well pleased with the *preaching* of Christ. Do you sometimes feel that your labour is in vain? Do you feel ineffective as you preach and teach His truth? Be encouraged today, for it pleases God "by the foolishness of preaching to save them that believe." God is pleased when Christ is preached.

—F. McC.

If it pleased God to smite Christ our Substitute, should anything please us better than to serve Christ our Saviour?
ALEXANDER SIMPSON

94

Living in the Present But Looking to the Future

But know thou, that for all these things
God will bring thee into judgment.

ECCLESIASTES 11:9

Happiness is not just a possibility; it is a command. The key to happiness is enjoying the present while looking to the future. Throughout Ecclesiastes, God has revealed that life and the ability to enjoy it are His gifts. The more we understand the nature of this life, the more we can appreciate each moment of it. Part of the secret to successful living is knowing that this life ends and after it comes the judgment. More than a creedal affirmation, this knowledge grasps the truth in such a way that it moulds and directs the way of life.

The sight of eternity puts the present in the proper perspective. Life is temporary and full of trouble. Young people think that they are exempt from the influence of time, and those not so young try to deny what they see in the mirror and feel in their bones. Nevertheless, youth must give way to age and ultimately death (12:1-7). That degeneration is part of life emphasizes the folly of living for this life only. Let us look eagerly to the future. How much better will be our eternal, heavenly home! The judgment that lies beyond this life reminds us that we are accountable to God. Knowing this should foster a fear of the Lord that drives us to please Him in all that we do and say. The thought of standing before our Lord is not a club that beats us into submission, but a sober reminder that Christ knows us for what we are. Though the judgment is future, we know that even now "all things are naked and opened unto the eyes of him with whom we have to do" (Heb. 4:13). Christ's estimation of us should be our overwhelming concern.

—M. P. V. B.

The future belongs to those who
belong to God. This is hope.
W. T. PURKISER

The Greatness of God's Mercy

God, who is rich in mercy.

EPHESIANS 2:4

One of the problems David faced when he came to the throne was how to treat the descendants of Saul. Many a cruel tyrant would have utterly destroyed the descendants of a previous regime in order to establish his own dynasty. But David showed great mercy when he took a helpless grandson of Saul and made him a guest at his table (II Sam. 9). Yet how infinitely greater is the mercy God displays in our salvation.

First, God's mercy is greater in His bringing us out from rebellion and sin. Though God's way is perfect, we chose to go our own way in fulfilling the desires of our flesh and mind (Eph. 2:3). We sided with the rebellion of this world rather than with God, and we served under "the prince of the power of the air" (v. 2). No one could fault God if He went to war against such "children of wrath" and utterly destroyed them. But we read that God was "rich in mercy, for his great love wherewith he loved us" (v. 4). By grace He saved us rather than give us the damnation we deserved. What a mystery! That the Lord of glory should treat us kindly is wonderful, but that He should *love* us surpasses imagination! Oh! let us never forget the love of God bestowed on us rebellious sinners.

Second, God's mercy is greater in His bringing us to a place of exaltation and glory. In uniting us to Christ, God has quickened, raised, and "made us sit together in heavenly places in Christ" (vv. 5-6). We now have a perfect standing before God. We read concerning Saul's grandson that he later fell out of favour with David (II Sam. 19:24-30), but we can never lose the favour of the Lord. His purpose of grace for us is eternal and unchangeable. He intends in the ages to come to "shew the exceeding riches of his grace in his kindness toward us through Christ Jesus" (Eph. 2:7). In the light of this surpassing mercy to us, ought we not to do the will and work of our Saviour with joy?

—M. W. A.

**Sin is brought in with birth,
and not removed save by the new birth.**
AUGUSTINE

Saved To Serve

Thus saith the Lord, Let my people go, that they may serve me.
EXODUS 8:1

Have you ever considered what a thriving institution the New Testament church was? I am often struck by the closing words of Acts 2, where we are given an insight into the life and labours of those converted on the day of Pentecost. Here is a demonstration of activity, involvement, participation—every member contributing to the work. It is a wonderful picture! The sad thing is that, in the eyes of many, Acts 2 is a mere historical document. They do not realize that this is God's blueprint for a vibrant, successful church! The Lord seeks for men and women committed and consecrated to His cause.

Have we forgotten the purpose of our redemption? That purpose is brought before us in the demand Moses was to carry to Pharaoh. The children of Israel were to be liberated so that they might serve God. Our deliverance, our redemption, our salvation, is to the end that we will serve the Lord. What a transformation would be effected in the witness of our churches if every member were fulfilling his obligations in the matter of Christian service. How much are you contributing to the witness of your church?

Do you serve by your presence? Is the pastor able to rely upon your attendance at every meeting? Do you serve by your prayers? Are you constantly interceding for your church and every avenue of its witness? Do you serve by giving practical support? Are you a good steward of that which God has given you? Do you serve by personal labours? Are you always ready to play a part, whenever possible, in the programme of your church?

"Saved to serve." Is that maxim true of your life?

—T. N.

Christ keeps no servants only to wear a livery.
WILLIAM JENKYN

97

Running the Race

*I press toward the mark for the prize of the
high calling of God in Christ Jesus.*
PHILIPPIANS 3:14

Here we have a master of illustration drawing spiritual lessons from the sporting arena of the Greek games. Whether it was the foot race or the chariot race Paul had in mind is not clear, but either one will do. One thing is certain: a race must have a starting line. The Christian race must begin by trusting Jesus Christ, who is "the author and finisher of our faith" (Heb. 12:2). As the runner must come to the starting line, so we must come to Christ and start for heaven at the cross. A good start is necessary; otherwise the race may be lost at the beginning. Like good athletes, we must maintain a steady pace and run with patience, for the Christian race is a marathon, not a sprint.

Many runners are content to think that they are as good as others. Some are even content with just being in the race, but the zealous Christian is devoted to "the high calling of God in Christ Jesus." This means that he will divest himself of every hindering thing. He will not be distracted by the successes or failures of the past. The things that are behind must be set aside, and the things that are before must take their place. It is necessary to renounce sin, and it is essential to lay aside doubtful things which are encumbrances to the race.

We must keep our eyes on the finishing line, which again is Christ. How wonderful it will be at the end of the course to receive the eternal prize from His nail-pierced hands and to hear Him say, "Well done."

> *Run the straight race through God's good grace,*
> *Lift up thine eyes, and seek His face;*
> *Life with its way before us lies,*
> *Christ is the path, and Christ the prize.*
>
> —D. C.

**Treasures in heaven are laid up only as
treasures on earth are laid down.**
ANONYMOUS

If We Sin...

If any man sin, we have an advocate with the Father,
Jesus Christ the righteous.

I JOHN 2:1

True Christians are painfully aware of their shortcomings. They feel sin with a keenness unknown to ungodly men. It robs them of their joy. It mars their fellowship with God. It destroys their service. So, what can we do when we sin?

Today's text teaches us a vital lesson: the free grace of God in Christ has not only provided us with a full forgiveness but also with a righteous Advocate who pleads our cause before God when we sin. We naturally hang our heads in shame when we sin and feel we are so unworthy that we should avoid God's presence. That is a fatal mistake. Lift your eyes into the heavenlies and behold at God's right hand a Friend, a Champion who does not forsake His blood-bought people when they fall.

As an advocate, Christ agrees that our sin is a breach of divine law and deserves to be punished. However, He goes on to say that He as our substitute fully bore all the wrath of God against all our sin. His blood argues that we have been redeemed from the curse of the law and have been justified freely by God's grace. In effect, Christ says, "Father, this one has sinned. But You laid that sin on Me. You accepted My obedience and sacrifice on this poor sinner's behalf. He is not accepted because of the perfection of his own obedience but because of the perfection of My obedience. Therefore, Father, restore this one whom You have accepted in Me to the joy of fellowship and useful service again." The Father accepts that plea, and fellowship is restored.

The basis of restoration for a believer when he sins is not his emotions. Nor is it some act of penance. It is the atonement and advocacy of Christ. Then let us penitently confess our sins and look to Christ our advocate to give us the peace and joy of restoration to fellowship.

—R. J. W.

Christ never lost any cause He pleaded.
THOMAS WATSON

Everlasting Love

Behold, I have graven thee upon the palms of my hands.

ISAIAH 49:16

Recently in our town some people discovered a newborn baby stuffed into a bag and left in a doorway to die. Though maternal love is proverbially strong, mothers can and do forget their sucking children. And if mother-love can break down, any human bond can snap, given enough pressure. The conditions—really, the sins—of modern society are applying that pressure to more and more people. Homes and marriages are breaking up at an alarming rate. Where once people professed love and devotion, they now express loathing and rejection.

Sometimes when we suffer such human rejection—and even when we do not—we are tempted to feel that the Lord also has rejected us. That is a horrible feeling. The Lord calls us to rejoice in His mercy (v. 13), but we are so depressed that we lament, "The Lord hath forsaken me, and my Lord hath forgotten me" (v. 14). Nothing could be further from the truth. Indeed, the Lord cannot forget us. He has graven us upon the palms of His hands.

That is a description of perpetual remembrance. It is the action of One whose love cannot bear that we should be out of His mind for a second. "The Lord thinketh upon me" (Psa. 40:17), and His thoughts are thoughts of peace (Jer. 29:11). Keep that in mind today. The Lord has not forgotten you. He cannot. He has graven you on the palms of His hands. That action denotes our indissoluble union with Him. Soldiers, slaves, and lovers etched the name of their commander, master, or loved one into their hands. The Lord does the same. He is not our slave, but He is the lover of our souls. Nothing can separate us from His powerful love. So, believer, let this text cheer your heart today. Whatever burden you may have to carry, however forsaken by man you may feel—remember, you are etched into the hands and heart of God. His power and His love are set for your security.

—A. C.

God never repents of His electing love.
THOMAS WATSON

The Death of the Righteous

Let me die the death of the righteous.   **NUMBERS 23:10**

The Scripture uses many terms to describe the death of the Christian. Paul said, "The time of my departure is at hand" (II Tim. 4:6). The word *departure* is a nautical term; it depicts the untying of the ship's moorings, the lifting of her anchors, and the slipping of the vessel away from the quayside and out to the ocean. Peter likens death for the child of God to the dismantling of a tent. Speaking of his own impending death, he said, "Shortly I must put off this my tabernacle," or tent (II Pet. 1:14). A tent is a frail, temporary structure. One day the Christian will exchange the tent of this life for the everlasting mansions of heaven. Peter also tells us that the Christian's death is an exodus, or a "going out." This is the meaning of the word *decease* in II Peter 1:15. It is used also in Luke 9:31 in reference to Christ's death. As the Lord was transfigured, Moses and Elijah appeared and spoke of His decease. Peter was there that day and obviously never forgot that word. He knew that as Christ took His exodus from this world in triumph, so would he. So death holds no terror for the righteous, or justified man. He dies with a quiet conscience; he dies in the arms of a Friend. He loses nothing, but gains everything.

Tragically, Balaam's expressed desire to die such a death was the vain talk of a hypocrite. How could he die the death of the righteous when he would not live the life of the righteous? He lived in rebellion against God. He would have cursed Israel had he not been restrained by the Lord. He actually died fighting against the righteous. No man has any hope of dying the death of the righteous unless he lays hold of the righteousness of God which is in Christ Jesus. To everyone who truly does so, "an entrance shall be ministered . . . abundantly into the everlasting kingdom of our Lord and Saviour Jesus Christ" (II Pet. 1:11).

—J. G.

With believers it may rain in the morning, thunder at
midday, and pour torrents in the afternoon, but it must
clear up ere the sun go down.
C. H. SPURGEON

101

From Gloom to Glory

He was taken from prison and from judgment:
and who shall declare his generation?

ISAIAH 53:8

With the great body of Protestant exegetes I take this text as a statement of Christ's resurrection and exaltation. Literally it means, "From prison, or oppression, and judgment He was taken away, or released." Death was not the end for Christ. He rose again the third day, the conqueror of death and hell. Thus there are two views of Christ in our text: Christ as prisoner, and Christ as conqueror.

Christ as prisoner. Prison speaks of oppression as well as of a place of incarceration. Our Lord was taken prisoner in Gethsemane and taken to Ananias. He was led a prisoner to Caiaphas, in whose house He could have spent time in the dungeon awaiting the Jews' verdict. He was taken as a prisoner to Pilate and from Pilate to Herod and back again. Finally, He was led as a prisoner to Calvary.

As a prisoner, the Lord Jesus endured a trial and a judgment that were a cruel mockery of justice and a crime unparalleled in human history. Jonathan Edwards preached a famous sermon called *Sinners in the Hands of an Angry God.* Here we are dealing with the reverse: God in the hands of angry sinners. No greater commentary on the depravity of man and the patience of God can be imagined. Christ endured all the ignominy and shame of His imprisonment, and when He had made a full atonement for our sins, He "gave up the ghost" and was laid in the tomb—the last stage of His imprisonment. His enemies thought the story was finished. They were wrong. It had only begun!

Christ as conqueror. Death could not hold Christ. He rose from the dead, and later God took Him to glory. *Taken* in our text is the word used in Psalm 49:15 to denote resurrection. God *took* Christ as He took Enoch and Elijah. He took Him bodily up to heaven. The tomb is empty, and the throne is occupied! Let us rejoice that we serve the risen, conquering Saviour.

—A. C.

Before Christ's resurrection,
it was twilight; it is sunrise now.
AUGUSTUS H. STRONG

Forsaking and Finding
Our First Love

Thou hast left thy first love.

REVELATION 2:4

In the light of today's text to the Ephesian church, Paul's emphasis in his epistle to the same people is prophetic. He urges them to "know the love of Christ, which passeth knowledge, [and] be filled with all the fulness of God" (Eph. 3:19). Nothing is better calculated to set our hearts on fire with love for Christ than a clear grasp of His love for us. That is why it is vitally important to keep ourselves in the love of God (Jude 21).

The Ephesians ought to have been able to maintain their first love for Christ. They were well taught. They had been led deeply into the glorious fulness of the love of God in Christ. As long as they bathed their souls in that love, they could never grow cold to Christ or to each other. In some way, however, they allowed the truth to become a dead letter to them. They remained as orthodox as ever and withstood the intrusion of error. That was all very commendable, but it was not enough. Even orthodoxy is no substitute for a heart aflame with love for Christ.

"You have left your first love." What an indictment! It is a very strong expression. Literally, it reads, "You have *forsaken* your first love." Does the Lord so upbraid us today? Let us examine ourselves. Do we love the Lord? Do we love Him as we once did? Or have our lives become mere dull shadows of the vibrant and joyous experiences of love they used to be? What a shame that so many of us have forsaken our first love and are trying to fob off the Saviour with some cold, mechanical observance of duty while our hearts are engaged elsewhere!

Yet shame alone will not resolve the crisis. We need to obtain a fresh sight of Christ's love for us. One glimpse of Calvary will remove our coldness and restore the warmth of our first love. For those suffering from this Ephesian disease, a constant dose of the epistle to the Ephesians is effective medicine.

—A. C.

I would hate my own soul if I did not find it loving God.
AUGUSTINE

Salvation on God's Terms

He sent his word, and healed them.

PSALM 107:20

The Word of God has been given to us to cure us of the greatest sickness of all, sin. It is not enough to admire God's remedy for sin; we must accept it and apply it to our hearts.

In II Kings chapter 5 we are introduced to Naaman, the general of the Syrian army. We are informed that he "was a great man with his master, and honourable, . . . but he was a leper" (II Kings 5:1). When God's word came to him from Elisha to dip seven times in the river Jordan, we are told that "Naaman was wroth, and went away, and said, Behold, I thought, He will surely come out to me, and stand, and call on the name of the Lord his God, and strike his hand over the place, and recover the leper. Are not Abana and Pharpar, rivers of Damascus, better than all the waters of Israel? may I not wash in them, and be clean?" (II Kings 5:11-12).

Naaman was like many in our day who are afflicted with the dreadful disease of sin. They want to be cured, but they object to the simple remedy of faith in Christ alone for salvation. Instead they turn to good works or church attendance, only to discover that these are totally inadequate to meet their need. It is only when we obey the gospel and look to Christ and trust Him as our Saviour that we can be healed and saved (Acts 4:12).

C. H. Spurgeon wrote of the Bible: "Remember dear souls, if you are sick, that the medicine that is to reach your case is somewhere between the covers of this Book. There is something here for every sin sick soul that seeks it."

—S. B.

There are two hopeless things, salvation
without Christ and salvation without holiness.
C. T. STUDD

A Dumb Bird!

She is hardened against her young ones, as though they were not hers:
her labour is in vain without fear; because God hath deprived her of
wisdom, neither hath he imparted to her understanding.

JOB 39:16-17

All nature portrays some degree of spiritual truth. The ostrich is described as a silly bird. Any lessons we may derive from it are of a negative and warning kind.

Its very appearance is a powerful example of double-mindedness and instability. It runs along the ground with its powerful legs, like an animal; yet it is a bird. It has feathers and wings; yet it does not fly. It gives the impression of being neither one thing nor the other. "A double minded man is unstable in all his ways" (James 1:8). Let us not be like the ostrich in our relationship with God. True Christianity demands a clear choice, a positive stand, and a firm commitment.

Again, the poor ostrich has no instinctive understanding of its circumstances. It has no ability to weigh up the consequences of its existence on earth. It lives with no regard for the future. That, alas, is the attitude of many in this world. "Eat, drink, and be merry, and the future will take care of itself" is their attitude. Their philosophy is "Sow, sow, sow, for there will be no harvest." How foolish! "The fear of the Lord is the beginning of wisdom" (Prov. 9:10). To make sure that our eternal welfare is secure is of the utmost importance. To know Christ as Saviour, and that for all eternity, is a paramount necessity.

Most of the creatures in the animal and bird kingdoms take care of their young. The ostrich does not. It displays no desire to advance the welfare and protection of its offspring. Many parents adopt a similar attitude toward the spiritual well-being of their children. They take care of them in temporal matters but, alas, have no regard for their eternal destiny. Let us behold this silly bird, the ostrich, and resolve not to adopt its attitude to the responsibilities of this life and the life to come.

—S. B. C.

He who has no vision of eternity
will never get a true hold of time.
THOMAS CARLYLE

Give Me a Blessing

She said unto him, Give me a blessing.

JUDGES 1:15

Here is a good prayer for every believer. We need the blessing of God. We cannot do without it. Wherever our pathway leads today, we must have the grace and favour of our heavenly Father.

Give me a blessing in my soul that I may enter into the full enjoyment of all that Christ has purchased for me. Let not my soul lie dry and barren. Make it like a well-watered garden. Give me a blessing as I read Thy Word and as I seek Thy face. Let my walk with God be blessed indeed.

Give me a blessing in my home. Let the presence of the Lord so fill my home that, as Moses said, we may there enjoy days of heaven upon the earth. In days when the world and the devil are attacking the Christian home and when there are great testings of our love and loyalty, give me the blessing of household salvation and household commitment to Christ. Then shall we enjoy the blessings of unity and fidelity.

Give me a blessing in my service for God. Without Christ I can do nothing. Without the power of His Spirit I am impotent. I cannot stand for God's truth or seek the souls of poor sinners without the blessing of the fulness of the Holy Ghost. Give me that blessing so that some word or deed of mine today will be used of God to further the work of Christ and bring some wandering one to Him.

Give me Thy blessing. Thou hast promised that Thy blessing is upon Thy people (Psa. 3:8). It is with confidence and great urgency, then, that I lift this petition to Thee today: *Give me a blessing.*

—A. C.

How strangely the Christian's blessings come to him. His strength comes out of weakness, his fulness out of emptiness, his joy out of sorrow, his life out of death.

W. S. PLUMER

A New Husband

Married to another, even to him who is raised from the dead.

ROMANS 7:4

What a tyrant our old husband was! One day we were married to the law of God, and how terribly it treated us! It beat us without mercy, for it demanded perfection of poor creatures who could not give it. It threatened us with awful punishment because of our stubborn rebellion. It gave us no rest but continually demanded work, work, and more work. We were sure this marriage would bring about our death unless death did part us! "The law hath dominion over a man as long as he liveth" (v. 1). But, thank the Lord, through the death of Christ we were delivered from this taskmaster. We died to the law in Christ, forever free from its threats, its scourgings, its punishment. And Christ did this for us that we might be "married to another, even to him."

Married to Christ. What a blessed union this! Just think of all that we receive at the hand of our Husband! We have, as do all brides, a new name. Christ's name is now our name. His name, as John tells us in Revelation 22, is in our forehead. What an honour to bear the name of Christ! How it ought to affect our walk in this world! Moreover, we receive a new standing in life. Look at that precious garment of His own righteousness that covers your sin. Rejoice in that new home that He is preparing for you even now. He takes us from the poorhouse of sin and brings us into His "house of wine."

And does not the bride receive the care and protection of her Husband? Our Beloved is the King of Kings and Lord of Lords. Who dares lift a finger against "the apple of his eye" (Zech. 2:8)? And why need we trouble our heads about tomorrow when "he that keepeth Israel shall neither slumber nor sleep" (Psa. 121:4)? But there is one more thing that our Lord gives to His spouse— a special love. How this love overcomes us! Such love to the unlovely must surely compel us to please Him by bringing "forth fruit unto God"!

—J. W.

We are never nearer Christ than when we find ourselves lost in a holy amazement at His unspeakable love.

JOHN OWEN

Remembering Christ's Death

My God, my God, why hast thou forsaken me? PSALM 22:1

Lest I forget Gethsemane,
Lest I forget Thine agony,
Lest I forget Thy love for me,
Lead me to Calvary.

This familiar hymn expresses well the way to keep Christ's love a reality in our hearts. When Paul confessed Christ's love as the motivating force in his life, he was thinking of Christ's death as the evidence of that love (II Cor. 5:14). Remembering Calvary is the cure for the doubts, frustrations, and clouds that frequently rob us of peace and joy. It is what gives direction and purpose to the Christian life.

Although written hundreds of years before Christ's death, Psalm 22 leads us directly to Calvary. It is a record of Christ's saddest hours, His dying words; it describes both the darkness and glory of the cross. As you read this minutely fulfilled prophecy, remember that Christ endured it all for you. Consider that He was forsaken of God (vv. 1, 2). Answering the question "Why hast thou forsaken me?" brings us to the heart of the atonement. Christ was not forsaken by God because of anything He had done, but because of what we were. As our substitute, He became a curse that we might be accepted by God. Consider that He was rejected by men (vv. 6-8). He experienced the depths of humiliation voluntarily that we might be exalted with Him. Although sinners mock Him in His death, we for whom He died rejoice. Consider that He was afflicted in body and soul (vv. 12-18). In His agony, shame, and death, He wove for us the garment of salvation and robe of righteousness. How can we live unto ourselves when our hearts are overwhelmed by the fact that Christ died for us?

—M. P. V. B.

If we would live aright it must be by
the contemplation of Christ's death.
C. H. SPURGEON

Marked Men

Set a mark upon . . . the men that . . . cry.

EZEKIEL 9:4

There is a pre-eminence about the Man in verse 2, clad in linen, with the writer's inkhorn by His side—the divine Registrar inscribing and keeping the names of God's dear ones in His book, the book of the Lamb slain. The instructions are to set a mark upon the men that cry over the hideous sin of the land.

The stamp of God is upon some men still, even in these dark times when Ezekiel ministers. These bear the mark of redemption. The saints are designated living epistles, "known and read of all men," with the Author's signature upon them wherever they go (II Cor. 3:2; cf. Acts 9:13, 15).

God wants identified men. This mark surely sets each man apart as God's own possession, his life well-pleasing to his Master. The Saviour knows the number of His redeemed. Thus He sets His seal upon every one of them.

Sin should alarm the saints. Abominations should distress them. Let us never allow ourselves to become hardened. The book of Hebrews—like Ezekiel, the book of the inner sanctuary—warns against being hardened by the deceitfulness of sin (Heb. 3:13). We must keep a tender conscience in all things.

Good men are marked by brokenness and prayer. They sigh and cry for all the abominations done in the midst of Jerusalem. Too many pray with dry eyes, dull hearts, and dilatory, wandering thoughts. God requires a contrite spirit, not much in evidence these days (Psa. 51:17; 57:15).

There is no exemption by class in God's sight. The little children, the ancients, the sanctuary men—all become answerable for what they do (Ezek. 9:6, 10). We must all bear the mark of the Lord on earth to be owned by Him in glory.

—J. D.

It is a human thing to fall into sin, a devilish thing to persevere in it, and an angelical thing to rise out of it.
AUGUSTINE

A Glorious Proclamation

Now is Christ risen from the dead.

I CORINTHIANS 15:20

The Bible foretells that in the last days there shall be a falling away from the faith. That apostasy can be seen today in the increasing attacks upon the cardinal doctrines of Christianity. Two areas are central to the devil's strategy, namely, the deity of Christ and His bodily resurrection.

What a gloomy proposition is the denial of Christ's resurrection! It would mean that all Christian preaching is vain and a waste of time. Even worse, it would be an exposition of falsehood. The faith of believing people would be empty and groundless, sin unforgiven, and our buried loved ones eternally perished. Salvation at best could be only for this present life. What a dark prospect!

However, the resurrection of Christ is one of the best-attested facts in history. There were over five hundred eyewitnesses whose testimony must be overthrown to deny the fact. It was prophesied by Christ. It was recorded in the Gospels.

The lives of the disciples, so depressed and discouraged by the crucifixion, were suddenly transformed by the resurrection of their Master. They went forth as fearless heralds of Christ and His gospel. A faked resurrection could not account for that transformation. The changed lives of millions of Christians attest to the veracity of Paul's statement, "Now is Christ risen from the dead."

Three philosophers—Karl Marx, Sigmund Freud, and Charles Darwin—have had a marked but debilitating effect upon modern society. Thank God, the Christian does not follow the mutable theories of dead philosophers, but the life-giving gospel of a living Redeemer. His resurrection is the capstone of all Christian doctrine. May we know "the power of his resurrection" (Phil. 3:10) today.

—F. McC.

Christians out-die pagans and the
resurrection of Christ is the reason.
T. R. GLOVER

The Inheritance of the Saints

*To an inheritance incorruptible, and undefiled,
and that fadeth not away, reserved in heaven for you.*

I PETER 1:4

Because we are elect, regenerate, and redeemed, we have a living hope of a glorious inheritance. Peter lifts the minds of his readers away from the reproaches, persecutions, and afflictions of this present world to the glorious anticipation of their promised and sure inheritance in the world to come.

Notice that it is an inheritance. It is not attained by our own exertions, but is bequeathed to us and is ours already by promise through the death of the Testator, our Lord Jesus Christ. How sure it is! We *must* inherit, for the Testator has already died, and the terms of His covenant must be fulfilled (Heb. 9:15-17).

It is an *undying* inheritance, incorruptible. There is no seed of death there, for there is no sin in heaven. Its glories, its felicities, and its joys are undying. They will never sour with the oft tasting.

It is an *undefiled* inheritance. This word indicates that there is nothing added to it. There is nothing to mitigate its holiness and happiness. In all our enjoyments of earth there is an admixture of infirmity and sorrow. But not so in heaven.

Our inheritance is therefore *unfading*. It will never cease to give joy. It is always fresh, satisfying, and new. As we follow the Lamb, we will be led to deeper, fuller springs of life eternal.

Then, it is *unremovable*. It is reserved in heaven for us. It is under the guardianship of divine wisdom and power, and so are we the inheritors—kept by the power of God. One day soon it will be revealed, and we will see it in perfect fulness and reality.

Let us count the trials of this life as but a light thing in the anticipation of such a promised and joyful inheritance.

—R. J. B.

**The road is not to be complained of,
as it leads to such a home.**
JOHN NEWTON

Horrible Horoscopes

Monthly prognosticators.

ISAIAH 47:13

Almost every daily newspaper feels it necessary to carry a column by some astrologer to advise its readers of their fate according to the stars. You would be surprised at the number of people who take such columns seriously. The wife of a former president of the United States regularly consulted an astrologer, and some high officials in the administration have averred that presidential action was at times influenced by the astrologer's advice. Even some Christians are foolish enough to check the astrology column in their newspaper. Of course, it is just for fun! The trouble is, there is nothing funny about astrology.

Astrology is ancient. The notion that the stars somehow control our destiny goes back a long way. In ancient times court astrologers made a lucrative if dangerous living by convincing their masters that the stars could direct their policy to the best advantage. The advent of the scientific age has not lessened the superstition to any marked degree.

Astrology is a counterfeit of the revealed truth of a personal, all-wise, sovereign Creator who rules all His creation according to His will. It is a substitute for the Word of God. It is sorcery (v. 12). It is fatalism at its worst. It is not only fatalistic, it is fatal. It is a slayer of souls. That is clear from today's text. The monthly prognosticators, or "stargazers," or "astrologers," as Isaiah also calls them, succeeded only in leading the people astray. By the time some people discovered their error, it was too late to recover.

We have God's infallible Word. It is the "light that shineth in a dark place" (II Pet. 1:19). It tells you how to be saved. It shows you how to live. It has the answer to every problem of life. And it lights the way through death to heaven. Go to the Bible today. It is not a horoscope you need, but the handbook of heaven. —A. C.

God assures us of a future that is better than all our past.
J. C. STERN

Runaway Christians

But Jonah rose up to flee unto Tarshish from the presence of the Lord.
JONAH 1:3

It is sad to see Jonah trying to get away from the presence of the Lord. Jonah was blessed as a prophet of God while he sought God's presence, but now he looks a forlorn figure as he hurries to get away from the Lord.

Many Christians spend much of their lives running away. They run away from witnessing, they run away from difficulties, they run away from the call to surrender fully, and all the time they are running away from God Himself. Maybe you are a "runaway" Christian. Once you loved to live close to the Lord, but something has happened to you. Now, if you are honest, you will have to admit that you seem to be keeping out of the Lord's way.

Have you ever thought of how foolish you are being? You cannot really get out of God's presence. Psalm 139, which Jonah would certainly have known, asks, "Whither shall I go from thy spirit? or whither shall I flee from thy presence? If I ascend up into heaven, thou art there: . . . if I take the wings of the morning, and dwell in the uttermost parts of the sea; even there shall thy hand lead me, and thy right hand shall hold me" (vv. 7-10).

In any case, no child of God should ever want to get out of the Lord's presence, for in His presence, as the Bible tells us, there is fulness of joy. It is only as we live close to God that we know that fulness of joy. The "runaway" Christian is miserable; the Christian who abides in God's presence is happy.

—G. F.

> The moment that Jonah made up
> his mind to act in disobedience he lost the
> sense of the Lord's presence in his soul.
> HARRY IRONSIDE

No God like Our God

There is none like unto the God of Jeshurun.

DEUTERONOMY 33:26

This is a sentence from Moses' last earthly utterance. What a way to leave the world! Facing death and reviewing the way in which the Lord had led him, Moses was at peace. He was absolutely sure that all those years before, when by faith he had turned his back on Egypt and had chosen to suffer reproach for Christ (Heb. 11:25-26), he had made the right choice, followed the right Master, and associated with the right people.

Happy is the man who can face death and eternity with the same assurance in the Lord. To choose Christ is often to choose earthly loss or painful persecution. Carnal men consider us lunatic if we turn our backs on the pleasures and treasures of Egypt to take up our cross and follow Christ. But those earthly baubles are useless in the hour of death. Only a living faith in Christ can comfort us as we enter eternity. If Christ is our Saviour in life, He will be our song in death.

Today, let us give much thought to the unique greatness of the Lord. He is the ever-living God. He is the ever-loving God. He is the everlasting God. The gods men worship are idols. They have no existence outside the imaginations of their creators. Our God is the true God, beside whom there is none else (Isa. 45:21-22). He controls all things. He keeps us continually in His thoughts. He protects and helps us. He daily loads us with benefits. Best of all, He has placed us in Christ, pardoning all our sins and clothing us in His imputed righteousness. Those whom He justifies He also glorifies (Rom. 8:29-30), thus establishing our eternal security in Christ.

Rejoice, O Christian, rejoice in the Lord! We have a great God and Saviour. Amid the trials of life He will not fail nor forsake us. When we come to die, He will carry us through in triumph. Therefore our testimony will forever be—as it now is—"There is no God like our God."

—A. C.

There is nothing little in God.
C. H. Spurgeon

114

God Speaks

The law of the Lord is perfect.

PSALM 19:7

God has revealed everything that we must know about Him, ourselves, eternal salvation, and daily life. He has not left anything to chance or imagination. God's Word to us is able to meet every need, whatever it may be. Throughout the history of the church, men risked their lives to translate the Scriptures and spread its message. To them the Bible was precious beyond words. Today we enjoy the blessings of their sacrifices; most of us possess multiple copies of Scripture. For us it is a common possession of uncommon worth. How precious is God's Word to us? We are ready to defend our right to have it and denounce governments who deny it to their people. That is good, but how is this Book affecting us day by day?

Psalm 19 begins with God's speaking to us through His magnificent creation. It ends with our speaking to God for aid in heeding His Word, a prayer for purity and pleasing behaviour in His sight. At the heart of the psalm is a beautiful description of the characteristics and effects of God's special communication. We read that the whole body of God's instruction is complete, restoring, reviving, and affecting every part of our being. It is reliable, meeting us at our need. It is straight, producing contentment in our inner man. It is radiant, giving us clear discernment and direction. It is refined and pure, standing forever. It is completely true and righteous; it reveals God's perfect will. Consequently, it is most desirable. More than material wealth or pleasure, God's Word should be our passion. We must not be content just to possess copies of the Bible. We must make our custom conform to our creed that the Bible is our rule for faith and practice.

—M. P. V. B.

Some people are critical of everything; some embrace anything. The wise weigh all things by the word.
H. T. MAHAN

The Cities of Refuge

We . . . have fled for refuge to lay hold upon the hope set before us.
HEBREWS 6:18

It is very evident that Paul has a particular illustration in mind here in speaking of Christ as the sinner's hope. He speaks of fleeing, and he speaks of refuge, a refuge found in the hope set before us. Paul is obviously thinking of the cities of refuge first spoken of in the book of Numbers. Under the law, certain cities were provided as a place of refuge for the unintentional manslayer. In the provision of those cities, there was a clear foreshadowing of the gospel, of Christ Himself, who is our hope.

The cities were built on mountains so as to be clearly seen by the searching fugitive. There is no obscurity in the gospel. Christ is set before us there with much clarity. Let us who would point sinners to Him always endeavour to use "great plainness of speech" (II Cor. 3:12). Remember that "a city that is set on an hill cannot be hid" (Matt. 5:14). Those citadels of safety were evenly located throughout the land: three on the west of Jordan—Kadesh, Shechem, and Kirjath-arba; and three on the east of the river—Bezer, Ramoth, and Golan. Thus refuge was available in every section, just as Christ is the strong tower into which sinners in every place may come. He is the Saviour for all men, men from all nations, all colours, all classes—sinners of every kind and every background.

In those cities alone was there shelter from the avenger of blood. Others may have looked just as safe, but only those of God's appointment offered shelter. Christ is the only hope for the sinner. Many would guide needy souls in other directions, but the Scriptures warn us against these false Christs and other gospels. You must enter that one refuge that God has set before us in His own Word, and you must enter in with urgency. The avenger follows and will strike you down. Flee to Christ today. To delay will bring certain destruction.

—J. G.

Everyone who is a man of God has
omnipotence as his guardian.
C. H. SPURGEON

A Light To Chase the Gloom

*I know the thoughts that I think toward you, saith the Lord,
thoughts of peace, and not of evil, to give you an expected end.*
JEREMIAH 29:11

Strange things happen to us at times. They baffle us, they distress us, and they try us. Often we feel like Jacob's sons when they asked in bewilderment, "What is this that God hath done unto us?" (Gen. 42:28). What in the world is going on?

There is nothing new in all this. The psalmist Asaph had so many troubles in his life that he felt the Lord had forsaken him (Psa. 77:7-9). Have not we all felt like this? And has not Satan used every such trial to try to embitter our souls and make us become wearied and faint in our minds (Heb. 12:3)?

Let us always remember this: when we do not know what in the world is happening, the Lord does. He is working out His purpose of grace toward us. "All things work together for good" to all His people. *All* things, not just some things, are for our good—even when we cannot see how.

When circumstances are difficult in the extreme, we should remember that the Lord is thinking about us. "I am poor and needy; yet the Lord thinketh upon me" (Psa. 40:17). Instead of worrying, think of Him who thinks constantly of us. Then see how much lighter the burdens of life are!

The Lord never intends evil to His blood-bought people. He never deals with us except in mercy. He constantly pursues a policy of peace toward us. Then begone, dull care and unbelief! I will stay my mind upon Jehovah my salvation, and He will keep me in perfect peace.

The Lord intends to give us our "expected end." He will not disappoint the hope of glory He has placed within our hearts. With God as our Father, Christ Jesus as our Saviour, the Holy Spirit as our Comforter, and heaven as our home, should we not soar above the worries of life and enjoy the peace of confidence in Him who knows what He is doing?

—A. C.

**As God did not at first choose you because you were high,
so He will not forsake you because you are low.**
JOHN FLAVEL

Christ Our Mediator

And Moses brought their cause before the Lord.

NUMBERS 27:5

What strong faith the five daughters of Zelophehad exhibited in the promise of God to Israel concerning the land of Canaan. Though it was yet unconquered, they petitioned for a share in it as if it were already their own. Such confidence was not presumptuous. Had not God covenanted to give Israel an inheritance? They knew that He would not break His covenant.

They had faith also in the power of God. They knew that the land was inhabited by fierce tribes and mighty giants; yet they believed that God would fight for them. Here were young women who were truly "five wise virgins." They were not living for the present, but had a clear eye to the future. The wilderness was not home to them. They relished the thought of the land flowing with milk and honey. What they had heard of stirred their souls—the grapes of Eshcol, the pomegranates, the olives, the well-watered soil, a veritable paradise compared to the barren wilderness they were traversing. With the eye of faith they could see themselves safely settled, their journeying finally ended.

These maidens knew that there was only one way to obtain an inheritance in the land—through the intervention of a mediator. Knowing that they had no rights of their own, no merit to entitle them to a portion in Canaan, they approached Moses, the man of God, and he "brought their cause before the Lord." Their cause was in many ways a hopeless one. Their father had died in the wilderness. Since they had no brothers, there was no one to claim the forfeited inheritance for them. Their only hope was to go to Moses and have him plead for them before God. Likewise, it is the Mediator between God and men who secures the heavenly land for sinners. Christ is the "door." Enter into Him today and look forward to that inheritance that is "incorruptible, and undefiled, and that fadeth not away" (I Pet. 1:4).

—J. G.

I have a great need for Christ;
I have a great Christ for my need.
C. H. SPURGEON

The Year of Jubilee

Cause the trumpet of the jubile to sound. LEVITICUS 25:9

In ancient Israel, after seven sabbaths of years, the fiftieth year was declared the Year of Jubilee. It began at the close of the Day of Atonement with the sounding of the trumpet. The holy convocations of Leviticus provide us with a picture gallery of Christ and the work of redemption. The Jubilee is a reminder of the great day when the trump of God shall sound and the eternal sabbath of rest in heaven begins.

It is a period of *rest*. The battles have all been fought. The sweat and tears are forever wiped away. All toil is ended, and the believer enters into that everlasting rest that remains for the people of God.

It is a period of *restitution*. Property in Israel that had been sold or alienated was returned to the original owners in the Year of Jubilee. Man in this present world is a dispossessed proprietor. He received much from God at creation, but lost it in the fall. Christ has redeemed His people, restoring what was lost.

It is a period of *release*. Chains were broken, prison doors opened, and captives set free. At the trump of God, tombs will burst and imprisoned bodies will be eternally freed. From sea floor and mountain top, and all places between, the resurrected bodies of dead saints will come forth in glorious liberty.

It is a period of *reunion*. In the Year of Jubilee the members of scattered families joined together in happy reunion. What a joyous occasion it will be when all the dispersed members of God's redeemed family will meet in heaven. What a glorious prospect!

It is a period of *refreshment*. There was no sowing or reaping, but the enjoyment of an abundant supply. The Israelites made preparation ahead of time for the Jubilee. On earth we are to lay up treasure in heaven. Dear Christian friend, sow today in righteousness and reap in mercy. The Lord will miss no deed of kindness done in His name. And listen for the trumpet sound; it may soon be heard.

—F. McC.

In heaven is no warfare but all well-fare.
JOHN BOYS

A Good Example

He was a good man.

ACTS 11:24

Barnabas is one of those minor characters in Scripture who are almost totally eclipsed by their relationship to a greater figure. He was a faithful fellow labourer with the apostle Paul. That is how he is known and also why he is sometimes forgotten. The figure of Paul is so captivating that we tend to forget everyone else when we see him. Yet the passages which relate to Barnabas set before us a true "son of consolation," a character worthy of imitation.

The first mention of him in the Bible (Acts 4:36-37) refers to his generosity in financial giving. Unlike Ananias and Sapphira, he gave all to the Lord, revealing something of the devotion he had to Christ and His cause. Someone has said that it is possible to give without loving, but it is impossible to love without giving. Barnabas's devotion held nothing back. The second reference in Scripture portrays him as one gentle in friendship (9:27). Saul of Tarsus, the persecutor, had been converted, but the church could not forget his past and treated him with coldness and suspicion. Barnabas supported him, encouraged him, and introduced him into the communion of the church. How important it is to be of help to those newly come to the faith!

The final passage relating to him in Acts (15:37) underscores his graciousness towards failures. John Mark had gone home once while on a missionary tour, but Barnabas was willing to give him another chance. How like the Lord's treatment of erring Peter, who, having denied Christ with oaths and curses (and that before the ungodly), was restored and subsequently fulfilled a powerful ministry as an apostle and elder.

Let us be generous, gentle, and gracious—that is the message of Barnabas's life.

—D. F.

We can do more good by being good than in any other way.
ROWLAND HILL

Hold Your Tongue!

*Whoso keepeth his mouth and his tongue
keepeth his soul from troubles.*

PROVERBS 21:23

There are many interesting entries in John Wesley's journal. On June 9th, 1742, he writes of attending an unusual court case. The magistrate was "a man of candour and understanding." He was to hear the complaints of some angry citizens who had brought to him "a whole wagon load of these new heretics." The magistrate enquired what they had done. One of the accusers answered, "Why, they pretended to be better than other people; and besides, they prayed from morning to night." "But have they done nothing else?" "Yes, sir," replied an old man. "They have converted my wife. Till she went among them, she had such a tongue! And now she is as quiet as a lamb." "Carry them back, carry them back," cried the justice, "and let them convert all the scolds in the town."

We may well smile at this story; yet the Word of God declares, "If any man among you seem to be religious, and bridleth not his tongue, but deceiveth his own heart, this man's religion is vain" (James 1:26). How deadly is the power of that little member! As the Puritan Thomas Watson put it, "The sword doth not make so deep a wound as the tongue." The hasty, hurtful word we immediately regret, but cannot recall. It is well said that "a word spoken is physically transient, but morally permanent." Christian, there is a time to be silent. "Learn to hold thy tongue. Five words cost Zacharias forty weeks' silence" (Thomas Fuller). Be slow to speak. "He that refraineth his lips is wise" (Prov. 10:19). It has been well said, "If you think twice before you speak once, you will speak twice the better for it." Pray the psalmist's prayer today: "Set a watch, O Lord, before my mouth; keep the door of my lips" (Psa. 141:3).

—M. P.

Give not thy tongue too great a liberty,
lest it take thee prisoner.
FRANCIS QUARLES

From Books to the Bible

The name of Debir before was Kirjath-sepher.

JUDGES 1:11

As soon as Caleb came into his inheritance, he attacked and conquered Kirjath-sepher, also known as Kirjath-sannah (Josh. 15:49), which he renamed Debir. The names are interesting and instructive. *Kirjath-sepher* means "city of a book," and *Kirjath-sannah* means "city of learning," while *Debir* means "place of the oracle." Evidently the town was a seat of learning among the Canaanites, a place where their records and such other literary works as they had produced were kept. When Caleb sent Othniel to conquer the city, he overthrew the learning and literature of the heathen and made the town a testimony to the oracle, or inspired revelation, of the Lord.

The gospel must challenge the seats of human learning, which nowadays are largely given over to ungodliness and heathenism. All too often God's people make no evangelical assault on these bastions of alleged "higher" learning. This is probably because of an ignorance of the deep theology of the gospel and a lack of experience of the power of the Holy Spirit. This double disability makes most Christians afraid to invade our modern Kirjath-sephers. These strongholds of ungodliness will fall only before the keen edge of the sword of the Spirit. Let us make sure to include in our evangelism those young people now being educated in the godless culture of Kirjath-sepher.

Each one of us has his own battle of Kirjath-sepher. We need to turn away from the *books* of the world to the *Book* of God. We must give pre-eminence to the Bible in our reading. Nowadays professing Christians spend hours before a television set or reading a book but give little time and study to the Bible. While with their lips they say it is the Word of God, by their behaviour they deny it. Our hearts should rightly be named Debir, the place of the oracle, the place where the Word of God holds absolute sway. Is your heart a Kirjath-sepher or a Debir?

—A. C.

It is a sad thing to be often eating of the tree
of knowledge, but never to taste of the tree of life.
THOMAS BROOKS

Reconciliation Through the Blood

Ye . . . are made nigh by the blood of Christ.

EPHESIANS 2:13

Though the heathen worshippers in Ephesus boasted that their city belonged to the goddess Diana (Acts 19:35), Paul emphatically states that they were "without God in the world" (Eph. 2:12). Their lifeless statue could never replace the living God. Paul further states that they were "far off" from God (v. 13). Only the man with clean hands and a pure heart (Psa. 24:4) can ascend into the hill of the Lord. All others must stand "far off." In contrast to these heathen worshippers, Paul makes the amazing statement that the Ephesian saints were now "made nigh" to God. What made the difference? Obviously, it was not their personal character that did. They were "by nature the children of wrath, even as others" (Eph. 2:3). What made the difference was the atoning, reconciling blood of the Lamb: "The blood of Jesus Christ his Son cleanseth us from all sin" (I John 1:7).

> *What can wash away my sin?*
> *Nothing but the blood of Jesus;*
> *What can make me whole again?*
> *Nothing but the blood of Jesus.*

Through the blood our position is one of being near God; therefore, Hebrews 10:22 exhorts, "Let us draw near with a true heart in full assurance of faith." In other words, let us lay hold of what Christ has purchased for us and draw near to God in prayer. There are many who refuse to come to God on the basis of the blood. They count "the blood of the covenant" to be "an unholy thing" (Heb. 10:29), or something to be despised. Such people can never draw nigh to God. Only the man who knows how to plead the merit of Jesus' blood knows how to pray. "Lord, teach us to pray," and may our plea in prayer ever be, "Nothing but the blood of Jesus!"

—M. W. A.

The blood keeps on cleansing. Its life is unabated; its power is undiminished; its merit is unimpoverished and its value is unlessened.

IAN R. K. PAISLEY

Caught in the Storm

But the Lord sent out a great wind into the sea.   JONAH 1:4

In Mark chapter 4 we see Christ stilling the storm that had terrified the apostles. Here we find Him sending a great wind into the sea. It is strange to see the Lord on one hand stilling a fierce storm and on the other sending one. But as the hymn writer has noted, the wind and waves obey Him.

The Lord never sends a storm without a very good reason. In Jonah's case it was because he was going in the direction opposite to where the Lord had sent him. He had to learn that he could not deliberately disobey God with impunity. To teach him that lesson, the Lord sent out such a storm into the Mediterranean Sea that no effort made by the most experienced sailors could avail in the unequal struggle between the waves and the helpless vessel being tossed about as a plaything.

Perhaps you are passing through stormy waters at this period of your life. You are not in the midst of the Mediterranean, but there is such a storm raging in your heart that you feel you cannot go on any longer. Hudson Taylor, founder of the China Inland Mission, once passed through a fierce conflict. He knew the Lord wanted him to go to the interior of China, but he was afraid to lead workers there lest the venture should fail utterly. His inner conflict was so intense that he thought he was going to lose his reason. At last Taylor was brought to a full surrender to God, and the subsequent work led to the salvation of multitudes of Chinese people.

Has the storm in your life has been caused by your refusal to surrender to the Lord and obey His voice? "Go through with God."

—G. F.

**There is no art that can elude or baffle the messengers
of Him who is the Judge of the quick and the dead.**
HUGH MARTIN

Under New Management

Ye are bought with a price.

I CORINTHIANS 6:20

Natural man has long considered himself master of his own destiny. He relies more and more on self and less and less on God. He exalts himself and is self-satisfied and self-sufficient.

The Christian rejoices, however, that he has been delivered from such self-worship. He knows that if left to himself disaster would strike, sooner or later. He is glad to know he is under new management. The failing company of his sinful life has been taken over by One whose resources are infinite.

He knows his body is the temple of the Holy Ghost. He is not left to muddle his way through life but has the blessed, indwelling Guide to direct his faltering footsteps from earth to heaven.

When the spiritual creditors come, God Himself takes the witness stand with the unanswerable question, "Who shall lay any thing to the charge of God's elect?" (Rom. 8:33). The believer has this great security, for he knows the bank of heaven stands behind him. He will not—nay, cannot—fail.

This new ownership brings new responsibilities to the Christian. No longer must the egotistical *mine* dominate, but the submissive *Thine*. "Thine be the glory" is the grateful song of the believer. We serve our new Master, Jesus Christ, because we love Him. We try not to have one foot in the world's camp and the other in the Lord's, but to serve Him wholeheartedly.

Service to Christ involves sacrifice, and at all times we are to give of our best to the Master. The key to such service is love, for we will always give our best to the one we love the most. What a thrill to know we are no longer under Satan's control, but are servants of the loving and merciful Christ!

—F. McC.

If Jesus Christ be God and died for me, then no sacrifice can be too great for me to make for Him.
C. T. STUDD

Seeking and Finding God

Ye shall seek me, and find me, when
ye shall search for me with all your heart.

JEREMIAH 29:13

Is there anything more miserable than to be or feel estranged from the Lord? In his distress Job cried, "Oh that I knew where I might find him! that I might come even to his seat!" (Job 23:3). The good news is that we know *where* to find Him, and *how!* So, however deep your need or your trouble, take heart, for you can find the Lord today. This is true for every sinner who longs to be delivered. It is true for every backslider whose heart feels estranged from God by unfaithfulness. And it is true for every faithful believer who longs for a clearer vision and a closer fellowship with his Lord. We can find the Lord today.

We know where He may be found. Paul tells us that it is at the throne of grace we meet with Him (Heb. 4:16). Moses called it the mercy seat. The meaning is the same. We meet God through the atoning blood of Christ. Christ has fully satisfied Him and has fully reconciled us. Let us by faith plead the merit of the blood, and we shall find the Lord.

We know how to find Him. We are to search for Him with all our heart. The Lord demands sincerity. He wants His people to be in dead earnest about seeking and finding Him. When we become earnest in our seeking of the Lord, He will surely reveal Himself to us. Our trouble is that while we say we are seeking Him, our hearts are cold and careless. Oh! how can we be lukewarm about searching for the Lord?

We will find Him. What a treasure! The seeking is itself a blessing, but who can describe the finding! There is no joy, no peace, no confidence, no thrill on earth to compare with our experience of all those blessings when we find the Lord. Then let us seek. Let us search. Let us this very day remove self-imposed obstacles from our way to the throne of grace. If we really mean business with God, He will do business with us.

—A. C.

God measures out His communion of love
according to diligence in seeking Him.
R. C. CHAPMAN

The Reign of Grace

Knowing this, that our old man is crucified with him, that the body of sin might be destroyed, that henceforth we should not serve sin.

ROMANS 6:6

The Church of Rome has always hated the doctrine of justification by grace alone. Since the days of the Reformation, she has asserted that such preaching will lead to licentious living. Of course, this is not a new charge against the gospel, for Paul had to face the same accusations in his day. Now it seems that today's popular "carnal Christian" theory is giving credence to Rome's allegation. In our day a person can make a "decision for Christ" without being made a disciple of Christ. He can be "saved" from his present troubles (or so he hopes!) or saved from hell, but never need to be saved from his sinful vices. Paul addresses both of these fallacies in the sixth chapter of Romans by proving that justifying grace will reign in the life of the true child of God.

By our union with Christ in His death, "our old man is crucified with him" (v. 6). As Christ died to sin's guilt, sin's condemnation, and sin's reign, so did we! That is, by bearing our sin on the cross, He destroyed all that sin could do to us. Not that our sinful nature was eradicated, but it lost its power to dominate us, "for he that is dead is freed from sin" (v. 7). Can it be any plainer than Paul's declaration in verse 14, "For sin shall not have dominion over you"?

What does this say to those who claim that this doctrine of free justification leads to immorality? And what does it do to the theory of the "carnal Christian," which says a man can be saved and never leave his sinful habits and wicked living? Most certainly, these notions are left high and dry. Thank God for the sanctifying power of the truth of justification! For how shall we who have been freed from the horrors of sin by the awful death of our Redeemer live any longer in sin? Let us therefore yield ourselves as servants of God unto holy living.

—J. W.

> He leads none to heaven but
> whom He sanctifies on the earth.
> JOHN OWEN

Transplanted

And he shall be like a tree planted by the rivers of water.

PSALM 1:3

Gardening enthusiasts know the significance of transplanting flowers, shrubs, and trees. The purpose of transplanting is to put the plant in a more advantageous setting, not to give it a better chance of dying. That which is transplanted is considered to be property and becomes the object of special cultivation and care.

This is the image suggested by the description of the blessed man as a tree "transplanted" by rivers of water. The believer has been transferred from the kingdom of darkness and placed in the kingdom of light. When God transplants us, He assures us that He makes us the object of His special care, concern, and provision. He puts us by a water source that never runs dry and thus supplies us with what we need for life, growth, and fruitfulness. Knowing that we are special to God will liberate us from the bondage of insecurities that easily rob us of spiritual joy. Experience testifies that this divine care may not appear as material prosperity, but then material things should not be the desire of the godly heart. Even though the benefits of God's special attention may not be visible to the physical eye, the benefits are absolutely certain. We will know them as we delight and meditate in God's law. To meditate means simply to become so consumed with God and His Word that we are oblivious to everything else. As we give our attention to the Lord, we will enjoy the blessings of His attention to us.

—M. P. V. B.

God looks over us but never overlooks us.
JOHN BLANCHARD

A Light for Dark Days

Who is among you that feareth the Lord, . . . that walketh in darkness?
. . . Let him trust in the name of the Lord, and stay upon his God.
ISAIAH 50:10

Somehow the notion has spread abroad that true Christians should never endure periods of darkness, trial, or trouble. Nothing could be further from the truth. Trials will come to every Christian. Satan will attack every Christian. When these things occur, we can become very confused and distressed. It appears that the Lord has forsaken us. Is that your experience today? Are you an heir of heaven walking in darkness? Today's text has a word for you.

Dark days are not necessarily a judgment on sin. Isaiah addresses those who fear the Lord. They obey the voice of His servant. This is a description of a believer walking according to the Word of God. Yet he walks in darkness. He is fighting a spiritual battle that depresses his soul. He reads his Bible but receives no light. He prays but obtains no relief. The devil tells him that all this is God's judgment on him and that He has forsaken him. Our text brands that as a lie. Faithful Christians face dark days. So what is the answer? Will the Lord leave a believer in such a condition indefinitely? No, but He may allow the darkness to continue until the necessary lesson of faith has been learned. What is that lesson? It is that we are not to base our assurance on good feelings or prosperous circumstances, but on the character and Word of our God. If you are compassed about by doubt or darkness, *stay*, or lean, upon the Lord. Trust Him. He will not fail you or forsake you. Stand upon His promises, and light will arise in the darkness.

—A. C.

> **He that rides to be crowned will**
> **not think much of a rainy day.**
> JOHN TRAPP

The Application of the Blood

The blood of sprinkling.

HEBREWS 12:24

The specific thought denoted by these words is the application to believers of all the saving virtues and benefits of the blood of Jesus Christ. This expression is borrowed from the Levitical economy, in relation to which the sprinkling of blood was a common feature. There were three outstanding occasions when the blood was applied in various ways.

In Egypt it was sprinkled on the doorposts and lintels of the houses of the Israelites (Exod. 12). That was the blood of redemption. God's people went out of Egypt because of that blood, leaving behind their bondage, their taskmasters, their labours, and their groaning. Through the redeeming blood sinners are set free from the power and thraldom of sin. They "have redemption through his blood" (Eph. 1:7).

The next outstanding reference to the sprinkling of the blood is in Exodus 24. Moses took a basin of blood, half of which he sprinkled on the altar and the rest upon the people. Here we see the Godward and manward aspects of the atonement. It was sprinkled on the altar first, for the atonement is objective in its primary effect. It satisfies the justice of God and appeases His wrath before it meets the need of the sinner. Thus it is the blood of justification. Sinners are declared righteous when they are covered with the satisfying merits of the blood of God's dear Son.

The final prominent reference to the sprinkling of blood is in Leviticus 16. On the great day of atonement Aaron sprinkled the mercy seat with the blood seven times. Thereby he was "reconciling the holy place" (Lev. 16:20). His action demonstrated that there is "peace through the blood of his cross" (Col. 1:20). Christ has made reconciliation for the sins of His people.

Truly the blood of sprinkling "speaketh." Hear its blessed tones today and rejoice in its power.

—J. G.

I hear the words of love, I gaze upon the blood,
I see the mighty sacrifice, and I have peace with God.
HORATIUS BONAR

Trust in the Lord

Whoso trusteth in the Lord, happy is he.

PROVERBS 16:20

How precious is the grace of faith! It is the gift of God. Faith unites us to Christ. "Other graces make us like Christ, faith makes us members of Christ" (Thomas Watson). It is a saving grace. "Thy faith hath saved thee; go in peace" (Luke 7:50). Happy indeed are those who, because they have been justified by faith, have peace with God.

The feet of faith take us in the ways of the Lord, ways of pleasantness and peace. The voice of faith cries out in the storm, "What time I am afraid, I will trust in thee" (Psa. 56:3). After all, as Thomas Kelly put it, "God is at the helm!" The eye of faith pierces through the darkest cloud and judges not the Lord by feeble sense, but trusts Him for His grace, believing that behind a frowning providence He hides a smiling face. The mouth of faith draws forth sweetness out of the flowers of promise, those exceeding great and precious promises. "These are the flagons that faith keeps by her, the apples she hath hoarded up in store, to revive and quicken in a day of swooning" (Thomas Lye). The prayer of faith delivers from fretting care by casting every burden upon the Lord. C. H. Spurgeon put it beautifully: "Faith lays a cool hand upon a burning brow, and removes the fever of the fearful heart."

"Thou wilt keep him in perfect peace, whose mind is stayed on thee: because he trusteth in thee" (Isa. 26:3). Here is the divine recipe for happiness: trust in the Lord at all times. Child of God, is He not worthy of your trust? Have you not proved His faithfulness again and again? May your heart be "fixed, trusting in the Lord" (Psa. 112:7).

—M. P.

If a man would lead a happy life, let him but seek a sure object for his trust, and he shall be safe.
THOMAS MANTON

Sheep Without a Shepherd

*That the congregation of the Lord be not
as sheep which have no shepherd.*

NUMBERS 27:17

What a love Moses had for the Lord's people! When informed that he could not lead the congregation of Israel into Canaan, his only concern was that someone else be raised up to do so. He voiced no word of murmuring; rather he pleaded with God that the Lord's people should not be as sheep which have no shepherd. What a Christlike concern that was! Many years later the Saviour Himself witnessed what Moses had feared. Matthew tells us that Christ "saw the multitudes . . . scattered abroad, as sheep having no shepherd" (Matt. 9:36).

What can cause God's people to scatter? Usually it is lack of a God-anointed leader. Notice how the Lord answered Moses' plea. He told Moses, "Take thee Joshua the son of Nun, a man in whom is the spirit, and lay thine hand upon him." Moses could not be mistaken. He was to ordain Joshua the son of Nun. But the leader of God's people was well acquainted with this Joshua. He had proved himself in many ways. At Rephidim he had been *faithful in warfare*, routing the Amalekites (Exod. 17). At the foot of Sinai he had been *fervent in worship*. He had "departed not out of the tabernacle" (Exod. 33:11); the revelry in the camp held no attraction for him. At Kadesh he had been *forthright in witness*. He had declared along with Caleb that the Lord would bring them into the land (Num. 14). The son of Nun therefore was no novice, but a tried and proven man who had displayed all the qualities necessary for leadership. As the Lord testified, the Holy Spirit was in him, giving him the ability his position required.

Let us, like Moses, pray for such men. Their scarcity has resulted in the scattering of the flock. May Christ Himself send forth many Joshuas and, through them, seek out His sheep and "deliver them out of all places where they have been scattered in the cloudy and dark day" (Ezek. 34:12).

—J. G.

None but He who made the world can make a minister.
JOHN NEWTON

The Last Drop of His Blood

Behold the man!

In this scene Pilate made his last attempt to avoid crucifying the innocent object of Jewish hatred. After the hours of scourging, a form of torture and whippings so awful that many died under it, Pilate remained still convinced that there was no fault in Christ at all (John 18:38).

He presented the lacerated, torn, and bleeding figure to the audience of enraged Jews. It seems Pilate hoped that one look at Christ's scourged form would appease and satisfy their thirst for revenge. He was wrong, for they still cried out, "Crucify him, crucify him" (19:6). Those enemies of the Son of God were not to be appeased with only some drops of Christ's blood, but with its last drop, resulting in His death.

The wonder of the gospel plan is that shameful as the Jews' treatment of the Lord Jesus was, it accomplished the very demand made by God's justice for justifying sinners. What the Jews insisted upon out of hatred, the justice of God had decreed from eternity (Acts 4:27-28). When Christ took upon Him the office of sin-bearer and became an offering for sin, He must not only bleed; He must also die. The law knew no mercy. The redemption of souls required more than some of Christ's blood; it required the very last drop.

As justified saints, we must never forget the ransom that was demanded for our release. Let us "behold the man" with humble, penitent hearts and rejoice that by the shedding of His blood He purchased our eternal salvation.

—I. G.

**Christ looked upon as bleeding and dying,
is the proper object of our faith.**
THOMAS WATSON

Promotion to Glory

Precious in the sight of the Lord is the death of his saints.

PSALM 116:15

I can imagine someone saying, "We have to live; don't talk about death. Death is a far-off event we don't need to think about just now."

It is true—we have to live. But it is also true that we have to die. Death for the Christian is not a morbid subject to be forgotten, but rather one that should be faced with confidence and assurance, knowing that our death is "precious in the sight of the Lord."

C. H. Spurgeon wrote: "The Lord watches over their dying beds, smooths their pillows, sustains their hearts, and receives their souls. Those who are redeemed with precious blood are so dear to God that even their deaths are precious to Him. He views the triumphant deaths of His gracious ones with sacred delight. If we have walked before Him in the land of the living, we need not fear to die before Him when the hour of our departure is at hand."

This cannot be said of any save of those who are washed in the blood of the Lamb. If you do not have Christ as your Saviour and Friend, you are without hope. If you are not saved, trust in Christ today, and you will be able to say with Paul, "To me to live is Christ, and to die is gain" (Phil. 1:21).

—S. B.

Live in Christ and the flesh need not fear death.
JOHN KNOX

Witnesses

Ye shall be witnesses unto me.

ACTS 1:8

One of the evidences of genuine conversion is a sincere desire to know and to do the will of God. Paul's prayer on the Damascus road, "Lord, what wilt thou have me to do?" (Acts 9:6), is proof that he had truly become a child of God. He had come to realize that he was not his own and that, in saving him, the Lord had a purpose for his life. That purpose for Paul was that he should be a witness for Christ. The same is true in the case of every believer. Surely our longing and prayer should be that we might be good witnesses. But what does this require?

First, in a court of law one is reckoned a good witness if he has confidence. There is clarity and certainty in his testimony. He knows what he speaks is true, for he has seen, heard, and experienced it for himself. The apostles used the same criteria in their witness for Christ: "We cannot but speak the things which we have seen and heard" (Acts 4:20). As believers, we declare the truth we have personally experienced (I John 1:3).

Then there must be character. Opposing counsel in a trial are aware that they can destroy the credibility of a testimony by discrediting the character of the witness. So the world and the devil are not slow to highlight the contradictions between what we profess to believe and how we actually behave. May God give us grace, that the message of our lips and of our lives will be the same.

Finally, there must be courage. Under cross-examination a witness's evidence and person will be subjected not only to scrutiny but even to scorn. He must have strength of conviction to endure the bombardment of disbelief and ridicule. How we need to pray that we will remain faithful in witness even when called to "suffer for his sake" (Phil. 1:29). What sort of witnesses are we?

—D. F.

Witnessing is not something we do; it is something we are.
ANONYMOUS

A Man Under God's Protection

There was a man in the land of Uz, whose name was Job.

JOB 1:1

The contents of the book of Job portray in vivid and at times poetic language the fierce conflict between the Lord and Satan concerning the faith and integrity of His servant Job. The devil was permitted to wreak havoc in his life. The dreadful misery, woe, and suffering of this sincere man of God remind us that the believer is a special target of the evil one. "All that will live godly in Christ Jesus shall suffer persecution" (II Tim. 3:12). The word *persecute* could be translated "pursue" or "follow after." The earnest Christian will be pursued by Satan. He will experience his fiery darts in all areas of his life, both physical and spiritual.

Close fellowship with Christ does not guarantee immunity from the forces of evil. The exact opposite is true. Nevertheless, the trials and afflictions of Job declare that the powers of darkness can go only so far and no further. In Job 1:10 we have a very precious and enlightening statement. Satan was forced to admit, "Hast thou not made an hedge about him, and about his house, and about all that he hath on every side?" What a blessed thought! What a glorious reality! This is the true position of every believer. The word translated *hedge* means "to cover" or "to protect." Concerning our salvation, we are hedged about by Christ's protecting love, secure for evermore. Even in this life, Satan is able to attack only with God's permission.

The message of Job is clear. Although Job's testings were exceptional, by looking to the Lord and trusting Him implicitly he was eventually delivered and came through his ordeal triumphant. At times the pathway of the Christian may be steep and difficult, our souls desolate within us, and the outlook seemingly hopeless. Remember Job. Yea, remember the God of Job. "Surely there is an end; and thine expectation shall not be cut off" (Prov. 23:18).

—S. B. C.

Security is not the absence of danger, but the presence of God, no matter what the danger.
ANONYMOUS

Christian Maturity

Perfect and entire, wanting nothing.

JAMES 1:4

We all tend to be a bit unbalanced or one-sided. Each of us is a strange mixture of virtues and vices, strengths and weaknesses, victories and failures. Maturity is supposed to take care of much of our moral and spiritual imbalance. That is what happens in everyday life. The child becomes a man and becomes a much more balanced and well-rounded person in the process. The same principle should hold true in the spiritual realm. New-born babes in Christ should develop into full-grown men of God. That is the norm, but we are seeing an increasing number of professing Christians who never seem to progress beyond the infant stage. Babies are beautiful, but they are a cause for grave concern when they do not develop and mature.

Maturity leads to completeness of spiritual experience. Zeal is wedded to knowledge. Practice goes hand in hand with doctrine. Prayer as if all depended on God is harnessed to a passionate energy that works as if all depended on us. "Complete" Christians live balanced lives. They do not go to an extreme in one direction to the detriment of another aspect of their Christian duty. Their testimony at home complements their testimony in church. They are in private what they appear in public. They act in business by the very principles that govern them in worship. To them life is indivisible, and it is all lived for the Lord. None of us has achieved this completeness to perfection. We are still in school. That is why the Lord sends us trials and afflictions. They are part of His plan of Christian education and character development. May the Lord help us to learn our lessons quickly and well.

—A. C.

**In apostolic times . . . no premium was given
to dwarfs, no encouragement to an old babyhood.**
E. M. BOUNDS

"Wee, Sleekit, Cow'rin', Tim'rous Beastie"

The mouse.

LEVITICUS 11:29

So wrote Scottish poet Robert Burns in 1785 when, with his plough, he disturbed a mouse's nest. Moses mentions the mouse as an unclean animal. God decreed certain animals to be clean and others to be unclean, to give the Israelites continual reminders of the difference between holiness and sin. Every time they saw an unclean animal, they were reminded of their own sinful nature.

The mouse, mentioned only six times in Scripture, is a powerful picture of sin. It is unclean, and *sin is moral uncleanness.* While certain animals are found only in some parts of the world, the mouse is to be found everywhere. *Sin is universal,* for all have sinned.

Burns described the mouse as *sleekit,* an old Scottish word for "sneaky." It darts quickly here and there and can get into a house through the tiniest of openings. How like sin! Give the devil the tiniest opening, and he will invade your life with the mice of sin.

Mice breed rapidly. One undisturbed pair in a house, with sufficient food and water, can multiply to three or four hundred in a year! *Sin breeds rapidly,* as David discovered when he sinned with Bathsheba. One look multiplied into adultery, lying, murder, and trouble in his own home that lasted for the rest of his life.

Mice are destructive and do great damage. *Sin is always destructive* and will adversely affect your life. Mice are attractive to some people—they keep little white mice. *Sin can be attractive,* and people talk of little white lies. Always remember, "Sin fascinates, but then assassinates."

Mice must be dealt with, or they will overrun the home and destroy the quality of life. Likewise *sin must be dealt with.* Only Jesus Christ can effectively eradicate sin. "The blood of Jesus Christ his Son cleanseth us from all sin" (I John 1:7). Be watchful today! Do not allow the devil's mice in to ruin your day, or your life.

—F. McC.

Our sorrows are multiplied when our sins are.
MATTHEW HENRY

God Is Our Refuge

The eternal God is thy refuge. **DEUTERONOMY 33:27**

"The eternal God!" How can we poor creatures of time ascend to His glorious majesty? We cannot. But the eternal God has come down to us in the person of the Lord Jesus Christ, who is God "manifest in the flesh" (I Tim. 3:16). We rest in Him for our salvation, and we do not trust Him in vain. He is our refuge, or our "dwelling."

In the eternal God our refuge we have salvation. Salvation is not in the church, but in the Christ; not in the sacraments, but in the Saviour. None but Jesus can do guilty sinners good. He gives us freedom from the haunting sense of guilt for a shameful past. He imparts to us the vital power to live in holiness and Christian victory. He admits us to the joy of real fellowship with our Father in heaven. He makes this life worth living, and in the darkest circumstances He breaks through the clouds with the sunlight of eternal love. What a joy to know that He who loved us before time began, and showed that love in the work of the cross, loves us still, whatever our earthly circumstances may be!

In the eternal God our refuge we also have security. The eternal God knows no change. "I am the Lord, I change not; therefore ye sons of Jacob are not consumed" (Mal. 3:6). Even the most timid believer in Christ is safe and secure. It is not the strength of our faith that guarantees our safety, but the strength of our refuge. All of the Israel of God "shall dwell in safety" (Deut. 33:28).

Fear not, for we who have God as our refuge are secure however fiercely storms or battles rage. As David said, "God is our refuge. . . . Therefore will not we fear, though the earth be removed, and though the mountains be carried into the midst of the sea" (Psa. 46:1, 2). Therefore, O Christian, fret not, and be at rest in God your refuge.

—A. C.

My faith has no bed to sleep upon but omnipotency.
SAMUEL RUTHERFORD

Waiting for the Dawning

Having a desire to depart, and to be with Christ; which is far better.
PHILIPPIANS 1:23

Paul the tent-maker here resorts to the language of his trade. The Greek word translated "depart" had various usages in ancient times. It could refer to the freeing of a slave, to the sailing of a ship, to the solving of a problem, and often to the breaking of camp by one of the Roman legions. Whenever a party of Roman soldiers reached the end of a long day's march, they set up an elaborate camp and settled down for an evening meal and for rest. In the morning the soldiers moved on, taking with them their weapons and baggage. Behind lay the camp with all its fortifications, like a discarded chrysalis.

The camping metaphor used by the apostle serves to remind us that death for the Christian is the exchange of what was at best a transitory tent-life for the "house not made with hands, eternal in the heavens" (II Cor. 5:1).

We may naturally have an aversion to death; yet it is the assurance of being with Christ that makes the departure for home desirable to the tried saint of God. Occupied many years against opposing forces of darkness, John Knox told a friend before his death in 1572 that he was "weary of the world and thirsting to depart."

Likewise, death held no terrors for Paul. It simply meant departing. What a picture of the believer's home-going! The "tent" we live in is taken down at death, and the soul goes home to be with Christ in heaven (II Cor. 5:1-8). Paul was not afraid of life or death. In either event he wanted Christ to be magnified. His equanimity in facing these alternatives is explained in that great utterance, "To me to live is Christ, and to die is gain" (Phil. 1:21). In his experience, the only life worthy of the name was that lived in union with Christ and spent in His service, and so for him death was gain because it gave entrance to the immediate presence of Christ.

—D. C.

Death is only a grim porter to let us into a stately palace.
RICHARD SIBBES

Advance Under Adversity

But the more they afflicted them, the more they multiplied and grew.

I am sure Pharaoh entertained great hopes of success when he introduced his plan to subjugate the children of Israel. The taskmasters set about their work with relish, with the result that the lives of the Hebrews were made "bitter with hard bondage" (Exod. 1:14). But Pharaoh's grand design was frustrated. Far from being destroyed, the children of Israel "multiplied and grew." It is no surprise that Pharaoh and his people should be "grieved because of the children of Israel" (v. 12).

Pharaoh failed to realize that he opposed not merely the Hebrews, but Jehovah—their God and ours. It is a mistake that many others have made over the years. At such times God laughs at man's presumption and pride. He will ensure that there is no lasting triumph for those who rebel against the purposes of heaven. Indeed, He turns times of affliction into times of multiplication for His people and His cause. History provides countless examples. When has the church advanced most obviously? When has she taken the greatest strides? In the day of ease and luxury, when there is acceptance and approval? No. She has succeeded most when she has been driven to the fields and the forests, when her name is no more than a term of reproach, when her sons are pursued and persecuted outcasts.

Surely there is a parallel in the experience of the individual believer. We rarely make much spiritual progress when the winds and the waves favour us. We often do best when all is against us. In times of persecution we are brought to realize the security that is in Christ. It is in seasons of illness, sorrow, and turmoil that there is a multiplication of those graces so pleasing to the Lord. Remember, adversity is often nothing less than God's way of enabling us to grow in Christian character and holiness.

—T. N.

In the day of prosperity we have many refuges to resort to; in the day of adversity, only one.
HORATIUS BONAR

Rejoicing in Redemption

*Unto him that loved us, and washed
us from our sins in his own blood.*

REVELATION 1:5

The angels of heaven have good reason to sing the praises of the Lord. Though they serve in the courts of glory and flawlessly execute His every command, they have no cause for self-congratulation. They owe their existence and happiness to the sovereign goodness of God, for, as Paul reveals, the reason they did not fall in Satan's rebellion was the electing purpose of God (I Tim. 5:21).

However, even angels have not so much cause to sing God's praise as do redeemed sinners. If creatures who never sinned rejoice in the power of God that kept them back from falling, how much more should we rejoice in His grace that saved us out of the depths of depravity and rebellion? That God would preserve sinless angels is one thing. That He should love and save foul and fallen sinners is something else. It is a miracle of grace. Yet that is what the Spirit records: *He loved us!* What a sublime statement!

He—the pure, holy, and just Creator, the One whose law we had trampled beneath our feet in arrogant rebellion; *loved*—fixed the purpose of His goodness upon us in divine tenderness so as not merely to wish us well but to ensure our eternal salvation; *us*—the most unloving and unlovely of His moral creatures, sinners who not only did not deserve His grace but did not even desire it.

The Lord's goodness to angels required the mere exercise of His will, the exertion of His power. The salvation of sinners required all that and more. It required the supreme self-sacrifice of the Son of God. Our salvation cost the Lord everything He could give. Out of love He gave it.

Whatever burdens we are called upon to carry today, let us lift our hearts to the Saviour who so loved us as to wash us from our sins. Think of it! All our sins—every spot, stain, and wrinkle—are washed away. As Jesus said, "Ye are clean" (John 13:10). Rejoice, Christian! Rejoice!

—A. C.

A drop of praise is an unsuitable
acknowledgment for an ocean of mercy.
WILLIAM SECKER

Our Strong Tower

The name of the Lord is a strong tower:
the righteous runneth into it, and is safe.

Here we are transported back to ancient times, back to days when roving bands of plunderers could so suddenly fall upon a helpless populace. As soon as the enemy was detected, the alarm would be raised. The peasants would catch up their children in their arms. A moment's delay could mean the enemy's sword in their hearts! They would flee to such a tower as that spoken of in our text. It is a testimony to their strength that many such towers stand to this day. In the great siege of Jerusalem by Vespasian, all of the Roman engines of destruction in one night succeeded only in disengaging four stones from the masonry of the tower of Antonia.

Our Lord Jesus is such a tower to His own dear people, those who are clothed in heaven's best robe, His own divine righteousness. They know His name. "I will declare thy name unto my brethren" (Heb. 2:12). The name of the Lord is expressive of all that God is, as He has been pleased to reveal Himself to us. There the child of God experiences protection from all the fiery darts of the wicked one. It is only in Him that we are safe from every attack of the enemy. There the child of God enjoys peace; even that "peace of God, which passeth all understanding" (Phil. 4:7), that is able to keep (literally, "to garrison about") both heart and mind through Christ Jesus. Thus it was that the psalmist, in spite of the increase of his enemies, could testify, "I laid me down and slept; I awaked; for the Lord sustained me. I will not be afraid of ten thousands of people, that have set themselves against me round about" (Psa. 3:5-6). Christian, in the moment of danger the bird flies to the cover of the thicket, and the fox hastens to its hole in the earth. Let us learn to run, with the feet of faith, to Him who is our strong tower. "They that know thy name will put their trust in thee: for thou, Lord, hast not forsaken them that seek thee" (Psa. 9:10).

—M. P.

Those who would have God for their refuge in the day of trouble ought to know or understand what a God He is.
BENJAMIN KEACH

The Christian Sabbath

There remaineth therefore a rest to the people of God.
HEBREWS 4:9

It is important to notice that the Holy Spirit employs a different word for "rest" in this verse from the one uniformly used throughout the chapter. Here the word literally means "a keeping of Sabbath." Therefore, there is a very specific reference here to the Christian Sabbath. Remember that Paul is writing to Jewish believers who have embraced Christ. Having renounced Judaism, the matter of the Sabbath must have troubled them deeply.

However, the apostle seeks to assure them by informing them that under Christianity there is a Sabbath to keep, one day in seven to observe as God's day. What that day is, is clearly revealed in the following verse, where Christ's rest from His work of redemption is plainly in view. Just as "God did rest the seventh day from all his works" (v. 4), so Christ has "entered into his rest" (v. 10). He did so by rising again, signifying the finished work of the cross. When did He rise? On the first day of the week, which day is now the Sabbath for the people of God, as the opening *for* of verse 10 indicates. In actual fact, Paul's reasoning here shows that the keeping of the Sabbath has a much fuller meaning now than it had in Old Testament times. It is not only a memorial of God's work in creation, it is also an emblem of the rest which Christ entered into when He completed His redemptive work. Observing one day in seven is therefore still binding upon God's people. The Lord has graciously given us six days during which we can attend to employment and recreation. Let us not rob Him of the other day. May God's people do all within their power to sanctify that day, calling it "a delight, the holy of the Lord, honourable" (Isa. 58:13).

—J. G.

**Any man who says there is no Christian Sabbath takes
direct issue with the New Testament Scriptures.**
A. W. PINK

The Complete Woman

Deborah, a prophetess, the wife of Lapidoth, she judged Israel.
JUDGES 4:4

Unlike many people, Deborah lived up to her name. *Deborah* means "bee," and it would be difficult to find anyone more deserving of the name than Israel's only female judge.

Deborah was as busy as her name suggests. She was a wife and mother (Judg. 5:7). She was a prophetess and a judge. She was practically co-captain of the army, for Barak would not go forth without her presence. She did enough work for half a dozen people, and obviously she did it well. Remember Deborah the next time you are tempted to complain of having too much to do.

Deborah made her busyness the means of spreading spiritual sweetness. She was faithful to the Lord as a prophetess. She was a woman of the Word. It governed her life. Consequently, when she judged the affairs of the people, she applied the light of the Word to them. Nor did she spread her sweetness only in public view; she brought it into her own home. Her role as a wife and mother allowed her to give to her loved ones what she had received from the Word of the Lord.

Here is a model for every wife and mother—indeed, for every Christian. Do not let the busy schedule of life crush your spirit and cause you to lose the blessing and joy you should daily derive from God's Word. Rather, let your daily fellowship with the Lord so nourish your soul that you will then spread the sweetness to your home and loved ones. Enjoying Christ is the key to being the person you long to be in the home.

Such a woman cannot be hid. Her influence will soon go beyond her own home. Deborah affected a nation. So has many another godly woman. Do not set your sights on being great. Aim rather to be godly, and let the Lord make as great a use of your godliness as He wills.

—A. C.

Be as busy as a bee, but never a busybody!
ALEXANDER SIMPSON

Trials and Temptations

Wherein ye greatly rejoice, though now for a season, if need be,
ye are in heaviness through manifold temptations.

I PETER 1:6, 7

Peter, after speaking of our heavenly inheritance, brings us back to earth again in these verses to face the reality of our present circumstances. We rejoice in our inheritance; yet while we are in the body and on the earth, there are of necessity manifold temptations and testings. Our faith is often sorely tried, and yet it is for the patient believer a precious thing. God is surely planning for us in love, for His own glory and for our good. How mysterious, very often, is the purpose and plan of God as it is wrought out in our lives. It was Luther who said, "We cannot always trace God, but we can always trust Him."

One of the major themes of I Peter is suffering. These New Testament believers were constantly being persecuted and harassed and their faith put to the test. God tests us, not that He may know what is in us, for He knows that already, but that we may know what it is to prove God in these trials.

These testings both prove and purify our faith. Gold is tested by the fire; it is thereby proved to be real gold, but it is also purified by fire. The furnace of affliction is necessary to prove us and to make us better Christians. We can be sure that our affliction will be found to be unto praise, honour, and glory at the appearing of Jesus Christ.

—R. J. B.

The anvil, the fire and the hammer are the making of us.
C. H. SPURGEON

The Arm of the Lord Revealed

Who hath believed our report? and to
whom is the arm of the Lord revealed?

ISAIAH 53:1

These words are in the form of a lamentation. To the prophet it appeared that the glorious message of the Christ, the suffering Saviour (Isa. 52:13-15), was universally rejected. The gospel seemed unsuccessful. Does it not still appear that way to us? We have cause to lament. There is a widespread slighting of the gospel message. There is little change of life, little evidence of true godliness, among professors of religion. Real conversions appear to be few. Churches have turned more to human psychology than to Biblical theology. They appear to engage more in entertainment than evangelism. Artistic expression is in, and Scriptural exposition is out. It is a bleak picture.

But today's text points the way of recovery. The answer to the spiritual problems of sinners and of the church is not a new programme. It is not some clever new method of doing things. It is "the arm of the Lord revealed." The Lord making bare His arm—demonstrating His power and assuming responsibility to see to the success of His own work—is the grand solution to the spiritual deadness and defeat of these dark days.

The power of God can create faith in the most faithless hearts. The most hopeless unbeliever will believe once the power of God goes to work on him. This is what Paul teaches in Ephesians 1:19-20. Men can believe only when the same power that raised Christ's body from the dead quickens their dead souls. No man is beyond the power of God. Let us then cry to Him to reveal His arm. It is vain merely to lament the spiritual conditions of our day. May they drive us to our knees and keep us there until the Lord makes known His power. —A. C.

It is easier to speak about revival than to set about it.
HORATIUS BONAR

Separation unto Christ

Let us go forth therefore unto him without the camp.

HEBREWS 13:13

Let us remember that Christ is without the camp because within it He has been rejected. In the apostate system, whether it be the Judaism of Paul's day or the ecumenical apostasy of our own times, another Christ has been set up, another gospel is preached, and another spirit controls. Consequently, the true Christ of God is so rejected, maligned, and blasphemed by His enemies that He has been driven forth. His people therefore are to go forth unto Him.

Note from this verse, then, that separation from apostasy is for Christ's sake. That is always the principle of the true separatist. One of the most vivid illustrations of that truth is found in Acts 19:9, where we read, "When divers were hardened, and believed not, but spake evil of that way before the multitude, he departed from them, and separated the disciples." As Paul preached in the Jewish synagogue in Ephesus, there was stiff opposition to the gospel. By a hardening of their hearts against the truth, by their unbelief of the truth, and then by their open hostility to the truth, the Jews manifested the apostasy of their system. In essence, therefore, apostasy is marked by being against Christ. The words *that way* refer to Christ Himself, who is the Way. Apostasy always strikes at the Saviour, at His person and His work. Thus apostasy is blatant antichristianity.

If we have any love for Christ, then we must depart from that which would crucify Him afresh. To do so is obedience to the expressed will of God in His Word. It is not being schismatic, as many allege. It is the apostate church which has rent the body of Christ by departing from the faith of the gospel. The Biblical separatist goes forth only to carry on the cause of Christ, free from any affiliation with those who would tread "under foot the Son of God" (Heb. 10:29).

—J. G.

Christ is the focus of our separation. No Christian should maintain fellowship in any church or movement where Christ is denied or betrayed.

ALEXANDER SIMPSON

Live!

When I passed by thee, and saw thee . . . , I said unto thee . . . , Live.
EZEKIEL 16:6

Christ is the one who passes by. We should recognize the similarity here to the good Samaritan, who passed by and brought
life and healing with his touch. In this case the picture is that
of an infant, newborn and cast out into the open field. It lies
there "to the lothing of [its] person" (v. 5), in the day it was born,
still unwashed and covered with its blood. It lies doomed and
ready to die.

What a picture of ourselves as we once were! God takes a poor,
helpless, unseeing, untaught, perishing infant, lying in the open
field, to show us how exposed we are to ruin, unable to do one
thing to save ourselves. Every man, by nature and by practice, is
under condemnation of sin. This is the plight of the babe from
birth. We are born in sin and shapen in iniquity. A babe like this
may in some way feel its miserable condition and sense that all is
not well, but it cannot intelligently discern the extent of its danger.
What a debt we owe to the Lord, who passed by to give us life!

All life is from the Lord, whether physical or spiritual.
Through the intervention of the Saviour the babe received a
new life. The true and full condition of this life came by the
word of His mouth (James 1:18).

Birth is the beginning of life, but birth alone will not sustain
life. There is just as great a miracle in the sustaining of life as
there is in the bestowal of it. The One who saved us has also kept
us—when we could neither save nor keep ourselves. As in this
chapter, He said to us, "Thou becamest mine" (v. 8). He has washed
us, clothed, nourished, anointed, and covered us. Best of all, He
has made us perfect through His comeliness, which He has put
upon us: "Thy renown went forth among the heathen for thy
beauty" (v. 14). Thus does the Lord confer His testimony upon His
people. Let us not think lightly of what He has done.

—J. D.

If God had not chosen me before I was born,
I am sure He would have seen nothing
in me to have chosen me afterwards!
JOHN NEWTON

149

A Hearing Ear

He that hath an ear, let him hear what
the Spirit saith unto the churches.

REVELATION 2:7

It is striking that the Lord Jesus used the expression *He that hath ears to hear, let him hear* (or, *If any man have* . . .) on seven different occasions during His earthly ministry. In the book of Revelation we learn that He used a very similar expression on seven occasions as He spoke from the throne of glory to His churches on earth.

The message is clear: the Lord Jesus Christ is insistent that His people attend to His Word. He demanded this while He was with them in the flesh. That sounds natural and reasonable. Which of us can imagine being inattentive or careless if we were listening to the Son of God speaking directly to us? But He demands the very same attention from us to the written Word. What He has to say to His churches is given to us in that Word. The Lord Jesus assures us that what is written there is what "the Spirit saith unto the churches."

Here is His challenge: You should pay the same close attention to what the Bible says as you would to anything spoken by the Lord Jesus Himself were He present with you in the flesh. Is that how you treat the Scriptures? You cannot pretend to be obedient to Christ while you are inattentive to His written Word.

To have an ear means to have the capability and willingness to receive God's truth. Unregenerate men are spiritually deaf. They need Christ to open their ears and give them faith to receive His saving truth. Sadly, some Christians who have the capacity to hear "are dull [or, slothful] of hearing" (Heb. 5:11). It is not inability that hinders you from receiving and profiting from the Scriptures. It is slothfulness or unwillingness.

The Spirit is still speaking to the churches. The written Word still carries His message to all His people. Take heed *that* you hear, take heed *what* you hear, and take heed *how* you hear (see Mark 4:24; Luke 8:18).

—A. C.

Backsliders begin with dusty Bibles
and end with filthy garments.
C. H. Spurgeon

Wisdom's Warning Against Wantonness

But her end is bitter as wormwood, sharp as a twoedged sword.
PROVERBS 5:4

The morality of the Bible differs from the morality of the world. One is the practical applications of the holiness of God. The other is licentiousness held in check by expediency.

There is a price to be paid for uncleanness. God makes that clear. The devil, with winning deviousness, denies this is so. Those who heed the devil discover that God is right.

The price of uncleanness is high. The wise man here lists for us the cost of rejecting the admonition of God. It is paid in the currency of dishonour (v. 9), poverty (v. 10), wasting (v. 11), and regret (vv. 12-14). Only sin can start out promising so much pleasure and in the end bring so much wretchedness. How deceitful it is!

The world's answer to the miserable consequences of sin is a ceaseless search for a means of avoiding them. God has decreed that "whatsoever a man soweth, that shall he also reap" (Gal. 6:7). Man has ever sought ways of escaping that divinely appointed harvest. The search for escape is a fruitless search. There is only one way of avoiding sin's curse, and that is avoiding sin.

As in the Garden of Eden, when the fruit of many trees could be freely eaten, so it is in life. The forbidden pleasures of sin (which are no pleasures in the end) have their counterpart in the many lawful pleasures God has ordained for man's comfort and good.

The evil pleasures of an improper liaison contrast starkly with the joys of a marriage ordained of God. For dishonour there is honour (Heb. 13:4), for poverty there is reward (Psa. 127:3), for wasting there is fruitfulness (Psa. 128:3), and for regret there is peace (Psa. 128:6).

The path God has ordained for His people is a path that leads us through paradise on the way to paradise!

—I. F.

Grace in the soul is heaven in that soul.
MATTHEW HENRY

Obedience

We ought to obey God rather than men.

ACTS 5:29

Obedience can be costly. The apostles had been threatened by the Sanhedrin (Acts 4:21) and then imprisoned (5:18) for their fidelity to the Lord in preaching the gospel. But they persisted in spite of the persecution which they had already endured and which they were sure was still to come. Had not Christ Himself told them, "Ye shall be hated of all men for my name's sake" (Matt. 10:22)? Believer, the Lord has not promised us an easy pathway, but He still requires that we be faithful to our calling and commission. We ought to obey God!

He has the right as our Creator to demand our allegiance and obedience. We are all the work of His hand (Isa. 64:8) and as such cannot question His dealings with us or demands of us (Rom. 9:20). And He has redeemed us! "I have redeemed thee, I have called thee . . . ; thou art mine" (Isa. 43:1). The precious blood has been shed that we might be His and His alone. Surely when we consider what Paul termed the "mercies of God," it is but a reasonable thing that we should obey without question or reservation His commandments. "The love of Christ constraineth us" (II Cor. 5:14). A further incentive to obedience is the reward that He gives. He has promised that in the keeping of His commandments "there is great reward" (Psa. 19:11). There is a crown that is incorruptible (I Cor. 9:25), a crown of life (James 1:12), and a crown of glory (I Pet. 5:4) assured to the faithful servant of Christ. But consider the result of disobedience—the blessings we forfeit, the troubles we incur, the chastisement we bring upon ourselves. Yes, it may cost to obey God, but how much will disobedience cost?

—D. F.

Every man obeys Christ as he prizes Christ, not otherwise.
THOMAS BROOKS

Ploughing Up the Heart

Sow not among thorns.

Few things can be more futile than sowing good seed among thorns. Even the most nonagricultural ones of us know that. Why then is it that so many people ignore the application of this simple truth to the spiritual realm? The message of today's text is clear. Unless our hearts are ploughed up by the Word of God and the thorns of wickedness are removed, no religious activity is of any spiritual value. Let us apply this truth to ourselves today. Let us each interrogate his heart.

Am I one of those who has never known repentance but seeks to buy the favour of God with some "good" deeds? Then I am sowing among thorns. Salvation does produce good deeds, but it is first a matter of the heart. Is my heart right with God? Has the blade of the plough of Scripture ever cut up my hard heart to make me feel my utter sinfulness and my urgent need for Christ? Has it yet produced repentance unto life?

Or, am I a Christian with a testimony as to when and how I was saved but whose life is not a fruitful field of consecrated service to Christ? Am I trying to mask the neglect of spiritual things and the presence of the weeds of backsliding with some apparently godly acts? It is good for me to go to God's house, to give to His work, and to do a host of other things Christians should do. But do they come from a clean heart, or are they my way of trying to hide what is really happening in me? If this is the case, I am foolishly sowing among thorns. I need my heart to be thoroughly ploughed by God's Word. Indeed, as Jeremiah's words in our text indicate, I need my heart to be ploughed and then ploughed again. I need to feel the Word cut into my soul, expose my sin, and show me my Saviour. When it gives me a clear sight of Christ it will break through all my hardness. When Jesus looked on Peter, the erring disciple wept. When I look on Him, I too will weep over my fallow ground and will never rest until it is broken up so that I may sow in righteousness (Hos. 10:12).

—A. C.

We must come to the withering of the flesh, before we can become spiritually strong and fruitful.
R. C. Chapman

A Tiny Instructress

Go to the ant, thou sluggard; consider her ways, and be wise.

PROVERBS 6:6

The Earth in its daily course is an animated lesson book teaching man, the highest of its inhabitants, how he ought to apply himself to his God-given duties. Nature, while giving man lessons in diligence, cannot tell man what his duty is. Only the Bible, the revelation of God's will for men, can do that. *The Shorter Catechism* states, "Man's chief end is to glorify God, and to enjoy Him forever." However, man's neighbours on this earth can teach him much about how he should perform the duty set forth in the Bible.

The ant is a tiny creature. Despite her size, she is God's example of diligent application to the duties He has given us. The duty of the ant is written in her instincts, which were given by God at her creation. Generation after generation, she is persistent in that duty. Her diligence brings its rewards. She has fully provided for her winters through her labours in summer and harvest.

Devotion to duty will pay as high a dividend for us as it does for the ant. The ant knows the seasons and applies herself to the appropriate duties. She is never guilty of slumbering when she should be toiling. Now is the summertime of opportunity for the sinner. Salvation is at hand for those who call upon the Lord. What an eternal store is laid by when the sinner calls upon the Lord while He is near! The sinner who takes the opportunity presented to him when the Holy Spirit strives with him about repentance will praise God's mercy throughout eternity that he was given grace to avail himself of Calvary's bounty.

Now is the season for the Christian to open the door unto his Lord and hold sweet communion with Him. Let us not sleep away our lives in indolence when we could be living them to the full in fellowship with Christ.

Sinners and saints may miss their opportunity (Song of Sol. 5:2-6), and all because they refused to be as the ant!

—I. F.

There are four steps to accomplishment:
Plan purposefully. Prepare prayerfully.
Proceed positively. Pursue persistently.
ANONYMOUS

Persevering Faith

These all died in faith.

Faith is the gift of God, the product of the Holy Spirit in the regenerate. Consequently, faith is supernatural in essence. It is like its divine Author, living and incorruptible. Since it is implanted by the Lord, faith can never be lost and cannot be conquered by the devil. That explains why the possessor of true saving faith will "persevere therein to the end" *(Westminster Confession of Faith,* XVII). Such is the truth conveyed by our text. The Old Testament saints "died in faith." What an obituary notice! It signifies that they lived in, or "according to," faith and continued steadfast to the end.

Faith perseveres, feeds upon, and is sustained by God's Word. Though these patriarchs did not receive the fulfilment of the promises, they did see "them afar off." Faith always comes "by hearing, and hearing by the word of God" (Rom. 10:17). Thus every one of these people received God's Word. Covenant promises were revealed to them, on which they set their faith. The expression *having seen them afar off* is nautical terminology, referring to a sailor descrying the coast at a distance. God's people in ancient times gazed into the distant future and saw Christ's day and were glad. They "were persuaded of" the promises. They had an assured confidence "that, what he had promised, he was able also to perform" (Rom. 4:21). In faith, therefore, they embraced such promises. That denotes a warm and hearty welcome of them. They appropriated all that the promises conveyed to their minds. Faith not only sees the meaning of the gospel promises and the faithfulness of God to fulfil them, it clings to them and in doing so clings to Christ. God's people were "strangers and pilgrims on the earth." Their inheritance was elsewhere. Like the New Testament saints, they looked "for new heavens and a new earth, wherein dwelleth righteousness" (II Pet. 3:13). They were not disappointed. Nor shall we be, for faith in Christ shall never be confounded.

—J. G.

Faith in God will always be crowned.
W. S. PLUMER

Friendly Advice from the Lord

The secret of the Lord is with them that fear him.

PSALM 25:14

Knowing the will of God should be the desire of every Christian. Although the Scripture reveals definite aspects of God's will, we all face questions that are not expressly addressed in the Bible. How can we know what God wants us to do in matters that seem unique to ourselves? Since the steps of a good man are ordered by the Lord, we should seek direction from the Lord more than anything else. While the counsel of godly friends is welcome, the counsel of the Lord is essential. God gives an assuring word that He will reveal His secret to those who fear Him. The word *secret* refers to the intimate advice that a friend would offer his friend.

Psalm 25, a prayer for guidance, steers us on the proper course to the Lord's special counsel. The first step is to hope in the Lord (vv. 1-3). Dependence, trust, and patient waiting are essential prerequisites to divine advice. Too many times we grow impatient and wander aimlessly, hoping to discover the right way on our own. The second step is to pray specifically that God will lead us by the truth (vv. 4-5). Apart from prayer, there is no hope of knowing with certainty God's will. Prayer is the means not for dictating God's will, but for expressing our submission to the Lord's will. Indeed, submitting to God's will prior to our knowing it is the secret to knowing it. The third step is to confess our sins (vv. 6, 7). Sin hinders our fellowship with God and prevents us from hearing His voice. But His mercy and goodness assure both forgiveness and the prospect of being taught by Him.

Whether for daily routine or potentially life-changing decisions, let us have our eyes ever toward the Lord and our ears ever open to His friendly advice.

—M. P. V. B.

The only way of arriving at a knowledge of the divine will, in regard to us, is by simplicity of purpose and earnest prayer.
JAMES HENLEY THORNWELL

Thy Righteousness My Glorious Dress

The righteousness which is of God by faith.

PHILIPPIANS 3:9

The verse for today summarizes the book of Romans, for it deals with the heart of the gospel. Salvation is to be found in Christ and in Christ alone. God is satisfied only with His own righteousness, which He offers freely to all who believe in Jesus Christ. He cannot be satisfied with any righteousness that comes from man.

Our righteousnesses are as filthy rags (Isa. 64:6). This truth is not very flattering to human pride. Yet the fact is that the best human righteousness is far from satisfying God, and so we are disqualified from any hope of acceptance or justification on the ground of our own merits.

However, the gospel brings the news of a righteousness that is adequate and acceptable to God. This righteousness is available to men because the Son of God became man and offered Himself without spot to God. He who knew no sin was made sin for us, that we who have no righteousness might be "made the righteousness of God in him" (II Cor. 5:21). The righteousness of God is ours by faith, because by receiving Christ Jesus the Saviour we are made one with Him, and all His merits and acceptance become ours also. Moreover, all His redeemed people are dressed in the glorious and precious raiment of His own righteousness, and they stand blameless before God, justified in Christ.

May the Lord enable us ever to glory in that righteousness imputed to us and received by faith alone. The more our hearts are gripped by the truth of Christ's imputed righteousness, the more calmly we can stand in the presence of God, because our righteousness is the righteousness of God.

—D. C.

In every period when God has awakened His people, the gospel of justification has come to the fore.
ROBERT M. HORN

The Divine Remedy for Sin

Every one that . . . looketh upon it, shall live.

NUMBERS 21:8

The healing of the Israelites who had been bitten by the fiery serpents was according to a divine plan. It was a means of healing that human wisdom would never have contrived. The victims were commanded to look upon a serpent of brass set on a pole. These instructions for cure were contrary to man's reason but brought instantaneous life and health to all who obeyed. God's way of saving sinners never fails. Though it be absolutely contrary to the wisdom of this world, the gospel of God alone brings healing to sin-sick souls.

Christ Himself shows us in John chapter 3 that this divine plan was a prefiguration of His own crosswork. Had He not done so, we might have been quite puzzled over the type. Doubtless we would have thought a brazen serpent an unlikely type of Christ. However, think carefully! The serpent was a reminder and emblem of the curse. Through "that old serpent," Satan, man sinned and came under the curse, but deliverance comes through Christ's "being made a curse for us" (Gal. 3:13). Thus there was no flaw in the type. Moses was told specifically to make a serpent of brass, for that metal in Scripture is an emblem of judgment. In coming under the curse, Christ suffered the judgment of a holy God. Yet He bore that judgment unflinchingly, just as brass, the hardest of metals, endures the scorching flame.

Moses lifted up the serpent in the wilderness to show that the gospel must not be obscured. Christ is to be plainly and clearly set forth. If the gospel be hid, "it is hid to them that are lost" (II Cor. 4:3). Let us ensure that we never lose sight of Christ. He is the divinely appointed object of faith. He Himself says, "Look unto me, and be ye saved" (Isa. 45:22). May you look today, for there is life for a look at the crucified One. —J. G.

The simplest word of faith is the deepest
word of theology: Christ died for our sins.
JAMES DENNEY

How To Be Wise

If any of you lack wisdom, let him ask of God, that giveth to all
men liberally, and upbraideth not; and it shall be given him.

JAMES 1:5

Wisdom in Scripture is the queen of virtues. In some places it is just another word for the entirety of revealed religion. In others it carries the idea of living according to the knowledge of God and of His truth. In yet other places it is a personal title of the Lord Jesus Christ (Prov. 8; I Cor. 1:24).

In whatever way we understand *wisdom,* we must confess we all lack it. Do we not yearn to grasp more fully the wonderful self-revelation of God in Scripture? Do we not constantly desire to enter ever more fully into the mighty truths of the Word and be able to live our lives constantly in the light of them? And do we not daily cry for more of Christ? Can we ever know enough about Him and His atoning sacrifice for us at Calvary? No! We confess we lack this wisdom and yearn to have it in a full measure.

There is only one way to obtain this true wisdom. We cannot learn it from others. They may teach us facts, but only God can teach us wisdom. To obtain wisdom, therefore, we need to "ask of God." It is on our knees that we will grasp—and be gripped by—God's truth. It is in prayer that we will have our souls overwhelmed with the knowledge of God and with the glory of Christ. It is as we ask for wisdom that we will learn to live by faith so that what we believe will dictate how we behave. So let us ask in the assurance that our God, who has done so much to make Himself known to us, will fully answer our prayer. We have no excuse. Why should we live like fools when the wisdom of God is ours for the asking?

—A. C.

The sublimity of wisdom is to do those things
living which are to be desired when dying.
JEREMY TAYLOR

Blessing out of Bitterness

*When they came to Marah, they could not drink
of the waters . . . , for they were bitter.*
EXODUS 15:23

It was just after crossing the Red Sea that the children of Israel
came to Marah. Here, at the first stopping point of any significance, they began to experience the sort of difficulties that would
plague them for the next forty years. In the wake of a great and
glorious moment, they had to face this most obvious setback. The
pattern is similar in the Christian life: often the soul newly
released from bondage is subject to immediate trial.

How shall we face the bitter experiences? That is the key
question. In the incident described at the end of Exodus 15 we see
two different responses. The people grumbled, but Moses cried to
the Lord. Often we are more like the Israelites than their leader;
the cry of complaint becomes almost a reflex action. It is our first
response to any test that is set before us. We forget the previous
mercies of the Lord. We forget that His hand overrules all for our
good, and we fail to see that there is purpose even in the bitter
moments. Moses did not question God's plan. There was not a hint
of rebellion. He cried to heaven, and his prayer was wonderfully
answered. Here is the way to face our troubles! Here is the way to
see the intervention of God. When He steps in, the situation is
altogether different, and the bitter waters can be made sweet.

—T. N.

**The one secret of getting sweetness out of
bitterness is loving acceptance of the will of God.**
ALEXANDER MACLAREN

The Holy Temple

In whom all the building fitly framed together
groweth unto an holy temple in the Lord.

EPHESIANS 2:21

The temple to Diana in Ephesus was one of the seven wonders of the ancient world. It was a huge structure some 425 feet long and 225 feet wide. Travellers came from all over the world to worship the idol Diana, and this gave the citizens of the city reason to boast (Acts 19:27-35). But Paul here speaks of a temple that is greater in splendour than that destroyed in A. D. 263 at Ephesus. Even the angelic host take interest in Paul's temple (Eph. 3:10). This is not a building of brick and mortar but is a living and growing edifice (cf. 4:16), for its chief corner stone is the living Christ (2:20). It does not merely house a few hundred people at one time, but is made up of the multitudes of believers throughout the ages. Its boundaries stretch well beyond the city limits of Ephesus. And the living God, not some lifeless image, inhabits it (2:21-22).

One of the greatest characteristics of the temple of the Lord is that it is holy. Again, Paul is not speaking of a physical building, but of the people of God. How often people labour to make a meeting house spotless for the day of worship, and yet they neglect to prepare the true temple. Brethren, we are the temple of the Lord. We ought to be clothed in the beauties of holiness (Psa. 110:3). If the world can look at us and see nothing of the character of Christ, then we must ask ourselves what part we have in the temple of the Lord. To be secure in Christ is no excuse for worldliness. Yea, when properly understood and believed, our union with Christ is the best motivation possible for a true holiness. May we adorn our profession with a life that is set apart for the use of Christ.

—M. W. A.

There is no place for any loose stone in God's edifice.
JOSEPH HALL

The Flawless Redeemer

I find in him no fault at all.

JOHN 18:38

In his attempt to release Christ from the hands of the Jews, Pilate stated a tremendous truth when he said, "I find in him no fault at all." Seven times the Gospels record Pilate's testimony to the innocence of Christ.

Every believer bears the same testimony. We find no fault in His walk on earth. Rather, we know that His perfect life earned a positive righteousness that God imputes to the Christian's account. We find no fault in His death. His sacrifice as an offering for our sins was without blemish. Peter says we were redeemed by "the precious blood of Christ, as of a lamb without blemish and without spot" (I Pet. 1:19). His was the blood of the God-Man, shed to make satisfaction for sin. Again, we can find no fault in His resurrection. On the third day, as appointed, He arose a victor over the powers of death and hell. He shook the world with terror and amazement by the appearance of His crucified but perfect body.

Not only do we find no fault in Christ, His Father also finds no fault in Him as He appears in His presence for us. The Father sees His Son who shed His blood to seal the everlasting covenant presenting that precious blood on our behalf, and He is well satisfied.

It is this faultless Saviour who shall one day present His redeemed people as perfect before the Father in heaven. Therefore, continue to look "unto him that is able to keep you from falling, and to present you faultless before the presence of his glory with exceeding joy" (Jude 24).

—I. G.

Christ takes possession *of* us on earth and *for* us in heaven.
Anonymous

It Is Time To Remember

Remember now thy Creator in the days of thy youth.
ECCLESIASTES 12:1

We seem to have no control over what we remember and what we forget. Things that would be to our advantage to remember seem to slip secretly away. Things that we would love to forget stay in our minds as unwelcome guests. Knowing the lack of control we have over memory makes the frequent Biblical commands to remember certain things and forget others beyond our ability to obey consistently. But God is never unreasonable. To remember in the Biblical sense is something we are capable of doing. Memory is something we can and should control. To remember God is to keep Him wilfully and consciously in our thoughts. Such recollection and reflection determine our behaviour.

If you are young, it is time to remember the Creator. If you are not young, it is time to remember the Creator. Youth marks the beginning of this duty, not the end. Remembering the Creator focusses our minds on God's majestic and uniquely infinite power. Our Creator is the only living and true God; our Creator is Christ, the eternal Word by whom all things were made. He who made man (Eccles. 7:29) is man's Sovereign, who holds man's destiny in His hands (9:1-2). As Creator, He has the innate right as Judge, whose judgments are correct (2:26; 3:17), comprehensive (12:14), and complete (3:14). That God is our Creator reminds us that He is infinitely superior to us, that He owns us, and that we are accountable to Him. He deserves our worship, respect, and reverence. Remembering the Lord does not just happen. We must think on His person, reflect on His perfections, acknowledge His goodness and grace, and meditate on His Word. **—M. P. V. B.**

Meditation keeps out Satan. It increases knowledge, it inflames love, it works patience, it promotes prayer, it evidences sincerity.
PHILIP HENRY

What a Fellowship, What a Joy Divine!

These things write we unto you, that your joy may be full.

I JOHN 1:4

When the apostle John penned these precious words, the Son of Man was no longer seen, heard, or handled as in the days of His earthly ministry. Nevertheless, the beloved disciple of Christ had not lost fellowship with the resurrected and exalted Saviour. Nor was his relationship and communion with the Lord less near and real than when he rested his head upon the Master's bosom or when he walked and talked with Him along the paths of Galilee. Our Saviour is just as sweet and dear to His people today as He was prior to His ascension. John speaks in the present tense and says, "Truly our fellowship *is* with the Father, and with his Son Jesus Christ" (v. 3). We are told that the close fellowship and intimate communion the apostle experienced with our Lord in the days of His earthly ministry can be ours through the Spirit. We know this is true because "Jesus Christ [is] the same yesterday, and to day, and for ever" (Heb. 13:8). Therefore, Christ was just as real and dear to the apostle John in spirit after His ascension as He was in the days of His humiliation. From this relationship with Christ, the apostle found joy and strength to endure hardships and remain steadfast unto the end.

Let us think right about our relationship with God. The Lord is very near unto His people and desires to be loved and worshipped for who He is and for what He has done for us. May we live in the reality that Christianity is a very personal fellowship with "the Man at God's right hand."

—R. J. W.

My God and I are good company.
RICHARD SIBBES

Christ Burdened, Christian Blessed

Surely he hath borne our griefs, and carried our sorrows.
ISAIAH 53:4

The gospel is a matter of divine certainty. *Surely* is a word of strong affirmation. It sets before us an eternal truth, not a mere temporal theory. Here, then, is a truth on which we may depend for time and for eternity: Christ bore what He did not have to bear in order that we might not bear what we otherwise must have borne to our souls' destruction. Christ was burdened that His people may be blessed.

Christ was burdened. "He hath *borne* our griefs, and *carried* our sorrows." Here is the real reason for His sufferings: He was the sin-bearer. The *griefs* here represent the guilt for which the griefs were punishment; the *sorrows* here represent the sins that caused them. That is what Christ bore for us on the tree. This is important because our text is referred to in Matthew 8:17, from which some people derive the theory that healing is in the atonement— that is, that Christ's death purchased healing from every sickness, not in the ultimate sense that He will give us glorified bodies, but here and now. This misunderstanding has caused sincere Christians untold confusion and misery. The simple truth is that Matthew 8:17 does not speak of healing in the atonement. It merely shows that if Christ bore the judgment of the sin that caused suffering, He had the right and power to heal. But as to the judicial act of *bearing* and *carrying* to which Isaiah refers, it was *sin* and *judgment* that He bore. In due course our bodies will be entirely free from sickness, but Christians should not misapply our text to deceive themselves that they need never be sick.

Indeed, we have a better immediate blessing than physical health. Because Christ was burdened for us, there are burdens we will never carry—unatoned guilt, unchecked corruption, unshared sorrows, unlightened death, and unending hell.

Can you say, "Surely He has borne my sin and my judgment"? No blessing on earth can compare to this assurance. Do not rest until it is yours.

—A. C.

Jesus is not a substitute for the symptoms—
He is the cure of the cause.
JOHN BLANCHARD

Cries in Crisis

Then the mariners were afraid, and cried every man unto his god.
JONAH 1:5

A time of crisis is a most revealing time. It is then we discover who our real friends are; we find out then what our true priorities are; we come then to value genuine religion. Before the *Titanic* struck the fatal iceberg, the ship's band was playing "Roll Out the Barrel and We'll Have a Barrel of Fun." Reportedly, when tragedy came the tune was changed, and the band began to play "Nearer, My God, to Thee."

In the first chapter of Jonah we see the reaction of heathen sailors to the greatest crisis they had ever faced. This crisis revealed how much these hardened men of the sea actually knew when they came face to face with death.

They knew that there was a Being superior to themselves. That is why they all cried to their gods. It is hard to be an atheist in the midst of a storm. The Frenchman Voltaire was a thorough-going atheist. His judgment on religion was "Crush the infamous thing." But when Voltaire came to his deathbed, his arrogant confidence failed him and he died in great fear. A nurse who attended him said she never wanted to see another infidel die.

The sailors knew also that God punishes sin. After crying to their gods, they decided to cast lots to find out who on the ship had offended so greatly as to cause the storm to come. In the crisis they could see the connection between sin and judgment. They could see that there is One who is holy, who can discover sin and deal with the guilty.

God uses the crises of life to show us what is of real value. Only then do we fully appreciate the true worth of the Saviour and His work for sinners on Calvary's cross.

—G. F.

There is a conscience in man;
therefore there is a God in heaven.
EZEKIEL HOPKINS

Packed Up and Ready To Go

Prepare thee stuff for removing.

EZEKIEL 12:3

The child of God must always be sensitive to direction from above. Ezekiel had a listening heart, a ready response to the promptings of the Lord.

The Lord often brings about radical, even dramatic changes in the expected circumstances of the day. He may call us to remove ourselves in some way. As with Ezekiel, removal may be necessary for us because of corruptions around us or because of rebelliousness within. We have things to learn from this message to the prophet.

The true disciple of Christ must never allow himself to become so enamoured of earthly things as to say, "I love my surroundings so much; it is so comfortable where I am; I cannot consider the thought of serving the Lord elsewhere." If the Lord so directs, a change of abode may have to come. Heaven on earth is desirable, but not at the expense of getting out of the will of God. God must sometimes change our location. Our roots tend to run too deep down into the earth. We sometimes forget that here we have no continuing city.

Putting the Lord Jesus first is the Christian's chief desire in obeying Him. With some, the big steps they have taken have meant much struggling, tears, and anguish of heart at the beginning of the way. Yet, upon a full surrender of all we know to relinquish, what joy, what victory we have when the peace and the assurance of God's presence come flooding in! There are never any regrets about doing the Lord's will. His way is best. He never makes mistakes.

The people of God are a people ready to go. Sooner or later, heavenly counsel will reach us: "Prepare thee stuff for removing." No one is here forever. The saved are set for a sign and a testimony to those who belong to the world. Before long we must take our flight hence to heaven. The ungodly move from this scene without the least sign of making preparation. For them, to remove hence means the loss of everything, the loss of their heaven. To the Christian there is one condition of life: "To me to live is Christ, and to die is gain" (Phil. 1:21).

—J. D.

If men are prepared to die they are ready for anything.
J. A. Alexander

The Greatest Subject in the World

The salvation of your souls.

I PETER 1:9

There is no greater subject upon which to discourse than the glorious theme of the salvation of the soul. It is so wonderful that even the angels desire to look into it (I Pet. 1:12). Here is a subject fit for holy angels' minds. The language of this verse speaks of bending down to examine the subject closely. These elect, unfallen angels have no personal need for salvation; yet they desire to ponder its inscrutable wisdom, holiness, and grace.

How much more must we poor mortals, the recipients of such a grand salvation, constantly ponder its depths and dimensions. A very telling example is set before us in the testimony concerning the prophets in verse 10. These prophets had much knowledge from the revelation that the Holy Ghost had given them. They had an understanding of the grace of God's salvation, for they prophesied of the grace that should come unto us. What a subject for contemplation—the grace of God! They had also a knowledge of the ground of God's salvation, for the Spirit of God testified beforehand of the sufferings of Christ. What further subject for contemplation—the love of God expressed in blood at Calvary! They also had some revelation of the glory of God's salvation, the glory that shall be hereafter. How wonderful to contemplate the glory! Yet we read that they inquired and searched diligently. They were not satisfied with their knowledge and understanding of these things. Whatever our knowledge and understanding of the Scriptures may be, let us likewise never be satisfied, but diligently search the Scriptures daily for fuller wisdom.

—R. J. B.

These are the gold mines in which the abiding treasures
of eternity are to be found and therefore worthy of
all the digging and pains we can bestow on them.

ROBERT LEIGHTON

Courage To Live

I shall not die, but live, and declare the works of the Lord.
PSALM 118:17

A young soldier was home on leave before being sent to the battle-front. He spent some time visiting with his grandfather, who was crippled with a painful disease. As they were both Christians, they spent much time in conversation about spiritual things. As he was about to leave, the young man asked his grandfather to pray for him that he might have the courage to die if he were required to do so. The old man looked up with eyes that revealed the terrible pain he was suffering and said, "I will, my boy, and please pray for me that I will have the courage to live." No one would deny that it takes strength and courage to die, but often it takes greater courage to live and face the difficult circumstances and problems that confront us day by day.

Some of the greatest of God's saints in the Bible wanted to die rather than live because they were so crushed by the situations they were facing. Think of Moses, who was so overwhelmed by the burdens and problems of the nation of Israel that he prayed to the Lord to kill him (Num. 11:14-15). Elijah also prayed that God would take his life (I Kings 19:4), and of course Jonah can be added to the list.

We learn from the experience of these men of God that the problems and pressures of life are real and that often it takes more grace and spirituality to face these situations in the strength of the Lord than it does to face death. The Lord does not promise us an easy road to heaven, but He does guarantee, "My grace is sufficient for thee: for my strength is made perfect in weakness" (II Cor. 12:9).

—S. B.

Sanctified afflictions are spiritual promotions.
MATTHEW HENRY

The Doctrine of Balaam

Thou hast there them that hold the doctrine of Balaam.
REVELATION 2:14

The greatest dangers to the church of Christ always come from the inside. The church of Pergamos was able to withstand the fiercest pressure from the outside. Though dwelling where "Satan's seat" was, it held fast the Lord's name and refused to deny His faith. Even the martyrdom of Antipas could not shake the believers' resolution to be faithful to Christ. But that same church was in danger from within. The same people who would not capitulate to outside pressure now tolerated evil men and evil doctrines within their ranks.

The particular evil was "the doctrine of Balaam." Balaam was the false prophet who recognized that the heathen force of Balak could never defeat Israel or deprive her of the protection of the Lord—that is, unless Israel brought herself under judgment because of sin. Thus he advised Balak to induce the Israelites to join his people in eating things sacrificed to idols and in immoral practices. Here, then, is the doctrine that threatened to wreck the work and witness of the church at Pergamos: the teaching that Christians could be lax in separation from their heathen surroundings and in their standards of personal morality.

This doctrine of Balaam is widely preached today. Satan is still attacking Christians on these two points. If we are to enjoy fellowship with the Lord and serve Him acceptably, we must be separated from the heathen spirit and practice of this world unto Him. This separation must particularly be seen in our church life and in our personal life. Ecclesiastical separation in an age of unscriptural ecumenicity and personal purity in an age of unbridled lust are the crying needs of God's people. Only let us keep ourselves pure out of love for Christ and His truth, and no power on earth can shake our testimony.

—A. C.

How careful should we be to keep clean the
house that is the dwelling of the King of Glory.
R. C. CHAPMAN

The Purifying Fire

*The fining pot is for silver, and the furnace
for gold: but the Lord trieth the hearts.* **PROVERBS 17:3**

The saintly Samuel Rutherford penned the following to a lady who had lost her husband and five children: "Oh, how Christ must love you! He would take every bit of your heart to Himself. He would not permit you to reserve any of your soul for any earthly thing."

The gold must be cast into the furnace. The Lord tries our hearts. This has been the experience of the godly in all generations. "Faith without trial, is like a diamond uncut, the brilliance of which has never been seen" (C. H. Spurgeon). Thus the sincerity of Job was evidenced and the lie given to Satan's slander. Fiery trial is one of the precious things of God. "Adversity is the diamond dust heaven polishes its jewels with" (Robert Leighton).

Affliction makes the Bible a new book to us. "Afflictions are a golden key by which the Lord opens the rich treasure of His Word to His people's souls" (Thomas Brooks). It is also a handmaid to prayer, to lead us to a neglected mercy seat. It weans us from this present evil world. Its voice says, "Arise ye, and depart; for this is not your rest" (Mic. 2:10). It discovers to us the plague of our hearts to humble us. It teaches us to lean hard on our Beloved. It calls our graces into exercise. Some Christians never shine so brightly as in the midnight of sorrow.

Our Lord sits as a refiner. It is a picture of exquisite beauty. "He bends in patient love over the furnace, until, when He looks down on the liquid metal He can see His own image perfectly reflected there. Then the process is completed, and the fire removed" (T. V. Moore). Welcome, then, thrice welcome to that discipline of grace that makes us more like the Lord Jesus!

—M. P.

**We often learn more of God under the rod that
strikes us, than under the staff that comforts us.**
STEPHEN CHARNOCK

A More Excellent Way

The greatest of these is charity.
I CORINTHIANS 13:13

Love, or charity, has rightly been called the "queen of Christian graces." Paul states that "the end of the commandment is charity" (I Tim. 1:5). It is a grace essential to true godliness. Many believers could not discourse upon the deeper points of Christian doctrine, but all know something of love. It is the chief of virtues.

A person may be great in faith, or be a notable philanthropist, or possess outstanding wisdom and knowledge. He may be a gifted orator and expounder of God's Word, but the absence of love is fatal to all of these gifts and negates their effectiveness.

Love is important, being the sum total of the law. The great commands direct our love first to God and then to our neighbour. On these, said Jesus, hang all the law and the prophets.

There are many mistaken views as to what love is. It does not involve just giving to the poor, as in the modern meaning of the word *charity*. It does not mean that one can never disapprove of another's conduct or religious views. Sometimes the greatest expression of love is to point out error and to attempt to guide a person away from sin and towards God.

There is also a strange love in some pulpits today that commends the wicked and condemns the righteous, that protects the guilty and exposes the innocent, that thrives on ritual but has lost touch with reality, that says "It is well" when the soul is in fact on the broad road to destruction. The Lord pronounces His woe upon such "love."

The first expression of the Christian's true love should be to the One who first loved us, Jesus Christ. Then it should extend to our family members, those of the household of faith, and the ungodly whom we hope to reach with the gospel message. True Christian love is the root of all true Christian service. "The love of Christ constraineth us" (II Cor. 5:14).

—F. McC.

Suspicions subtract, faith adds, but love multiplies.
It blesses twice—him who gives it and him who gets it.
C. T. STUDD

Perverse and Foolish

Who hath sent out the wild ass free?
or who hath loosed the bands of the wild ass?

JOB 39:5

All creation, with a proper, Biblical interpretation, is a spiritual textbook. In every realm of nature there is a message for our souls. The Lord directs Job to consider the characteristics and abode of the wild ass.

The wild ass is a powerful example of a nature that cannot be tamed or governed. The whole tenor of God's description of this beast shows its nature to be one of unrestrained lawlessness and unbridled licence. It will not be subject to rules and regulations. Even when captured, it cannot be entirely domesticated. It is noted for its stubbornness, obstinacy, and perverse determination. To the surprise of many, the Bible uses this animal to picture the state of man before God (Exod. 34:20). Under the law of the firstborn, some kinds of animals were declared unclean and could be delivered from death only by being redeemed by the sacrifice of a lamb. One of these animals was the ass.

It is with good reason that we see in the ass a picture of the perverseness of man. "The carnal mind [that is, the natural mind of man] is enmity against God: for it is not subject to the law of God, neither indeed can be" (Rom. 8:7). When faced with the commandments of God, man behaves like the wild ass. He rebels against divine authority and, with dogged perseverance, pursues his own way. Moreover, if left to his own devices, he will always remain in a state of enmity against God. Like the ass, he is doomed to die unless he is redeemed by the sacrifice of the Lamb of God. It is only when the precious blood of Christ has been applied and the Lord Himself has entered into the human heart that it can be conquered, its perverseness rendered powerless, and its service freely given to God.

—S. B. C.

**Let God have your life; He can
do more with it than you can.**
D. L. MOODY

173

The Burnt Offering

If his offering be a burnt sacrifice of the herd.

LEVITICUS 1:3

The first chapters of Leviticus are taken up with detail of the five offerings—the burnt, meat, peace, sin, and trespass offerings. All these offerings speak of Christ and His work of redemption. The burnt offering occupies a prominent position and pictures Calvary. Let us learn its unmistakable lessons.

The first lesson that comes to mind is that man is separated from God by reason of his sin. When man fell in sin, the communion between God and man was broken. The second lesson is that God speaks to man through a mediator. Moses acted as mediator between God and Israel, and a Greater than Moses is here, even Jesus Christ. The third lesson is that God demands a blood sacrifice. It may seem unpleasant to proud man, but God has the right to dictate the terms of reconciliation. Such extreme measures speak of the extremity and heinousness of man's sin. The fourth lesson is that the burnt offering pictures Calvary. The sacrificial animal or bird was a male. The first Adam brought death. The last Adam brought life. It was "without blemish," speaking of the sinlessness of Christ. It was to be "of the herd," telling of the accessibility of the sacrifice. Christ is near to all that call upon Him.

The offerer "put his hand upon the head" (v. 4) of the victim, identifying his sin with the sacrifice. The sinner's touch always brings death. It was killed "for him," teaching us the truth of the substitutionary sacrifice. It was a voluntary offering, picturing the voluntary nature of Christ's death on the cross. It was to make "at-one-ment," to reconcile lost sinners to God.

Let us rejoice this day in Christ our Saviour. We are not worthy of the least of His mercies, but He has blessed us with the greatest.

—F. McC.

God requires satisfaction because He is holiness,
but He makes satisfaction because He is love.
AUGUSTUS H. STRONG

Riches of Righteousness

*Therefore being justified by faith, we have peace with God
through our Lord Jesus Christ: by whom also we have
access by faith into this grace wherein we stand.*

ROMANS 5:1-2

In seeking to define grace, someone has turned this word into an acrostic, reading thus: God's Riches At Christ's Expense. That would be an apt summary of the fifth chapter of Romans. Having shown God's method of justifying the ungodly through faith in Christ's crosswork, Paul now reveals the riches of righteousness that belong to every believer in Christ.

We are, in the first place, reconciled to God—"we have peace with God." One day we were at war with God, "alienated and enemies in [our] mind by wicked works" (Col. 1:21). But through our Lord Jesus Christ, the "mediator between God and men" (I Tim. 2:5), all was changed! Christ our Priest took our sin away in His own body on the tree and covered us with His own spotless righteousness. Christ our Prophet, through His Word, made us see our state before God, convincing us of sin. Christ our King subdued our rebellious hearts and caused us to put down our weapons. Never will those reconciled experience what John called the "wrath of the Lamb." Never will the believer feel the heat of hell's flames, the darkness of the pit, or the unquenchable thirst of the damned.

But grace has also given us access to God. We ever stand in a state of acceptance before God. Not only is there peace between us and God, but there is fellowship. We can go directly and immediately into the Father's presence. We can boldly approach the throne of grace without fear of rejection. After having failed the Lord in some way, we often feel that we cannot draw near to Him, that we must first make ourselves "respectable." But grace will always keep the door of heaven open to the weakest of saints! We can, with Paul, "rejoice in hope of the glory of God."

—J. W.

He hides our unrighteousness with His righteousness, He covers our disobedience with His obedience, He shadows our death with His death, that the wrath of God cannot find us.

HENRY SMITH

Brokenness Before Blessing

The people lifted up their voice, and wept.

JUDGES 2:4

The people of Israel had good cause to weep. They had wilfully disobeyed the voice of the Lord. They had compromised with the idolatry of the nations they were sent to dispossess. They were going headlong to ruin, and so "an angel of the Lord came up from Gilgal to Bochim" to warn them of the inevitable consequence of their sin.

Gilgal was the place where the reproach of Egypt was rolled away (Josh. 5:9) and speaks to us of separation from sin. "It was the place where flesh came under the execution of the sentence of death" (W. Kelly). Israel had forsaken that separation just as too many Christians go easy on the flesh and fail to bring it under the power of the cross. Such compromise with sin calls forth divine chastening. Sin never makes happy Christians.

Bochim means "weepers" and signifies the place of sorrow for sin. Great as Israel's sin was, it was not so great as that of many of us, for at least those Jews had grace enough to weep when confronted with their backsliding. More often than not we rationalize our sin, we excuse our compromise with the world, and we harden our hearts and do not weep.

Sin should break the heart of a Christian. Let us ask ourselves today, "Does it break my heart? Do I not need to weep over broken vows and coldness of heart?"

But weeping alone is not sufficient. We need to confess our sins and plead the merits of the blood of the Lamb for their remission. In Bochim Israel sacrificed unto the Lord and proceeded to enter into their possessions (Judg. 2:5, 6). So it is with us. "If we confess our sins, he is faithful and just to forgive us our sins, and to cleanse us from all unrighteousness" (I John 1:9). Then we will enter into the enjoyment of our inheritance in Christ.

—A. C.

**Mortification of the flesh is the
true place of power in the Spirit.**
W. KELLY

Conviction of Sin

Cause Jerusalem to know her abominations. EZEKIEL 16:2

The fifteenth chapter of Ezekiel is all about the vine, a type of Israel. The Lord shows by this figure that He has not chosen His people because of their fitness or goodness, even at their best (15:1-5). Now in chapter 16 God begins to lift the curtain on Jerusalem to give depth to the message of the vine.

Men are blind when it comes to the treachery of the heart. Sinners on the road to hell have no conscience of sin. They know nothing as they should of its guilt or danger, its power or damnation. But the blindness in this instance is in Jerusalem—surely the last place we would expect to find this dreadful malady. Jerusalem is the best place on earth at the time, remember. God put His name there. Yet He grieves over the sin they do not see.

It is necessary for God to open men's eyes to reveal their true condition. The striking thing is that God is not talking here about some sort of obscure sin, the kind of sin some would excuse on that account. "Abomination" is the worst kind of sin. We concede the small spots we do not see. Here are the glaring faults we have failed to see.

There is a showing of sin that we may feel the intensity of guilt and the sense of gravity in the offence. We do not consciously *know* what sin is. Ezekiel could not see this in chapter 9 verses 5, 8-10, when he willingly would have held back the angels on their mission of judgment. God will not hide the truth from us. In this chapter we see why there is ruin, heartbreak, death, and hell in the way of the transgressor. There is a showing of sin so that we can thankfully begin to comprehend the mercy of God unto eternal life in Christ.

—J. D.

It is our duty to feel sin, to fear sin,
and to fly as far as we can.
JOHN BOYS

Created by Jesus Christ

God, who created all things by Jesus Christ.

EPHESIANS 3:9

The ransomed in heaven praise the Lord for creating all things for His own pleasure (Rev. 4:11). Strange that on earth many who hope to go to heaven are ashamed to confess the same truth. That was not the case with the apostle Paul. He gloried in the sovereign Lord who could make and uphold all things by the word of His power (Heb. 1:2-3). In our text Paul is speaking of the original creation, but he also saw God's creative power in what theologians call our regeneration. We were dead in sins when God quickened us (Eph. 2:5). Twice Paul uses the term *create* to describe this life-giving act of God (2:10; 4:24). He also sees God's creative power in the formation of the church. Christ brought Jew and Gentile together in one body, or as Paul put it, He made, or created, "in himself of twain one new man, so making peace" (2:15).

Modern man likes to view himself as autonomous. He wants to make his own laws and be answerable only to himself. We can understand then why he rebels against the truth of creation, though he does so to his own destruction. What is baffling is the one who says he knows Christ, who is the Creator, and yet is ashamed of the Biblical record of God's direct creative acts. Even more puzzling are those who say that Christ is their Saviour, and yet they will not be answerable to Him as Lord (II Pet. 2:1). They are doubly condemned. First, if Christ is their Creator, they owe allegiance to the one who made them. Second, if Christ is their Saviour, He must also be their Redeemer. What He redeems or buys, He owns (I Cor. 6:20). Let us, like Paul, glory in our Creator and boldly bear witness for Him in the midst of His rebellious creatures. Then let us demonstrate our faith in God our Creator by our obedience to Christ our Redeemer.

—M. W. A.

Did Christ open His veins for our redemption,
and shall we not open our mouths for His vindication?
WILLIAM SECKER

Christ Our Sin-bearer

*He was wounded for our transgressions, he was
bruised for our iniquities: the chastisement of our peace
was upon him; and with his stripes we are healed.*

ISAIAH 53:5

Here we have Calvary unveiled. It is a holy scene depicting the
greatest work ever done on earth, even by God. What is here
described is the deep, mysterious transaction that took place in
the darkness of the crucifixion day, when the Son of God died as
our substitute and sacrifice. Isaiah mentions four particular
aspects of that work.

First, *the physical agony of the cross. Wounded, bruised,* and
stripes are all words that describe deep bodily pain. *Wounded*
means "pierced," or "stabbed." *Bruised* means "broken in pieces,"
or "smitten most severely." *Stripes* are weals or bruises, the marks
or prints of blows to Christ's body. What unspeakable physical
torment our Saviour endured! We should never be able to read of
His bodily suffering without tears (see Psa. 22).

Second, *the spiritual conflict of the cross.* Wounding and
bruising also denote the penetration of Christ's heart with sorrow
and the severe inward sufferings He bore. When men had done
their worst, all hell sought to conquer Christ. Satan bruised
His heel (Gen. 3:15), but, praise God, He bruised Satan's head
and spoiled principalities and powers, making a show of them
openly (Col. 2:15).

Third, *the penal sufferings of the cross.* "The chastisement of
our peace was upon him." This was from the hand of His Father
as He judged our sin in our sin-bearer. What a mystery! And, oh,
what love, that God should so afflict His Son to spare His enemies!

Finally, *the finished work of the cross.* "With His stripes we
are healed." We have healing by virtue of the work of Christ
alone. He paid our debt. He bore our judgment. He removed our
curse. He cures our disease. He redeemed us to God. Hallelujah!
What a Saviour!

—A. C.

**Calvary shows us how far men will go in sin,
and how far God will go for man's salvation.**

H. C. TRUMBULL

179

Silencing the Adversaries

*They were not able to resist the wisdom
and the spirit by which he spake.*

ACTS 6:10

Stephen's preaching had silenced the enemies of the gospel. While they were unwilling to accept the message, they were unable to answer it. There was a power in Stephen's witness that was irresistible. He had proved by experience the truth of the Lord's promise, "I will give you a mouth and wisdom, which all your adversaries shall not be able to gainsay nor resist" (Luke 21:15). Beloved, the world is full of gainsayers, and the need of the hour is for wisdom and power "to silence the ignorance of foolish men" (I Pet. 2:15). What were the characteristics of Stephen's preaching?

First, it was founded on the Scriptures. An examination of his defence in chapter 7 shows how completely he based his message upon the Word of God. Speaking to men who boasted that they possessed and knew the law of God, he used that Biblical truth to expose their folly and exalt Christ. The simple fact is, child of God, it is His Word that God has promised to bless (Isa. 55:11). Philosophical arguments, human logic, and worldly reasoning are of no avail. It is by "sound doctrine" that we are able "to exhort and to convince the gainsayers" (Titus 1:9).

Then, Stephen was filled with the Spirit. The church had recognized this characteristic of his life when they chose him to be a deacon. We all are commanded to "be filled with the Spirit" (Eph. 5:18), that our thoughts, words, and walk might be under His divine control. The disciples thus filled in Acts 4:31 "spake the word of God with boldness." They experienced "great power" and were endued with "great grace" (Acts 4:33).

How are we to stop the mouths of the enemies of the truth? Our wisdom is the message of the Scriptures; our power is the might of the Spirit.

—D. F.

There is something in the very countenance of those
who walk with God, that gives authority to all they say.
R. C. CHAPMAN

The Bible Stands

Every word of God is pure.

PROVERBS 30:5

It cannot be otherwise. The Holy Scriptures are holy because their Author is holy. They are the "oracles of God." An oracle is something that is spoken. Every word from the mouth of Him who cannot lie must be absolutely pure. The God of truth has spoken. How unthinkable that His Word be tinged with falsehood! God has graciously revealed Himself. How dreadful the consequences if that divine revelation were marred with inaccuracies! J. C. Ryle put it succinctly: "Once admit the principle that the writers of the Bible could make mistakes, and were not in all things guided by the Spirit, and I know not where I am. I see nothing certain, nothing solid, nothing trustworthy in the foundations of my faith. A fog has descended on the Book of God, and enveloped every chapter in uncertainty!"

Let us hold fast to the absolute trustworthiness of the Bible. No other book has been so tried and tested. "The words of the Lord are pure words: as silver tried in a furnace of earth, purified seven times" (Psa. 12:6). The divine volume has been cast into the furnace of the fiercest criticism. It has passed through the hottest of fires; yet it has come forth without even the smell of burning upon it. "Come," C. H. Spurgeon challenged, "search, ye critics, and find a flaw; examine it from its Genesis to its Revelation and find an error. This is a vein of pure gold, unalloyed by quartz or any earthy substance. This is a star without a speck; a sun without a blot; a light without darkness; a moon without paleness; a glory without a dimness." Rejoice, Christian. The foundation of God standeth sure!

—M. P.

**The Word of God is perfect; it is
precious and pure; it is truth itself.**
MARTIN LUTHER

181

Be Not Deceived

For the ear trieth words, as the mouth tasteth meat.

JOB 34:3

Elihu makes an important statement as to how people ought to formulate what they believe, especially in spiritual matters. As the mouth tastes food before the stomach receives it, so we ought always to test all we hear before we believe it.

One of mankind's most common sins is an inability to tell the truth. "The wicked are estranged from the womb . . . , speaking lies" (Psa. 58:3). If a person is noted for believing everything he hears, people's opinion of him is not complimentary. He is classed as a simpleton, one without discernment or judgment. Deception is one of the traits of the human heart. If discretion is so important in worldly matters, it is even more vital in the spiritual realm. The Bible is filled with somber warnings against allowing ourselves to be spiritually deluded. Alongside the true gospel that upholds the true Christ in the power of the true Spirit, there is another gospel, energized by another spirit, proclaiming another Christ. When our Lord was asked questions concerning the last days (the age in which we live), the first exhortation He gave was, "Take heed that no man deceive you" (Matt. 24:4). One of the inspired proverbs of Holy Writ commands, "Cease, my son, to hear the instruction that causeth to err from the words of knowledge" (Prov. 19:27).

The Bible is the reservoir of all spiritual truth. The death and resurrection of Christ form the basis and beginning of all spiritual light and life (Luke 24:26-27). Like the blessed man of Psalm 1, by meditating upon this inerrant guide of heavenly wisdom, we shall grow in grace and be enlightened and strengthened in our Christian experience and service. Thus we will be equipped to test all we hear and to discern the false from the true, and thereby be in a position to help others who are in danger of being carried away by every wind of doctrine.

—S. B. C.

Keep the truth and the truth will keep you.
WILLIAM BRIDGE

Transformed by the Sight of Christ

When he shall appear, we shall be like him;
for we shall see him as he is.

I JOHN 3:2

We become what we behold. When our glorious Lord returns, we shall be changed and made "like him." No sin will mar our souls, and even our bodies will be transformed into the likeness of His glorious body. Thus perfected in Christlikeness, both in body and in soul, we shall be "made perfectly blessed in the full enjoying of God to all eternity," as the *Shorter Catechism* puts it.

The promise of today's text not only sets before us the reality of our future glorification; it also reveals the secret of our present sanctification. What motivates and enables us to live a life of growing holiness? The sight of Christ! As we will be perfected in holiness when we see the Saviour in person, so now we are more and more conformed to His image as we look upon Him by faith. This is what Paul taught in II Corinthians 3:18: "We all, with open face beholding as in a glass the glory of the Lord, are [being] changed into the same image from glory to glory, even as by the Spirit of the Lord."

Let us then remember this truth: as we journey as pilgrims in the wilderness of this world, what we behold will have a great effect on what we become. The beauty of Christ's person and the all-sufficiency of Christ's work must be our constant meditation and focus. God makes Christ central in His plan of redemption. Let us make Him central to every thought and action in our redeemed lives.

—R. J. W.

We must be constantly making progress both in the knowledge of God, and in conformity to His image.
JOHN CALVIN

The Open Bible

*Open thou mine eyes, that I may behold
wondrous things out of thy law.*

PSALM 119:18

Robert Murray McCheyne of Dundee died at the early age of twenty-nine. His short but successful ministry continues to touch and bless lives through his memoirs, letters, and sermons. Writing to a young believer, he shared this spiritual advice: "Turn the reading of your Bible into prayer. Thus, if you are reading the first psalm, spread the Bible on a chair before you and kneel down and pray, 'O Lord, give me the blessedness of this man; let me not walk in the counsel of the ungodly.' This is the best way of knowing the meaning of the Bible and of learning to pray."

Speaking of the psalmist, McCheyne writes: "He was not blind—his eye was not dim . . . and yet he felt that he needed to see deeper, to have the eyes of his understanding opened. He felt that if he had nothing but his own eyes and natural understanding, he would not discover the wonders which he panted to see. He wanted divine teaching—the eye salve of the Spirit; and therefore he would not open the Bible without this prayer."

If the man after God's own heart felt like that, how much more should we? We must confess our natural inability to grasp divine truth and apply it to our lives. But natural inability is no barrier to a spiritual education. The psalmist's prayer is one the Lord delights to answer. The Holy Spirit will always reveal spiritual truth to praying saints. He will open the eyes of our understanding and direct our hearts into the knowledge of our God.

Will you take McCheyne's advice and cry for the eye salve of the Spirit? Learn to make the Bible your prayer book, not just your reading book, and you will be amazed at how much more you see in it.

—S. B.

**A humble and prayerful spirit will find a
thousand things in the Bible which the proud,
self-conceited student will utterly fail to discern.**
J. C. RYLE

The Attraction of the Cross

And I, if I be lifted up from the earth, will draw all men unto me.

JOHN 12:32

We little understand the dreadful gulf between sinful men and the God of heaven until we begin to grasp how bitter the cup was which our Lord drained upon the cross. That cup of suffering and shame is what constituted the deep agony of Calvary. It reveals the twofold message of the cross—the curse of God upon sin and the only course out of sin.

The preaching of this message of Christ's dying in the sinner's place has moved the hearts of multitudes to flee from the wrath to come. The crucified Lord is the object of saving faith. In fact, there can be no saving faith where the bleeding Lamb of God is not set forth.

Paul the apostle depicted Christ's death so vividly to the Galatians that he described his preaching as "placarding" Christ crucified before their very eyes (Gal. 3:1). Surely this is the secret to gospel preaching. The death of Christ must not be trivialized by the jargon of the salesman. It must not be hidden under the abstruse terms of vain philosophy. Rather it must be declared with plainness of speech. As Paul put it, our speech and preaching must not be "with enticing words of man's wisdom, but in demonstration of the Spirit and of power" (I Cor. 2:4). We must go back to the original commission of lifting up the crucified Saviour. Only then will we enjoy the original power of the gospel in our churches and in our daily lives.

Do you feel a distance between your soul and the Lord? Then lift up the cross before your eyes, and by studying the crucified Christ you will know afresh His drawing power in your life.

—I. G.

It may take a crucified church to bring a
crucified Christ before the eyes of the world.
W. E. ORCHARD

185

The Battle Against Sin

Now these are the nations which the Lord left, to prove Israel by them.
JUDGES 3:1

There were two distinct peoples in the land of Canaan: the heathen and the people of God. The Lord did not remove the enemy nations before Israel took possession of the land, but left them there to prove His people. The continued presence of the heathen, with the threat and temptation they presented, was intended to keep Israel in constant dependence upon the Lord and in perpetual separation from them.

These two peoples in Canaan remind us of the two natures in every believer. The old man is not eradicated when we are saved. His hatred of all things godly is not altered. He remains a bitter enemy of the Lord and of our enjoyment of our inheritance in Christ.

The old man must be opposed. We must make no provision for him. "Put ye on the Lord Jesus Christ, and make not provision for the flesh, to fulfil the lusts thereof" (Rom. 13:14). The fact that the old man still resides within us is no licence or excuse for sin.

The way to victory over indwelling sin is to "keep the way of the Lord to walk therein" (Judg. 2:22). A life of holiness is not achieved through a single decision. Victory over sin is never once and for all. "The Lord left those nations, without driving them out hastily," or speedily (v. 23). Our battle with sin must be constant. Our mortification of the flesh must be daily. The proof of the reality of our walk with God will be our attitude to our old man. He who pampers and provides for the flesh and smiles upon his own sin deceives himself if he thinks he is walking with God.

Like Israel in today's text, we have received our inheritance without any personal effort, but we can enjoy its rich fulness only as we faithfully battle the fleshly lusts that war against our souls.

—A. C.

The vigour, and power, and comfort of our spiritual life depends on the mortification of the flesh.
JOHN OWEN

Mercy and Judgment

He shall have judgment without mercy, that hath shewed no mercy.
JAMES 2:13

Anyone who has truly experienced the mercy of God will be a merciful person. Anyone who shows no mercy to others, especially within the church, cannot receive mercy from God. These are radical sentiments, but they are the sentiments of the Holy Ghost. They expose and condemn the selfishness and self-righteousness that all too often infiltrate the ranks of God's people.

Salvation is a holy root that produces holy fruit. If like produces like, then the mercy of God toward us must produce Godlike mercy from us to others. Any man who can live with a hard, indifferent heart to the needs of others simply testifies that he is a stranger to the mercy of God: "He shall have judgment without mercy." On the other hand, "Blessed are the merciful: for they shall obtain mercy" (Matt. 5:7). We are not saved by virtue of the mercy we show to others, but our behaviour shows what is in us. The existence of the fruit of grace in us is evidence of the root of grace in us.

We show mercy when we respond with the love of Christ to meet the needs of others. They have physical, emotional, and material needs. They need our mercy in these areas. But the greatest need men have is spiritual. They need the gospel, and it is the highest form of mercy to present it to them. No Christian can be indifferent to dying sinners. Can you?

—A. C.

**He who demands mercy and shows none ruins
the bridge over which he himself is to pass.**
THOMAS ADAMS

Joy Is Abounding

Rejoice in the Lord alway.

PHILIPPIANS 4:4

Paul was growing old. The sufferings he had experienced had certainly taken their toll. Yet despite the catalogue of afflictions he had endured while preaching the gospel of Christ, he had not lost his sense of the vibrancy of life. The words *joy* and *rejoice* (which is a variant form of the word *joy)* occur sixteen times in this epistle.

These words express triumph in the face of the disappointments and hardships of the Christian life. The command "Rejoice in the Lord alway" sounds the keynote of the entire epistle. The Christian can rejoice at all times and under all circumstances, because the source of his joy is the Lord. Thus rejoicing, like joy, is supernatural. It issues from the very nature of God and is intended to well up within those in whom God's Spirit dwells.

Those who have trusted Christ have the privilege of experiencing "fulness of joy" (Psa. 16:11). The "Man of sorrows" was possessed of a deep joy. As He faced the cruel death of the cross, He said to His followers, "These things have I spoken unto you, that my joy might remain in you, and that your joy might be full" (John 15:11).

The unusual thing about Paul's situation was that there appeared to be no reason for him to rejoice. He was a Roman prisoner awaiting trial. He might be acquitted, or he might be beheaded. Yet in spite of his danger and discomfort, Paul overflowed with joy.

He could testify, "I rejoiced in the Lord greatly" (Phil. 4:10). All our joys must terminate in God, and our thoughts of God must be delightful thoughts. The psalmist said, "Delight thyself also in the Lord" (Psa. 37:4). Even in the midst of grievous and afflicting experiences he could say, "In the multitude of my thoughts within me thy comforts delight my soul" (94:19).

Earthly joys vanish, but when you rejoice in the Lord, you have something that lasts.

—D. C.

**Joy is the flag that is flown from the citadel
of the heart when the King is in residence.**
ANONYMOUS

A Lesson from the Raven

Who provideth for the raven his food?

JOB 38:41

Under the Mosaic law, the raven, or crow, was an unclean bird. Yet the Lord saw fit to care for it. This was the implication of the Lord's question to Job. Even by natural standards, the raven is not an attractive bird. It has a tendency to feed upon dead carcases like a vulture. Yet despite its lack of appeal, the Lord has His eye upon it for good. It is unclean, yet a recipient of God's mercy. How like man, defiled in thought, word, and deed, yet the object of the Lord's kindness and grace! "While we were yet sinners, Christ died for us" (Rom. 5:8).

The raven, as any farmer will testify, is a very noisy bird. In fact, God's care for it is in answer to its cry, a sound that is not pleasant to the ear. It does not warble or cheep. Its call is more aptly described as a harsh, rasping squawk, repeated incessantly to the annoyance of all within range. Nevertheless, the Bible impresses upon us that the cry of the raven is heard on high. "He giveth to the beast his food, and to the young ravens which cry" (Psa. 147:9). Every believer should remember the raven. The Lord is not interested in dry, formal prayers with well-constructed sentences and fine-sounding phrases. Rather would He hear a "squawk" from the heart, a fervent lifting up of the soul to seek His face in earnest supplication.

Again recall that God's treatment of this bird is an encouragement to every believer to trust Him more. That is what the Lord wanted Job to do. He was enduring hard days and difficult times. Bitter thoughts had arisen in his heart. Did God really care? Had He forgotten him? The Lord directed Job to the raven. If He would extend mercy and care to a creature that was basically useless and of no real value to anyone, how much more would He care for those who look to Him from a contrite heart!

—S. B. C.

God never fails those who trust Him.
ALEXANDER SIMPSON

Love Which Passes Knowledge

And to know the love of Christ, which passeth knowledge.

EPHESIANS 3:19

The spiritual eye often sees the weakness in a man that others do not detect. Perhaps when the apostle expressed his desire that the Ephesians be rooted and grounded in love (Eph. 3:17), he saw that weakness which later drew the Saviour's rebuke: "Thou hast left thy first love" (Rev. 2:4). How often could those same words be applied to us? Truly, "we love him, because he first loved us" (I John 4:19). If then we would keep our love for Christ strong and vibrant, we must do so by continually viewing His love to us (Gal. 2:20).

Paul describes Christ's love as passing knowledge (Eph. 3:19). The love of Christ is a vast ocean that has no bank or bottom. Its shoreline is always beyond our farthest vision. While all God's people have begun to experience Christ's love to some extent, none of us has ever scaled its heights or fathomed its depths. There is always more to know. The greatest minds cannot take in all that this love entails, but the simplest believer may know and experience it. Let us immerse ourselves in this unspeakable love until it makes our daily fellowship with God a little heaven.

Paul also speaks of this love as a sacrificial love (5:2). Our Lord demonstrated His love to us by His giving Himself on the cross (John 10:11). If we have any real love for Christ, it will show itself in our actions. Certainly by looking at His wounds on our behalf, our hearts are stirred to give back to Him in love. Finally, Paul tells us that Christ's love is a covenantal love (Eph. 5:25). The eternal Son of God has bound Himself to us in an everlasting covenant. How can we be unfaithful to a Saviour who loves us beyond comprehension, gave Himself for us, and has bound Himself to us forever?

—M. W. A.

Since He looked upon me my heart is not my own,
He hath run away to heaven with it.
SAMUEL RUTHERFORD

Help!

*This thing is too heavy for thee; thou art
not able to perform it thyself alone.*

EXODUS 18:18

Self is the governing factor in many areas of human life, and it is with considerable difficulty that this principle is kept outside the door of the church. We are familiar with that type of church member who views his association with the local church merely as a means of advancing himself in his own circle—here is another avenue through which he may satisfy his craving for personal popularity and self-glorification. Such a display is always distasteful to the believer who knows anything of the humility of his Master.

Self is prone to manifest itself in another way—less obvious, less blameworthy, but no less dangerous. It is in that attitude which says, "No one is able to do this job to my satisfaction; I must do it all myself." Perhaps all of us have been guilty on this count at one time or another! Moses was in danger of falling into this trap, whether consciously or not. Jethro counselled him to delegate some responsibility to other able men, and his was sound advice. What if Moses had continued without help from those around him? Would he have completed each task in a wholly satisfactory manner? Would the immense burden have caused him to suffer personally? His motives may well have been honourable, but there is always the need to listen to the kind of practical good sense provided in this instance by the words of Jethro.

The work of God is not the work of one man, just as the body does not function because of the contribution of one sole member. Let us never feel that we do not need the help of our fellow labourers, and let us not hesitate to offer such help to those who stand in the forefront of the battle.

—T. N.

It is always better to set one hundred men to work,
than attempt to do the work of one hundred men.

F. B. MEYER

191

Sowing the Gospel Seed

*He that goeth forth and weepeth, bearing precious seed, shall
doubtless come again with rejoicing, bringing his sheaves with him.*

PSALM 126:6

There can be no doubt that of all the promises in God's Word, the
promise of Psalm 126:6 is one of the best known and loved. Who
can tell how many Christian workers have claimed this blessed
promise and found it to be true? In this wonderful text we have
some of the great principles of soulwinning.

First, there is the *sowing*—"bearing precious seed." Just as the
sower must sow the seed, we must spread the Word and carry the
good news of the gospel to every creature. C. H. Spurgeon was once
asked if he thought the heathen would be saved if they did not
hear the gospel. The great preacher's reply was, "Will we be saved
if we don't tell them?"

The sowing is to be followed with *weeping*. The sower weeps
like his Saviour, the Man of sorrows who wept over the city of
Jerusalem because of her unbelief and rejection of the gospel. A
young Salvation Army officer wrote to General Booth complaining
that he was not having any success. He asked what should he try
next. "Try tears" was the reply he received from the general.

After the sowing and weeping comes *rejoicing*—"shall doubtless come again with rejoicing, bringing his sheaves with him."
If we sow the seed, the Lord will take care of the results. Barry
Goldwater once said, "The political battles of this generation
will be won on the doorstep." The false cults, such as Mormonism
and Jehovah's Witnesses, are harvesting on doorsteps across
this world. May the Lord enable each one of us to do our part
in the sowing and weeping so that we, too, will rejoice as the
harvest is gathered in.

—S. B.

Witnessing is the whole work of the
whole church for the whole age.
A. T. PIERSON

Changed!

Lord, what wilt thou have me to do?   ACTS 9:6

That God's salvation makes the greatest conceivable change in the life is powerfully demonstrated by the experience of Saul of Tarsus. Observe this once proud, Pharisaical persecutor of the church as he lies humbled in the dust of the Damascus road and then rises a new creature in Christ Jesus. His brief, heartfelt prayer, uttered when face to face with the Saviour, reveals characteristics that are true of every regenerated soul.

Notice that there was submission. He addressed Christ as "Lord," indicating a turning away from self-will and rebellion to surrender to the Master's control. To receive Christ truly is to accept Him as Saviour and Lord—to give ourselves entirely, for time and for eternity, to Him alone. It is ours to hear and obey His voice and "not to please ourselves."

Then obviously there was supplication. These words constitute the first prayer that Saul ever prayed. They demonstrate the reality of his conversion, for the proof given by God to Ananias that Paul was truly saved was "Behold, he prayeth" (Acts 9:11). A prayerless Christian is really a contradiction in terms. Life does not exist without breath, and prayer is the Christian's vital breath.

Finally, there was service. The cry of Saul's soul was to know what he must do. He immediately recognized and acknowledged that he was now a servant called to invest his life in doing his Master's bidding for His glory.

May submission, supplication, and service ever demonstrate the reality and quality of our faith.

—D. F.

Service is the overflow of superabounding devotion.
OSWALD CHAMBERS

A Time for Everything

He hath made every thing beautiful in his time.

ECCLESIASTES 3:11

We believe that whatever the Bible says is true. Yet sometimes experiences cause us to question whether certain things are personally relevant. The tension between doctrine and experience is a common test of faith. Solomon's conclusion that God has made every time beautiful and appropriate is one of those great statements easy to believe in good times and easy to apply to others in their bad times. The key is to believe it during our own bad times. Believing that God has a purpose that embraces everything in life and that His plan is beautiful regardless of its manifestation is the secret to enjoying the life that God has given us.

Solomon leads up to this all-embracing statement by setting forth all the times ordered and ordained by God. Ecclesiastes 3 begins with a list of fourteen pairs of defined times that together represent all possible times in life. Nothing, absolutely nothing, happens by chance, accident, or fate. Everything, absolutely everything, happens according to God's design. Our efforts and worries cannot alter His eternal plan for us. Whereas unbelievers may regard themselves as the masters of their fate or the captains of their souls, we as believers know that our times and destinies are not only in God's good hand, they are part of His infinitely wise plan. Our life is a privilege; our life is God's purpose. In the good times, we should humbly acknowledge that God has made all times beautiful. In the hard times, we should confidently rest in that beauty. That God is sovereign over the affairs of life is true whether we believe it or not. Believing it is the only thing that gives sense to life.

—M. P. V. B.

**We must believe in the grace of sovereignty
as well as the sovereignty of grace.**
AUGUSTUS H. STRONG

That Woman Jezebel

*Thou sufferest that woman Jezebel, which calleth herself
a prophetess, to teach and to seduce my servants.*

REVELATION 2:20

Jezebel is to be understood not as a woman, but as a doctrine
(v. 24). Yet the character of the Sidonian seductress whom Ahab
made queen of Israel was clearly in mind as the Lord exposed
and condemned the false doctrine of the church at Thyatira.

False doctrine is imported into the church just as Jezebel was
imported into Israel. It can gain a foothold only when the church
departs from the Word of God as its sole and sufficient rule of faith
and practice. What enormous errors have been imported from
pretended apostolic traditions, from spurious ancient writings,
from heathen religions, and from science falsely so called! When
a church either abandons God's Word and turns to the opinions of
men or entertains any other standard of belief in addition to the
Bible, it has imported a Jezebel.

Like Jezebel, false doctrine knows how to paint its face to
appear most attractive. When the old, austere doctrines of Protestant evangelism came to be despised, it was because the
church was enamoured with the painted face of the Jezebel of
a more "liberal" theology. Under the cosmetic mask, however,
Jezebel remains a soul-destroying emissary of the devil. False
doctrine ruins souls. We need to go beyond appearances and
examine every doctrine in the light of the Word of God.

Jezebel is always intolerant of any competition. False doctrine
demands to be tolerated, but once tolerated, it takes control and
seeks to stamp out all adherence to the truth. This Jezebel is hard
at work in the church today. She aims to lay hold of the vineyard
of every Naboth and to slaughter every Elijah. There is no room
for compromise with her. To arms, Christian! Learn the truth, love
the truth, live for the truth. On behalf of his Master, John says, "I
have no greater joy than to hear that my children walk in truth"
(III John 4). That is always the answer to Jezebel.

—A. C.

A thousand errors may live in peace with one another,
but truth is a hammer that breaks them all in pieces.

C. H. SPURGEON

Life Observed Through the Palace Window

For at the window of my house I looked through my casement.
PROVERBS 7:6

Monarchs rarely see life as it truly is. Efforts made to secure their lives are so necessary and extensive that ordinary activities must be denied them. To be born a member of a royal family is to be born to a perpetual prison sentence from which there is no reprieve. Do not envy the rich and the famous. Sometimes they inherit great deprivation with their wealth.

Solomon was well aware that the scenes which met his gaze when he was on royal business amongst his people were most likely contrived, a show for his benefit. He was wise enough to seek a true view of his city by occasionally looking out on it secretively from his window.

Do you ever stop and take a long, unobserved look at the world? If you do, you will, like Solomon, see a world in darkness in which many are made fools by the enticements of sin. Are you ever moved to exclaim, "By the grace of God I am what I am"?

There is a vantage point within a king's palace from which mankind is seen for what it is. Such is the position occupied by the believer. "He . . . lifteth up the beggar from the dunghill, to set them among princes, and to make them inherit the throne of glory" (I Sam. 2:8). Oh! how our hearts should be lifted in thanksgiving every time we look out on the world from which we were delivered by the Lamb of God! How unprofitable will sin appear when viewed from the palace window. Nor shall we ever forget the needs of men who remain still in the darkness of sin when we see them from this vantage point. The king's window ought to be a place of intercession for those still trapped in nature's night.

If you have been washed in the blood of Christ and made to be a king and a priest, then go today and look out from the palace window. It may give you a new perspective on life.

—I. F.

Thanksgiving is good but thanks-living is better.
MATTHEW HENRY

Obedient Servants

And the living creatures ran and returned.   **EZEKIEL 1:14**

The cherubim ran. The King's business requires haste. Work for God should be done with alacrity and not tardiness and indifference.

These four living creatures call for attention as soon as we commence the reading of this prophecy. This focus of attention is not due merely because of the prime place accorded to them or the peculiar strangeness of the language attending their arrival, appearance, and activity. While these are important, one point about their symbolic function is to be noted: "they had the likeness of a man" (v. 5).

The cherubim are here *likened to the redeemed.* God's dear ones see a comparison in their being granted access into heavenly places. They too are in God's presence, close to the throne. All is done as before Him, unto Him. Their life attains to fulness only as it is conducted in the heavenlies, giving a full dimension to the words, "Thy will be done in earth, as it is in heaven" (Matt. 6:10).

The cherubim are also *careful to go as directed.* The prophet expresses this astutely: "their feet were straight"; "they went every one straight forward: whither the spirit was to go, they went; and they turned not when they went" (Ezek. 1:7, 12). They were as men governed by the Word and led by the Spirit—resolutely obedient, unitedly active, supremely guided, wholly single-minded.

Finally, the cherubim returned, *ready for new activity in service.* Oh, to be at God's beck and call! He would then have more for us to do. The running not only suggests zeal and instant response; it points up the promptitude of obedience, which opens the door to future fruitful service.

—J. D.

Obedience is the crown and honour of all virtue.
MARTIN LUTHER

A Plea for Humility

*Not to think of himself more highly than he ought
to think; but to think soberly, according as God
hath dealt to every man the measure of faith.*

ROMANS 12:3

It is somewhat surprising to find that the first Christian grace the apostle exhorts believers to possess after his strong exhortation in verses 1 and 2 is that of humility. You would think that love would be first in line, love to God and man being the two greatest commandments. Paul does deal with the virtue of love in the remaining verses of chapter 12 and into chapter 13. But before he does so he makes a very strong plea for humility to the Christians at Rome. Until we are emptied of self and pride, we will know very little of what it means to love! The very essence of love is selflessness. "Greater love hath no man than this, that a man lay down his life for his friends" (John 15:13).

Having shown that transformation into Christlikeness begins with the renewing of our minds, we are not surprised to find Paul using the word *think* three times in verse 3. The first part of the verse calls for soberness of mind. A Christian whose thoughts are in line with God's thoughts will not have a lofty opinion of his talents and abilities. "Who maketh thee to differ from another? and what hast thou that thou didst not receive?" (I Cor. 4:7). Whatever we have is a gift, and there is no room for boasting.

The last part of the verse gives us the standard of measurement for judging ourselves. Men are high-minded because their standard of judgment is all wrong. God's standard is the "measure of faith" that He has given to every man. In other words, do not form an opinion of yourself by your talents, intelligence, wealth, or education, but judge yourself by the extent of your faith in God! Men of humility are men of faith, because faith casts its entire dependence upon Christ. High-minded Christians betray a confidence in self.

Let our boasting be confined to the cross of Christ. We will find that the desire for man's praise will fade away into the shadows of Calvary.

—J. W.

God's choice acquaintances are humble men.
ROBERT LEIGHTON

The Sabbath in the Twentieth Century

The seventh day is the sabbath of rest. LEVITICUS 23:3

The keeping of the Sabbath comes as a Christian obligation by divine example and by divine command. God rested after creation, and in the fourth commandment He instructed us to keep the Sabbath.

Its importance can be seen in its *priority.* It was first mentioned in Genesis and in the wilderness before the law was given on Sinai. Notice also its *perpetuity,* lasting from Genesis through life on earth to heaven (Heb. 4:9). As to its *position,* it is the keystone in the arch of the law, spanning man's duty to God and to his fellow man. Its *primacy* among the holy convocations of Leviticus 23 is evident, as it is the only moral command, the rest being ceremonial.

Christians observe the first-day Sabbath. It is the day of rejoicing and gladness, commemorating the resurrection of Christ (Psa. 118:22-24). By contrast, the seventh-day Sabbath was a day of intense sorrow and sadness when Christ was in the grave.

The Christian Sabbath, or Lord's Day, was observed by the disciples. They met together for the preaching of the Word, sat together in remembrance at the Lord's Table, and collected offerings for the support of God's work. It was also the day when the apostle John had a vision of the risen and exalted Christ.

Observance of the Lord's Day is an intelligent practice. We must have rest from toil, perhaps all the more with the pressures of late twentieth-century life. We must stop and worship God.

There should be solemn preparation for the Lord's Day. We should take time to meditate upon the Lord and His goodness by way of soul preparation. We should pray the Lord to impart some special blessing from His Word as we meet to worship. The Sabbath then will not be a drudgery, but a delight to the soul.

—F. McC.

People who cannot abide the Lord's day, cannot abide the Lord.
THOMAS WATSON

Covetousness and Its Cure

Let your conversation be without covetousness.

The word *conversation* today refers only to verbal communication. However, in Scripture it has a much broader meaning, for it refers to our behaviour and our character. In those areas Paul commands us to be free from the sin of covetousness.

Literally, the word *covetousness* means "lover of silver," and certainly the love of money is one of the principal forms of this sin. However, it is not the only one, for covetousness is an inordinate lusting after anything. It is a most subtle sin, for it can be committed only in the heart. Consequently, many professing believers look on it as a trifling matter, while the world applauds it as ambition, shrewdness, or prudence.

Very different is the Holy Spirit's estimate, for in Colossians 3:5 He calls it idolatry. To covet anything is to idolize it, which means that the Lord is no longer the supreme object of our delight and love. We have instead become discontent with the things of the Lord and with our situation in life, because the lust of other things has entered in. Furthermore, unbelief follows rapidly in the wake of covetousness. To covet means that we are not prepared to trust the Lord for those things that we need. Notice, therefore, that Paul proceeds in this verse to urge us to "be content with such things as [we] have." His plea is based on that great promise, "I will never leave thee, nor forsake thee." The point is that the things we covet will fail, but the Lord never will. Consequently, we can be content with Him and with whatever He provides. Elsewhere Paul tells us that "godliness with contentment is great gain" (I Tim. 6:6). There we have not only the cure for covetousness, but the preventative as well.

—J. G.

Covetous men, though they have enough to
sink them, yet have never enough to satisfy them.
JOHN TRAPP

No Latter Rain

There hath been no latter rain.

JEREMIAH 3:3

Spiritual drought makes a wasteland where once there was a Canaan. It reduces a land flowing with milk and honey to poverty and want. It produces spiritual famine, powerlessness, and despondency.

No generation knows this better than ours. We are living through a prolonged and terrible drought. Gone are the days of great awakenings when the preaching of the old evangel caused a deep fear of God to fall upon multitudes and led them to faith in Christ. Where once there were floods of blessing we have only dried-up river beds that testify to what used to be and mock our present deadness.

The lack of spiritual fulness is evident on an individual level, too. Do you not lament that in your own experience you have lacked the latter rain? The latter rain is the rain shortly before harvest. Without it the harvest is scorched. Ah! where are the fulness and fruitfulness we know we should experience? Where is the freshness we should have in prayer? Where is the power we should have in witness? Where are the results we should see for our preaching? Alas! "There hath been no latter rain."

This drought is not accidental. Jeremiah says, "Therefore the showers have been withholden." When the heavens are as brass it is because God has shut them up in response to our sin (II Chron. 7:13). The worldliness so prevalent among God's people today is the direct cause of our spiritual drought.

The answer to our needs is clearly the opening of heaven and the outpouring of the latter rain. II Chronicles 7:14 tells us how to obtain this blessing. It can come only by self-humbling, prayer, and repentance. Can we endure another day of drought? May God drive us to our knees and keep us there till we hear the "sound of abundance of rain" (I Kings 18:41).

—A. C.

It is an alarming condition for a Christian
man . . . when there is more *knowledge*
of the truth than *experience* of its power.
OCTAVIUS WINSLOW

201

Sleeping Saints

What meanest thou, O sleeper?

JONAH 1:6

While everyone else on Jonah's boat was praying and working, Jonah was fast asleep. The only saved man on the boat was doing absolutely nothing to help the increasingly desperate passengers and crew on board. Ah, but Jonah was a backslider! Not that that excuses him, but it helps to explain his uselessness and his prayerlessness.

The backslider is prayerless. He not only does not pray—he cannot pray, for prayer begins with submission to God's will. When the Lord Jesus Christ taught His disciples to pray, He told them to say: "Our Father which art in heaven, Hallowed be thy name. Thy kingdom come. Thy will be done in earth, as it is in heaven." Jonah could not have prayed like that. He could not have asked for the Lord's will to be done on earth while he himself was deliberately disobeying God. If you are a backslider, you cannot pray. Once you start to pray, you stop backsliding. Backsliding and praying cannot exist together. They are like oil and water; they simply do not mix.

The backslider is a pretty useless person. Just as Jonah did nothing to help make the ship lighter and thereby increase everyone's seemingly slim chances of survival, so backsliders do very little to help perishing souls come to a place of safety in the Lord Jesus Christ. Backsliders do nothing for God and are of no benefit to themselves, their family, their friends, their church, or the community in which they live.

It was a rough hand that aroused Jonah from his slumber. God may have to use a rough hand on us to arouse us from the prayerlessness and uselessness of backsliding.

—G. F.

Sometimes God makes use of a rough hand to arouse us from our lethargy, and we should be thankful that He cares sufficiently for us to do so.

A. W. PINK

The Power of a Surrendered Life

But what are they among so many?

JOHN 6:9

Five thousand men, as hungry as hunters, were commanded to sit down to eat on a lonely hillside where the grass was turned into pews. It was a strange command, for the only food in sight was a little meal a lad had brought to satisfy his personal needs. The demand for food so outweighed the supply that a small boy's lunch might have been expected to cause a riot among so many men, but when given into the hands of the Creator of heaven and earth, it became the means of blessing and satisfying all.

We learn from this that serving God is not by talents or by great resources, but by an unreserved surrender of our all to the Lord. While we seek to utilize our own resources we will miserably fail, but when we surrender our few talents to the Lord for His service, who can tell what He will do with them? Should we not place our all in the Saviour's hands? If we rightly understood that all we have is the Lord's sovereign provision for us and that we have nothing but what He has given us, we would realize that we may withhold nothing from Him. How can we call ourselves His disciples if we do less?

Yielding his total reserves to the Saviour was this boy's best investment ever. He himself feasted more fully than he could otherwise have done from the food created by the Master's hands, and he had the added joy of watching as the fish and bread were distributed around the rows and rows of men, satisfying the needs of the whole multitude.

This is the joy of Christian surrender. God will multiply our smallest offerings and make them great and mighty instruments of blessing when they are yielded to His use. Let us start with what we have to offer today. Multitudes of hungering souls may be reached with gospel food by our surrendered lives and ready witness.

—I. G.

Since the first day that God put the poor of London upon my heart God has had all there was of William Booth.
WILLIAM BOOTH

The Merits of Christ's Atonement

And he stood between the dead and the living.
NUMBERS 16:48

Had Aaron not interposed himself between the wrath of God and the people as he did, none would have lived in Israel. The position he occupied was designed to stop divine vengeance from smiting any more of the congregation. He occupied it successfully. However, it must be carefully noted that it was not Aaron himself who turned aside the plague. Rather, it was the atonement that he had made that secured safety. A priest without an atonement is powerless to save. Furthermore, it must be a proper atonement. It must be according to God's requirements.

In making this atonement, Aaron burned the incense ordered by God in the Levitical law—incense comprised of various spices and giving off sweet odours which were acceptable to God. Thus the incense which Aaron carried in his hand propitiated God. Behold in that incense a type of the merits of our great High Priest, the merits of His perfect obedience and spotless purity. What a sweet savour those merits emit! What a covering they provide for the soul! Aaron's spices could give off their sweet odours only when they were burned. Fire from off the altar of burnt offering ignited the incense and produced the atoning cloud. It was fire, therefore, that had already fed upon and consumed the innocent sacrificial victim. Only the death and suffering of the sacrifice released the savour of the spices in the incense. Likewise, the merits of Christ are available to make atonement only because He has died under the fire of God's wrath due to us for sin. By death through blood-shedding, the merits of Christ's righteousness are released to make atonement for guilty sinners. That atonement is complete and is totally satisfying to God. It is as sweet incense before His face. Are you sheltering beneath the cloud of Christ's atoning merits? If not, you face certain death. Come today, and hide under the propitiation of our great Saviour and High Priest.

—J. G.

**The power of the blood of Christ may be seen
in this: not one blood-washed soul will be lost.**
ALEXANDER SIMPSON

The Silent Sufferer

He was oppressed, and he was afflicted, yet he opened not his mouth.
ISAIAH 53:7

There is an old saying, "Speech is silver; silence is golden." Of Christ it was said, "Never man spake like this man" (John 7:46). We do well to mark every utterance of the one who is called God's Word and God's Truth (John 1:1; 14:6). His speech is certainly of great importance.

When that speech suddenly ceases, we are immediately struck and must ponder, "Why?" As we stand at His trial, His scourging, and His crucifixion, we are wrapped in the golden silence of the cross. No more eloquent silence has ever been known. Think for a moment of what it teaches.

It teaches that the Lord Jesus Christ willingly gave Himself to be the ransom for His people. The Hebrew word translated "oppressed" has a wide range of meaning. It carries the idea that Christ was vexed and ill-treated by men. That is plain. But it also means "to exact a tribute or ransom" (see Deut. 15:2-3; II Kings 23:35). Something was exacted from Christ as a ransom. The context shows what that something was. It was the full payment for our debt of sin that the Saviour paid in the shedding of His own blood. What an awful price He paid!

He paid it willingly. *He was afflicted* may be translated, "He willingly humbled or submitted Himself" to pay the price. Christ was not forced to die either by God or by man. He *gave* His life. He died because He loved us enough to pay for our salvation. That is why "he opened not his mouth." He did not complain of His Father's rod upon Him. He had no word of condemnation for us. He did not even reproach His revilers. Thus He made a perfect expiation and provided a perfect example.

As we consider this silent Sufferer, we feel the glorious fulness and freeness of our salvation. And we feel the compulsion of all saved people to be more like our Saviour, who yielded Himself in perfect and uncomplaining obedience to His Father's will.
—A. C.

The whole world in comparison with the cross of Christ is one grand impertinence.
ROBERT LEIGHTON

Time To Get Up!

Awake to righteousness, and sin not.

I CORINTHIANS 15:34

A most amazing, and amusing, human practice is sleep. It is amazing that one who has reached the Biblical seventy years has already spent about twenty-three years in bed. It is amusing that we all, overcome by an uncontrollable urge, climb into bed, put the lights out, and wait—until the phenomenon of sleep turns down our hearing volume, closes our eyes, and quietly slips the brain out of gear. During the hours of sleep, millions of tiny "workers" are very much awake, reconditioning and recharging the body for another day's toil.

There is, of course, a time to sleep and a time to be awake. The Lord counselled His disciples to "rest awhile" after a period of strenuous labour for Him and His kingdom. Some believers get things mixed up; they sleep when they should be awake and are awake when they should be resting.

Some can sleep in the most unlikely of places and times. These hardy souls can sleep sitting bolt upright on a hard pew whilst their eardrums are assaulted by the preacher's strident voice. They are the ones who invariably say, "Good message, Pastor," as they file out after the service. They must measure its "goodness" by the speed with which the sermon puts them over!

But Paul here speaks of those who sleep in the Lord's work. Their eyes are closed, and they have no vision of the great need of a perishing world. Their eyes are blinded to their own sinful and slothful ways. They are unconscious of those who have never heard the gospel of redeeming grace. Their spiritual sleep prevents any action, and so they do little or nothing for Christ. Hence Paul's strident alarm, "Awake to righteousness, and sin not; for some have not the knowledge of God: I speak this to your shame." May this day be one of wide-awake service for Christ.

—F. McC.

Salvation is a helmet, not a nightcap.
VANCE HAVNER

The Single Greatest Desire

One thing have I desired of the Lord.

PSALM 27:4

Adversity always seemed to bring out the best in David. Whether pursued by Saul or betrayed by family, his soul longed for God's power and presence to sustain him through fears, doubts, and temptations. Psalm 27 gives insight into that devout heart that could be content in any situation as long as his experience of God's fellowship was real. Dwelling constantly in the Lord's house ought to be the single greatest desire for every Christian. The benefits of the abiding presence of the Lord are far more important than the form of the dwelling place. Whether a kingly palace, common tent, or cave in the wilderness, any place can be the house of God when the Lord is present. Too often we judge the measure of God's presence by the nature of our circumstances. Walking by sight will never lead to satisfaction.

Two things happen when we earnestly and persistently seek after the Lord: we behold His beauty, and we inquire after Him. To behold means to gaze with our eyes fixed on a special object. The special object of our gaze is the beauty, the pleasant delightfulness, of the Lord. As the bridegroom finds joy in the bride, so should we see the grace and goodness of our Lord. To inquire means to meditate, contemplate, and reflect. We should be preoccupied with our God. All our wants and wishes should converge in Him. If our minds and hearts are filled with Him by faith, then we, like devout David, can know true happiness in the Lord, who is our light and salvation.

—M. P. V. B.

> If there is anything in your life more
> demanding than your longing after God, then
> you will never be a Spirit-filled Christian.
> A. W. Tozer

The Guarding of the Mind

Wherefore gird up the loins of your mind.   I PETER 1:13

Here the apostle sets before us what should be the resolve of every Christian through grace—to guard the mind. There is in this evil day a constant, concerted attack upon the minds of God's people. We are daily exposed to a brainwashing process. Radio, television, videos, the press, and various publications are all instruments hijacked by our subtle enemy to reach our minds. The media constantly presents sin as acceptable in modern society. Drinking, adultery, and unfaithfulness are presented as socially acceptable and the common norm. The unsavoury filth of the world should never be allowed to seep into or sully the mind of the Christian. He must gird up the loins of the mind, as the pilgrim on a journey girded up his robes with a girdle so that he might walk unhindered. So let us keep our garments unspotted from the world and gird our minds lest they get caught up and entangled in the philosophy and thinking of the worldling.

Paul speaks of "loins girt about with truth" (Eph. 6:14). Here is the mind girt and encircled with the word of truth and hedged about with the power of truth. Feed your mind and soul on the manna of Christ in His Word. Keep your mind's eye on Christ, and it will not be able to fix itself on the world. Remember, loose thinking must inevitably lead to loose living.   —R. J. B.

> The same eye cannot both look up to heaven
> and down to the earth at the same time.
> JOHN BROWN

Loved with Everlasting Love

I have loved thee with an everlasting love. JEREMIAH 31:3

When the Lord speaks of His everlasting love, He means the love that gave His Son to be our Saviour and Redeemer. He means His eternal, saving purpose whereby He engages all His divine perfections to bring us safe to glory to enjoy forever the deepest fellowship with Him. This is no passing feeling. It is no surface emotion. It has its source in the depths of the Divine Being. It has its expression in the person of the Lord Jesus Christ. It has its exercise in the ministry of the Holy Spirit, applying Christ's merit according to the Father's purpose to our souls.

This everlasting love had no birthday. It is eternal. Amid the vastness of God's creation I am less than a speck, but from all eternity He set His love on me. What a mystery! What a miracle! How it humbles the heart! God's love obviously did not commence because of some good feature in me. No! It long predates my very existence. God loves me because He loves me. It is a sovereign love.

This everlasting love has no change. It is immutable love. Satan would have me believe that my God will give me up, but he is a liar. My Saviour cries, "How shall I give thee up?" (Hos. 11:8). "Having loved his own . . . , he loved them unto the end" (John 13:1). Despite my changes, His love never fluctuates.

This everlasting love knows no defeat. It infallibly draws to Christ all on whom it rests. God's love is the source of every desire after Him that I have ever felt. I come to Him because He draws me. What an assurance that He will meet with me and answer me! His love will give place to no foe. It will allow no usurper to hold my heart. It is an all-conquering love.

This everlasting love has no end. It lasts as long as God lasts. Here is the prospect I enjoy with every believer: eternity in the full enjoyment of all the love of God. Then let me enjoy a foretaste of that heaven today. God loves me. Nothing must dull my heart to the joy of the greatest sentence God could ever speak to me.

—A. C.

Love so amazing, so divine,
Demands my soul, my life, my all.
ISAAC WATTS

The Triumph of Mercy

Mercy rejoiceth against judgment.

JAMES 2:13

Mercy rejoices against judgment in the salvation of sinners. It glories in the fact that God has found a way to be just and yet justify sinners (Rom. 3:26). God's mercy could never ignore, deny, breach, or weaken the divine law and its just sentence, but it could rejoice that the law was satisfied without the destruction of the sinner. God's mercy is embodied in the Lord Jesus Christ. In Him it bore all the force and fury of the judgment of God against us and our sin and came forth triumphant. Mercy triumphed because Christ exhausted the judgment of God against His people.

Mercy rejoices against judgment in the sanctification of the saints. Mercy makes men merciful. It does not make us indifferent to the pursuit of justice, but it does keep us from hypocrisy. We are all wont to practise a double standard. Like the wicked servant in Christ's parable (Matt. 18:23-35), we want mercy from the Lord but are loath to give it to others. That is our old nature at work. But the Lord sanctifies those He saves so that they delight to treat others as He has treated them. This is why Christians love their enemies and seek the good of those who have wounded them. The triumph of mercy in us, therefore, is to make us more like Christ.

Mercy triumphs over judgment in the happiness and holiness of heaven. The great songs of heaven will all be sung by sinners who are there because of the mercy of God. Every note glories in a perfect justification that stood the rigours of the judgment day. Triumphant mercy justifies, sanctifies, and glorifies believers in Jesus. Can you join in its song?

—A. C.

If God should have no more mercy on us than we have charity one to another, what would become of us?
THOMAS FULLER

210

Enjoying Life

That every man should eat and drink, and enjoy
the good of all his labour, it is the gift of God.

ECCLESIASTES 3:13

Giving gifts is enjoyable; receiving gifts is not so bad either. Our desire in giving presents is to bring happiness to someone. A parent does not set out to give a gift to his child that will make the child unhappy. A husband does not give a present to his wife to make her life miserable. The gift is a token of concern. Although we give gifts to show our love and to make people happy, it would be most distressing if the one to whom we gave the gift became so obsessed with it that they forgot all about us. It would be bad if a wife received her husband's gift and shut him out, claiming that she did not need him since she had such a wonderful gift.

How we respond to God's gift of life says much about us. Some people have become so enamoured of life and its potentials that they see no need of God. The gift is a perversion when separated from the Giver. Others are not satisfied with their gift and assume that God is unfairly making life miserable for them. Solomon declares the proper way to receive the gift of life: eat, drink, and enjoy. Unfortunately, like many statements in Ecclesiastes, this one has been misunderstood. This is not an epicurean recommendation to pleasure. Rather, Solomon means exactly what Paul meant when he said he was content in whatever state God put him. What we drink, eat, and do daily is from the hand of God. We should with grateful contentment receive it from His hand. God has our best interest at heart. No matter what our lot in life or our labour, God has given it for our good.

—M. P. V. B.

Content makes poor men rich;
discontent makes rich men poor.
BENJAMIN FRANKLIN

Faithfulness

They that were scattered abroad went every where preaching the word.
ACTS 8:4

Every Christian ought to be a preacher! That statement may startle some and raise the protest, "But I could never stand before a congregation and speak publicly." Maybe not, but this is not the only sense in which the word *preach* is used in the Scriptures. Public declaration is certainly the intended meaning in verse 5, with reference to Philip's ministry in Samaria, but the word in our text today indicates "conversing" or "gossiping" about the gospel. This is surely something we all can do, and nothing should be allowed to hinder us.

Lack of education did not prevent these disciples from preaching. Many of them could not have written their names, but academic qualifications are not demanded by God as essential to witnessing. An experimental knowledge of Christ enables one to say, "Come and hear . . . what he hath done for my soul" (Psa. 66:16). "It is not great talents that God uses but great likeness to Christ" (R. M. McCheyne). Neither were the disciples silenced by persecution. They had been scattered abroad by the ferocity of Jewish opposition, losing homes and possessions, leaving friends and comfort; yet they ceased not to preach Christ. Threats, losses, imprisonment, the martyrdom of their brethren—none of these could restrain them from declaring the love of Jesus. Nor could their strange and new situation stop them. They may well have reasoned that as newcomers to alien environments they should not make trouble for themselves, but, no, they went "every where preaching the word." Nothing stopped them. What stops us?

—D. F.

The test of your character is what it takes to stop you.
BOB JONES, SR.

Opposite Ends of the Spectrum

A righteous man regardeth the life of his beast:
but the tender mercies of the wicked are cruel.
PROVERBS 12:10

These words, concerning the cruelty of the wicked, have an application to every Christian. How many foolish parents, with feelings of what they conclude is tenderest mercy, spoil their children, give them their every desire, and so hasten them down the road to ruin and damnation. Unenlightened mercy results in the cruelest of conclusions.

These words give an explanation of why the works termed good by men are rejected by God. Man's works are so tainted as to render the best of them utterly unacceptable. Primarily, this verse declares man's depravity. Even the tenderest of feelings within the breast of the wicked are cruel. The record of man's highest endeavours is stained with cruel bloodletting. History rarely gives the full details of the shameful acts that surround mankind's most applauded achievements. The garments of man's noblest adventures are soaked with the blood of innocent suffering. "Man's inhumanity to man" is how we aptly describe his self-inflicted misery.

The grace of God has put a difference between the saint and the sinner. It is a difference of immeasurable magnitude. There is a gulf as broad as that which separates the East from the West. The difference is seen in simple, everyday matters such as the treatment of the dumb beast. Long before there were animal welfare groups there was the grace of God in the heart of the saved sinner. Long before there was national legislation respecting the treatment of animals there was the law of the Word of God. The concern of God for His creatures is inscribed in the law He gave to Moses and Israel. It is also etched upon the new nature which He imparts to the regenerate. The saved man has a concern for his beast. Saved men will cherish the creation that God described as "good."

—I. F.

Every moment is the right one to be kind.
ANONYMOUS

Into Canaan

Go in and possess the land.

DEUTERONOMY 1:8

The Lord has made an unspeakably rich provision for us in Christ. He has given unto us "all things that pertain unto life and godliness" (II Pet. 1:3). It is not God's will for His children to live as spiritual paupers. Yet how many of us are doing just that! It is a contradiction in terms for us to testify that we are "heirs of God, and joint-heirs with Christ" (Rom. 8:17) and live a spiritually impoverished existence. Are you living this contradiction? Are you living in a spiritual wilderness despite the fact that the fulness of Christ and of His Spirit are set before you? Do you long to enter into the personal experience of these blessings? If so, today's text is for you.

"Go in and possess the land." All that is in Christ rightly belongs to every child of God. There is no reason that we should miss the Lord's fulness in our lives, except our own sinful disobedience and unbelief. We must realize this and grasp the fact that it is the Lord's will for us to lay hold of what Christ has purchased for us.

Our progress will be challenged. There is no such thing as a life beyond spiritual conflict this side of the grave. Our flesh would join forces with the devil to keep us out of Canaan. We must therefore mortify the deeds of the flesh and press on with God in full surrender to His will.

What hinders our spiritual life? If we deal with the flesh, we will find God's power to deal with the world and the devil. The land is before us—a land of rich spiritual experience, warfare, and usefulness. Let us not be content to dwell on the borders of Canaan, but "go in and possess the land."

—A. C.

**Shame on us for being paupers
when we were meant to be princes.**
D. MARTYN LLOYD-JONES

Blessings in Afflictions

Before I was afflicted I went astray: but now have I kept thy word.
PSALM 119:67

Martin Luther once said: "I never knew the meaning of God's word until I came into affliction. I have always found it to be one of my best schoolmasters." Notice in today's text the wonderful words that speak of affliction in the life of the child of God.

First of all, we have the psalmist's confession. He confesses the fact that he had gone astray. In the last verse of the psalm he says, "I have gone astray like a lost sheep" (v. 176). The child of God, because of the world and the flesh and the devil, lives always with the possibility of going astray. We will be safe only when we reach the land that is fairer than day.

Second, we have his correction: "I was afflicted." "Such affliction," writes Charles Bridges, "marks Christ's wisdom no less than His love. This is the gracious rod by which He scourges back His prodigal children to Himself." One of the marks of sonship is chastening. In Hebrews 12:5-11 we read how the Lord chastens those whom He loves.

Finally, there is his consecration: "But now have I kept thy word." The psalmist, because of affliction, was now restored to the place of obedience and consecration. This is one of the great sanctifying purposes and blessings of divine affliction. It will bring us back to the place of obedience and dependence upon God and into a deeper and closer walk with Him. This is why the psalmist affirms, "It is good for me that I have been afflicted; that I might learn thy statutes" (Psa. 119:71).

—S. B.

Thy vessels of mercy are first seasoned with affliction, and then the wine of glory is poured in.
THOMAS WATSON

The Word of the Cross

The preaching of the cross. I CORINTHIANS 1:18

The apostle Paul was an extremely well-educated man, and no one can read his epistles without being impressed by his giant intellect. Yet Paul renounced the preaching that uses "wisdom of words" (I Cor. 1:17) for a plainness of speech that left none of his listeners in any doubt about the thrust of his message.

The gospel is not hindered by plainness, but there is an eloquence, an elegance of language, that deprives the gospel of its proper effect. Paul renounced that "wisdom of words," choosing rather to employ "the Word of wisdom."

The word translated "preaching" in the text is *logos,* which simply means "word." So Paul expounded the word of the cross, telling us that it has its own message. It has one message, and it is a distinct one. What is the cross saying to us today?

It tells us that God is just. When man sins, he must die. The Judge of all the earth does right. Sin must be punished. But it also tells us that God is merciful and loving. As a righteous God, He hates evil; yet He gave His sinless Son to be sin for us, that we, through His death, might be reconciled to God. Justice and mercy meet on the cross.

The cross also bears the message that redemption is complete. It is an empty cross leading to an empty tomb. Jesus accomplished a *finished* work. The atonement is complete in Him.

The vertical stake of the cross reaches down into the ground and points up to heaven. Jesus came down to this sin-cursed earth to point sinners to heaven. The horizontal bar points out to mankind and in effect beckons, "Come, and welcome." The gospel of Christ is "the power of God unto salvation to every one that believeth" (Rom. 1:16). Have you experienced its saving power? Why not heed its message now?

—F. McC.

There are no incurable diseases under the gospel.
Any sinner may be healed if he will only come to Christ.
J. C. RYLE

Aaron's Rod Budding

The rod of Aaron . . . brought forth buds,
and bloomed blossoms, and yielded almonds.

NUMBERS 17:8

The rebellion of Korah, Dathan, and Abiram was against the divinely instituted priesthood. However, that insurrection was swiftly crushed, and the Lord gave unmistakable proof that the house of Aaron was the only priestly family in Israel. Aaron's rod supernaturally budded, bloomed, and brought forth fruit—a divine testimony to his priesthood.

The gospel type is clear. Just as Aaron's rod was conspicuous among all the other rods, so Christ our great High Priest stands pre-eminently above all pretended mediators between God and men. Aaron's rod became alive after having been a dead, lifeless branch. It is the resurrection of Christ, the Rod out of Jesse's stem, which gives incontrovertible evidence that He alone is the Priest for sinners. Christ's rising signifies a finished work, a sufficient sacrifice, a satisfactory atonement. As Aaron's living rod was placed in the Holiest of All, so the risen Christ has entered into the holy place not made with hands, to continue His high-priestly ministry.

What *vitality* there is in Christ! Aaron's rod showed the signs of life without being part of a tree. Christ had life in Himself and had power to rise again. That supernatural life is what gives vitality to the church. Because He lives, His people live also. What *beauty* there is in Christ! In the days of His humiliation, there was no beauty in Him that men would desire him. But He rose with the blossoms of a fragrant beauty about Him, having left the grave clothes behind. What *fertility* there is in Christ! As Aaron's rod was covered with buds, blossoms, and almonds simultaneously, so the fruit of Christ's death never ceases to come forth. It is apparent at different stages in His people. Some are budding. Some are blossoming, giving the promise of greater things to come. Some have reached maturity and are fully ripe for glory. What stage have you attained? May we each bear much of His fruitfulness today.

—J. G.

A saving relationship with Christ always
produces spiritual fruitfulness for Christ.
ALEXANDER SIMPSON

Wisdom's Wealth

Wisdom is better than rubies.

PROVERBS 8:11

There is no more likely a place to find Christ than in a chapter which sets forth wisdom's virtues. Wisdom is one of our glorious Saviour's glorious titles. When reading this chapter, for *wisdom* read *Christ Jesus*.

Nothing is freer than wisdom. Its voice is heard crying out its free offer of mercy wherever men are found (vv. 1-9). The Lord Jesus comes at no cost to anyone who accepts Him. All other gifts cost dearly in the end, but not the Saviour. There are no hidden clauses with Him.

Nothing is more precious than wisdom. It is to be desired more than silver or gold. It is of more worth than rubies (vv. 10-11). Christ is the same in value today as He was yesterday and will continue so tomorrow. There is no devaluation with Christ, the treasure of heaven.

Nothing is more beneficial than wisdom. It opens the way to a right application of all the knowledge we gain. It teaches the fear of God. It guides the thrones of kings and princes. It handsomely rewards those who follow its counsel (vv. 12-21). Those who are endued with this wisdom shall shine as the stars forever (Dan. 12:3).

Nothing is more glorious than wisdom. Its imprimatur is found on the architecture of the universe (Prov. 8:22-31). Christ made all things and upholds all things by the power of His Word (Heb. 1:2-3). The life that is yielded to the divine Architect will take on the beauty of holiness, a beauty that outshines earth's glories.

Nothing is more foolish than to close our ears to wisdom's voice. He that finds wisdom finds life. He that sins against wisdom wrongs his own soul (Prov. 8:32-36).

How is this wisdom to be obtained? Why, by receiving Christ. "Christ Jesus . . . is made unto us wisdom" (I Cor. 1:30). There is none wiser than those who are possessed by Christ!

—I. F.

The greatest wisdom on this earth is holiness.
W. S. PLUMER

A Balm for Our Sorrows

*Joint-heirs with Christ; if so be that we suffer
with him, that we may be also glorified together.*

ROMANS 8:17

Thomas Watson, the Puritan divine, wrote: "Man is born to trouble. . . . He comes into the world with a cry, and goes out with a groan." Indeed, the word of the curse in Genesis 3 is *sorrow*. There are no exceptions to this eternal rule, not even for Christians. No, not even for the godliest of Christians. Yet it is quite common for believers to feel that God has left them to themselves when troubles and afflictions come in like a flood. Our text is a remedy for such thinking.

See the light in which Paul views suffering. Note that he says we "suffer with him." What a thought! Not that we suffer *for* Him—although that we do—but that we suffer *with* Him. That is, we suffer not alone, but Christ suffers with us. "In all their affliction he was afflicted" (Isa. 63:9). Do not think for a moment that the Lord has left you in the midst of your sorrow. By faith cast your gaze upon the "friend that sticketh closer than a brother" (Prov. 18:24). Rest your weary head upon the Saviour's bosom. Jesus knows all about your troubles!

But learn beyond this that suffering is God's way of preparing us for glory. "We suffer with him, that we may be also glorified together." Here Paul takes us back to the sorrow of Christ at Calvary. Before Christ could enter into the "joy that was set before him" He had to endure the cross (Heb. 12:2). Always remember that the way to the crown is through the cross. If we suffer together with Christ, it is a sure sign that we will be "glorified together." Perhaps today your heart is breaking with sorrow. Fear not; all is well. God has not left you. He is only stamping the image of His Son deeper upon your heart. Lift up your head, for your redemption draweth nigh!

—J. W.

**All the stones that came about Stephen's
ears did but knock him closer to Christ.**
THOMAS BROOKS

What Does It All Mean?

Vanity of vanities; all is vanity.

ECCLESIASTES 1:2

What is the meaning of life? Philosophers, thinkers, and ordinary men have pondered this question for ages. Man has both an innate desire to know and an inherent inability to know completely. Rationalism answers the question by assigning a reason to everything and denying the existence of anything inexplicable. Existentialism answers by denying meaning to anything; nothing makes sense. Apart from God, man has no hope of escaping the despair and frustration of not knowing the answers to life's questions. Having a saving relationship with God in Christ enables us to live at peace in a world of frustration even if we do not understand everything about life. We may not know all of life's meaning, but our God does. Trust in Him eliminates the frustration of not knowing.

The book of Ecclesiastes is God's revealed philosophy of life for His people. The first thing He wants us to know is that life is vain. The word *vain* literally means "breath." Everything in life is merely a breath. This does not mean life is useless, futile, or meaningless; it does mean that it is transitory and unsubstantial. It agrees exactly with the New Testament answer to the question, "What is your life?" "It is even a vapour, that appeareth for a little time, and then vanisheth away" (James 4:14). Understanding the brevity of life is essential to enjoying and using life as God's precious gift to us. If this life is transitory, we can never find ultimate satisfaction in the things of this life, because God has made us eternal creatures. Jesus said, "This is life eternal, that they might know thee the only true God, and Jesus Christ, whom thou hast sent" (John 17:3). To live without this knowledge of the eternal God can lead only to despair in life and doom in death. Only God can satisfy, both for time and for eternity.

—M. P. V. B.

Make sure the thing you are living for is worth dying for.
C. MAYES

Blessings of God

Blessed be the God . . . who hath blessed us.

EPHESIANS 1:3

While most men bless God for those blessings they can see with their physical eyes, Paul blesses Him for the unseen blessings as well. He describes these blessings as "spiritual" and "in heavenly places." God has chosen (Eph. 1:4), adopted (v. 5), redeemed (v. 7), and forgiven us (v. 7) in Christ. Just as we have never physically seen Christ, so we cannot behold with the eyes of the flesh these many blessings that are connected to His person and work. However, God says they are ours, and by faith in His Word we count them ours.

Although our blessings in Christ are described as spiritual blessings, we must not consider them as less than real. Spiritual reality is greater and more enduring than the "real world" we see around us. In another epistle Paul states, "The things which are seen are temporal; but the things which are not seen are eternal" (II Cor. 4:18). What Paul lists for us in Ephesians chapter 1 remains with us even after we have reached our eternal home and the joys of our earthly existence have faded from our memories. In this world of change and decay, where everything we see and touch is transient, we have this abiding joy: the Lord's saving blessing is everlasting. His election, adoption, redemption, and pardon will never be removed from us. He loves us with an everlasting love.

We must be careful to note that each of God's benefits comes to us through Christ. It is as we walk by faith in Christ that we enjoy our great spiritual possessions. Walking by faith includes believing and laying hold of what we are and have in Christ. Believing these great truths moves our hearts to bless God in our worship. Let us but grasp them, and like the psalmist we will cry, "Bless the Lord, O my soul, and forget not all his benefits" (Psa. 103:2). Truly, we have every reason to bless the Lord.

—M. W. A.

Indeed this is one of the greatest mysteries in the world—
namely, that a righteousness that resides with a person in
heaven should justify me, a sinner, on earth.
JOHN BUNYAN

Judging Righteous Judgment

They came . . . to mourn with him and to comfort him.

JOB 2:11

The book of Job is filled with questions, queries, and puzzling circumstances. On the surface we learn that nothing can be judged by mere outward appearance. The central character was robbed of his possessions, bereaved of his children, deprived of his health and strength, and afflicted by a dreadful disease that gave him a hideous appearance. These fearful calamities befell him, not because of his sin, but because of his spirituality. That in itself is a great mystery.

When Job's three friends heard of his woeful condition, they determined to come and comfort and console. However, when they arrived and saw his wretchedness and utter misery, they immediately concluded that he was a wicked man, a great sinner, and an hypocrite. In this verdict they were entirely wrong, and by the end of the story, they had to apologize to Job and seek to obtain forgiveness from on high. All who bear the name of Christ should ponder these events carefully and beware how we judge others, especially our fellow believers. If we follow in the footsteps of Job's friends, let us not be surprised if the same treatment is returned to us with good measure (Matt. 7:1-2).

Some go to the other extreme and think that no judgment of any kind should be passed upon others. This position cannot be sustained by Scripture. We have a right to examine a person's words and scrutinize his actions. If a preacher who purports to be a servant of Christ stands up and by his words rejects the truth of God, he should be Biblically judged. He is guilty of deceiving and deluding many, and the true minister of the gospel has every right to expose his error, denounce his teaching, and seek to persuade as many as possible to cleave to the truth. The One who was love personified not only preached the Word of God, but publicly and openly denounced all who proclaimed "another gospel." Let us constantly be aware of our responsibilities in Christ and ever seek to make our judgment "righteous judgment" (John 7:24). —S. B. C.

It is but a short step from the critical to the hypocritical.
ANONYMOUS

The Heart a Gift for God

My son, give me thine heart.

PROVERBS 23:26

We were not always "sons." Once we were slaves, bond-slaves to sin. We were held captive under its dreadful and ruinous dominion. Then our great and glorious Redeemer came in all the omnipotency of His grace and broke the power of cancelled sin and set the prisoner free. Once we were strangers, afar off. Now we are made nigh by the blood of Christ. We are fellow citizens with the saints and members of the household of God. "Behold, what manner of love the Father hath bestowed upon us, that we should be called the sons of God" (I John 3:1). Oh, amazing, astonishing love!

Here is the demand of that love, what one preacher called the "most condescending and most affectionate command of the great God of heaven and earth"—*My son, give me thine heart.* How freely, gratefully, and unreservedly it ought to be given! What is it, then, to give our heart to the Lord? It is to love Him supremely. What a man loves most, he gives his heart to. Shall we fail to love the Lord our God with all our heart? Of course, to give our heart to the Lord is also to delight in Him supremely. What a man loves, he delights in. It is to say with the psalmist, "Whom have I in heaven but thee? and there is none upon earth that I desire beside thee" (Psa. 73:25).

Ah, Christian, until the heart is given, nothing is given. Everything is as sounding brass and a tinkling cymbal. Yet when the heart is given, all is given. The heart given stamps the cup of cold water with an untold value and converts the two mites of the widow into a magnificent offering to God.

—M. P.

No man is conquered until his heart is conquered.
GEORGE BARLOW

The Believer's Mandate

Go, and sin no more.

JOHN 8:11

The trial of the woman taken in adultery demonstrates Christ's power to cancel the guilt of sin. The law, represented by the accusing Pharisees, is swift to condemn, but Christ, who came to redeem sinners from the law, here shows that He can silence all accusation against those He pardons. On that day He convicted the hypocrites, cleansed the guilty, and commissioned a new saint with a gospel purpose to live in the world.

To every pardoned soul the Lord says, "Go, and sin no more." Christ cleanses and keeps. He justifies and sanctifies. He plants the seed of holiness in each convert to enable him to strive to sin no more. "Whosoever is born of God doth not commit sin; for his seed remaineth in him: and he cannot sin, because he is born of God" (I John 3:9). The imperative need is to be born of God. Only then does the indwelling Christ control the life.

Holiness of life is the Christian's earnest principle as long as he lives. Augustine prayed, "Lord, save me from that wicked man, myself." We who are born of God are transformed to a new life by Christ's grace in our hearts. One day soon we shall fulfil our mandate perfectly when we shall see the Lord face to face. Then shall we be entirely without sin.

—I. G.

Everything in Scripture has in
view the promotion of holiness.
A. W. PINK

The Secret of Spiritual Power

The Spirit of the Lord came upon him.

JUDGES 3:10

Othniel, the first judge of Israel, was undoubtedly a courageous man and a good soldier. But neither his courage nor his military skill provided the real reason for his victorious campaign against the king of Mesopotamia through which he delivered Israel from bondage. No, the real reason is given in the statement *The Spirit of the Lord came upon him.* That is why he succeeded. Othniel was filled with the Holy Spirit's power for the work to which God had called him.

God's work can be done only in His power. God's power can be communicated only by His Spirit. Thus he who would do a work for God must be filled with the Holy Spirit. Nowadays there is so much emphasis on talent, on training, and on methods that the importance of the fulness of the Holy Spirit is largely overlooked.

The Spirit's fulness of power is necessary for every servant of God. "The flesh profiteth nothing" is never more true than in Christian service. It was in the power of the Spirit that our Lord and His apostles went forth upon their missions. Can we then hope to succeed without the fulness of the Spirit?

That fulness is available to every believer. When the Bible commands us, "Be filled with the Spirit" (Eph. 5:18), it is commanding not what is possible for only a few, but what is the will of God for all His people.

The fulness of the Spirit is closely identified with prayer (Luke 11:13). Let us cry to God that His Spirit will come upon us and our service. It is not some wild charismatic experience we need, not some manufactured state of euphoria. What we need is the power of God to render our service effective to the pulling down of the strongholds of the devil. Let us pray for that power until we receive it.

—A. C.

After a person has become a Christian, the greatest
goal of his life is to be completely filled with the Spirit.
EDWIN H. PALMER

The Joy of Forgiveness

Blessed is he whose transgression is forgiven. PSALM 32:1

Luther called Psalm 32 one of the Pauline psalms because of its glorious message of forgiveness of sins. This song of thanksgiving looks back to the sorrow of sin that could be relieved only by the gracious act of God. It was good for David, and it is good for us, to reflect on the joy of forgiveness. The blessedness of the forgiven man refers to the benefits and fortunes that characterize his state. Whereas the estate of sin is misery, the estate of forgiveness is one of true happiness and fellowship with God.

The first two verses of this psalm are theologically profound and personally precious. When Paul quotes these words in Romans 4, he makes it clear that this justifying forgiveness is completely due to God's grace and not to any merit or worth on our part. In fact, not only do we lack positive merit before the Lord, we have so many demerits that we could never hope to be accepted by Him. We have rebelled against His law; we have missed the mark of His inviolable standard; we have twisted and perverted His ways. Nonetheless, He forgives us by lifting up and taking our sin away as far as the east is from the west. He covers our sins, concealing them from His sight by the atoning blood of Christ. How powerful is that blood to hide our heinous sins from the all-seeing God! He justifies us by not regarding our sins against us. This is the essence of pardon: God reckons our record clean on the merits of Christ's perfect life and death. We are accepted in Christ. It may be impossible for us to understand completely the theology, but we can rejoice in its reality.

—M. P. V. B.

Sins are so remitted as if they had never been committed.
THOMAS ADAMS

An Antidote to Anxiety

*The peace of God, which passeth all understanding,
shall keep your hearts and minds through Christ Jesus.*

PHILIPPIANS 4:7

Paul offers here a timeless and universal remedy for anxiety as
he counsels his readers not to be overly anxious about human
problems. Instead of giving way to such corroding care, the
Philippians are exhorted to commit everything to God in prayer
with thanksgiving for past mercies and present blessings (v. 6).
The antidote to anxiety and prelude to the enjoyment of peace
are to be found in the joint exercise of prayer and thanksgiving.
In prayer, anxiety is resolved by trust in God. That which causes
the anxiety is brought to the One who is totally competent and
in whose hands the matter may be left. In thanksgiving, anxiety is resolved by the acceptance of the worrying circumstance
as something which an all-wise, all-loving, and all-sovereign
God has appointed (Rom. 8:28).

Despite all the excitement and danger of his busy ministry,
Paul had a deep-settled peace: peace with God and the peace of
God, both of which passed all human understanding. Therefore he
could write from experience to the Philippians to encourage them
as they fought the good fight of faith.

Through the ages many saints of God have enjoyed this
blessing, even in times of persecution and deep sorrow. The
peace of God is "perfect" (Isa. 26:3), and it is therefore suited for
every circumstance and adequate for all the burdens we may be
called upon to bear. The city of Philippi was guarded by a Roman
garrison; so Paul's statement that God's peace would keep—
literally, "guard"—their hearts would appeal to his readers. The
peace of God is the garrison of the soul in all the experiences of
life. To all His believing people, God has pledged His guardian
peace and His own presence as the God of peace. —D. C.

> **Peace comes not from the absence of
> trouble, but from the presence of God.**
> ALEXANDER MACLAREN

What Happens When a Believer Sins?

He shall bring a ram . . . for a trespass offering.
LEVITICUS 5:18

Christians ought to live holy lives. Their sins have been blotted out by the precious blood of Christ, and their lives should be examples of godly living. But what happens when a believer sins? Most Christians do not commit open sins, but what about those sins committed even in ignorance? Is there cleansing from these?

The Lord in His infinite wisdom gave the children of Israel a series of sacrifices, each one having a different emphasis. The burnt offering was a picture of the sacrificial work of Christ on the cross. The meat offering, an unbloody sacrifice, pictured the work of sanctification, in which we are to give of our best to the Master. The peace offering again pictures Calvary, but centres on the benefits the believer receives from Christ's death, namely, peace. The sin and trespass offerings were made after the others had been offered. In other words, these offerings had to do with the lingering defilements of contact with this sinful world.

As guilty sons and daughters of Adam's fallen race, we must acknowledge our natural bent towards sin. It is only the sustaining grace of God that keeps us from sin. With all his efforts, the best Christian is still faulty. And Leviticus makes it clear that ignorance of our sin is no excuse. We are guilty before God.

But God made a way for Israel to deal with these lingering defilements. The sin and trespass offerings foreshadow Christ on the cross. Thank God, we have a trespass offering in Christ. The apostle John encouraged the saints not to sin, but he went on to say, "If any man sin, we have an advocate with the Father, Jesus Christ the righteous" (I John 2:1). Does some sin, known or unknown, steal your peace today? Come, confess it to Christ, and He will cleanse it. Start this day with a clean conscience, trusting the merits of the shed blood.

—F. McC.

The way to cover our sin is to uncover it by confession.
RICHARD SIBBES

The Precious Blood

*Ye were not redeemed with corruptible things, as silver
and gold, . . . but with the precious blood of Christ.*

I PETER 1:18, 19

Hugh Brown as a young man on the threshold of his ministry read
these words in an old volume in his library: "The blood must stand
out in solitary splendour." He determined to make that the basis
of his ministry as he set out to witness for the Lord.

The blood stands out in solitary splendour in this chapter.
There are three incorruptible things mentioned, and they are all
in heaven. In verse 4 the incorruptible inheritance is in heaven; in
verse 23 the incorruptible Book is settled in heaven; and in verses
18-19 the incorruptible blood is likewise in heaven. Who can speak
highly enough of this precious, incorruptible, living blood of Christ?

It is invaluable blood; it is precious. The value of the blood
resides in the value of the Person to whom it belongs. Who can
value the unique Person of the God-Man? The blood of Christ is
the blood of incarnate deity. Thus the Holy Spirit estimates the
value of Christ's blood not only according to His sinless humanity,
but according to His divine nature. He speaks of "the church of
God, which he hath purchased with his own blood" (Acts 20:28).

It is impeccable blood, "as of a lamb without blemish and
without spot" (I Pet. 1:19). In order to ensure the purity of the
blood, God wrought the miracle of the virgin birth. How inscrutable was the wisdom of God in producing Christ's true humanity
while safeguarding the purity of His blood! Let us constantly
make much of the blood and praise God for its efficiency to save
and to cleanse.

—R. J. B.

Its value it eternal, its worth is infinite, its energy
is omnipotent, its sufficiency is everlasting.

ANDREW MURRAY

229

God Is on Our Side!

I am for you.

EZEKIEL 36:9

Ezekiel 35:3 contains the very worst words the enemies of God can hear: *Behold, . . . I am against thee.* Chapter 36 has the very best words for the feeble saint: *Behold, I am for you.*

These words are a reminder that *God's purposes will be opposed.* All which is not of God is against us. The devil is against us. The world is against us. Our own failings are against us. But God is for us. All which is of God is for us. God's Word is for us. God's mighty power is for us. God's sovereignty is invincible. He will carry out His own purpose. On this account Paul inquires, "Who can be against us?" (Rom. 8:31).

We are also reminded that *God's purposes will work to our ultimate advantage.* In Romans 8:28 Paul argues, "We know that all things work together for good to them that love God, to them who are the called according to his purpose." In Ezekiel 36 the prophet builds line upon line in obvious progression: "I will turn unto you"; "I will multiply men upon you"; "the wastes shall be builded" (vv. 9, 10). Best of all, the God of Israel promises, "I will settle you after your old estates, and will do better unto you than at your beginnings: and ye shall know that I am the Lord" (v. 11). The best is yet to be—all things working for good and His people knowing God as never before.

Finally, *God's purposes are related to His people.* "For, behold, I am for you." The promise is irreversible. There is a message in this for Israel, too. The chapter is specifically addressed to them. God will bring His own people back to Himself. What a promise for the backslidden, the unworthy, the defeated, the discouraged! There is victory in Christ. "Who shall separate us from the love of Christ?" (Rom. 8:35). "Who shall lay any thing to the charge of God's elect?" (v. 33). "Nay, in all these things we are more than conquerors through him that loved us" (v. 37).

—J. D.

All of God's giants have been weak men
who did great things for God because
they reckoned on His being with them.
J. HUDSON TAYLOR

Apathy Rebuked

*Is it time for you, O ye, to dwell in your
cieled houses, and this house lie waste?*

HAGGAI 1:4

Apathy is a real problem to the work of God. The literal meaning of *apathy* is "without feeling." Christians often have to lament that they have little or no feeling for the things of God.

The prophet Haggai was raised up to rebuke the Jews for a prolonged season of apathy. For thirty years no work had been done on the rebuilding of the temple, and the people were making the excuse that the time was not opportune for the recommencement of the building programme. With withering scorn, Haggai asked the Jews whether the time was opportune for them to be building ornate houses for themselves while nothing was being done for God's house.

Haggai put his finger on the real cause for the people's failure to get on with the building work: their apathy had been brought on by worldliness. The word *cieled* indicates that the Jews' own houses were covered and panelled with the most expensive timber. It is hard to have much feeling for God's house when your heart is set on your own, on making it beautiful and ornate and better than your neighbour's. Haggai showed the Jews that apathy brings disappointment and dissatisfaction, and he encouraged them to get back to the work that God had appointed for them.

While your heart is set on the things of the world, you cannot have any real feeling of satisfaction or fulfilment. You are sure to encounter continual disappointments and frustrations. The reason the church so often lacks its note of praise and triumph is that the people of God are caught up in the world and are cold and unfeeling towards the Lord and His work. It is time we recognized this unfeeling attitude as sinful and repented of it.

—G. F.

**Nothing is so offensive to Christ
as lukewarmness in religion.**
J. C. Ryle

231

Printed for Thomases

Except I shall see in his hands the
print of the nails, . . . I will not believe.

JOHN 20:25

Thomas was slow to believe, but was totally convinced at the end. He paid dearly for being absent from the fellowship of the disciples when the risen Lord first appeared to them. His absence left him in doubt and despair for a further week. It must have been a week of coldness and blank numbness within his soul as he wrestled with the events of Christ's death and reports of His resurrection. There were no comforts or blessings through Thomas's witness during those days of scepticism. Unbelief is a rotten and fruitless plant.

However, Thomas was present when the Lord appeared again to His disciples eight days later. On that occasion the Lord, knowing full well of Thomas's struggle, singled him out and invited him to behold the print of the nails in His hands. Thomas's unbelief disappeared at the sight of Christ, and he expressed his total belief in the risen Lord, stating, "My Lord and my God" (v. 28). The nail prints were enough to dispel all doubts and to create a living faith in doubting Thomas.

It is the sight of those nail prints in the Saviour's hands that transforms doubters into believers today. What was printed in the Saviour's hands for Thomas to see and believe is recorded in Holy Scripture for us to read and believe. The written Word of God is printed for us to deliver us from all doubts. May the Lord show us all the truth that He "died for our sins according to the scriptures; and that he was buried, and that he rose again the third day according to the scriptures" (I Cor. 15:3, 4), that we may not be faithless, but believing.

—I. G.

The Scriptures are in print what Christ is in person.
The inspired Word is like a faithful portrait of Christ.
A. W. TOZER

The Ribband of Blue

Remember all the commandments of the Lord, and do them.
NUMBERS 15:39

The setting of these words is very instructive. The Lord commanded the Israelites to put a "ribband of blue" in the fringe along the borders of their garments. Each time they looked upon those ribbons they were to "remember all the commandments of the Lord, and do them." The colour blue in Scripture speaks of heaven. Thus these ribbons reminded the believing Israelites that the commandments of the Lord were heavenly in origin. The ribbons also taught them that they were a heavenly people with laws from heaven for life on earth, and thus a people who must not do just as they pleased. They were not to walk after the way of the flesh, which is interpreted in the same verse as seeking "after your own heart and your own eyes." Hence the ribbon of blue was a visible warning against the outbreak of the corruption of the flesh. If we are of the heavenly people of God, then let us "make not provision for the flesh, to fulfil the lusts thereof" (Rom. 13:14). Rather let us walk "in all the commandments and ordinances of the Lord blameless" (Luke 1:6).

The ribbon of blue is a reminder also that there is deliverance from the weakness, failure, and corruption of the flesh, deliverance through Christ. Do you remember the woman in the Gospels who came and touched the border of Christ's garment? When she did so she was appropriating all that the fringe with its ribbon of blue stood for. Christ is the only one who ever perfectly remembered the commandments of the Lord and satisfied their demands by rendering flawless obedience. Thus the hem of His garment signified redemption from the curse of the law. The law is "holy, and just, and good" (Rom. 7:12). It is spiritual, but we are "carnal, sold under sin" (v. 14). Is there any hope for a poor, dying sinner? Thank God there is. Reach out the hand of faith today and rest in Christ's finished work, for those who touch Him are made perfectly whole.

—J. G.

**An obedient Christian lives his life amid the things
of earth but sets his love on the things of heaven.**
ALEXANDER SIMPSON

The True Teaching of Christ

Ye have not so learned Christ.

EPHESIANS 4:20

Paul taught daily in the school of Tyrannus for the space of two years. Judging from his epistles, the content of his teaching would differ greatly from that in schools today. There are many schools that pride themselves on their communication of knowledge, but they say little of Christ. In contrast, Paul taught that in Christ "are hid all the treasures of wisdom and knowledge" (Col. 2:3). How much real knowledge and wisdom are received in a school that shuns Christ? Many a diploma could read, "Ye have not learned Christ." There are also churches over whose doors the same statement could be hung. Moral truths or principles of Christian living are taught with little mention of, or no reference to, Christ. This condemnation can even apply to many Christian homes. The home is to be the centre for the teaching of God's Word (Deut. 6:7-9). Do we neglect this responsibility or try to give it to others? If the light of Christ does not shine in these places of learning, then darkness reigns no matter how much other so-called knowledge is imparted.

But Paul says, "Ye have not *so* learned Christ." Paul is dealing with the manner in which Christ is taught and the effect this teaching has on the heart. Some know about Christ in their heads, but this knowledge has never changed their hearts. The Ephesians did not learn such theoretical knowledge from Paul. We must guard ourselves from an armchair theology that does not work in the battles of life. In the last three chapters of Ephesians, Paul takes the great truths concerning Christ and applies them to every area of our lives. May we diligently so learn Christ in our day.

—M. W. A.

Teachers may put good things into our heads but
it is God only that can put them into our hearts.
MATTHEW HENRY

The Comfort of Predestinating Grace

Before I formed thee in the belly I knew thee.

JEREMIAH 1:5

The Lord clearly intends the fact of His predestination to bring comfort and consolation to His people. Jeremiah found this out when God appointed him as His prophet to the nations. The young man was not surprisingly overawed by such a task. He protested, "Ah, Lord God! behold, I cannot speak: for I am a child" (v. 6). The Lord's response was to give him a glimpse of His eternal purpose. "I knew you; I formed you; I sanctified you; I have appointed you."

God's foreknowledge of His people is more than foresight of what they would naturally become. It is the knowledge of a personal, loving choice in Christ (Eph. 1:4, 5). It is the predetermination of a gracious purpose toward us. All He does subsequently is based on this sovereign goodwill and favour.

The eternal purpose of God is made known in time by His effectual call to His people. It is vain and sinful for men to try to discover, "Am I elect? Did God predestinate me to salvation?" Such questions are usually employed as excuses for refusing to receive Christ as He is freely offered in the gospel. The Lord made known His predestination to Jeremiah only after He had called him. Once we receive God's call by His Word and Spirit, we can rejoice in the hidden springs of such grace in His eternal predestination.

That predestination is a source of great comfort. The Lord knew and loved us from eternity. He formed us for this hour. Our circumstances do not disturb His plan. "We know that all things work together for good to them that love God. . . . For whom he did foreknow, he also did predestinate . . . , [and] them he also called . . . , [and] them he also justified . . . , [and] them he also glorified" (Rom. 8:28-30).

Let us then rejoice in the eternal, electing, distinguishing, and unchangeable love of our God to us. Let that truth really grip our hearts, and nothing in the world will move us from serving Him.

—A. C.

Nothing makes a man so truly bold as to feel he is God's elect. He shall not quiver, he shall not shake, who knows that God has chosen him.
C. H. Spurgeon

How To Run the Race

Looking unto Jesus the author and finisher of our faith.

HEBREWS 12:2

Christ Himself is to be the single object of our attention in the spiritual race which we pursue. The word *looking* comes from a verb which means "to look away from." It denotes the idea of viewing with undivided, fixed, earnest attention.

This is the look of *total dependence* upon Christ for all we need as we run. Christ is the source of all our requirements. Thus the verse can be read, "Looking *into* Jesus"—a deep, penetrating look, filling our minds with all that Christ is, constantly communing with Him and drawing out of Him strength for the course.

To run "looking into Jesus" also indicates *total obedience*. In the context, Paul reminds us that there is a race set before us (v. 1). We must fix our purpose on that race and allow nothing to divert our attention. That is possible only as we are taken up with the Lord. What obedience is generated in us as we keep our eyes on Him! You see, He ran His race with full commitment to the Father. Nothing could prevail upon Him to keep Him from doing the Father's will. As He obeyed because He loved His Father, so love for Christ alone will stir up our hearts to run the race set before us. The more we love Christ, the more we will lay aside those things which would hinder us—our besetting sins, which are our inward corruptions, and the things of the world, the weights that would hold us back.

Furthermore, this "looking unto Jesus" refers to *total steadfastness* in our running. We should want to run well and complete the race. Christ did so. He is the "author and finisher of our faith." The word *author* also means "prince" or "captain," denoting a leader. He has gone before us; so He has covered the ground already. What an example of steadfastness! Thus "let us run with patience" (v. 1).

—J. G.

Too much occupied with our work, we
can forget our Master—it is possible to
have the hands full and the heart empty.

THEODORE MONOD

236

The Revelation of the Lord

The heathen shall know that I am the Lord.

EZEKIEL 36:23

These words or their equivalent occur some sixty-four times in Ezekiel. This key theme in the prophecy speaks of the manifestation of the Lord in grace or glory. God is going to make Himself known mightily among men. It will be a revelation—epochal, consummate, glorious. The whole earth shall know it (38:23).

This is significant news for *the Christian.* There is progression in the Christian life. Salvation is knowing the Lord. After salvation the child of God will want to know more of Him. Paul, some thirty years on the road, testified that knowing the Lord more and more was his goal in life: "That I may know him, and the power of his resurrection" (Phil. 3:10). The believer anticipates that glad day, eclipsing all other days, when he will see Jesus. Now he sees through the glass darkly, but then face to face. What shall the coming of the Lord Jesus mean to me? I shall know Him as never before.

This news is also significant for *restored Israel.* How remarkable has been their history! The patriarchs and the prophets knew God, as did some others, but on the whole the nation did not. At length the Messiah came. He first saw the light of day as an infant in the land. He walked among the people, performed His wonders, and proclaimed His Word. Yet they knew Him not. They rejected Him and nailed Him to a tree. What shall the coming of this Christ be, when men shall look on Him whom they have pierced, when they shall know that He is the Lord?

Finally, this news is significant for *the heathen,* the wicked of the earth who have hated God, blasphemed His name, and abused His people. All such have a discovery to make. They will find out at last who God is, but they will find out too late. O Lord, let me truly come to know Thee now.

—J. D.

When Christ comes again, the remains
of ignorance shall be rolled away.
J. C. RYLE

Faith That Works

Faith without works is dead.

JAMES 2:20

There is a faith that does not save. It is not even worthy of being called faith. It is but a counterfeit of true, saving faith in Christ. This counterfeit faith may be very orthodox in its doctrine. Indeed, it may be vociferous in its stand for the doctrines of the Bible. It can dot every *i* and cross every *t*. It loves theological hair-splitting and will make a man a heretic for a word. This false faith is very religious. It looks good. It sounds good. But in truth it is an evil thing. It has the stench of death about it, because when all is said and done, it simply does not work. A faith that does not produce good and holy works is a faith that is no better than what the devil has (James 2:19). Oh! let us take this personally and seriously. If your professed belief allows you to live comfortably in sin, if it does not work repentance and holiness within you, it is a dead faith. It is true that we are saved by faith without works. It is equally true that we are saved by a faith that works.

Does your faith work? Does it stir up your heart to do the will of God and to seek the welfare of men? If godly works are the evidence of saving faith, is there any evidence that you are saved? Now is the time to face this question, because a faith that does not work for God now will not work for you on the judgment day.

—A. C.

It is faith alone that justifies, but
the faith that justifies is not alone.
JOHN CALVIN

A Prayer from the Depths

Then Jonah prayed unto the Lord his God out of the fish's belly.
JONAH 2:1

The Lord Jesus Christ told His disciples that when they prayed they should go to their room, shut the door, and pray to their Father in secret. Jonah could not quite manage that; he was in a fish's belly! But while the place of prayer was unique, the prayer itself could have been prayed anywhere on earth at any time.

When Jonah prayed, he was in a desperate situation. Physically he seemed lost in the belly of the fish. He felt as if the mountains were standing on top of him and the earth had closed and bolted its doors against him. He said, "Out of the belly of hell cried I. . . . I am cast out of thy sight" (vv. 2, 4). Unparalleled loneliness and despair must have gripped the prophet's heart.

In this seemingly hopeless situation, Jonah prayed. He prayed at the best possible time, for when there are no props left, that is the time to look to God. He prayed in the best possible way, for he looked towards God's holy temple, the place of sacrifice and reconciliation. In prayer Jonah used the best possible arguments, for he kept quoting the Word of God, particularly the book of Psalms. And Jonah's prayer was answered: verse 10 tells us that "the Lord spake unto the fish, and it vomited out Jonah upon the dry land."

Whenever you find yourself in a hopeless position, when it seems that all is lost beyond hope of recovery, you must pray. The devil will tell you it is no time to pray; God's Word shows you otherwise. Pray, quoting God's Word to Him; pray in the best possible way, looking to the Saviour who died for sinners and made reconciliation for them at Calvary. "Men ought always to pray, and not to faint" (Luke 18:1).

—G. F.

> The angel fetched Peter out of prison,
> but it was prayer fetched the angel.
> THOMAS WATSON

A Cause for Tears and Joy

Rejoice for joy with her, all ye that mourn for her.

ISAIAH 66:10

Lamentation and laughter have always followed hard on each other's heels in the church of Christ. There is "a time to weep, and a time to laugh" (Eccles. 3:4), because there is good cause for each.

There is much cause for mourning in Zion. This is a day of spreading apostasy. Entire churches are returning to the medieval delusions from which they were rescued by the Reformation in the sixteenth century. The gospel of free grace is denied or down-played. What is preached as the gospel in most quarters today is far removed from the message of Christ and His apostles. Ruin by the fall, regeneration by the Spirit, and redemption by the blood are out of date as far as most churches are concerned. The grand truth of justification by faith alone—the article of a standing or a falling church, according to Martin Luther—is conspicuous by its absence. Even evangelicals have shared in the debacle. Most of them see no relevance in the gospel for the problems and pressures of everyday life. That is why they turn to psychological gimmicks and are disappointed. We could go on listing causes for mourning—compromise with sin and error, spiritual power-lessness, and little real praying.

The depressing catalogue should convict us. It should drive us to our knees in confession and in repentance. Surely no Christian can contemplate such a situation without a fervent cry to God for pardon and quickening.

Despite everything, there is much cause for joy in Zion. Our God is still on the throne and has power to hear our cry for restoration and revival. The victory is His, and He will make it ours. Lament your sin. Turn from it, and the Lord will turn your tears to joy.

—A. C.

There may be joy *in* God when there is little joy *from* God.
STEPHEN CHARNOCK

Three Urgent Needs

*Gold ... that thou mayest be rich; and white raiment, that thou
mayest be clothed, ... and ... eyesalve, that thou mayest see.*
REVELATION 3:18

Only the Lord Jesus Christ can give us what our souls need. If you
are trying to satisfy your soul with what the world has to offer, you
are doomed to disappointment. This is particularly true of every
blood-washed Christian. You are spoiled for the world. Only Christ
can satisfy your soul. He offers us real wealth, "gold tried in the
fire." The riches of His grace are no fool's gold. They are the true
wealth of heaven. Ephesians chapter 1 gives us an inventory of
this wealth. Blessed with all spiritual blessings in Christ, we are
rich indeed. Lay hold of this wealth. Stretch out the hand of faith
and take all that the Saviour offers you. There is no need for you
to live as a spiritual pauper even for one more day. The rich fulness
of Christ is yours to enjoy.

He offers us the perfect answer to the guilt and shame we
often feel. In this Laodicean age we need to learn this truth.
Laodicea was famous for the clothes it made from black wool.
Jesus says, "Have done with the garments of Laodicea, and put on
My white robes of perfect righteousness." God imputes to His
people the righteousness of Christ. Indeed, He makes Christ to be
our righteousness (I Cor. 1:30). Lay hold of that truth and you will
have the perfect answer to every lingering feeling of guilt for the
sins of your unregenerated past.

How to lay hold of these things is the problem. The Lord Jesus
says we need eyesalve to enable us to see, or to understand, these
spiritual truths. Ask for sight to perceive the fulness you as a
Christian have in Christ. Pray that you may perceive and grasp
the riches and the righteousness He has made over to you. When
you see these things you will feel like David when he said, "By my
God have I leaped over a wall" (Psa. 18:29).　　—A. C.

**There is no hurdle too high for those
who live in the fulness of Christ.**
ALEXANDER SIMPSON

Lessons in the Night

Weeping may endure for a night, but joy cometh in the morning.
PSALM 30:5

For one reason or another the people of God have always experienced afflictions, persecutions, and opposition. The apostle Paul endured trouble after trouble in his service for Christ. Through it all, he found God's grace sufficient. The Christian life is one of faith; it is a life of self-insufficiency. From the moment of salvation to every aspect of daily living, the Christian must be dependent on God. One of the reasons trouble comes into our lives is to increase our sense of that dependence. When the night comes, it is good to pay attention to what God wants to teach us.

Psalm 30 shows the way God uses darkness to make us better. *Before affliction*, the psalmist felt secure in himself (vv. 6, 7). Everything was going smoothly—no battles to fight, no opposition. His ease was pleasurable, but not spiritually profitable. Human nature being what it is, the sunshine is usually more dangerous than the storm. In the providence of God, the night came. *During affliction*, the psalmist first misunderstood what was happening (v. 9) and then sought the Lord for deliverance (v. 10). That is the way it usually is for us. As soon as things go wrong, we feel sorry for ourselves and misread God's dealings as harsh and uncaring. The sooner we quit moping and groping in darkness and seek the Lord, the sooner we will see the light. *After affliction*, the psalmist was able to put things in the proper perspective. What seemed to be such a long night was just a brief moment compared to the daylight of God's favour (vv. 5, 11). There will always be a morning to end the mourning. When we learn the lessons of the night, we, like the psalmist, will celebrate God's goodness with joy and thanksgiving (vv. 1-4).

—M. P. V. B.

I never knew the meaning of God's
Word until I came into affliction.
MARTIN LUTHER

Habitual Holiness

Ye shall be holy men unto me. EXODUS 22:31

There is no argument for the message of the gospel like a holy life. The children of the world may never take time to listen to the loudest and most eloquent professions of faith, but they cannot fail to be impressed by a clean, Christlike life. It is no surprise that the counsel of the Lord to each one of His disciples is simply "Be ye holy" (I Pet. 1:16).

A holy life will tell in our habits. There will be no place in our daily behaviour for those practices which are out of step with a testimony for Christ. We will not indulge the flesh, even in those areas that are considered legitimate for a man of the world. Life is made up of habits—mundane, routine, everyday actions. We must be careful to see that they are all consistent with our profession of Christ.

A holy life will tell in our speech. The Bible warns against the use of "filthy communication." As Peter was betrayed by his Galilean accent, so the Christian should be betrayed, in a positive sense, by the language he uses. Our speech should be pure. Christ was commended to the crowds by His speech. "Never man spake like this man" (John 7:46).

A holy life will tell in our thoughts. The mind is the ground on which many a battle is fought. Temptation will assail us. When it comes we must turn from it, pleading all the help of Christ. If we are to cultivate the fruits of the Spirit, then we must keep the seedbed clean.

Christian living is holy living. Holiness for the believer is not an option, but an obligation.　　　　　—T. N.

Let the main sermon of your life be illustrated by all your conduct, and it shall not fail to be illustrious.
C. H. SPURGEON

Guidance

Being sent forth by the Holy Ghost.

ACTS 13:4

Paul and Barnabas laboured in the certain knowledge that they were selected of God, separated unto God, and servants of God. In His harvest field, it is the Lord alone who can appoint the men, the task, and the sphere of service. God's people must seek to be certain of the will of the Lord for them individually. Moses had no doubt from his experience at the burning bush what his duty was; Isaiah would always be sure of his responsibility because of the vision he had in the temple; Gideon could be certain from his meeting with the Lord at the winepress what he must do. Such knowledge makes all the difference in a Christian's ministry.

First, it inspires *faithfulness*. "It is required in stewards, that a man be found faithful" (I Cor. 4:2). What keeps a man pressing on consistently and determinedly in his task is the firm conviction that he has a divine commission to fulfill. A solemn responsibility rests upon him. He has been appointed by God and is accountable to Him.

This awareness will also promote *fearlessness*. The Christian speaks as the ambassador of Christ (II Cor. 5:20). He knows that he brings the Word of the King, and there is a solemn and weighty "thus saith the Lord" in his message. Authority marks his ministry, and he speaks the Word of God with boldness (Acts 4:31).

Finally, it assures *fruitfulness*. God never calls a believer to a specific task to mock him. Our labour is "not in vain in the Lord" (I Cor. 15:58). Let us seek to know God's will for us and faithfully and fearlessly labour, assured that "in due season we shall reap, if we faint not" (Gal. 6:9).

—D. F.

The will of God is not something we are just to understand; it is something we are to undertake.
G. B. DUNCAN

A Seed To Sow

Being born again, not of corruptible seed, but of incorruptible,
by the word of God, which liveth and abideth for ever.

I PETER 1:23

The Bible assures us of the reliability and uniqueness of this seed spoken of by Peter. It is first of all a *precious* seed (Psa. 126:6). How precious is the Word of God to you? It is precious because there is none like it. We say of it as David said of the sword of Goliath, "There is none like that; give it me" (I Sam. 21:9). Sadly, familiarity does breed contempt; we have Bibles in our homes, but too often they are dust-covered and neglected. May God renew to our souls the preciousness of the holy seed of the Bible.

It is also spoken of as a *pure* seed (Psa. 12:6). The Word of God is as pure as God Himself. There are no tares among this wheat. Every grain is pure. Yet an enemy has sown tares in the host of perverted versions that have lately appeared purporting to be the Word of God. God says in Leviticus 19:19, "Thou shalt not sow thy field with mingled seed." What a sad harvest such perverted seed must eventually produce!

Then it is spoken of as a *powerful* seed (Heb. 4:12). The power of God is in this Word. A dying infidel commanded that his grave should be covered with a massive slab of concrete and then said, "If this should ever crack, then there might be a resurrection." His grave was thus covered, but beneath it a little seed of a tree was buried. Nature took its course, the seed germinated, and the plant wound its way upwards towards the light, cracking the concrete as it grew. The infidel was condemned, and God's Word was vindicated. So the powerful seed of God's Word vindicates God and silences the infidel.

—R. J. B.

The Word generates faith and regenerates us.
JOSEPH ALLEINE

Right Words

A word fitly spoken is like apples of gold in pictures of silver.
PROVERBS 25:11

A servant of God called on a businessman, having felt led to speak to him about Christ. A conversation something like this ensued:

"What can I do for you?"

"I would like to speak with you, if I might, about your soul and its eternal interests."

"Oh, I am very sorry, but I am just far too busy."

He was so insistent that the Christian man put out his hand to say good-bye and, drawing closer to the astonished listener, said quietly, "Suppose I had been Death?" This solemn reminder of the brevity of life and the necessity of being prepared for a visitor that would not be put off, however unwelcome his appearance, brought that man to the Saviour. A word fitly spoken indeed!

Solomon speaks here of a beautiful work of Oriental art, one of painstaking skill and labour. It is precious; it is rare. Alas, so is the "word fitly spoken." How many a thoughtless word is spoken! Carefully weigh your words. Strive to find out acceptable words. How essential is that wisdom that comes from above, if we are to speak the right word to the right person.

How many a good word is lost by being spoken out of season! Our Lord is one who ever knows how to speak a word in season to him that is weary. How often He has spoken such a word to our hearts! The soulwinner needs a holy tact. The word *tact* comes from the Latin *tangere*, "to touch." The word fitly spoken will always touch the heart. How precious is such a word! It will be as a nail in a sure place. As Job said, "How forcible are right words!" (Job 6:25).

—M. P.

The best tact in soulwinning is prayerful contact.
ANONYMOUS

Overcoming in Adversity

Redeeming the time, because the days are evil.

EPHESIANS 5:16

Paul was looking at the world from God's viewpoint when he said, "The days are evil." From the standpoint of man they may have been days of trouble or distress. Or some may have considered them days of mighty accomplishments. Yet the Lord said, "The days are evil." He sees the great wickedness in the heart of man and judges the days, not by the standard of discovery and invention, but by the spiritual climate of the times. How often we hear someone describing our century as days of great scientific advancement or educational achievement. Man is able to speak in glowing terms of what he has done while overlooking his own crimes against the Creator and his fellow man. The discerning eye, however, agrees with the apostle: "The days are evil."

Other men, although they agree with Paul that the days are evil, see only the evil. They are completely ignorant of the work of God taking place in the midst of evil days. While Paul could honestly assess the wickedness of his generation, he was also convinced that the gospel of Christ could overcome that evil (Rom. 1:16). To hear some Christians talk, you would think that the church ought to retreat to a monastery and hide from this evil age. Paul was of the opposite opinion, and he proved the power of the gospel in his day.

Our Christ is seated at God's "right hand in the heavenly places, far above all principality, and power" (Eph. 1:20-21). This is not the time for us to sound the retreat, but to move ahead by looking to Christ. For this reason Paul exhorts us to redeem the time. We are to seize the opportunities that lie before us and proclaim the gospel whose light can dispel the darkness of this age (Col. 4:5, 6).

—M. W. A.

The Lord has a golden sceptre and an iron rod. Those who will not bow to the one, shall be broken by the other.

THOMAS WATSON

God's Immutability

*God is not a man, that he should lie; neither
the son of man, that he should repent.*

NUMBERS 23:19

Not only did Balaam find it impossible to curse Israel, he also found himself stating the reason he could not: the immutability of God. God is unchangeable, confirming the security of His people. "I am the Lord, I change not; therefore ye sons of Jacob are not consumed" (Mal. 3:6). Since the Lord is immutable, so then is His Word, hence Balaam's emphasis on the impossibility of God's either lying or repenting. Men change their minds and therefore break their word, but God does neither. He never changes His mind and therefore never recalls His promise.

What a great comfort this is in a world of constant change! With God there is neither variableness nor shadow of turning. Consequently, what God has promised concerning His people, He will do. This truth is intended to strengthen and increase our faith. Do you find that the canker of unbelief often eats at your soul? If so, meditate much on this great doctrine, that God's promises, like Himself, are unalterable. It was that assurance that kept Abraham from staggering at the promise of God in unbelief. He was persuaded "that, what he had promised, he was able also to perform" (Rom. 4:21).

Another result of God's unchangeability is that His blessing of His people cannot be reversed. Even Balaam was made to recognize that, for he proceeded to say, "He hath blessed; and I cannot reverse it" (Num. 23:20). God's blessings are irreversible because they are based on His immutable covenant. He will never break nor be unmindful of that covenant. Its blessings are sealed to His people by the precious blood of the Mediator of the covenant, the Lord Jesus Christ. Every benefit He secured by His death, His people will surely receive. God's immutability guarantees that.

—J. G.

**God may change our circumstances, but
our circumstances can never change God.**
JOHN BLANCHARD

Tribulation

We must through much tribulation enter into the kingdom of God.
ACTS 14:22

The Lord has not promised His people an easy pathway to heaven. He assured His disciples, "In the world ye shall have tribulation" (John 16:33). Those who preach a Christian life of ease and prosperity, free from discomfort and adversity, do not proclaim the message of Christ and the apostles. "Beloved, think it not strange concerning the fiery trial which is to try you, as though some strange thing happened unto you" (I Pet. 4:12), but regard it as the certain lot of Christians.

But while tribulation is certain, we can rejoice that it is controlled. By whom? By Him who "worketh all things after the counsel of his own will" (Eph. 1:11). He is the Refiner who places the precious gold in the fire. He knows the intensity of heat and duration of time that it must endure in the furnace until His purpose is accomplished. To change the figure, we are the clay in the hands of the Potter, who knows how much pressure to apply and when and where to apply it. Nothing that we are as believers is outside the control of our sovereign God and loving Father. The comfort in all our afflictions is to remember that His intention is not our detriment or destruction, but our good (Rom. 8:28). His purpose is good, and His presence is guaranteed. He will never leave us nor forsake us (Heb. 13:5), and He will give us grace sufficient for every test (II Cor. 12:9).
—D. F.

**The refiner is never very far from the mouth
of the furnace when His gold is in the fire.**
C. H. SPURGEON

The Hope of the Hypocrite

For what is the hope of the hypocrite, though
he hath gained, when God taketh away his soul?

JOB 27:8

Poor Job had many woes to bear during his time of devilish affliction. Alongside the heavy burdens of poverty, bereavement, and disease was the dreadful stigma of hypocrisy. This was the shameful accusation of his so-called friends. Job vigorously denied all such charges, and eventually he was vindicated by the Lord Himself.

The word *hypocrite* has several meanings. It chiefly refers to a pretender, one who is like an actor, playing a part. It can also describe a profane man who, while rejecting the truth, professes allegiance to God. Job was neither. He was no hypocrite, but the whole of Biblical history is littered with real hypocrites. Jude 11 lists three prominent hypocrites in the Old Testament. All were outwardly religious men. Cain denied the blood atonement. Baalam could not come to terms with the doctrine of justification, seeking to curse a people who in their standing before God could only be blessed. Korah refused to recognize the unique mediatorial position of the high priest of Israel. In the New Testament we have the example of Judas, a professed follower of Christ, yet without the grace of God in his heart. Job points out a common denominator in the religion of such people. They all have a hope that they can gain acceptance with God without coming to Christ in repentance. Locked up in their souls is the conviction that they do not need a Saviour, that at the end of the journey of life, somehow all will be well. How tragic, how dreadful is such logic! The hope of every pretender to Christianity will perish. Such are like the man of whom the Lord Jesus speaks, who built a beautiful and well-constructed house upon sand. All was well while the sun shone, but once the storm came it fell, and great was its ruin. What a blessed experience it is to take the position of Job, who recognized that while there are hypocrites in the world, he was not one of them, God Himself being witness.

—S. B. C.

We must not think to dance with the
devil all day and sup with Christ at night.
JOHN TRAPP

Limitations No Barrier to Service

A man lefthanded.

JUDGES 3:15

For some reason or other, the tribe of Benjamin produced a remarkable number of left-handed men (Judg. 20:16). Ehud, the slayer of the Moabite king Eglon, was left-handed. In fact, he may have been left-handed because of some deformity or weakness in his right hand. The Hebrew text simply states that he was "shut of his right hand." Were it not for the fact that the same description is given of the seven hundred Benjamite warriors in chapter 20, we might suspect that Ehud had a crippled right hand. Probably it means simply that through disuse and a natural tendency to use his other hand, his right hand was weak and unskilful. At any rate, Ehud was "shut of his right hand." It was an impediment and surely a real drawback for a man of war. But Ehud made up for his deficiency by his increased skill with his other hand.

Too often we use what we are not, or what we cannot do, as an excuse for doing nothing. "If I had this talent or that ability, I would certainly serve the Lord." Such thinking is hypocritical. It is a dishonest excuse to avoid our present responsibility. We do not need to be supermen in order to serve God. Throughout the book of Judges we have examples of the Lord making weak things His instruments to defeat His enemies. The same is true in the New Testament. The Lord Jesus Christ chose "unlearned and ignorant men" to be His disciples. However, they had the essential qualification of every good servant: "they had been with Jesus."

Christian service—doing something worthwhile in the cause of Christ—is open to all who walk in fellowship with the Lord. Instead of making your limitations an excuse for idleness, use the ability and opportunity God gives you and look to Him to bless your service for His glory.

—A. C.

Do all you can,
By all the means you can,
To all the people you can.
JOHN WESLEY

251

Bridling the Tongue

Even so the tongue is a little member, and boasteth great things.
Behold, how great a matter a little fire kindleth!

JAMES 3:5

To illustrate controlling the power of the tongue, James speaks of putting a bit in the horse's mouth to make it obedient and of steering a great ship with a small helm. His message is clear: control a horse's mouth and you control its immense physical strength so that you can direct it where you will; control a ship's helm and you can turn it about despite the influence of wind and tide. Likewise, the man who exercises godly control over his tongue holds in check his natural perverseness and impetuosity, and withstands the powerful influences from without that would blow his life off course.

This appears to claim too much for control of the tongue, but actually it does not. Our words are important. The Lord Jesus taught that we must give account to God for every idle utterance. He clearly saw our words as indicators of the state of our hearts and said that by them we will be condemned or declared just (Matt. 12:36-37). Sanctimonious phrases spoken at opportune times to impress men do not hide from the Lord the words of bitterness, anger, scandal, and lying that are habitual to so many of us.

A tongue that indulges in these is a fire that is "set on fire of hell" (James 3:6). It can rapidly cause widespread destruction. It inflicts terrible injury and loss. Is this how you use your tongue? Despite the fact that you can say very nice prayers and sound very holy at times, do you fail to bridle your tongue and let it blaze out of control, causing insult and injury to those around you? If so, you need to know two things. First, your conduct is inexcusably wrong. Second, you need to submit to the control of the Lord and let Him be the rider and the steersman (to use James's illustrations) who will curb your natural temperament and turn you to do His will despite the tempest and tides of passion and provocation that would conspire to blow you off course.

—A. C.

The only cure for a tongue set on fire of hell is the purifying touch of the live coal from off the altar of heaven.

ALEXANDER SIMPSON

The Offering of False Fire

Nadab and Abihu . . . offered strange fire.

LEVITICUS 10:1

The early chapters of Leviticus bring us face to face with the five offerings, followed by the consecration and service of the priests. The children of Israel are reconciled to God, happily worshipping. All was done God's way, and His blessing is on the people.

But now comes a dreadful event. Just as night follows day and war follows peace, disaster strikes Israel. Two of Aaron's sons, Nadab and Abihu, offer strange fire in the tabernacle. Fire from God bursts forth and consumes them. Aaron is plunged into deep sorrow.

Their sin was one single act, but it resulted from a complex build-up. The command of God immediately following, "Do not drink wine nor strong drink" (v. 9), suggests that their error had its genesis in drink. The consumption of alcohol has left mankind with a history of tears, ruin, and blood. Individuals and empires have been destroyed by it.

Nadab and Abihu then substituted human "will worship" for God's commands. Depraved human nature always wants to add to, or subtract from, God's Word and His way. They paid for their sin by the swift judgment of God. "Be sure your sin will find you out" (Num. 32:23).

Fire in the Bible is symbolic of the Holy Spirit. God also makes His ministers a "flaming fire," and incense in the Bible is a picture of prayer. Sadly, there is much strange fire being offered today. There are *strange spirits*, leading to *strange preaching* and *strange praying*. Christians must be careful not to ascribe to the Holy Ghost that which is actually the work of a strange spirit.

Had Nadab and Abihu obeyed the Word of God, they would have lived, Israel would have been delivered from disaster, and Aaron the high priest would have been spared his grief. How important it is for us all to read, study, and obey God's Word. Obedience prevents much heartache. Disobedience brings disaster.

—F. McC.

We cannot rely on God's promises without obeying His commandments.
JOHN CALVIN

In Christ

*There is therefore now no condemnation
to them which are in Christ Jesus.*

ROMANS 8:1

The believer's spiritual union with Christ is a doctrine of which Paul never wearied. Over seventy times in his epistles Paul uses those precious words *in Christ*. All that Paul enjoyed at the hand of God, all that he was and was going to be, traced its roots back to his union with Christ. After leaving the struggles of chapter 7, he enters the security of chapter 8 with those words of assurance: *no condemnation to them which are in Christ Jesus.* See what security such a position affords!

Our union with Christ began in eternity, and this can never end. As the apostle stated in Ephesians 1:4, God's people were chosen in Christ before the foundation of the world. That means that when God chose you in Christ in eternity past, He did so knowing all about you—every sin, every failure, every backsliding. He knew then your lack of faith, love, and obedience. Still He put you in Christ! And as it is *God* who put you there, only someone greater than God can remove you! Where is he?

Further, this position in Christ delivers us from any and every charge that could be brought against us by the law of God. The law demands perfect obedience and punishment for offenders. Our destruction would be sure had we not kept the law *in Christ*. God's wrath would be our portion had we not been "baptized into his death" (Rom. 6:3). The law has no condemning word to say to Christ's people now; it must be silent. By His vicarious life and death, Christ satisfied the law's demands.

And so real is this union that God can never deal with us apart from dealing with His Son, and never deal with His Son apart from us. If the believer is sent to hell, so must Christ be, for the head and body must ever be together. But if God forever loves and accepts His beloved Son, then He must forever love and accept those who are in Christ! Rejoice, dear child of God, in the Lord.

—J. W.

Union is the ground of communion.
JOHN TRAPP

The Value of the Bible

*The law of thy mouth is better unto
me than thousands of gold and silver.*   **PSALM 119:72**

Archibald Naismith, who invested over forty years of his life in
India as a Christian teacher, tells that when his family returned
home to Great Britain for a prolonged holiday, one of his sons, a
boy of about six or seven years, attended school for the first time
in Britain. One day the young boy came home and reported that
he had to write a short essay on the topic "My Greatest Treasure."
When he finally showed his parents his completed composition,
they were overjoyed to read his first sentence: "My greatest treasure is my Holy Bible."

This young boy's testimony should be the testimony of every
child of God. Each believer should be able to say, "Therefore I love
thy commandments above gold; yea, above fine gold" (Psa. 119:127).
The question is, can we honestly give this as our testimony? It
is easy to pay lip service to the value of the Bible while largely
ignoring it.

If we truly esteem God's Word, we will *read* it. It will be our
most read book. Day by day we will peruse its pages.

Furthermore, if we honestly hold God's law to be more valuable than gold and silver, we will not allow the pursuit of gold
and silver, the business of the world, to hinder us from spending
time in it. We will *esteem* Scripture above our very food and will
not latch on to vain excuses to neglect it.

Again, if we really set such a value on God's Word, we will
obey it. Our regard for God's law will be evidenced by our submission to it.

Of course, such an esteem for the Word of God will express
itself in *spreading* the Word. When we recognize what a treasure
the Bible is, we cannot rest while multitudes lie in ignorance of
its message.

Is this the value we place on the Word of God?   —S. B.

**I never saw a useful Christian
who was not a student of the Bible.**
D. L. MOODY

Something To Think About

Think on these things.

PHILIPPIANS 4:8

We live in a stressful age. Even Christians can suffer from complex physical and psychological problems. In such circumstances, however, the inspirational advice of the apostle is most helpful.

Paul counsels his readers to fill their minds with things that are true, honest, just, pure, lovely, and of good report. Surely much of the anguish of body and mind today is caused by dwelling on things that are untrue, dishonest, impure, unlovely, and of ill report. Wrong thinking leads to wrong feeling, and before long the heart and mind become restless like troubled waters. We need to realize that our thoughts are real and powerful, even though they cannot be seen, hence the need to bring "into captivity every thought to the obedience of Christ" (II Cor. 10:5).

There are many things that Christians should not think about. This does not mean that we hide our heads in the sand and avoid what is unpleasant and displeasing. It does mean, however, that we do not focus our attention on dishonourable things and allow them to control our thoughts. The believer must dwell on high and noble thoughts, not the base thoughts of this corrupt world. "Set your affection on things above, not on things on the earth" (Col. 3:2). Just as a carnal mind is the surest passport to the downward path, so a mind drilled in the things which God approves is the best way to a life of practical holiness. Let your mind therefore be under the constant control of the truth of God and the Spirit of God (John 17:17; I John 5:6).

A good parallel passage for today's text is Psalm 19:7-9. The Christian who fills his heart and mind with God's Word will be able to discern wrong thoughts. Right thinking is the result of daily meditation on the Word of God. "Great peace have they which love thy law" (Psa. 119:165).

—D. C.

When filled with holy truth the mind rests.
C. H. Spurgeon

No Small Promise

For by me thy days shall be multiplied,
and the years of thy life shall be increased.

PROVERBS 9:11

When searching for treasure, the hardest part is finding where to start. Man has been seeking the treasures of wisdom for as long as time itself. From every nation under heaven there has gone up the cry *Eureka!* at some time or other as men have voiced their belief that they have discovered the fount of wisdom. But all such claims are false—all, that is, except the cry of the Bible. "The fear of the Lord is the beginning of wisdom: and the knowledge of the holy is understanding" (Prov. 9:10). The fear of the Lord is nothing more than the giving to God that reverence that is due to His name, that wholesome regard for the majesty and power of God. We must recognize the glorious character of Him with whom we have to do. Today there is little regard for the glory of the Lord God omnipotent. Let us fear the Lord.

From such a fear there springs a wisdom that is beyond value. By it "thy days shall be multiplied, and the years of thy life shall be increased." When we fear the Lord, wisdom takes hold of our hand and guides us in the paths of safety. When we fear the Lord, the host of heaven takes up our cause (Psa. 34:7). Such care as this will ensure that the God-fearing will come to their grave "in a full age, like as a shock of corn cometh in in his season" (Job 5:26).

There are many who claim to have the means of adding to our wealth. Their claims usually involve relieving us of some of the possessions we have managed to lay by. The world is filled with hawkers of all descriptions. Some make very outlandish claims. Few dare make the claim that wisdom does. None but wisdom can substantiate the claim and actually add to our days. If you would see "good days," then fear God. As a result, this day may become for you the beginning of days of richness and blessing. —I. F.

He who fears God has nothing else to fear.
C. H. SPURGEON

The First and the Last Adam

The first man Adam was made a living soul;
the last Adam was made a quickening spirit.

I CORINTHIANS 15:45

Jesus Christ is here referred to as "the last Adam." The two Adams are alike in that they had a supernatural generation. Adam was made by God from the dust of the ground, and Jesus Christ was virgin born. Each Adam had an unparalleled pedigree.

They were both sinless in their birth, untainted by human iniquity. They both had a powerful influence upon the human race. The first Adam left a trail of sin as a result of his fall. The last Adam brought redemption to fallen man.

The sinfulness of the first Adam is evident. He was created with a positive holiness, but by the exercise of his mutable will he fell. He was tempted and conquered, and because he fell, we fell in him. He was an earthy man (*Adam* means "red earth"), and by his own efforts he could not rise above the earth from which he was made. The living soul died in sin, and "in Adam all die" (I Cor. 15:22). We died in him.

The superiority of the last Adam, Jesus Christ, is equally evident. He is more than just a divine man; He is the Son of God. He had a superior holiness, for it was impossible for Christ to sin. He was tempted but triumphant. He rose from the earth in glorious resurrection. He rose above the earth and entered heaven for us. Whereas all in Adam died, those in Christ shall be made alive. The first Adam brought death. The last Adam brings eternal life.

One final similarity exist between the two Adams. They each needed a bride. The first Adam slept, and bore a scar in the area from whence God took Eve. Jesus Christ slept the deeper sleep of death and bears in His body the marks of the purchase price of His spotless bride, the church. There is a question every Christian needs to ask: Is the influence of the first Adam or the last Adam the dominant force in my life today?

—F. McC.

All that Adam lost, Christ recovered, and more—for now there is no possibility of our losing paradise.
ALEXANDER SIMPSON

Setting Affections on Things Above

He that loveth silver shall not be satisfied with silver.
ECCLESIASTES 5:10

Whereas heavenly treasure is eternally secure, all earthly treasure stands in jeopardy of loss (Matt. 6:19-21). Because hearts and treasures are inseparable, we must set our affections on things above, not on things on the earth (Col. 3:2). Understanding this logic is easy; putting it into practice is sometimes difficult. As creatures of time, we become more consumed with preparing for earth than for heaven. Our materialistic society compounds the problem. Everywhere we look, we see struggles to achieve pleasure, possessions, and property. The world, and unfortunately some Christians, measure success by "things." Life becomes a race for things. The more people get, the more they want. Experience, however, testifies to the truth of Solomon's conclusion that money cannot satisfy.

Solomon was well qualified to condemn things as the secret to a happy life. He had unsurpassed wealth, a large retinue of servants, and extensive property. Ecclesiastes 2 recounts his thorough investigation of these things as they related to life. After all was done, he concluded that things provided no advantage; they were as empty as breath and as futile as chasing after the wind (v. 11). The quest for things can never bring happiness or satisfaction. We must learn this lesson. We must thankfully receive whatever God gives us in this life and use it for His glory. But regardless of what we have or do not have in this world, we must by faith be more committed to heaven than to earth. We will be when we remember that our greatest asset in heaven is Christ Himself, who causes us to possess all spiritual blessings in Him.
—M. P. V. B.

If your treasure is on earth, you are going
from it; if it is in heaven, you are going to it.
ANONYMOUS

Workaholics

This is the work of God, that ye believe on him whom he hath sent.

JOHN 6:29

Man would rather do than believe. Many came to Christ asking what they must do to be saved, but they stumbled at the truth because of the heresy of salvation by works. Because of the widespread proclamation of the social gospel today, people think of Christianity as a gospel of man's deeds. It sounds wonderful for people to be doing works for God, but the real and primary need is to have the work of God wrought in your own soul. The inward operations of the gospel in your heart cannot be replaced by any system of good works.

Lest men should miss this fact, Christ emphasized the need to accept God's way of saving souls. He calls you to faith in His own person as the only Redeemer of sinners. This action of believing is not merely a work of the mind, but of the heart. Nor is it any earning of merit for heaven. Simply put, it is a resting upon the merit of the finished work of Christ's sacrifice. Dr. John Duncan once addressed a beggar-woman in Edinburgh: "Now, you'll promise me that you'll seek: but mind, seeking will not save you, yet it is your duty; and if you seek you'll find, and finding will save you."

Have you fallen into the age-old trap of seeking to work your way to peace with God? Have you tried to earn God's favour by your works of self-righteousness, which you may be calling the works of God? Then heed the voice of the Saviour: the only true work of God in your heart is believing in Him and trusting in His work alone for salvation. Workaholics will accumulate no merit for heaven. Ceasing from works and resting in Christ's merit is the sole way to glory.

—I. G.

**Faith is the outstretched hand of
the soul taking what Christ offers.**
S. M. ZWEMER

Revival in Nineveh

So the people of Nineveh believed God.

JONAH 3:5

The ancient city of Nineveh was the scene of an amazing revival in the ninth century B.C. This vast city, which had a huge population, was so full of sin that God said its wickedness had come up before Him. The Ninevites were so evil they almost seem to have compelled God to take notice of them. And yet there was revival in Nineveh—Nineveh, of all places!

Now, if God could send revival to Nineveh, He can surely send it to the place where we live and work. Some people are far too pessimistic. They are so taken up with the end-time apostasy that they would feel somewhat let down if God were to send a spiritual awakening. Let us not be like that! Christians should be positive in their outlook; they should be looking for a harvest of souls. The man who hid his talent in the earth did so because he thought his lord was a mean man who could hardly be pleased. Christ is not mean. He died to save a vast multitude, and He will have that multitude with Him in heaven, out of "all nations, and kindreds, and people, and tongues" (Rev. 7:9).

The revival in Nineveh affected all classes of society, all age groups, and all types of people. It led to a thorough reformation of the lives and manners of the people. The Ninevites turned from their sin to God, and God looked down from heaven approvingly and blessed them.

As we read of what happened in Nineveh, we should long to see revival in our district. The devil has been blinding our neighbours and friends for far too long. Let us pray for a mighty outpouring of the Spirit of God.

—G. F.

We cannot organise a revival but we can set
our sails to catch the wind from heaven when
God chooses to blow upon His people once again.
G. CAMPBELL MORGAN

Memory's Aid to Praise

He brought me up also out of an horrible pit, out of the miry clay.

PSALM 40:2

"Look unto the rock whence ye are hewn, and to the hole of the pit whence ye are digged" (Isa. 51:1). This is good advice. Remembering where we were before God's grace rescued us will not only teach us humility, but will bind us firmly in love and thankfulness to God. Remembering past misery makes us appreciate the great measure of His present mercy. Remembering the horrors of the slimy abyss that held us highlights the wonders of Christ's redemption. Psalm 40 begins with such contemplation, goes on to gratitude for grace received, and ends with desire for renewed displays of God's mercy.

We well remember our unsaved state. The words David uses to describe our sin and guilt actually mean "the pit of tumult" and "the mire of mud." But the greatness and grace of God were greater than our sin. He heard our cries for mercy and delivered us. He *inclined* to us, or extended His heart toward us in favour. He gave us a complete deliverance. He took us out of the pit and placed our feet on a rock, the peak of a high crag. This is how the Lord always works when He applies His saving grace to a lost soul. He raises us from the depths to the heights, from the slippery mire to the firm footing of spiritual security in Christ our solid rock and sure foundation.

As we contemplate such a full deliverance, we cannot help but lift our hearts in praise. The Lord has taken away the frightening noises of the pit of tumult and has given us the new song of spiritual freedom. Let us sing that song with grateful hearts. If we ever forget the melody, we need only remind ourselves of the words of today's text. The memory of where we were and what the Lord has done for us will soon restore our song.

—M. P. V. B.

The only song worth singing is the song of
Christ's redemption and its tune is *Amazing Grace*.
ALEXANDER SIMPSON

Come into My Heart, Lord Jesus

Behold, I stand at the door, and knock.

REVELATION 3:20

The Lord Jesus has many ways of making His people hear His knocking. From verse 19 we may gather that His rebukes, His chastisements, and His calls to repentance are all knocks on the doors of our hearts. Who will hear His voice? He speaks in mercy, even when He chastens. Who will hearken to His knocking? All His blows upon our hearts are but calls to closest fellowship.

Christ wants an entrance to our affections. He is not satisfied with our cold acts of duty. "Give Me thy heart" is His demand. Has He obtained it? Or is He still standing outside? Remember, the people to whom He addresses this message are professing Christians. Like all too many, they are lukewarm—indifferent to spiritual things. They are too busy with worldly concerns to pay much attention to the spiritual reality of the gospel they profess. The Lord Jesus refuses to allow such a situation to go unchallenged. He must have the heart's throne of anyone who professes His name.

The mark of a true Christian, as distinct from a mere professor, is that however cold in heart he has become, he cannot ignore the voice, or the knocking, of the Saviour. Do you hear that voice, that insistent knocking, today? You may think that the way to renewed fellowship will be long and difficult, but you are wrong. Jesus says that all that is required is to hear His voice and open the door. Throw open your heart—your affections, your will, your inmost being—to the Saviour, and He will enter and establish a fellowship with you that will be sweet, satisfying, and unbroken.

The King of Glory wants to dine with you today, and He wants you to dine with Him forever. Will you heed His call?

—A. C.

**Carelessness about the friendship of
Christ is the crying sin of the church.**
R. C. CHAPMAN

Valiant for the Truth

Buy the truth, and sell it not.

PROVERBS 23:23

What a great stir Christian and Faithful provoked in Vanity Fair! It was crowded with merry people, busily engaged in buying trifles. These held no interest to the pilgrims. One merchant, "mockingly, beholding the carriage of the men, said unto them, 'what will ye buy?' But they, looking gravely upon him said, 'We buy the truth.'"

The Scriptures alone are absolute truth, essential truth, authoritative truth, undiluted truth, and eternal truth. How precious to the Christian! It is "the word of truth, the gospel of his salvation (Eph. 1:13). It is the excellency of the knowledge of Christ Jesus our Lord (Phil. 3:8). Who can put a value on it? It is beyond price.

This treasure, the Christian is to make truly his own. As Will Houghton put it, "Lay hold on the Bible until the Bible lays hold on you." It is only by prayerful, patient, and persevering study that the mine of divine revelation will yield the golden nuggets of truth. Tell me, Christian, how much of the unbounded ocean of Scripture is yet uncharted? How much of the vast continent of Holy Writ is yet to be explored? Cry prayerfully, "That which I see not, teach Thou me."

Having obtained this treasure, sell it not! Every temptation is a persuasion to sell the truth. Do not barter it for anything this world has to offer. "Give not an hairbreadth of truth away, for it is not yours but God's" (Samuel Rutherford). The Bible in your hand is a blood-stained volume. It is the precious legacy of the martyrs of Jesus, those who prized the truth above life itself. "I have settled myself through the strength of God's Holy Spirit, patiently to pass through the torments and extremities of the fire now prepared for me, rather than to deny the truth of God's Word" (John Hooper, Bishop of Gloucester, at his martyrdom).

—M. P.

We must read our Bibles like
men digging for hidden treasure.
J. C. RYLE

An Antidote for Discouragement

Consider him.

HEBREWS 12:3

It is the plan of Satan so to attack and harass the people of God that they will become "wearied and faint" in their minds. The word *wearied* means "exhausted," being so despondent and discouraged as to have one's spirit broken. The consequence of that is to be "faint" of mind. *Faint* literally means "to lose out," or "to relax." It signifies an abandonment of one's stand for the gospel and the Word of God. Surely this is Satan's aim in these days. He is determined to break the spirit of the faithful remnant and cause them to relax in their stand against the enemies of truth.

How can such a tragedy be prevented? The words of our text signify the only preventative: *Consider him.* The word *consider* means "to compute by comparing things in their due proportion." In the context here, Paul is urging believers to form an accurate estimate of Christ's suffering and compare their own with it. The apostle speaks of Christ enduring "such contradiction of sinners against himself." The idea is that Christ's sufferings were unprecedented, unparalleled, and unsurpassed. In effect, therefore, Paul is drawing our attention to the cross and Christ's agony there. Ultimately he is directing us to the love of Christ for His church. When we "behold, and see" (Lam. 1:12) that there is no sorrow like Christ's, we are reminded of Christ's mighty love for the elect. It is an unconditional, sacrificial, and immutable love. Such love calls for faithfulness and steadfastness for Christ. May each of us catch a fresh glimpse of Christ's love in His crosswork and be strengthened as we strive against sin.

—J. G.

Joy fills our heart to the extent that Jesus fills our mind.
ALEXANDER SIMPSON

Bible Study

Set thine heart upon all that I shall shew thee.

EZEKIEL 40:4

Ezekiel is told to fix his heart on the Word of God. If he, the watchman-prophet, intimate with God and renowned for wisdom, receives such a command, how much more must we give heart attention to what God says?

Every word of God is important. God has revealed Himself in the Scriptures. The words there are important because they are His. While there is undoubted emphasis upon the certainty of Scripture throughout this prophecy, these last chapters contain some particularly strong personal admonitions. There is a three-fold injunction here: *Behold; hear; set thine heart.* For example, in chapter 44 verse 5 Ezekiel is told, "Mark well, and behold with thine eyes, and hear with thine ears all that I say unto thee." Ezekiel is an example to us in this.

We may hear God's Word and yet not have a listening heart. The ear picks up the message, but the heart is set upon something else. We do a dishonour to the Lord if we hear with a divided heart. Ezekiel learns two things. First, God has a purpose in speaking to him. God has providentially placed him before Him, just so that he can hear what God has to say. Second, it is God's will that Ezekiel should now go forth with what he has learned in his heart and declare it to the house of Israel. Teaching is before preaching.

The Lord assures the prophet of a reward for his assiduity. The verse offers a guide to the study of Scripture, for the prophet is here enrolled as a student at the feet of his Lord. There are four conditions for each one to adopt in this "Bible college." First, our heart must be in what we learn. Second, obedience is necessary to the favour of God. Third, God requires submission to *all* that He says. Fourth, we must have absolute conviction as to the divine origin of the written Word: "I shall shew thee."

—J. D.

**What we take in by the Word we digest
by meditation and let out by prayer.**
THOMAS MANTON

Behold the Lamb of God!

Christ . . . hath given himself for us . . . a sacrifice to God.
EPHESIANS 5:2

A new convert reading through the Scriptures for the first time finds in the Old Testament books things that perplex him. In Leviticus 7:8 an animal is entirely consumed on the altar and the skin is given to the priest. Another animal is consumed by the worshipper, the priest, and the altar (vv. 11-36). On the day of atonement the priest takes an animal and puts him to death, while on the same day another animal is sent into the wilderness (16:7-10). The new believer cries, "What does all this mean?"

As he continues his journey through the Bible, God provides an answer to his question. While many passages point to Christ as our sacrifice before God (Isa. 53:4-12; John 1:29-36), none is clearer than this text, which states that Christ gave Himself "an offering and a sacrifice to God for a sweetsmelling savour" (Eph. 5:2). With this key in his hand the believer is able to unlock the mysteries surrounding the Old Testament sacrificial system. It is Christ who received the wrath of God and gave to His people a robe of righteousness (Rom. 3:24-28). It is Christ who reconciles the worshipper, the priest, and God by His atoning work (Rom. 5:10-11). And it is Christ who once and for all bore all our sins away into a wilderness, never to be found again (Heb. 10:12-18). Christ's sacrifice takes away all the sins of all God's people for all eternity (I John 1:7-9).

With the light of this glorious gospel shining in the soul, new and old saints alike confess:

> Jesus, Thy blood and righteousness,
> My beauty are, my glorious dress;
> 'Midst flaming worlds, in these arrayed,
> With joy shall I lift up my head.
>
> —M. W. A.

He suffered not as God, but He suffered who was God.
JOHN OWEN

Complaining Christians

And when the people complained, it
displeased the Lord: and the Lord heard it.

NUMBERS 11:1

The book of Numbers is replete with references to the complaints of the nation of Israel. On most of the occasions when this discontent arose, it was vented against the leaders of the people. Yet the solemn fact is that the murmuring was actually against the Lord. Unjust murmurings against God's men are regarded in heaven as rebellion against the Lord Himself.

How terrible is this sin! It is the basest ingratitude. What wonders God had wrought for Israel in their exodus from Egypt, but how quickly they forgot! Scarcely had they left their bondage when the first signs of revolt appeared, and though the Lord was longsuffering, the discontent continually surfaced from their hearts. In the book of Hebrews the Holy Spirit shows us the real nature of murmuring. He indicates that it arises from an evil heart of unbelief. Referring to the rebelling Israelites at Kadesh, Paul concludes that they "could not enter in because of unbelief" (Heb. 3:19).

To murmur against God is to doubt His wisdom. Every time Israel complained, they questioned the wisdom of God in bringing them out of Egypt. Indeed, they openly expressed that doubt. To murmur is to doubt God's love. In effect, as they complained, the Jews were saying that the Lord did not love them. To murmur is to doubt God's power, His providence, and His promises. All these were called into question each time Israel complained, and they still are when that spirit emerges among us.

Murmuring is a crippling sin. It robs us of the blessing of the Lord. It causes us to forfeit enjoyment of Christ and all His covenant mercies. It will leave us wandering in a spiritual wilderness. It will rob us of the joy of going on to take the land set before us. Has this sin taken root in your heart? If so, repent of it and flee to Christ for cleansing. He will forgive you and give you victory over it.

—J. G.

Complain without cause and
you will have cause to complain.
THOMAS TAYLOR

Unfeigned Love

Seeing ye have purified your souls in obeying the truth through the Spirit unto unfeigned love of the brethren.

I PETER 1:22

A major evidence of the grace of God in our lives is love of the brethren. Throughout the New Testament it is presented as such. In John 13:35 the Lord singles it out as the badge and ensign of discipleship. John points to it as evidence of quickening to life (I John 3:14), as an evidence that God dwells in us by His Spirit (4:12, 13), and as an evidence of our love for God (4:20).

Love, then, is a pre-eminent evidence of grace. This verse speaks of the love of God in our hearts for both the Word of God and the Holy Spirit. This love is both Biblical and spiritual. As such it is sincere. It is not a pretended love, but is born of the Spirit, bears the stamp of God's Word, and spurns all hypocrisy. How different from that love which ecumenism parades in hypocrisy!

It is also a grace that is linked to purity. It germinates, develops, and matures in the heart that is pure. True love is always accompanied by purity. Much of what the world terms love is linked to impurity; this is not true love, but rather lust with all its unclean associations.

The Spirit's love is fervent love. The pure heart is set alight with this love. It is warm, compassionate, and outgoing to others in sympathy, support, and self-forgetfulness. Let us pray for such an unfeigned love in our hearts.

—R. J. B.

One loving heart sets another on fire.
AUGUSTINE

Rejected Confidences

The Lord hath rejected thy confidences. JEREMIAH 2:37

Proud flesh has no place in the work of God. That message is not a popular one nowadays, when even professed ministers of Christ have jumped on the humanistic bandwagon of self-love, self-esteem, self-expression, and self-gratification. However, it is still the message of God, and people desperately need to hear it.

The Lord rejects all confidence in the flesh for salvation. Some people have an easy confidence that it is well with their souls. They rest in carnal security. They fear no judgment, for they have never felt any great burden of sin. They have easy methods of dealing with guilt, ranging from denial, to vain excuses, to blaming someone else, to adopting just enough religion to salve their conscience. Such people may expressly state their dependence on their own good works. Or they may place their confidence in a "decision" that has never yielded a true heart relationship with Christ. In all these cases, unsaved people are confident of their soul's salvation. To all such, today's text comes as a thunderbolt: "The Lord hath rejected thy confidences." If you would be truly confident of your salvation, you must come to the end of yourself and unreservedly cast yourself upon the merits of Christ. Only in and through Him have you access to and acceptance with God.

The Lord also rejects all confidence in the flesh for Christian service. It is "not by might, nor by power, but by my spirit, saith the Lord of hosts" (Zech. 4:6). This condemns so much of what masquerades as Christian service nowadays—the Hollywood entertainment, the preacher personality cult, the man-centred messages. On the other hand, the Lord's rejection of all such reliance on the flesh is an encouragement to all of us who desire to see a genuine work of the Spirit. We may confidently trust the Lord's promise that we have access to Him and His power through the blood of Christ (Heb. 4:14-16; 10:19). He rejects all confidence in the flesh, but He rewards all true confidence in Christ. —A. C.

A mite of spirit is of more worth than a mountain of flesh.
STEPHEN CHARNOCK

True Riches

Hath not God chosen the poor of this world rich in faith?
JAMES 2:5

There are poor rich people and rich poor people. The rich fool in Christ's parable (Luke 12:16-21), the rich young ruler (18:18-25), and the rich man who fared sumptuously every day while the godly Lazarus lay starving at his gate (16:19-31) are all examples of poor rich people. They did not perish because they made a lot of money. They perished because money was the only wealth they had; they were not rich toward God.

There are many just like them in the world today. The pursuit of material wealth consumes them. To obtain it they sacrifice time with their families, they sacrifice their marriages, and they neglect their souls. Then they hear the awful summons from God: "Thou fool, this night thy soul shall be required of thee" (Luke 12:20). To their eternal horror they discover that "riches profit not in the day of wrath" (Prov. 11:4).

In contrast, there are people who are poor as far as worldly possessions go but are truly rich, for they are "rich toward God" (Luke 12:21). By faith in Christ they are "heirs of the kingdom which he hath promised to them that love him" (James 2:5). Here is true wealth. It does not fluctuate with the stock exchange. It does not disappear at death. It does not impoverish our spirits to pursue it. This wealth is called "the unsearchable riches of Christ" (Eph. 3:8). To know God's love and God's pardon; to have peace of heart because we have peace with God; to have joy in life, certainty in death, and heaven in eternity—this is to be truly rich. Let us make sure we have this treasure whatever the earthly cost.
—A. C.

Worldlings make gold their god; saints make God their gold.
MATTHEW HENRY

Riches Without Remorse

The blessing of the Lord, it maketh rich,
and he addeth no sorrow with it.

PROVERBS 10:22

It is good to allow God to manage our finances. In that way we avoid the snare of riches and the pit of poverty. Seeking after riches always proves to be a terrible snare: "They that will be rich fall into temptation and a snare, and into many foolish and hurtful lusts, which drown men in destruction and perdition" (I Tim. 6:9). When money and not God governs our will and engages our love, then we are like the wasp drawn to the honey smeared on the inside of the trap. Greed blinds us to the consequences of our reckless search, and we pay the penalty.

There are riches that are not measured in monetary terms. Such are the treasures of the gospel of God's grace: forgiveness of sin, reconciliation with God, eternal life in Christ, and grace to live in victory over sin. Gold and silver decay and lose their value. They carry no esteem in eternity. But not so the riches of God's blessing. They enrich our lives here and in eternity. Some investments take quite some time to mature, but when they do they show tremendous returns. Wise men invest in such and patiently abide their maturing. Often such investments are passed on so that they mature in the lifetime of the investor's descendants. So it is with the riches that spring from the blessings of God. The gospel forecasts high returns for those who invest their life, their soul, their all in Christ. That forecast is accurate. The full riches of God's kindness and grace await our laying claim of them in heaven. Here on earth we constantly enjoy immediate returns from our heavenly investments. Where else can an investor begin enjoying returns that far outweigh the investment the moment it is made? Eternal life and blessing begin immediately upon placing our faith in Christ. These are riches that bring no sorrow in their wake. All other riches are but an alloy of much and misery!

—I. F.

In the day of judgment a pure conscience
will be worth more than full purses.
BERNARD OF CLAIRVAUX

Murmuring

There arose a murmuring.

ACTS 6:1

A striking characteristic of the church in the book of Acts was its spirit of unity. *With one accord, of one soul,* and *of one heart* are expressions used to describe the atmosphere that prevailed. Unity of the spirit based upon the truth has especially marked the church in days of revival and is singled out as a thing well pleasing to God (Psa. 133). That being the case, we can be sure that Satan will seek to destroy it.

The murmuring that arose among the disciples in Jerusalem created a division that threatened the very future of the work. How little we realize the potential for evil there is in an unrestrained tongue. When we begin to murmur and complain and thus cause division amongst brethren, the Spirit of God is grieved, the blessing of God is absent from us, and the adversary is pleased.

What was the source of the problem in Jerusalem? Something of fundamental importance? Not at all—something comparatively trifling, something of a temporal and material nature. Relatively insignificant matters have often caused much bitterness among saints and thus hindered blessing. Let us consider the possible results of our words before we speak and decide whether the issue is important enough to outweigh the risk of harming God's work.

Thankfully, there were men in the church in Jerusalem determined to give themselves "continually to prayer, and to the ministry of the word . . . and the word of God increased" (Acts 6:4, 7). When tempted to complain, let us press on with our responsibilities in the work of the Lord and pray continually. In this way Satan's plans can be defeated and the kingdom of Christ extended.

—D. F.

Our murmuring is the devil's music.
THOMAS WATSON

The Upper and the Nether Springs

Caleb gave her the upper springs and the nether springs.

JUDGES 1:15

Our Father always gives with a bountiful hand. We come like Caleb's daughter, requesting a blessing, and He gives us a double portion, "the upper springs and the nether springs."

There are upper springs and there are lower springs in the Christian life. We need both, and the Lord gives both. His grace is sufficient for every need and flows freely to us in every situation.

His upper springs may be taken to speak of the spiritual blessings in heavenly places that He gives us in Christ (Eph. 1:3). What rich springs of grace are the blessings Paul goes on to list in Ephesians chapter 1—election, predestination, adoption, acceptance in the beloved, redemption through the blood of Christ, the revelation of God's will, the sealing of the Holy Spirit, our eternal inheritance, and a place in the body of which Christ is the exalted Head. Too often Christians dismiss these glorious truths as impractical or reduce them to the deadwood of theological controversy. These spiritual blessings are the wells, or springs, of salvation, and we should learn to do what Isaiah the prophet speaks of: "With joy shall ye draw water out of the wells of salvation" (Isa. 12:3).

The lower springs may be taken to speak either of the special grace the Lord gives to us in those times when we are passing through some valley experience, or of His provision for our earthly needs. There are lower springs that meet the needs of the body as well as upper springs that meet the needs of the soul. There is grace to enable us to live in the joy of the Lord in this present world as well as grace to bring us safely to the Celestial City. There is no valley so deep, no suffering so great, and no affliction so trying but that God's grace can make our experience of it fruitful and beneficial.

O Christian, look up. Cry for a blessing. The river of God is full of water (Psa. 65:9). There are springs of divine help and favour for every believer in every situation.

—A. C.

Christ has springs of living water to turn our wilderness into an Eden of fellowship and fruitfulness.
ALEXANDER SIMPSON

The Shepherd's Watch-Care

Behold, he that keepeth Israel shall neither slumber nor sleep.
PSALM 121:4

Jill, our American guide, conducted our party of tourists to one of Jerusalem's newest attractions, the Scripture Gardens. These gardens seek to take the visitor back in time to Bible days and give him an insight into Bible manners and customs. It was fascinating to look at the various exhibits, which range from a shepherd's tent to an oil press.

One of the things which made a lasting impression upon me was the sheepfold. Our guide explained that the sheepfold had no door, simply a gap in the hedge, and that at night the shepherd would have slept across the gap. He was the door himself. This gave me new understanding of the Saviour's words, "I am the door."

Another verse which took on new meaning was today's text: "Behold, he that keepeth Israel shall neither slumber nor sleep." Our guide explained that some sheepfolds, like the one we were looking at, had a watch tower, and that the shepherds would take it in turns to watch the flock. The sheep were always under the watchful eye of the shepherd, who neither slumbered nor slept. Does this not remind us of the "shepherds abiding in the field, keeping watch over their flock by night" (Luke 2:8)? How comforting it is to know that the Lord is our keeper and that as our Shepherd He watches over us twenty-four hours a day. We can rest in confidence, knowing that He neither slumbers nor sleeps.

—S. B.

To destroy one of Christ's sheep Satan must first deceive or defeat the Shepherd. Who could ask for greater security?
ALEXANDER SIMPSON

Bible Cutting Destroys Axes

The scripture cannot be broken.

Sometime before his death in 1809, Thomas Paine wrote, "In five years from now there will not be a Bible in America. I have gone through the Bible with an axe and cut down all its trees." He was only one of many who have lifted their axes to God's Book. The infidel Voltaire set up a printing press to publish attacks on the Scriptures, but after his death his presses were used for printing Bibles, and his home became a centre for the Genevan Bible Society. The puny little axe-men and their vaunted blades have disappeared, but the Bible stands unmoved.

When the Lord Jesus stated that the Scripture cannot be broken, He confirmed the absolute authority of Scripture. The Lord established that no matter how men may choose to argue and reason on any subject, the Word of God is final. What God has decreed and written in the Scriptures cannot be discarded, changed, superseded, or worn out.

God has magnified His Word above all His name. It is eternally bound up with His own veracity and authority. The gospel message declared by the Word of God is the sure and certain way to heaven. As the Scripture cannot be broken, neither can the Saviour's redemption, for He fulfils the Scripture's every type and precept. "For all the promises of God in him are yea, and in him Amen" (II Cor. 1:20). The axes of atheists will wear out, but through all the tests of time the Bible will stand victorious.

—I. G.

He who wrests the Scriptures will never find rest in them.
ANONYMOUS

The Rule of Faith and Practice

To the law and to the testimony: if they speak not according to this word, it is because there is no light in them.
ISAIAH 8:20

We must learn to judge all things by the written Word of God. The Lord has given the Bible to us as the only infallible rule of faith and practice. It is our yardstick to measure every doctrine, every claim, and every movement. We dare not adopt any other standard. We will not add tradition to Scripture, for soon we would end up trimming the Word to accommodate our traditions. We will not add science to Scripture, for soon we would be denying the Word to accommodate some passing scientific theory. We will not add church councils to Scripture, for soon we would be twisting God's truth around our denominational shibboleths. We will not add experience to Scripture, for we would surely make the Bible agree with our experience, even if we had to defy all sound principles of interpretation. The Bible and the Bible only must be the standard of our belief and behaviour. Anyone who teaches otherwise has no light in him. He is an agent of darkness and of the prince of darkness.

Bible rejectors are not brilliant. They are darkened fools. Their folly has wounded many churches. Rationalism has spread its poison, undermining faith in Scripture and frightening humble Christians by the claims to scholarship of its exponents. It is not scholarship but sin that leads men to deny the Bible.

As rationalists have taken away from Scripture, so traditionalists and the purveyors of immediate revelation have added to—and often replaced—Scripture. This also is darkness.

We are called to walk in the light. That means that we must learn the Scriptures. We must live the Scriptures. And we must hold everything that claims our attention to the touchstone of the Scriptures. If it is Biblical, believe it or do it! If it is not, shun it as you would shun the devil.

—A. C.

We must surrender ourselves to the authority of Holy Scripture, for it can neither mislead nor be misled.
AUGUSTINE

The Signature of Peter

Peter, an apostle of Jesus Christ.

I PETER 1:1

Every letter has a signature. It is our custom to put the signature at the end of the letter, so that we have to wait until after we have digested the contents to identify the writer—that is, if we can resist the temptation to turn first to the last page and see the signature. Not so in this letter. Peter places his signature at the beginning. Immediately we are prepared for the communications that this letter brings.

What emotions the name of Peter will conjure up in the minds of the readers! Many will know him personally; all will no doubt have heard of him. They will remember his obedient call from the fisherman's boat, his lucid confessions concerning the Son of God, his walking on the sea, and his revelation on the mount, but they will also remember his weakness and failure. How impetuous he was, how boastful at times before Christ's resurrection! They will remember his tears over his denials. They will remember that Peter, though an apostle, was only a man.

Yet they will see in this mere mortal material that God shaped, formed, and sanctified into a chosen vessel which He filled with His Spirit and made one of the most blessed servants in the New Testament. Short-sighted men would have written Peter off, but the Lord took up the marred vessel and made him a vessel unto honour, sanctified and meet for the Master's use. What can God not do with each of us, despite the infirmities and weaknesses we know so well, if we will but yield ourselves to God and His Holy Spirit?

—R. J. B.

**The greatness of a man's power
is the measure of his surrender.**
WILLIAM BOOTH

Keeping a Right Balance

A false balance is abomination to the Lord:
but a just weight is his delight.

PROVERBS 11:1

Napoleon is said to have referred scornfully to the English people as a race of small shopkeepers. In this day of supermarkets and hypermarkets, the small shop is almost a thing of history. Considered as no longer having any commercial value, it has been swept away by the tide of what is called progress. In other days, God considered small shops of such importance that He inspected their affairs!

The Lord has an interest in the business ethics of businesses large and small. Few things are so disliked by God that they are called an abomination. Among those few things are the cheating merchant and his false balances.

The religion of many never reaches their store or their office or wherever they carry on their business. It never affects their dealings with others. It has no impact upon the quality of the service they render others. True religion will always influence us, our affairs, and those we encounter every day. It will make us persons with whom it is safe and pleasant to do business. The businessman or merchant who is converted to Christ will be "under new management"—a management whose policy is one of scrupulous honesty, a management that pays particular attention to the accuracy of the balances, a management that loves its customer as itself.

Such an honest policy pays. It really is true that honesty is the best policy. It will never cost you money or profit to honour God by maintaining His business standards and dealing with others as you would have others deal with you. God delights in a "just weight." He also delights in those who "deal truly" (Prov. 12:22). Any venture in which God delights will surely prosper. The great Arbitrator of men's affairs will see to it that "with the same measure that ye mete withal it shall be measured to you again" (Luke 6:38).

—I. F.

Honesty is one business policy that will never
have to be changed to keep up with the times.
ANONYMOUS

God Is Still on the Throne

One sat on the throne.

REVELATION 4:2

The throne of heaven is not vacant. Nor is it impotent. It is occupied by our God and Father, who omnipotently controls all the affairs of angels, demons, men, and events according to His own sovereign purpose.

This is what John said and what he wanted his readers to grasp. Those early Christians appear to have been somewhat troubled by all that the throne of the Caesars meant. At times it must have appeared to them as if that idolatrous, persecuting throne was supreme and unchallengeable. John's message was that there is a throne above every human throne from which God sovereignly dispenses His purpose.

Forty-seven times in this book John uses the word *throne*. Clearly it is something of supreme importance to God's people. Surrounded by the apparently dominant power of sin and Satan, we need to have John's vision of our God upon His throne. He is doing His will. He has a purpose of grace in the world through the gospel. He has a purpose of government whereby He will by powerful interventions in the natural world show His sovereign authority. Of course, ultimately His purpose is a purpose of glory that will be completed only when "in the dispensation of the fulness of times he [gathers] together in one all things in Christ, both which are in heaven, and which are on earth" (Eph. 1:10).

We desperately need to have this vision of the total sovereignty of God. This is no mere academic truth. Nor is it only a theological position of those called Calvinists. It is a truth that is vital to inspire Christians with confidence and courage. Having once gazed on the throne of God, will we ever be intimidated by any show of the power of man? Will we ever despair to pray and preach? Behold the throne set in heaven today, and you will walk on earth in the light of its purity and power.

—A. C.

God's ways are behind the scenes, but He
moves all the scenes which He is behind.
J. N. DARBY

The Day of Atonement

Make an atonement for the children of Israel.

LEVITICUS 16:34

The Day of Atonement, *Yom Kippurim,* is of great significance to the modern Jew, but it should mean much more to the Christian. The events of the day form a very appropriate picture of the crucified Christ and what He accomplished for His people on the cross.

The Day of Atonement came after the serious sin of Nadab and Abihu. They were religious but wrong. Here the great climax of the true offerings points to Jesus Christ. It was celebrated once a year, once in a full period of time, just as Jesus made "one sacrifice for sins for ever" (Heb. 10:12), once in the lifetime of this world.

Only the high priest could enter the Holiest of All. Jesus, our High Priest, entered into the presence of God to make an atonement for us. Aaron divested himself of his glorious garments for a plain linen robe. Jesus left the splendour and glory of heaven to wear the plain robe of humiliation and condescension. Its whiteness speaks of His purity.

Two goats were central to the sacrifice. One was killed, its shed blood picturing Christ's death for the sins of His people. The other, the scapegoat, had the sins of Israel confessed on it and was freed to leave the camp for the wilderness. It is a beautiful picture of Christ the Lamb of God bearing away our sins.

When Aaron had presented and sprinkled the blood in the Holiest of All, he came forth. His blood-stained robe was exchanged for the garments of beauty and glory. The bells on the hem rang, indicating that he had entered the presence of God, made an atonement, and come forth alive. What joy there was in Israel!

Jesus died on the cross, shed His precious blood, made atonement for His people, and came forth from death in glorious resurrection. What joy that should bring to believers! We serve, not a dead philosopher, but a living Redeemer. Let us rejoice this day in Him.

—F. McC.

**The wounds of Christ were the greatest
outlets of His glory that ever were.**
ROBERT MURRAY MCCHEYNE

281

Election and Evangelism

I have great heaviness and continual sorrow in my heart
. . . for my brethren, my kinsmen according to the flesh.

ROMANS 9:2-3

Let him who thinks that the doctrine of sovereign and unconditional election kills the spirit of evangelism weigh these words very carefully. Let him who tenaciously holds to this doctrine do the same, for in these words one finds an answer to much of today's misunderstanding and misrepresentation of this truth.

Before Paul delves into those deep waters of election, predestination, and reprobation, he speaks of his sorrow and burden for the lost sheep of Israel. Here was a man who believed and preached these doctrines, yet lived with a continual burden for the lost! Lest we think he exaggerates, the apostle declares, "I speak the truth in Christ, I lie not" (v. 1). What happens then to the allegation that "Calvinism" destroys one's zeal for the lost? Indeed, a close look at Paul's burden will put many a modern-day "soulwinner" to shame! This was a real burden. Paul did not evangelize out of a sense of guilt or human pressure. Further, his burden stood the test of the Holy Spirit, for he says that the Spirit was bearing witness with Paul's own conscience that what he was saying was true. I wonder how many professed "burdens for the lost" would stand the test of God's Spirit in our day? Burdens to have the fastest-growing church, the largest Sunday school, or the most baptisms are not burdens to which God's Spirit will bear witness!

But there is another side to all this. If this is the kind of burden under which Paul lived, what does it say to the "Calvinist" who strongly defends the doctrine of election, but has little if any burden for the lost? Where is the weeping for sinners without Christ? Where is the evangelistic fire?

These are vital issues. Let us take them before the Lord and ask Him to search our hearts and our understanding. We need both sound doctrine and a zealous love for souls in the work of the gospel.

—J. W.

If we can view, unmoved, the perishing condition
of our fellow-men, . . . we are very different from
Paul, and from Him who wept over Jerusalem.
CHARLES HODGE

The Profit of Knowing God

Acquaint now thyself with him, and be at
peace: thereby good shall come unto thee.

JOB 22:21

"Be at peace." Such is the blessing God offers. Society at large knows nothing of this mercy. We live in a world of strife, envy, and hatred. On a personal level, how easy it is to be bowed down with worry. Practically every day we contend with stress and strain that make our very existence a burden. Responsibilities and duties press in upon us from every side. In every heart there is a need for an inner peace that will conquer the trials and tribulations of life. We urgently need a rest of soul that will comfort, a sustaining strength in the depths of the soul which nothing in this world can destroy. Such a peace is above rubies and worth more than gold.

Today's text declares that this rest of soul and peace of mind come only from God Himself. "Acquaint now thyself with him, and be at peace." *Acquaint* literally means "make profit." It is always to our profit to get to know God. John the Baptist asserts that no one has seen God at any time. Only Christ can reveal Him and bestow His blessings on our hearts (John 1:18). In Christ, the God of peace takes up residence within our souls. He not only delivers us from the consequences of our sins, but grants us a rest that sustains and supports our souls amid the ever-changing patterns of our lives.

The proffered blessing of peace proclaims a promise for the future: "Thereby good shall come unto thee." To be a Christian, to be acquainted with God, will not only profit us in this world but, best of all, in the world to come. Today we enjoy the presence of the God of peace amid the discordant sounds of this life. One day we will be with Christ and will dwell in the bliss of His presence in "the glory that shall be revealed" (I Pet. 5:1).

—S. B. C.

There is but one thing in the world really
worth pursuing—the knowledge of God.
R. H. BENSON

Preparing the Instrument

Peter went up upon the housetop to pray.

ACTS 10:9

The Lord's commission (Acts 1:8) stated that the disciples would be witnesses "unto the uttermost part of the earth." The gospel, having spread abroad from Jerusalem through Judaea and into Samaria, was about to be preached to the Gentiles, but first God must prepare His instrument for this mission. When the Lord has a work for us to do, He will fit us, as He did Peter, to fulfil the task.

In Acts 10:9 Peter is retreating from the affairs of life to seek the face of God in prayer. He had a set place, "the housetop," and a set time, "about the sixth hour." This was evidently his usual habit, as it should be for every Christian, but on this occasion he was to make a discovery of God's will that would surprise him. It is often in our daily converse with the Lord that He opens our understanding of His plan for us. Yet in verse 10 we discover Peter's flesh resisting, for as the apostle sought to pray, "he became very hungry, and would have eaten." Perhaps there is no time when we feel the old nature's power more than in the place of prayer. The weariness of the body and the wandering of the mind hinder us as we seek to transact business with God. But God, in His power, overcame in Peter's case and revealed to him truths he needed to understand. He needed to learn the truth concerning sin to be repudiated. The sin of Peter's prejudice as a Jew against the Gentiles needed to be exposed to him by the Lord (vv. 11-16). It would hinder his usefulness for God unless it was dealt with. He also needed to learn the truth concerning souls to be reached (vv. 10, 20). Providentially, the Lord had just written these truths upon the apostle's heart as the men from Cornelius's household arrived to seek him. The mission was plain; the man was prepared. The time in the secret place with God was essential before the great work of winning the lost could be accomplished. It still is. Be much alone with God if ever you would speak with power to needy souls.

—D. F.

To pray without labouring is to mock God: to labour
without prayer is to rob God of His glory.
ROBERT HALDANE

The Light of Scripture

Thy word is a lamp unto my feet, and a light unto my path.
PSALM 119:105

The author of Psalm 119 compares the Word of God to many things. In verse 105 he likens the Scriptures to a lamp. If David was the writer of the psalm, as I believe he was, he would have known from experience the importance of the shepherd's lamp. On a cold night the shepherd would put the lamp between his feet to warm them; on other occasions he used the lamp to light up the pathway before him in the darkness.

Let us consider for a moment three ways in which the Word of God can be likened to a lamp. First of all, it gives illumination: "The entrance of thy words giveth light" (v. 130). It shows us our sin and reveals to us God's remedy for sin, the precious blood of Christ, which alone cleanseth us from all sin (I John 1:7).

Second, it gives us direction. Just as the lamp shining on the pathway of the shepherd guided and guarded his feet, so the lamp of God's truth is given to us to enable us to walk uprightly before the Lord. David's prayer was, "Order my steps in thy word" (Psa. 119:133).

Finally, the Word of God, like the lamp, is for restoration. Last thing at night the shepherd counted his sheep going into the fold. If one were missing, he left the rest in the care of a porter, lit his lamp, and went looking for the sheep that was lost. David, at the end of this psalm, confessed that he had gone astray like a lost sheep. God sent Nathan His prophet to preach the Word of God to him that he might repent and be restored to the Lord. As Christians, we need the Word of God for restoration and recovery. Listen to the words of the Chief Shepherd in John 15:3: "Now ye are clean through the word which I have spoken unto you."

—S. B.

I am a Bible bigot. I follow it in
all things both great and small.
JOHN WESLEY

Rigourous Self-Examination

Let a man examine himself.
I CORINTHIANS 11:28

Honest self-examination is a healthy exercise for a Christian, especially before sitting at the Lord's Table. When we consider the many symptoms of the leprous disease of sin, we realize that self-watch is necessary if we are to "worship the Lord in the beauty of holiness" (Psa. 29:2).

The Bible variously describes the evidences of sin in the soul by likening it to the diseased body. The *head* is sick, the *eyes* blind, the *ears* deaf, the *tongue* set on fire of hell, the poison of asps under the *lips*, the *throat* an open sepulchre spewing forth the sounds and smells of death. The *mouth* is full of cursing and bitterness. It goes on to speak of the *neck* as being stubborn and rebellious, the *heart* deceitful and desperately wicked, the *legs* unequal with a natural bias to sinful pathways, the *feet* swift to run to evil, and the *hands* wicked. The *whole body* is full of putrefying sores. The Lord does not paint a very flattering picture of the natural man, but He reveals him exactly as he is, a sinner in need of God's salvation.

But there is a balm in Gilead. The Sun of righteousness has arisen with healing in His wings. The believer is a new creature in Christ. However, the old man still lurks within and will not be completely eradicated until we enter heaven.

That is why Paul encouraged the Corinthian Christians to examine themselves before sitting at the Lord's Table. We all need to carefully examine ourselves to make sure no symptom of the leprosy of sin manifests itself in our lives. Let us therefore come to the mirror of the Word of God and examine ourselves in the light of its holy precepts. Where sin, seen or unseen, lurks, let us confess it and claim the cleansing and healing of the blood of Christ. "Wherewithal shall a young man cleanse his way? by taking heed thereto according to thy word" (Psa. 119:9).

—F. McC.

Secret sins, like secret conspirators, must be hunted out.
C. H. SPURGEON

The Sound of an Alarm

Thou hast heard, O my soul, the sound of the trumpet, the alarm of war.
JEREMIAH 4:19

We all like to hear good news. However, "good news" that ignores the truth is not good news. It is a fatal invention.

We see evidence of this all around us. People today are like those of whom Isaiah spoke, who refuse to hear the law of the Lord but who still say to His prophets, "Speak unto us smooth things" (Isa. 30:9-10). These are people who want to hear no word of condemnation of their sin, no imperial summons to repent. They want no message of the holiness and wrath of God. "Only tell us smooth things."

False prophets will always accommodate that desire (Jer. 6:14), but God's servants cannot do so. We have heard the sound of the trumpet. We have heard the alarm sounding the approach of the wrath of God. We cannot be silent. We cannot trim the message. We must bear witness to dying men and women in the light of the soon-coming judgment of God.

Of course, the message of judgment does not remove the real good news we have to tell. The good news is not that there is no judgment or hell. Our news is infinitely better than that! It is that there is a hell, but God has made known a way of escape. His wrath is real and furious, but Christ bore that wrath as our substitute on Calvary. Now, that is good news! Whether men will hear us or whether they will despise us, we must be faithful to sound the gospel alarm. We owe it to men to tell them the truth.

That goes for our witness to professing Christians, too. This is a time of glowing optimism in some sections of evangelicalism. In reality, it is a day of awful apostasy. Many Christians want "smooth things," but we have heard the sound of the trumpet. Amid the false ecumenism of our day we are called—and we call our brethren—to war. Let not the noise of the world deafen us to the Lord's alarm. It calls us to Him, to serve Him faithfully unto death.

—A. C.

A good man, in such a bad world as this,
cannot but be a man of sorrows.
MATTHEW HENRY

287

Sulking Saints

But it displeased Jonah exceedingly, and he was very angry.

JONAH 4:1

Some people are noted for their sullen disposition. They are so gloomy that they cast a cloud over every activity in which they become involved. Jonah's ill humour, which is faithfully recorded by the inspired penman, throws light on the unhealthy activity of sulking and shows us how much we grieve the Lord when we behave in this way.

Jonah sulked because God spared Nineveh, and Jonah did not want Nineveh spared. Of course, we know that the Ninevites were bitter and vicious enemies of Jonah's nation, and it was natural for Jonah to desire their destruction. But what is natural is not necessarily spiritual. God spoke to Jonah about his attitude and asked him, "Doest thou well to be angry?" (v. 4). It is clear that God did not approve of Jonah's sulking, but that did not stop Jonah. He dared to defend his bad temper even before God.

Sulking is evidently very hard to overcome. It is an obstinate vice that men are reluctant to give up or even admit to be sinful. The root cause of sulking is self-love. Sulking Jonah was completely taken up with himself. His language in chapter 4 shows this. There is a great deal of emphasis on the first-person singular—*I, me,* and *my.*

Jonah's sulking was quite disgraceful. He sulked in spite of the fact that he knew God was gracious and merciful, slow to anger, and of great kindness. Indeed, he even sulked *because* he knew this. He was happy when the Lord showed mercy to the Israelites, but not when He favoured heathen Ninevites.

It is bad to sulk when we see someone else being blessed. Shame on all sulking Christians!

—G. F.

I dare not fret any more than I dare curse and swear.
JOHN WESLEY

A Great High Priest

*Seeing then that we have a great high
priest, . . . let us hold fast our profession.*   HEBREWS 4:14

One of the real conflicts the Lord's people have to experience is the
constant pressure upon them to turn back from Christ. To coun-
teract such pressure the apostle Paul uses one emphasis the whole
way through his epistle to the Hebrews: the superiority of the Lord
Jesus Christ. Since the Hebrew Christians were being pressured
to return to Judaism with its dead, defunct ceremonies, Paul proves
conclusively that Christ is superior to all that was highly esteemed
in that system. He is superior to the Old Testament prophets, to
the angels, to Moses the lawgiver, and, above all, to the Aaronic
priesthood. The apostle demonstrates beyond all doubt that the
Old Testament priesthood and the entire ceremonial system which
revolved around it were not only inferior to Christ but had in fact
been utterly abolished by Him.

So Paul uses Christ's priesthood as an encouragement to those
Jewish believers to remain true to the gospel. He tells us that
Christ as High Priest is great, something that is never said of any
other high priest in Scripture. He is great because He is the only
priest between God and men, since He alone has offered a sacrifice
that satisfies divine justice. He is great because He never dies. The
priests of Aaron's line died, "but this man . . . continueth ever"
(Heb. 7:24). He is great because at God's right hand He prays for
us and is "touched with the feeling of our infirmities" (4:15). Why
then should we ever abandon this great High Priest? That is the
sin of those who do not hold fast their profession. It is a sin true
Christians refuse to commit. Rather than repudiating our Saviour,
we will come continually to Him, and He will give us mercy and
grace to help us in every time of need.

—J. G.

Once we grasp by faith the truth of our standing *in* Christ,
we will be greatly strengthened to stand *for* Christ.
ALEXANDER SIMPSON

What Is Real?

Why art thou cast down, O my soul?

PSALM 42:11

We tend to believe what we see. We understand the logic of discerning the existence of ducks. If it looks like, walks like, and quacks like a duck, it must be a duck. Faith, however, adds another dimension. By faith we know things that we cannot see. Faith sees the invisible, but it does not see the nonexistent. By faith we know that whatever God says is real. Our senses may be deceived, but never our faith. One of the greatest lessons faith teaches is that appearance and reality are often not the same.

Although we know that we are to walk by faith and not by sight, sometimes sight dominates and we draw wrong conclusions: "I will say unto God my rock, Why hast thou forgotten me?" (Psa. 42:9). How many times have our souls become cast down because we interpret what we see as evidence of God's disinterest in us? Having eternity in our hearts and time before our eyes creates tension for us. Psalm 42 portrays this common experience. The inspired poet became depressed when he focussed on his separation from God's house, on the oppression of his enemies, and on the waves of difficult circumstances that billowed over him. Though he knew better, he listened to the taunt, "Where is thy God?" If appearance was reality, he had every reason to be cast down. But what appeared to be was not the reality. When he focussed on the reality of the Lord and allowed his desire for God to overwhelm him, anxiety gave way to praise. The lovingkindness of the Lord became the life-jacket that preserved him in the rough seas. For the psalmist, faith was the answer to despair. The answer is the same for us. Let us learn to be more overwhelmed with the God we know by faith than we are by the circumstances we see surrounding us.

—M. P. V. B.

Let us never despair while we have Christ as our leader!
GEORGE WHITEFIELD

Strength for Warfare

Be strong in the Lord, and in the power of his might.
EPHESIANS 6:10

David and his men returned to their home in Ziklag only to find their houses burned to the ground and their families taken captive (I Sam. 30:1-6). They could not appeal to the local government for help, because at this point in his life David was rejected by the Philistines and a fugitive from Israel. Even worse, David's men, who had stood by him in the midst of other grave difficulties, in this situation spoke of stoning him. It was in this crisis that we read that David "encouraged [or, more literally, strengthened] himself in the Lord his God" (v. 6).

Now Paul commands us, like David of old, to "be strong in the Lord." This is not advice from an armchair theologian but from a great warrior for Christ. In Ephesus the demon declared, "Jesus I know, and Paul I know" (Acts 19:15). The powers of hell lost many a conflict to this soldier. It is this same Paul who says, "Be strong in the Lord." In earlier chapters of this epistle to the Ephesians he tells us that to be in Christ is to be chosen (1:4), forgiven (1:7), quickened (2:5), raised (2:6), and seated with Christ (2:6). But we must go further than mere intellectual apprehension of these truths; we must by faith embrace them. After David strengthened himself in the Lord, he then was able to conquer his enemies. When we lay hold of Christ and what we are in Him, we will conquer as David did.

Paul also admonishes us to lay hold of the power that is available to the believer because he is in Christ. The strength of Christ's might is omnipotence. This power is communicated to the believer through the Holy Spirit. Therefore let us seek to be filled with the Spirit of Christ (5:18). —M. W. A.

> Get God's arm, wherewith to wield His armour, and then you may do anything.
> JOHN TRAPP

Because

Because their waters they issued out of the sanctuary.

EZEKIEL 47:12

The picture here is of trees whose leaves do not wither and whose fruit will be gathered in abundance *because*, we are told, "their waters they issued out of the sanctuary."

No doubt these final chapters of Ezekiel have a much more extensive fulfilment than can be indicated by a spiritual review of God's great work as the prophet saw it. However, with a brief look we can mark out the spiritual lessons quite clearly.

The blessings in the chapter turn upon the flowing of the waters. These waters issue from the door of the sanctuary. In their onward flow, they begin in a small way and become increasingly deeper. Everywhere these waters go, they bring about a tremendous transformation: "every thing . . . which moveth, whithersoever the rivers shall come, shall live: and there shall be a very great multitude of fish, because these waters shall come thither: . . . and every thing shall live whither the river cometh" (Ezek. 47:9). On either side of the river grow "very many trees" (v. 7). The ground is bringing forth an abundance of good fruit. This fruit appears every month and is the product, not of the artificial labour so necessary in the world we know, but of natural development. The ground that before by nature brought forth thorns and briars now brings forth good fruit. These trees are sources of meat and medicine—the latter for bruises and sores. All this occurs "because their waters they issued out of the sanctuary." These blessings are all benefits of redemption.

If there is a spiritual parallel here, it lies in the mighty reviving work of the Holy Spirit through the life-giving Word. The Lord brought the prophet again to the door of the sanctuary to let him see it and to enrich his experience of it. May He bring us to the same place and give us a rich experience of this reviving stream.

—J. D.

The best definition of revival is "times of refreshing from the presence of the Lord."
J. Edwin Orr

Abolishing All Slavery

And ye shall know the truth, and the truth shall make you free.
JOHN 8:32

On February 27, 1991, President George Bush announced to the world that Kuwait had been liberated by Allied forces. After seven months of oppression under cruel Iraqi dictatorship, the people of Kuwait were delivered from bondage or exile. Television pictures captured many of the images of that joyous event of liberation for the Kuwaiti people.

Tragically, multitudes in the free world who enjoy unrestricted freedoms of the press, of free association, and of democratic government are in spiritual captivity. That is the worst form of captivity of all. The freedom offered by the Lord in our text deals with this dreadful bondage. It is not political or military, but spiritual liberty Christ promises.

To some, sin may appear to be an abstract evil. It is not. It is a very real evil. Its tentacles wrap around the lives of multitudes. Drink, gambling, passions for worldly pleasures, and illicit connections are all so many tyrants holding men captive. Bitter indeed is the condition of such prisoners.

Rejoice, however, because Christ is the liberator of His people. He came into the world to preach deliverance to the captives (Luke 4:18). He totally frees His people from the guilt and consequences of sin by His blood. He frees them from an accusing conscience. He liberates them from the thraldom of lust and from the dominion of the devil.

This is the message of the gospel of saving grace. How blessed is this truth when it shines into darkened and imprisoned souls and leads them into victorious fellowship with God! This freedom comes through Christ indwelling you by His Spirit. Without this emancipation, all other freedoms are ultimately worthless, for they will soon give place to the everlasting imprisonment of hell. But if Christ has saved you from sin, your future is one of eternal liberty and blessedness. "If the Son therefore shall make you free, ye shall be free indeed" (John 8:36).

—I. G.

The union of faith and freedom is the essential genius of Protestantism.
JUSTIN WROE

The Man with the Two-edged Sword

Ehud made him a dagger which had two edges.

JUDGES 3:16

When we engage in spiritual warfare, we need to be well armed. Ehud believed that, and so he armed himself with a two-edged sword (the word translated *dagger* is the usual Hebrew word for "sword"). It was ideally suited for his purpose, and he used it with devastating effect.

The Lord has provided every gospel warrior with such a sword, the Word of God (Eph. 6:17; Heb. 4:12). We should ever be prepared to use this weapon: "Let the high praises of God be in their mouth, and a twoedged sword in their hand" (Psa. 149:6).

Those who would serve the Lord must get a thorough grasp of the Bible. There is no other sword as sharp. All the training the world can give you in logic, philosophy, literature, science, and even theology cannot compare with a deep knowledge of God's Word. The Lord has promised to bless His Word. It can never return to Him void (Isa. 55:11). He uses it to convince men of their sin, empty them of all hope in themselves, and then point them to the Lord Jesus Christ as the only way of salvation. The devil's grasp on souls cannot withstand the power of the Word of God applied by the Spirit of God to the heart. Even a text of Scripture borne home to the heart by the Holy Spirit is enough to bring a soul to eternal life.

Satan fears this two-edged sword. That is the reason for his sustained but totally unfounded attack on the Bible. Let us never be ashamed of God's Word or substitute some other sword for it. Let us learn it and obtain a thorough knowledge of what it says on the all-important issues of sin and salvation. But do not just learn it. Use it with confidence. Its thrusts are just as successful in the spiritual realm as Ehud's sword was in the physical.

—A. C.

There are some who . . . suppose the old sword
is rusty, and worn out, but *we* can say,
"There is none like that; give it me!"
C. H. SPURGEON

Christians in Conflict

But I am carnal, sold under sin.

ROMANS 7:14

Strange words from the lips of such a man of God. Or are they? Some would say this is Paul in his Christian infancy, still struggling with the basics of holy living. But if that is true, there are few, if any, *mature* believers. The seeming difficulty of these words is resolved upon the consideration of what prompted them.

Paul has been showing the work of God's law in his own conversion. It was seeing the spiritual nature of the law that brought this one-time Pharisee to call upon Christ. But once he understood this truth, he could never forget it—not even as a Christian. The more Paul matured in his spiritual life, the more he came to understand the law's spiritual standards and the fact that holiness does not consist in an outward conformity to the law, but an inward conformity of heart. As the law's light grew brighter and brighter, Paul saw more of his own sin and cried out, "I am carnal!" His was the same conviction that men like Luther, Calvin, Rutherford, and McCheyne felt in their own lives.

But this law also revealed Paul's true Christian character, for he states in verse 22 that he "delight[ed] in the law of God after the inward man." Thus Paul declares that he does the things he hates, and does not the things that he loves in God's law. You see, it is only in a Christian that such a battle rages. The unsaved have no delight in God's law nor desire to obey it, and hence no struggle.

Now it is because of this conflict brought on by the law of God working in our hearts that we see our wretched, helpless condition. "O wretched man that I am! who shall deliver me from the body of this death?" (v. 24). And it is this realization that drives us back again and again to Christ and His righteousness. Blessed law that brings us to Christ! Blessed Christ that brings us to victory!

—J. W.

There is no holiness without a warfare.
J. C. Ryle

The Best Friend

A friend loveth at all times.

PROVERBS 17:17

Cicero said, "Friendship is the only thing in the world concerning the usefulness of which all mankind are agreed." In all ages men have esteemed, extolled, and treasured friendship. It has been well described as "the most beautiful and fragrant flower that man meets in his earthly pilgrimage." What heart is not stirred by the loveliness of that bond of friendship between Jonathan and David? Truly, "friendship is the marriage of affections" (Thomas Watson). Alas, such friendship is rare indeed. How wondrous is that grace that enables us to say of the Lord of glory, "This is my friend" (Song of Sol. 5:16).

The true extent of friendship must be measured not in word, but in deed. "Greater love hath no man than this, that a man lay down his life for his friends" (John 15:13). This is the greatest act of friendship among men—"love's crowning deed," as C. H. Spurgeon called it. How unparalleled, therefore, is the friendship of our Lord Jesus. He loved us and laid down His life for us, His enemies (Rom. 5:10)! O matchless love!

True friendship is ever characterized by constancy. "Swallow-friends, that fly to you in summer, but are gone in winter; such friends there is no loss of" (Matthew Henry). The Saviour is the Friend who loveth at all times. There is no fickleness about Him. He is the same yesterday, today, and forever. It has been well said, "Christ's friendship prevails when human friendship fails." He is an unfailing Friend. He never forsakes His friends. He loves unto the end. Jonathan Edwards, on his deathbed, asked, "Where is Jesus of Nazareth, my old and faithful friend? I know He will be with me now that I need His help." And so He was, for that faithful servant died triumphantly. Christian, rejoice daily in this thy Friend.

—M. P.

God is the sweetest friend, but the worst enemy.
Thomas Watson

Growing Christians

*As newborn babes, desire the sincere milk
of the word, that ye may grow thereby.*

I PETER 2:2

The spiritual life of the Christian, once born, is a developing and progressive one. The origin and development of that life are pictured for us by the apostle in this verse. First, it is a life that is generated within us and is manifested through a spiritual birth. We are as newborn babes. The moment a child is born it manifests life—it cries. So it is with the born again. The first evidence and expression of our spiritual life is that we cry. We pray the sinner's prayer. So it was with Paul the apostle. It was said of the transformed and regenerate Saul of Tarsus, "Behold, he prayeth" (Acts 9:11).

But if the life of Christ has been truly implanted in our soul, it will prove to have a healthy appetite. Its desires and appetites will be a reflection of its own nature—holy and pure. It will desire the sincere milk of the Word that it might grow and mature thereby. Feeding on the milk of the Word, we will soon begin to grow, to grow spiritually, to "grow in grace, and in the knowledge of our Lord and Saviour Jesus Christ" (II Pet. 3:18). It is a natural growth—as natural as for a child to grow. An infant that does not grow is unnatural. So is a Christian who does not grow spiritually.

Growth is gradual. No infant becomes a man at once, but each day sees it coming nearer adulthood and full growth. Let us labour for that gradual but strong and consistent growth that comes with daily nourishing of the soul by the manna of God's holy Word. This sincere milk of the Word is divine truth understood, believed, and adopted.

—R. J. B.

There is enough in one of the articles of our
faith to hold you in study all your lives and
afford you still an increase of knowledge.
RICHARD BAXTER

Death's Contribution to Life

*It is better to go to the house of mourning, . . . for that is
the end of all men; and the living will lay it to his heart.*
ECCLESIASTES 7:2

Every so often death comes to someone we know and reminds us
of our own mortality. The Bible says that this is an important
reminder. Although we know that death is unavoidable and does
not discriminate according to age, sex, colour, social status, or
wealth, we somehow convince ourselves that we might be the
exception. If not forever, we think that at least for the moment,
death will keep its distance until we fulfil all our hopes and aspirations. The future holds great fascination for us. That is perfectly
good, but it is important for all of us to face the fact that this life
is not all there is. We must prepare for what will follow this earthly,
temporary existence. It is particularly important for Christians,
who know what lies beyond this life, to use life to bring honour and
glory to our Lord.

It is significant that Ecclesiastes, a book that shows us how
to live, says much about death. The best philosophy of life is one
that recognizes the brevity of life and the certainty of death.
There is much about death that is disagreeable to self-esteem.
The body returns to dust (Eccles. 12:7), and life goes on without
us (1:4). We will not be gone very long before we are completely
forgotten (1:11; 2:16; 9:5, 15). It is vital to be ready for death,
for though its coming is determined by God (3:2), it is unknown
to us (9:12). We are not to have a morbid worry about death; we
are just to remember that we will die. Death puts life in the
proper perspective. We must live in the light of eternity, not time.
—M. P. V. B.

I am packed, sealed and waiting for the post.
JOHN NEWTON

What Is Your Life?

*What is your life? It is even a vapour, that appeareth
for a little time, and then vanisheth away.*

JAMES 4:14

These words are most frequently used to warn sinners of the urgent necessity for them to get right with God. They certainly should make every careless soul think of the brevity of life, the certainty of death, and the solemnity of eternity. If you come to this day still in your sins, you should stop and consider this word from God. You know the gospel. You know you should call upon the Lord to have mercy upon you. You know that tomorrow it may be too late for you to call. Call upon Him today and you will find that He will have mercy and will abundantly pardon (Isa. 55:7).

Yet James originally directed these words to Christians. They had become very careless about spiritual things. They were consumed with the here and now, this life with its pleasures and profits. They took time for granted and made their plans as if they were certain to be around for a long time.

Is that not how all too many of us live? We need to take James's rebuke seriously and personally. We need to grasp again some basic facts. First, our hold on life is very tenuous. Second, at best our life will be brief. Third, in this brief life what matters is not where we have travelled or what we have gained, but how we have responded to the will of God.

In the light of these things, how does your life measure up? What is your life? What motivates it? What has it accomplished? The Lord asks the questions, and He will have honest answers.

—A. C.

**The business of our lives is not to
please ourselves but to please God.**
MATTHEW HENRY

The Joyful Sound

Ye shall be remembered before the Lord your God,
and ye shall be saved from your enemies.

NUMBERS 10:9

Such a promise as this strongly implies that God's people sometimes feel that they are forgotten in heaven. When the enemy surrounds the feeble believer and the battle rages more and more fiercely, he fears that his God has forgotten him. However, the text for today draws our attention to the impossibility of such forgetfulness on God's part. There is a blessed note constantly sounding in the ears of Almighty God, acting as an unceasing reminder of His own people. It is the clear, sweet note of redemption. When Israel went forth to battle, the priests blew the two silver trumpets, and the Lord remembered His people.

Silver speaks of redemption, as is shown in the third chapter of Numbers, when the firstborn males who had no Levites to represent them were each redeemed with five shekels of silver. That redemption money was given to Aaron and his sons, and there is good reason to believe that it was used to make these trumpets. Thus each time they were blown, the note of redemption was sounded, and Israel was comforted by the fact that that sound was ascending to heaven. What a blessed illustration of why the believer cannot be forgotten. He has been brought under the gospel of redemption, which sounds forth the certainty that the price of his liberty from sin has been paid. He is remembered in heaven because of the redeeming blood of the Lord Jesus Christ.

It is interesting to note that the two trumpets were both fashioned from one whole piece of silver. Consequently, the metal of each trumpet was of the same consistency, so that when blown they were in perfect unison. The message of redemption contains no discordant notes. Christ has done all things well. What a pleasing melody reverberates around the throne of God! He is satisfied, and so are His saints. "Blessed is the people that know the joyful sound" (Psa. 89:15).

—J. G.

The Christian's joy is in proportion to his
understanding of his full and free acceptance by
God on the sole merit of Christ's righteousness.
ALEXANDER SIMPSON

Heart-to-Heart Fellowship

If we walk in the light, as he is in the light,
we have fellowship one with another, and the blood
of Jesus Christ his Son cleanseth us from all sin.

I JOHN 1:7

Beloved, for God to have fellowship with us in this sin-cursed world, we must walk in His light. The apostle John is not addressing merely our manner of living, but the motivation for doing what we do. Dear Christian, God must have your heart before you can give Him your hands and feet. Our conduct before God must be the expression of our hearts. For us to walk with God, our hearts must be in agreement and in harmony with Him.

God is light, and in Him is no guile, deceit, or hypocrisy, but rather truth, purity, and righteousness. Therefore we must have an enlightened heart to walk with God. The light of God's purity has revealed our sinful condition and our dreadful state and has moved us to embrace the beauty of Christ crucified. Our hearts now desire to walk in purity and in truth.

We must have a sincere heart to walk with God. Christianity is not a fleshly performance, but a joint participation with the Lord. Our seeking for mercy and our reverence of the Lord are very real in our lives.

We must have a holy heart to walk with God. We absolutely abhor falsehood and all the filthy things of the world. Our hearts are in total agreement with God. We love what He loves, and we hate what He hates. As Amos 3:3 points out, "Can two walk together, except they be agreed?"

Finally, we must have an open and transparent heart to walk with God. Our hearts must be so open to the truth of God that the doctrines of grace touch us and we readily accept what God says about righteousness, sin, hell, and judgment. Our hearts must be so open to God in prayer that we hide nothing from His holy face. Can the Lord testify of us, as He did of Nathanael, "Behold an Israelite indeed, in whom is no guile"?

—R. J. W.

**Live near to God and all things will appear little
to you in comparison with eternal realities.**
ROBERT MURRAY McCHEYNE

301

Praying on the Merit of Christ

There was given unto him much incense, that
he should offer it with the prayers of all saints.

REVELATION 8:3

A very precious lesson awaits us in this text. Once grasped, it will revolutionize our prayer lives and lead us into the joyous experience of truly being able to plead the blood of Christ in our praying. It is this: the prayers of God's people ascend to His throne with the sweet incense of the merits of Christ and therefore obtain His answer.

We are not heard for our much speaking (Matt. 6:7). Our oratory has no effect on God. On the other hand, our stumbling sentences are no hindrance to His hearing our cry. What renders our praying acceptable to God is the merit of Christ's atonement. That is the "sweetsmelling savour" (Eph. 5:2) that merits the favour of God. Hebrews 10:19 tells us that we have "boldness to enter into the holiest by the blood of Jesus."

We have a great high priest at the right hand of God. For His sake God hears our cry. His perfection covers the weak pleas we send to God. Therefore let us no longer labour under the delusion that "I cannot pray. My words are too mean. My best efforts are too weak." Let us place all our trust in the perfect merits of Christ. The Father will never deny Him or His blood. What leaves our lips as a puny cry reaches His throne as a powerful plea that has all the sweetness and strength of the Lord Jesus in it.

Let us then expect answers to our prayers. What God does on earth is in answer to the prayers of the saints. Even the mighty cataclysmic judgments of God upon the earth in the last days are sent in answer to the prayers of the saints (Rev. 8-9). Can anything, then, bar the progress of a Christian or a church that knows how to pray on the merits of Christ? May the Lord teach us so to pray, and we shall move heaven and earth for the glory of Christ our Saviour.

—A. C.

Christ's intercession is grounded in His
atonement; and so is the prayer of faith.
R. C. CHAPMAN

302

The Missing Ingredient

Cause the lamps to burn continually.

LEVITICUS 24:2

This is an unusual chapter, coming after the holy convocations of Israel and before the instructions for the year of Jubilee. Its seems to bear little relation to either the preceding or following chapters. It is also unusual in its contents, because the first nine verses deal with instructions for tabernacle service, and the rest tells of an apparently unrelated incident of blasphemy.

Something is unusual also about the sanctuary instructions; something is missing! Let us search for the missing piece. The tabernacle consisted of the rectangular outer court, approximately 150 feet by 75 feet. Inside and towards the rear of the outer court was the tabernacle proper, roughly 45 feet by 15 feet. It was divided into two sections: the larger sanctuary, and the smaller Holiest of All, where resided the ark of the covenant and the mercy seat.

In the sanctuary there were three pieces of furnishing: the table of shewbread, the candlestick, and the golden altar of incense. In this chapter instructions are given for the provision of bread for the table and oil for the lamp, but strangely there is no mention of the altar of incense. The altar of incense is the missing ingredient.

The table pictures for us the *church profiting,* feeding on the living Bread, Jesus Christ. We must read and study the Word. The candlestick shows us the *church preaching,* holding forth Jesus Christ, the Light of the world, by the power of the Holy Spirit. We must preach the Word.

The golden altar typifies the intercessory ministry of Christ and the *church praying.* Sadly, the *church praying* is often the missing ingredient in many assemblies today. Power has ebbed away because there is little or no prayer.

Is the altar of incense missing from your life today? Is prayer the missing ingredient from your Christian witness? Your feeding and profiting on Christ, and your preaching and witness for Him, will be much more blessed and effective if they are sanctified by prayer.

—F. McC.

Prayer meetings are the throbbing machinery of the church.

C. H. Spurgeon

Gospel Satisfaction

The fulness of the blessing of the gospel of Christ.

ROMANS 15:29

One of the devastating consequences of the fall was that it left man with a deep void in his soul. Something is missing. Ever since that dark day, men have spent their lives looking for something to fill their souls' emptiness. Sadly, they "spend money for that which is not bread . . . and . . . labour for that which satisfieth not" (Isa. 55:2).

But God's child has discovered that "blessed are they which do hunger and thirst after righteousness: for they shall be filled" (Matt. 5:6). Paul beautifully expresses this truth in the words *the fulness of the blessing of the gospel of Christ*. Because he was filled with the gospel, the apostle was fully satisfied. Paul knew well the truth that so few believers seem to experience: none but Christ can satisfy! Doubting, seeking acceptance from man, thinking that fame or fortune will bring happiness are all the sad lot of a Christian who has yet to learn what Paul enjoyed.

First, he was *satisfied with Christ's merits*. This one-time Pharisee learned that he could never earn God's pardon, God's peace, or God's righteousness. But he rejoiced in the glorious truth that Christ had earned them for him by His perfect life and sacrificial death. There is no power that can ever take Christ's merits from us. What a ground for assurance!

But Paul was also *satisfied with Christ's mercy*. Some believers are always looking for the love and affection of others. But dear, lonely child of God, what love is there like Christ's love? To think you are loved without limit, at all times, in all your weakness and failure—surely His "love is better than wine" (Song of Sol. 1:2).

And was not Paul also *satisfied with Christ's mind?* Paul suffered the loss of all his privileges in the Jews' religion and counted them as dung that he might know Christ. That meant being filled with the mind of Christ (Phil. 2:5-8), a mind of self-denial, service, and sacrifice. Oh, that we might enjoy more of this fulness today!

—J. W.

**When Christ reveals Himself there is satisfaction
in the slenderest portion, and without Christ
there is emptiness in the greatest fulness.**
ALEXANDER GROSSE

Knowing the Times

Doth the hawk fly by thy wisdom,
and stretch her wings toward the south?　　JOB 39:26

As the Lord questioned His tried and afflicted servant Job, He referred to many aspects of His creation to illustrate His wisdom and power. Here He refers to the hawk, one of the swiftest birds in the sky. For example, a falcon-hawk once escaped from a town in France and reached the island of Malta, 1350 miles away, twenty-four hours later. Moreover, the hawk is not only swift, but is instinctively wise. In northern climes, long before winter approaches, it flies south to the heat. Its annual flight displays its innate knowledge of the times and seasons of the year. Not only does it have understanding of its present condition, but it is aware of what is ahead.

We may raise this thought to the spiritual realm. The believer is taught of God, that he may have understanding of the times in which he lives so as to be aware of what lies ahead. Large portions of the Bible are given over to prophecy. The climactic event of all prophetic utterances is the second coming of our Lord Jesus Christ. The Christian life is depicted as turning to God from idols to serve the living and true God and to wait for His Son from heaven (I Thess. 1:9-10). The same sentiments of patiently waiting for the coming of the Lord are expressed in James 5:7-11. As the momentous event approaches, the believer who is walking in close fellowship with the Lord will, like the hawk, have insight into the times and seasons. He will not be in darkness that that day should overtake him as a thief (I Thess. 5:1-4). As the Lord's coming approaches, let us be found faithful—faithful in our worship, our supplications, and our service.

　　　　—S. B. C.

A man full of hope will be full of action.
Thomas Brooks

Security Through the Blood

*If the Lord were pleased to kill us, he would
not have received a burnt offering.*

JUDGES 13:23

Samson's mother had a grasp of gospel theology! Manoah, her husband, had an attack of doubting and said, "We shall surely die." Many a Christian has had the very same feeling. There are times when terrible doubts about our salvation assail our soul. Many people are driven to the depths of depression and despair as they struggle with the thought that though they have trusted Christ, they may ultimately perish.

These are not days when such struggles of soul are much understood. Even preachers can give little help in this area. Gone are the old Puritans who were such Biblical physicians of the soul, and in their place, alas, we have mostly men to whom deep spiritual conflict is foreign. Souls battling doubt are led to another "decision," and then another, and another, until the confusion is like darkness that may be felt.

The trouble with all the emphasis on the human decision is that it pays more attention to the work of man than to the work of Christ. Add to this the widespread denial of the truth of particular redemption and the sweet-sounding but fatal notion that on the cross Christ did exactly the same for all men without distinction, and the trouble is compounded. If Christ did the very same work for those who ultimately go to hell as for those who go to heaven, *then obviously going to heaven does not depend entirely on the merit of Christ.* With that theology, is it any wonder men lack assurance?

However, Christ's sacrifice is all-sufficient. Has God accepted His blood for us? Then He will never fail to give us everything that blood purchased for us (Rom. 8:32). How are we saved? By looking in faith to Christ (Isa. 45:22). How can we be sure we are saved and will not ultimately perish? By looking in faith to Christ. Let us learn the theology of Samson's mother: If God has accepted the blood of Christ, He cannot reject anyone whose faith is in Christ.

—A. C.

**Until God can be unjust, and demand two payments for
one debt, He cannot destroy the soul for whom Jesus died.**
C. H. Spurgeon

Protected by the Power of Prayer

*Holy Father, keep through thine own name those whom
thou hast given me, that they may be one, as we are.*

JOHN 17:11

There is an ongoing miracle in the life of each Christian as he lives in this hostile world. As one quaintly said, "It is more wonderful to maintain a candle in a bucket of water than in a lantern." The preservation of the saints in this world is a work ascribed to all three Persons of the Trinity. In this high-priestly prayer of Christ we learn that God the Father keeps His people in His own name. This is remarkable. It indicates that the Father keeps His saints through His own attributes, such as His power, His love, and His wisdom.

For the three years that the Lord had been with His disciples in the world, He guarded them from all harm through the Father's power. His success as Shepherd of the sheep is a blessed encouragement to His people. Not one of them has ever been lost. The whole flock has been folded safely, and all the church of Christ will assuredly be presented with full attendance on the latter day.

Knowing that He was soon to die and leave this world, Christ interceded with His Father for His blood-bought saints to be kept in the fulness of mutual fellowship with the Father and be delivered from the evils of sin, scandal, and despair. This is a great comfort and source of strength to the child of God while serving the Lord amongst the ungodly. While the world is laughing at us, our Advocate above is praying for us. Such intercession is the peculiar privilege of the saints and one grand reason for their continuance in grace.

—I. G.

Souls in heaven are more holy but not more secure.
ROBERT MURRAY MCCHEYNE

Thoughts for a Bad Day

In the day of prosperity be joyful, but in the day of adversity consider.
ECCLESIASTES 7:14

Everybody has good and bad days, ups and downs. The tides of life come in and go out; life constantly ebbs and flows. The command to rejoice when everything is good, up, in, and flowing is probably the easiest command in the Bible to obey. But on the bad days we are to think about something: that our God has put the day of adversity next to the day of prosperity so that we might "find nothing after him." The fluctuations of life increase our sense of dependence on the Lord. Because we have a tendency to forget God when everything goes well, God brings trials to remind us that He is in control. By the providence of God, nothing happens by accident; everything happens for our ultimate good and God's glory.

Do not judge a book by its cover. This adage reminds us that things are not always what they appear to be. The difference between appearance and reality is an important lesson to learn. Ecclesiastes 7 depicts this in several ways: the day of death is better that the day of birth; mourning is better than mirth; sorrow is better than laughter; rebuke from a wise man is better than praise from a fool; the end is better than the beginning. At first glance, the opposite of these seems to be true. Too often we judge God and what He does by the first glance. We fail to look beyond sight to the reality only faith can discern. Faith sees that prosperity without God is worthless and adversity with God is worth everything. Faith in the good, wise providence of God means that we look beyond appearances to the reality of God's purpose in every circumstance of life.

—M. P. V. B.

Life asks no questions that faith cannot answer.
ANONYMOUS

Praying for Boldness

Praying . . . that I may open my mouth boldly.
EPHESIANS 6:18-19

The great prophet Elijah serves as an example for us in the place of prayer. In James 5:17 we read that Elijah "was a man subject to like passions as we are." Were it not for this reminder, the humble saint would faint at the prospect of trying to follow in the footsteps of such a giant in prayer. Likewise, Paul gives us a testimony to his own weakness when he asks the believers in Ephesus to pray that his witness would be with boldness. This is truly an amazing request. Was not this the apostle who preached the gospel to both Jew and Gentile in public and from house to house at Ephesus (Acts 20:20)? And did not Luke record that "all they which dwelt in Asia heard the word of the Lord Jesus" from the lips of Paul (Acts 19:10)? And yet now he requests prayer for boldness.

This request of Paul ought to help us in at least three areas of our own witness. First, Paul recognized that true boldness is not necessarily something found in a man's character, but is something God gives in response to prayer. When the early church received threatenings from men, she prayed to the Lord for boldness to witness. The result was that the Holy Spirit came upon those believers, and they found the power they sought (Acts 4:24-33).

Second, if Paul had to ask for prayer, then certainly no believer is exempt from this need for spiritual boldness. Would that every minister had such prayer warriors calling on God for his ministry!

Third, Paul, like many believers, knew enough of the gospel to save the world. The problem was not a lack of knowledge, but the need to give out the gospel in a manner becoming the gospel. It is a great message we proclaim. May God grant us each one the power to proclaim it boldly wherever we go today and every day.
—M. W. A.

The more holiness any man attains to, the more bold, courageous and heroic that man will be for God.
THOMAS BROOKS

Praise in Every Part

Upon . . . an instrument of ten strings will I sing praises unto thee.

PSALM 144:9

An old saint of God prayed the following prayer at a prayer meeting: "Oh, Lord, we will praise Thee, we will praise Thee with an instrument of ten strings." Those present in the meeting wondered what the ten strings were, but they soon discovered them as the brother continued in prayer. "We shall praise Thee with our eyes by looking only unto Thee. We shall praise Thee with our ears by listening only to Thy voice. We shall praise Thee with our hands by working in Thy service. We shall praise Thee with our feet by running in the way of Thy commandments. We shall praise Thee with our tongue by bearing testimony to Thy lovingkindness. We shall praise Thee with our heart by loving only Thee. An instrument of ten strings, Lord. Keep the instrument in tune. Lord, play upon it. Ring out the melodies of music. Keep it in harmony. Make it to speak out Thy glory—an instrument of ten strings. Two eyes, two ears, two hands, two feet, one tongue, and one heart."

Horatius Bonar wrote:

> *Fill Thou my life, O Lord my God, in every part with praise,*
> *That my whole being may proclaim Thy being and Thy ways.*
> *Not for the lip of praise alone nor e'en the praising heart*
> *I ask but for a life made up of praise in every part.*

—S. B.

We should be always wearing the garment of praise, not just waving a palm-branch now and then.
ANDREW BONAR

The Source of Our Strength

*The spirit entered into me when he spake
unto me, and set me upon my feet.*

EZEKIEL 2:2

Superhuman strength is needed for an evil day. The prophet grows lonely in exile, parted from his homeland forever. There will be no return for Ezekiel, for the city of Jerusalem is doomed. His visions show its temple reduced to ashes. The sanctuary is profaned, the glory of God is departed, and God is hiding His face from the nation. Yet God has called Ezekiel to minister to a captive people like himself in such a dark hour.

The indwelling Spirit is Ezekiel's source of strength. Ezekiel has an anointing from above. One like unto the Son of Man sets him apart. The Holy Spirit enters in as the Lord begins to speak. However hard the circumstances, Ezekiel's ministry will now leave its mark. The people "shall know that there hath been a prophet among them" (Ezek. 2:5). There is no justification for anything less in the way of divine ordination nowadays.

The Holy Spirit works in conjunction with His Word. God Himself did the speaking; the Holy Spirit did the work. He will never work contrary to what God says in His Word.

God's purpose at this time is to stand the servant of the Lord upon his feet (vv. 1, 2). The serpent loosed a flood on the woman to prevent her from standing in the midst of the tide of secularism, temptation, worldliness, and sin (Rev. 12:15). God puts us on our feet so that we can listen at our best.

Here is the answer. This work of the Holy Spirit brings Ezekiel into closest communion with God. He says as of now, "I heard him that spake." May the Holy Spirit open up our hearts to the Word of God in like manner.

—J. D.

Messages from God are for standers, not
prostrate ones. They require utmost *attention* of
body, *intention* of mind, and *retention* of memory.
JOHN TRAPP

It Is Going To Get Better

But God will redeem my soul from the power of the grave.

PSALM 49:15

The inequities of life have bothered saints for a long time. Whereas hard-working, God-fearing people often have little of the wealth or fame of this world, known scoundrels seem to prosper at will. If this life were everything, this inequity would be impossible to understand. But this life is not all there is. The philosophy of the rich man in Christ's parable who sought prosperity in this life at the expense of his soul is shared by many. Christ declared that he who provides for this life but takes no thought for eternity is forever a fool.

Death is the great equalizer; it comes to all, rich or poor, sinner or saint. What happens after death is infinitely and eternally more important than what happens in life. It is foolish for us to fret over what happens in such a temporary arena. Psalm 49 reveals that man's life is nothing more than an overnight lodging (v. 12), after which comes the morning when the upright will have dominion (v. 14). For those who die without Christ, death is horrible. Earthly wealth and fame have no value in redeeming the soul. Death becomes the sinister shepherd who leads to destruction. But God will do for us what riches cannot do: He will redeem us from the power of death. He will not abandon us. As He received Enoch and Elijah, so will He receive into glory all who belong to Him. The words of the old song ring true: "This world is not my home—I'm just a-passing through." If we are more concerned about eternity than about time, we can easily endure our "light affliction, which is but for a moment" (II Cor. 4:17).

—M. P. V. B.

He whose head is in heaven need not
fear to put his feet into the grave.
MATTHEW HENRY

Acceptable Sacrifices

I beseech you therefore, brethren, by the mercies of
God, that ye present your bodies a living sacrifice, holy,
acceptable unto God, which is your reasonable service.
ROMANS 12:1

Here is the beginning of the believer's duty in sanctification. After having expounded what God had done for them, Paul now tells these Roman Christians what they ought to do for God. But why does Paul begin with the *body?* Because the body is the instrument of sin or of righteousness. The body carries out the desires and intentions of the heart, will, and mind. And because sin still dwells in our flesh, we must present our bodies as a living sacrifice—literally, a "living-slain" sacrifice. These words mean far more than the popular notion of "surrendering your life to Christ." God calls for an *active* sacrifice of the flesh, a crucifying of the lusts of the flesh. We are to be dead indeed unto sin but alive unto God.

We should, with David, set no wicked thing before our eyes, but rather behold wondrous things out of God's law. We must present our ears as a living sacrifice, refusing to listen to the world's music and message, while applying our ears to the words of knowledge. And, like the psalmist, we should purpose that our mouth shall not transgress. This is what Paul meant when he said the sacrifice must be holy. How can we present ourselves to God for service if, to change the metaphor, the vessel is dirty? A dirty pot is of little use—much less a "dirty" believer (II Tim. 2:21).

But Paul describes this bodily presentation with one more word: *acceptable.* What a word of encouragement this is! This sacrifice of ourselves must be acceptable unto God. There was only one way God would accept the Old Testament sacrifice: it must be presented by the high priest. And as we would present ourselves unto God for service, let us always do so through Jesus Christ, our great High Priest. His blood will cover all our failures, sins, and blemishes and make our service acceptable in the Father's sight.

—J. W.

Nothing less than a living sacrifice is demanded.
Not a loan, but a gift; not a compromise but
a sacrifice; not our poorest, but our best.
J. PEARCE

313

The Peace of God and the God of Peace

He shall offer of the sacrifice of the peace offering.
LEVITICUS 3:9

Many Christians find Leviticus a difficult book to study. One of the reasons is that the intricate details of the offerings and other services are hard to decipher. It is good to note the similarities and then the differences, and also to regard the names. That approach will help you understand, for example, how the peace offering is different from the burnt offering.

The peace offering shows more the results of Christ's sacrifice than the manner. It signifies the peace, prosperity, and joy which should characterize the believer's life. There are some today who are gloomy, dull, dark-spirited, and unsociable, and who seem to labour under the delusion that gloominess is a sign of piety. Nothing could be further from the truth. When the Jew brought his peace offering, it was with a heart moved by the mercy of God. Any remarkable favour from God was a fit opportunity to bring the peace offering.

Let us bring our peace offerings to God today and thank Him for the enjoyments of life that are common to all. God is seen in all the world around us. Thank Him for beauty, domestic happiness, friendships, and for a multitude of His tender mercies.

Let us thank the Lord for the enjoyments of eternal life. These are meats sacred to the Christian. We know God not only as Creator but also as Redeemer. The turbulence of a sinful life is replaced by the peace of God. We can sing, "It is well with my soul."

Thank Him also for the guidance of His Word. The riddle of life is explained. The Christian sees himself tracing the steps of Moses and Paul and a host of God's chosen servants. He does not have to muddle his way through life. God has shown in His Word that "this is the way, walk ye in it" (Isa. 30:21). What a joy to know the peace of God and the God of peace (Phil. 4:7, 9)!

—F. McC.

What peace can they have who are not at peace with God?
MATTHEW HENRY

314

Victory in the Valley

Maschil of David; A Prayer when he was in the cave.

PSALM 142

The title of this psalm tells us that it was written by David when he was in a cave. We are not told which cave he was hiding in, whether it was at Adullam or Engedi. King Saul was now seeking to kill him, and David was fearful for his life. Three thousand men were searching the countryside for him. It was against this dark background that David penned this psalm. In verse 4 we have his sorrowful words, "No man cared for my soul." It seems that the man after God's own heart had forgotten about Jonathan, the king's son in the palace, who loved David even as his own soul. How often we find ourselves in some dark cave of spiritual depression and feel that no one cares for us. Like David we forget about the King's Son, the Lord Jesus Christ, who loves us with dying yet undying love. Peter, writing to those who were passing through a time of trial and testing, wrote these wonderful words: "Casting all your care upon him; for he careth for you" (I Pet. 5:7).

> *Said the robin to the sparrow, "I should really like to know*
> *Why these anxious human beings rush about and worry so."*
> *Said the sparrow to the robin, "Friend, I think it must be*
> *That they have no heavenly Father such as cares for you*
> *and me!"*

The Lord in His love never ceases to care for His children. Look to Him now by faith and trust Him to give you the victory in the valley.

—S. B.

To carry care to bed is to sleep with a pack on your back.
THOMAS HALIBURTON

The Foolishness of Preaching

It pleased God by the foolishness of preaching.

I CORINTHIANS 1:21

An earnest young Christian prayed that the Lord would bless his pastor, for "it pleased God by the *preaching of foolishness* to save." That unconscious mistake is near the truth in many pulpits today.

It is a "preaching of foolishness" that exalts a human, mutable philosophy and neglects the life-saving Word of God. Likewise when the cardinal doctrines are omitted or buried under a mass of human tradition. It is foolish preaching where everything is a mist and a haze and the unfortunate sinner has no idea from his preacher of the way to heaven. Preaching that never mentions the name of God, or the Holy Spirit's essential regenerating work, or justification by faith alone, or redemption by the shed blood, is foolishness indeed.

But Paul speaks in our verse of the "foolishness of preaching," and in so doing he gives the world's view of the preaching of the cross. Why should it be seen as foolishness in the eyes of the world?

Perhaps because ordinary people receive it. There is a snobbery of intellect that believes its superiority could not stoop to something as simple as the gospel of Christ. The gospel does not come by human speculation, but by divine revelation. Proud man does not like to acknowledge that fact.

The world regards preaching as foolish because it punctures man's pride. He does not like to be told that he is nothing and a nobody. Yet that is exactly what the gospel does to the pride of man. Not many mighty are called, but God has called the weak, the foolish, the base, and the despised into His kingdom.

Proud man wants to retain some of his glory, but the Bible shows us that man has nothing to glory in save the cross of Christ. That which is foolishness to the world is wisdom with God. And it is "the power of God unto salvation to every one that believeth" (Rom 1:16).

—F. McC.

We have the truth and we need not be afraid to say so.

J. C. RYLE

Our Daily Bread

Thy words were found, and I did eat them.

JEREMIAH 15:16

True Christians have a taste for God's Word. They read it; they study it; they feast on it. Empty professors may be content with a religion that pays scant attention to the Bible, but believers indwelt by the Holy Spirit can never be indifferent to what the Spirit has written. Like Job they testify, "I have esteemed the words of his mouth more than my necessary food" (Job 23:12).

To eat God's words is to receive them into our hearts by faith so that we live them out in obedience. It is to receive our inner strength, not from circumstances, but from what the Lord has said. His Word is always the final word on any subject. It drives away our fear. It establishes our assurance. It informs our conscience. It judges our sin. It guides our steps.

The Bible, then, is no mere ancient document. It is a living Word that is the Lord's means of grace to our souls. By it He convicts us of sin, converts us from sin, and builds us up in the comfort of the gospel. No other book can take its place. Never allow any other literature, secular or religious, to take the place of the Bible itself.

Make the Bible more than mere reading material. Read in order to understand. Understand in order to learn. Learn in order to obey. The Lord has plainly made known to us His will in the gospel of His Son. Let us then embrace all He has said. Let us count His Word a feast of royal dainties. What a rich provision He has given us there! There He reveals the majesty of His person, the glory of His grace, and the preciousness of His Son. There He expounds to us the power of the blood of the Lamb and the security of our standing in Christ. There He meets with us to feed us and strengthen us. We need never go away hungry from His table. Feast richly on the divine Word today.

—A. C.

The great cause of our neglecting the Scriptures is not want of time, but want of heart, some idol taking the place of Christ.
R. C. CHAPMAN

Longing for Revival

Where be all his miracles which our fathers told us of?
JUDGES 6:13

Christians should never despise the day of small things. We tend to look for the extraordinary and discount the ordinary, but this is wrong. God's ordinary dealings in and through His people are worthy of our deepest gratitude. People saved here and there through the normal ministry of the church are just as truly saved as those saved in revival, and their salvation is just as much a miracle of grace.

Yet we cannot be indifferent to the need for revival. We have read in Scripture and in church history of the great outpourings of the Holy Spirit. We have thrilled at the record of the powerful revelation of the majesty of God, causing men to fall under great conviction of sin and to cry for mercy through Christ. As we have read, we have yearned to see the working of His Spirit. We are grateful for every token of the Lord's presence as we worship and serve, but we long to see greater things than we have yet seen. Where are the mighty works of grace our fathers have described?

It is tragic that all that most Christians today know about revival is what they have read. It is not the knowledge of experience. What is being touted in some circles as a great movement of spiritual renewal is mostly a manufactured phenomenon and is largely divorced from the solid preaching and the awesome sense of the majesty of God that mark true revivals. Crusades and crowd psychology are no substitute for a real movement of the Holy Spirit in the fulness of His power.

Where are God's mighty works? We do not see revival today. But we may see it. The Lord is sovereign in dispensing His grace, but we have every reason to pray that He will send us a true revival. Each of us can personally enter into the experience of being filled with His Spirit, which is revival on an individual scale. Let us cry for such a reviving. Then may the Lord enlarge it to touch multitudes.

—A. C.

I pray daily for revival.
D. Martyn Lloyd-Jones

Fulness

But he, being full of the Holy Ghost, looked up stedfastly into heaven.
ACTS 7:55

In choosing the first deacons, the early church was instructed to look out men "full of the Holy Ghost" (Acts 6:3). Fulness of the Spirit is therefore something that is recognizable—we can know a person who is living in this experience. But how? We need to know, since every believer is commanded, "Be filled with the Spirit" (Eph. 5:18). Consider the marks of fulness as revealed in the life and death of one of those men chosen by the early church, Stephen.

We find him in the hour of his death looking up "stedfastly into heaven." He had a vision of and concern for heavenly things. So will a child of God submitted to the control of the Holy Ghost. His affections are set "on things above, not on things on the earth" (Col. 3:2); he looks "not at the things which are seen, but at the things which are not seen" (I Cor. 4:18). He has his eyes fixed upon Christ. Stephen testified that he saw "the Son of man standing on the right hand of God" (Acts 7:56). This must be the logical consequence of yieldedness to the Spirit. Jesus said, "He shall glorify me: for he shall receive of mine, and shall shew it unto you" (John 16:14). His delight is to give to the believer a deeper and fuller appreciation of the person and work of Christ. This will in turn lead to a Christlike spirit more in evidence in the life.

Observe how this martyred saint, like his Master, prayed for his persecutors in the hour of death (Acts 7:60). This is the love for souls that we need, and this we will have when we are filled with the Holy Ghost.

—D. F.

**He who has the Holy Spirit in his heart and
the Scriptures in his hands has all he needs.**
ALEXANDER MACLAREN

Dishonouring the Lord

And when they entered unto the heathen,
whither they went, they profaned my holy name.

EZEKIEL 36:20

Ezekiel chapter 36 has something to say about the necessity of sanctifying God. This Israel did not do. The wicked looked on while God's professed people profaned His name. They made it just like any other name before the ungodly, as many Christians of today have begun to do. Israel dishonoured God's holy name, and the heathen said, "These are the people of the Lord."

To profane is the opposite of to sanctify. We do either one or the other with God. There is no middle ground in the Bible. Sometimes we use the word *profane* to indicate blasphemy. The word derives from the Latin, meaning "outside the temple," hence that which is secular, irreverent, impious, or ungodly. Israel made God's name a byword by dragging it in the gutter. The Christian is not to use profane language or be dishonest or deceitful. He is not to act wickedly and bring the testimony of the Lord into reproach. A sanctified man will sanctify God's name in private and in public, in character and in actions. A relevant question here is not just, "Is God sanctifying me?" but rather, "Am I sanctifying God?"

The Israelites, as the verse shows, were no power for good outside the land. They left everything of God, including the song, behind them. Their greatest sin was not sanctifying God. Christian, do not be picked out at your place of work by your sin or your gloomy face, as one who has left God behind him at church.

—J. D.

There is a great difference between the
sheep that by weakness falls into the mire, and
a swine that delights to wallow in the mire.
THOMAS BROOKS

320

The Death of Death's Champion

*That through death he might destroy him that
had the power of death, that is, the devil.*

HEBREWS 2:14

Satan, by alluring man into disobedience against God at the fall,
is the instigator of death in this world. Physical, spiritual, and
eternal death exist because of this malicious foe. Furthermore,
Satan uses death as an instrument of torment upon the minds of
sinners. "Through fear of death . . . all their lifetime" they are
"subject to bondage" (Heb. 2:15). The devil, having brought them
into a state of death, then terrorizes their souls with the thought
of impending doom. He "had the power of death" in the sense that
he monopolized a just claim against sinners. They deserve eternal
death—man must receive the wages of his disobedience. Satan
takes advantage of this fact and uses it as a weapon of fear, bondage, and torment.

However, the gospel tells us of One who came to destroy Satan.
This truth is set in the context of the incarnation. From that point
the battle lines were drawn. Christ was "manifested, that he might
destroy the works of the devil" (I John 3:8). How interesting it is
that the very weapon that Satan was using against man, Christ
seized and used to destroy him. The word *destroy* means "to make
null," "to render powerless," "to bring to nought." It is not that the
devil has been annihilated, but that his ability to use death in this
fashion against God's redeemed has been taken from him. By His
own death Christ has suffered the penal infliction of the law, enduring the wrath of a holy God. As a consequence, He has taken
the sting out of death for His people, and Satan no longer is able
to bring us under the fear of death. Thank God, the "prey of the
terrible" (Isa. 49:25) has been delivered, and the "strong man" has
been bound (Matt. 12:29). God's people no longer have the spirit
of fear. Now in Christ they have the spirit "of power, and of love,
and of a sound mind" (II Tim. 1:7).

—J. G.

**As the law is vindicated, sin put away, death
swallowed up, Christ has destroyed the Devil.**
ADOLPH SAPHIR

Effective Prayer

Thou shalt make an altar to burn incense upon.

EXODUS 30:1

The altar of incense, in common with the other pieces of tabernacle furniture, is rich in meaning for the child of God. Incense is the symbol of prayer. Remember how the psalmist expresses the desire of his heart: "Let my prayer be set forth before thee as incense" (Psa. 141:2). The essence of prayer, in its best form, is typified by that cloud of sweet odours that is offered up to God. True prayer, like incense, ascends towards God. We must be sure that our prayers are not merely a form of words, a series of vain repetitions spoken to salve our conscience or to impress those around us. Such prayers do not touch heaven.

True prayer, like incense, if it is to soar upwards, must be kindled. The stick of incense is alight before its sweet odour is set free. Our prayers, even should they ascend to the Lord, will be of no delight to Him and no benefit to us if they are but the product of a heart that is cold and without passion. Earnest prayer is the prayer that wins the day, not eloquent prayer.

True prayer, like the altar of incense, lies at the centre of things. The altar stood in the centre of the inner court, between the lampstand and the table with the loaves. How plainly does this suggest the significance of prayer in the Christian life! The light will burn dimly and the work of our hands will be stale and dry unless they are enlivened and sustained by prayer.

Yes, we often say our prayers, but do we really pray? The question needs to be asked. How can we answer it?

—T. N.

When thou prayest, rather let thy heart be
without words, than thy words without a heart.
JOHN BUNYAN

The Exemplary Sufferings of Christ

*For even hereunto were ye called: because Christ also suffered
for us, leaving us an example, that ye should follow his steps.*
I PETER 2:21

This book was written to a suffering church, and therefore one of
the main themes of the book is the sufferings of Christ both in
Himself and in His church. Some of the sufferings of Christ we
cannot enter into—those sufferings by which He expiated, or removed, the guilt of our sins. We cannot follow His steps there, for
in the secret, mysterious place of agony only Christ could suffer as
He suffered for our sins.

However, this verse introduces us to a part of His sufferings
that we can exemplify. We are called to these sufferings; indeed,
we are appointed to them. He has left us a pattern in them that
we should follow. Here is the fellowship of His sufferings.

His sufferings were *unavoidable*. He did not seek to avoid or
mitigate them (Mark 15:23). As God the Son, He embraced them
as being necessary and unavoidable in God's eternal will and covenant. Likewise, suffering is unavoidable for the Christian—"For
even hereunto were ye called" (I Pet. 2:21).

Christ's sufferings were also *undeserved* (v. 22). We cannot, of
course, be like our impeccable Lord in this respect, but if we suffer,
let it not be for evil-doing or unrighteousness. Let it rather be for
the sake of righteousness (3:14) and well-doing (3:16, 17).

His sufferings were also *unanswered* (2:23). The patient
forbearance of the Lord is emphasized here. He neither threatened nor reviled again. May we exemplify that spirit of patience
and forbearance when we suffer for well-doing. We are so prone
to hit back and bite back in such circumstances. How happy we
will be if, by the grace of God, we take the spoiling of our goods
joyfully and commit ourselves and our case to Him that judgeth
righteously (v. 23). May the Holy Spirit even in this conform us
to the image of Christ.

—R. J. B.

**Christians are never more Christ-like
than when bearing their cross.**
ALEXANDER SIMPSON

To Everything a Season

Canst thou bind the sweet influences
of Pleiades, or loose the bands of Orion?

JOB 38:31

The Lord has questioned Job concerning the wonders of the earth and the sea, and the variety of meteorological conditions. Now He bids Job to look up and behold the glory of the sky at night. He speaks to him of Pleiades and Orion, two star groups that have a special seasonal significance.

Orion is seen at its best in the autumn of the year and heralds the approach of winter. Pleiades, a cluster of seven stars intensely bright and beautiful, appears in the middle of April and announces the coming of spring, the time of bursting forth of life, vitality, and colour. In Greek, Pleiades is associated with sailing, implying that safe travel on the seas could now be assured. Thus the Lord is actually saying to Job, "Can you stop the arrival of winter, with its frost and cold and sense of deadness? On the other hand, in any year, can you prevent the sweet approaches of spring?"

Every year has its seasons and times that must run their appointed course. As such, they must be accepted from the hand of our all-wise, all-holy, all-powerful God, who rules and reigns in the affairs of all men and who works all things for the good of those who trust in Him. That is the teaching in these words. Every year has a winter season. No one can halt the bands of Orion. Every year, even in the lives of those who know Christ, there are upsets, trials, disappointments, and days of heartache and trouble. "Man is born unto trouble, as the sparks fly upward" (Job 5:7). Nevertheless, as in the natural realm, so in the spiritual: every year has its springtime, a time of refreshing from the hand of our bountiful God. He gives us moments of blessings and joy. No year is all winter. Orion does not rule forever. In our own lives as believers, thank God, we experience the sweet influence of Pleiades. Therefore let us rest upon the mercies and faithfulness of our blessed Redeemer, who gives us what is meet for us in every season.

—S. B. C.

Christ never allows any faithful servant of His
to suffer loss, but He turns that loss to great gain.
R. C. CHAPMAN

Using What We Have for God

Shamgar . . . slew of the Philistines six hundred men with an ox goad.
JUDGES 3:31

When there are no conventional instruments available, the Lord does not hesitate to use the unconventional. Shields and spears were hardly to be found among the Israelites, so complete was their enslavement by heathen invaders (Judg. 5:8). Without shields and spears, how could they possibly have military success against the well-equipped armies of the Philistines? The case seemed hopeless.

Enter Shamgar with his ox goad. Shamgar? Who was he? And, really, with an ox goad! What on earth could he do with that besides prod a few Philistine oxen? Nothing more derisory could be imagined. Yet that unknown Shamgar with his primitive and apparently useless weapon was God's man to deliver Israel. And he did. No doubt he would have preferred the latest in military technology, but he realized that God's work is done by consecrated men using what instruments God has given them in the power of the Holy Spirit.

Shamgar's example leaves no room for excuse from any of us. "What is that in thine hand?" (Exod. 4:2). That question to the reluctant Moses is still the Lord's question to us. Like Moses, we may have to confess that what we have holds no promise in itself of much usefulness in such a great work as the Lord's. What matters, however, is not what we have, but what the Lord can do with it. Too many Christians do nothing for the advancement of Christ's kingdom, always waiting for better training or more advantageous circumstances. Take what you have and give it to the Lord for His service today. After all, it is not human greatness God blesses in His service, but true love and faithfulness to Him. "Not by might, nor by power, but by my spirit, saith the Lord of hosts" (Zech. 4:6) is still the word that every servant needs to learn.
—A. C.

**Give what Thou commandest,
and command what Thou wilt.**
AUGUSTINE

Worthy Is the Lamb

Worthy is the Lamb that was slain.

REVELATION 5:12

The apostle John had long known the Lord Jesus as the Lamb. That was the very first description of Christ he ever heard. As a disciple of John the Baptist, he was present at Bethabara when his master saw Jesus and cried, "Behold the Lamb of God" (John 1:29, 36). Later he saw the Lamb crucified. Later still he made the atonement offered by the Lamb the great theme of his message (1 John 1:7; 2:2; 4:10). Finally, in closing the canon of Scripture, he refers to Christ as the Lamb no less than twenty-nine times. Now it is the Lamb glorified that occupies his attention. "The Lamb is all the glory in Immanuel's land."

The Lamb is worthy of all praise. Without His sacrificial work on the cross there would be no redeemed souls in heaven at all. Heaven would be empty and hell full. Every soul in heaven will feel His entire indebtedness to the Lamb. None will sing of his own self-righteousness. None will prate about his own inherent self-worth. No! The song on every tongue will be "Worthy is the Lamb!"

In this world men make light of the blood atonement of Christ. Even professed Christian scholars often seek to denigrate it and deny it. In heaven there is no such attitude. There the Lamb and His precious blood are freely and forever praised.

Should not our song be the same as heaven's? We can sing it for the same reason and with the same certainty as the glorified throng. As we sing, we can proclaim the power of the blood of the Lamb to a world of sinners. After all, every saint in heaven is only a sinner washed in Jesus' blood.

Let us then praise the Lamb that He is bringing us to glory and tell abroad His power to save, that we may see Him bring others with us.

—A. C.

Christ's blood is heaven's key.
THOMAS BROOKS

The Marketplace

It is naught, it is naught, saith the buyer:
but when he is gone his way, then he boasteth.

PROVERBS 20:14

Truly there is no new thing under the sun. "It is naught, it is naught," cries the buyer in the marketplace. "It is not worth that price. I can buy it cheaper elsewhere. I don't really want it anyway." Thus he spins his web of deception until the purchase is made. Now it is a different story. He boasts in this once worthless article and laughs at how he tricked the seller. All such double dealing is an abomination in the sight of the Lord (Prov. 20:10).

How much is excused today! Deceit and dishonesty are hidden under many a guise:

"Business is business."

"It's just one of the tricks of the trade."

"You've got to make a living, after all."

"Competition is so tough!"

"Ah, well, everybody does it!"

Martin Luther well said: "Holiness consisteth not in a cowl, nor in a garment of grey. When God purifies the heart by faith, the market is sacred as well as the sanctuary." The grace of God should be operative in our everyday lives. Holiness to the Lord should be stamped on all our transactions. "The Christian must not only mind heaven but attend to his daily calling. Like the pilot who, while his eye is fixed upon the star, keeps his hand upon the helm" (Thomas Watson). The fear of God should govern all that we do. "Thou God seest me" (Gen. 16:13). The Christian should be scrupulously honest, knowing that "a false balance is abomination to the Lord: but a just weight is his delight" (Prov. 11:1). The child of God is not to be slothful in business, but fervent in spirit, serving the Lord (Rom. 12:11).

—M. P.

The trade of lying hath crept into all trades.
GEORGE SWINNOCK

327

The Gospel of Christ

*I am not ashamed of the gospel of Christ: for it is the power of God
unto salvation . . . for therein is the righteousness of God revealed.*
ROMANS 1:16-17

What is the gospel of Christ? We live in a day when the gospel is
little understood, its power seldom experienced, and its message
too often muddied by the notions of men. Paul, on the other hand,
sounds the gospel trumpet very clearly in our text. Here you have
the essential elements of the gospel of Christ.

First, at the heart of the gospel there is a *Person*, for it is
the gospel *of Christ!* He is the Son of Man (v. 3) and the Son of
God (v. 4), bone of our bone and flesh of our flesh, yet very God
of very God. What a message is this! "Oh who am I, that for my
sake / My Lord should take frail flesh, and die?" How tragic it
is that the gospel has come today to centre on a "plan" or "principles." Above and beyond all else, the gospel is a revelation of
Jesus Christ, of His glorious person and His atoning work. The
more you see of Christ in God's Word, the more you will come
to know and enjoy the liberty of the gospel.

Further, the gospel carries a divine *power,* as it is the "power
of God unto salvation." Sin left man absolutely powerless to do
anything to save himself, for he is "dead in trespasses and sins"
(Eph. 2:1). But what men cannot do, Christ does through the plain
preaching of the gospel. The Spirit of Christ begets faith in the
heart by the Word, and that faith brings Christ and His saving
grace to the sinner. Paul would unashamedly go to Rome, home
of the scholars and philosophers, and preach Christ crucified because he knew that saving power was not in his learning or finely
spun arguments, but in the declaration of Christ's crosswork!

Finally, the gospel tells of a divine *perfection*. It reveals the
righteousness of God. Christ, who knew no sin, was made sin for
us, who knew no righteousness, that we might be made the righteousness of God in Him. Through faith in His blood, we are made
righteous, perfect in the eyes of God. Who can condemn us? Then
believe the gospel, trust it, and obey it.

—J. W.

The gospel is not so much a miracle as a
marvel, and every line is suffused with wonder.
MARTIN LUTHER

Smiling Saints

*Happy art thou, O Israel: who is like
unto thee, O people saved by the Lord!*
DEUTERONOMY 33:29

Are we enjoying this happiness today? No people on earth have the reason to be happy that blood-washed saints have. The happiness of the world is shallow and temporary. Ours is deep and permanent. Yet all too often we become so engrossed in the concerns of this world that we lose the smile of happy contentment in Christ.

If we have Christ, we are saved. That alone should make us happy. We are justified by grace through faith in the merits of Christ. We are accepted by the Father in Christ. We can never be robbed of this full and free salvation. We are as sure of heaven as if we were already there.

Not only are we saved, but we are "saved by the Lord." The eternal God has thought on us. He has loved us with an everlasting love. He has pledged Himself in all the fulness of His glorious attributes, to accomplish our eternal salvation. Thus He is our shield to defend us against every foe. He is our sword to cut through all opposition to our progress to heaven. This is the essence of true happiness. The miserable masses of this world desperately need to see true, happy Christians living their Christianity to the full. Are we allowing some passing trouble to wipe the radiance of salvation from our face? How then can we ever convince the world that Christians are the only truly happy people on earth? Oh! let us cry to the Lord for grace to live in the overflowing happiness of the gospel.

—A. C.

If you have no joy in your religion, there's
a leak in your Christianity somewhere.
BILLY SUNDAY

Getting Back to God

Draw nigh to God, and he will draw nigh to you.

JAMES 4:8

Do you ever wish that you could know the presence of the Lord in a much more intimate way? Surely every Christian has longed for this many a time. We have been saved for fellowship with God. It is a denial of our very reason for existence not to enjoy this close fellowship. We can never be satisfied without it.

Perhaps we can look back to times when we did enjoy a great intimacy with the Lord. We remember the sweet sense of His presence in the place of prayer. We cherish the memory of hours spent in the Word of God when the Author of the Book drew very near and blessed us. But somehow the old closeness is gone. There is not the same joy in our spiritual exercises, and we long for the former fellowship. Is there any hope? Praise God, there is.

Draw nigh to God. There is a way of approach. The blood of Christ assures our access to the Father (Heb. 10:19). There is not only an access for us, but there is an invitation. The Lord calls us to Himself. Draw near. Let us lay aside the follies that took our attention off our God. Let us plead the blood against every obstacle that stands in our way. Neither sin nor Satan can withstand the power of the blood of Christ; so let us cry to the Lord to overcome them and bring us near.

He will answer that cry. Indeed, as soon as we approach He will draw near to us. He will come with forgiveness; He will come with a smile. Let us come today, and we will wonder why it took us so long.

—A. C.

As soon as it is our *settled purpose* to please
Christ, He takes us for His bosom friends.
R. C. CHAPMAN

Men of God

Though these three men, Noah, Daniel, and Job, were in it.
EZEKIEL 14:14

God speaks of these men by name. He knows all His servants, and He knows their character and exploits, too.

The Bible has a true history. Each man named appears authentically in the Biblical narrative. Noah, Daniel, and Job were men who lived exactly as the Bible says. Significantly, all three have been called into question by the adversaries of truth, in one way or another. Daniel is the only one of the three currently alive at the time of Ezekiel's writing. Ezekiel mentions him as one already known. By now he has been in Babylon at least fourteen years. Thus Daniel is indisputably shown to be Ezekiel's contemporary and not a mythical Maccabean folk hero. Further, this reference belongs to a time three years before the siege of Jerusalem, definitely fixing the date of Daniel's lifetime.

All three men are noted in the New Testament—Noah for preparation, Daniel for Scripture, and Job for his patience under trial (Heb. 11:7; Mark 13:14; James 5:11). Together these verses present an all-round picture of the child of God. He has made preparation for the saving of his house. He reads that he may understand. He must endure manfully against all odds in the evil day.

The meaning of these men's names tells forth the victory of Christ. *Noah* means "rest"; *Daniel,* "the judgment of God"; and *Job,* "assailed by the enemy." There is rest through the judgment of God against the adversary. Noah overcame the world. Daniel triumphed over the flesh. Job stood against the devil until God gave the victory. The victory of these three is all the more heroic in that each man had to stand alone in his fierce fight of faith.

—J. D.

When you tell me what a man is in the pulpit, you must also tell me what he is out of it, or I shall not know his size.
JOHN NEWTON

The Expiatory Sufferings of Christ

For Christ also hath once suffered for sins, the just
for the unjust, that he might bring us to God.

I PETER 3:18

Peter in this epistle speaks much of our Lord Jesus Christ's sufferings for our sins. These were the penal sufferings of Christ, whereby He expiated our guilt and propitiated God's wrath. No one but Christ could suffer so. How severe those sufferings were! Their severity is underlined in the words *suffered for sins.* His sufferings were in proportion to our sins. Our Lord Jesus suffered in all parts of His body, from all kinds of men, from His enemies and from His friends. He suffered much from the devil and from the powers of darkness. But His most trying suffering came when in the darkness of the cross He was smitten of God and afflicted. What agony the holy, sensitive soul of Christ endured when the fiery indignation of the Father's displeasure fell on His dear Son at Calvary!

That suffering and anguish was for sinners. It was the Just for the unjust. How simple but profound is the testimony of the repentant soul: "I am a guilty sinner, but Jesus died for me." He, God's Lamb who knew no sin, was made sin for us that we might be made the righteousness of God in Him. He dies that we might live and lives that we may never die.

How singular that sacrifice was! He "once" suffered for our sins. In His sufferings and death, He made full and perfect satisfaction to God's justice for all those for whom He died. There is no more sacrifice for sins required. The work of Christ is perfect, final, and complete. In that death He has accomplished something definite. He suffered that He might bring us to God. He brings us to God here and will bring us to God hereafter. "Believest thou this?"

—R. J. B.

One drop of Christ's blood is
worth more than heaven and earth.
MARTIN LUTHER

Tithing

Bring ye all the tithes into the storehouse, that there may be meat in mine house, and prove me now herewith, saith the Lord of hosts, if I will not open you the windows of heaven, and pour you out a blessing, that there shall not be room enough to receive it.

MALACHI 3:10

Some people become very irritated when the preacher starts to preach about money. No doubt some have cause to feel uneasy because they have been guilty of robbing God, as Malachi puts it, by not paying their tithes and offerings. There are those who would tell us that tithing is legalistic, and they can point to the self-righteous Pharisee who gave tithes of all that he possessed. To show us how much superior they are to the legalistic Pharisee, they in their generosity generally give less than he did to the support of God's work!

Whether we want to face up to it or not, the subject of our giving is dealt with in the Word of God, and we cannot expect to prosper spiritually until we are right in this matter. Tithing, giving a tenth of our income to God, is not legalism. Jacob promised to tithe before the law was given (Gen. 28:22). Abraham, again before the giving of the law, gave tithes of all he possessed to Melchisedec, a type of Christ if not Christ Himself, as some people believe (14:18-20).

C. H. Spurgeon preached from Malachi 3:10 at the reopening services in the enlarged New Park Street Church in London in 1844. He reminded his people that if they wished to have the promised blessing, they must comply with the conditions attached to it. Spurgeon later commented, "This they were quite ready to do, and from the time of our return to our much-loved sanctuary until the day when we finally left it, we never had 'room enough to receive' the blessings which the Lord so copiously poured out for us."

—G. F.

If we would have God open His treasury, we must open ours.
T. V. MOORE

Where To Begin

In Jerusalem, and in all Judaea.

ACTS 1:8

The problem of where God would have us to serve Him is one that has perplexed many of God's people. Every genuine convert has a sense of obligation to the Lord, but knowing the place of service is what some believers profess to find difficult. Here the Saviour plainly told the disciples where their ministry was to begin—at Jerusalem. To the recently delivered demoniac of Gadara, Christ commanded, "Go home to thy friends, and tell them how great things the Lord hath done for thee" (Mark 5:19).

Clearly our first mission field must be our homes, our families, our friends. We are told of Andrew that "he first findeth his own brother Simon . . . and he brought him to Jesus" (John 1:41, 42). Why should this be? Obviously we feel concern for the souls of our loved ones keenly immediately after our own conversion. Having received spiritual sight, it breaks our hearts that those near to us by nature's ties should be in danger of hell-fire. Then, too, it is among those who know us best that our testimony can be the most powerful. Friends who knew us intimately in our days of following after sin are more likely than others to see the change that divine grace has wrought in our lives. It is possible to play the hypocrite before strangers, but before family and close acquaintances the reality of our profession is most noticeable and speaks most loudly. Of course, it is to our near kinfolk that we have the best and most frequent opportunities for witness. Others we may see and speak to but once in a lifetime. Those with whom we live can hear the Word from us every day. Would you witness for the Master? Then begin at home.

—D. F.

The only possessions you can bring to heaven with you are your loved ones.
ALEXANDER SIMPSON

Christ Is Altogether Lovely

Thou art fairer than the children of men. **PSALM 45:2**

Happy marriages are those in which the husband and wife are consumed with each other. It is not surprising that marriage describes the union between Christ and His people. Psalm 45 is an inspired picture of the spiritual marriage between Christ, the kingly Husband, and the church, His royal bride. When the psalmist began to write this "Song of loves," his heart boiled up as he considered the wonder of the King's beauty and grace. So we, the spiritual bride, should be consumed with thoughts of our royal Husband, who is altogether lovely and altogether ours.

Within the natural realm, love may be blind to faults and blemishes, but spiritual love removes the blindness that hides Christ's beauty from faithless eyes. To us He is "fairer than the children of men." He is also our hero who defends us with majestic weapons (vv. 3-5). Many young girls have dreamed of knights in shining armour only to be disappointed when the shine gave way to tarnish. But Christ never disappoints. He is mighty to save; He is mighty to love.

Christ is also the Head of His bride (v. 6). As a godly wife submits to the headship of her husband, so must we submit to Christ. We may not always understand why He rules as He does, but we should recognize the benevolence of His rule. Whatever He does is right.

The everlasting throne of our King-Husband is our great confidence. As in human marriage the wife is bound to her husband as long as he lives, so are we bound to Christ as long as He lives.

> *While God and I shall be,*
> *I am His, and He is mine.*

Let us have eyes and hearts for Christ only. Let us see more of Him and less of ourselves. That is a good formula for any marriage.
—M. P. V. B.

**He values not Christ at all who
does not value Christ above all.**
AUGUSTINE

Praying in the Will of God

If we ask anything according to his will, he heareth us.

I JOHN 5:14

Nothing more immediately touches a Christian's happiness and usefulness than his prayer life. All God's people admit the importance of prayer. All feel that they cannot live without prayer. Yet in a great many cases they are frustrated by a lack of confidence in prayer and an inability to know the difference between asking in faith and mere make-believe. Today's text goes a long way toward supplying the solution to the problem.

We need confidence when we pray. Here is our confidence: "If we ask anything according to his will, he heareth us." God will hear us every time we pray according to His will. Once we know that God has heard us, we know that we have the petitions we have desired of Him (I John 5:15).

The crux of the matter, then, is ascertaining the will of God. That means finding out what the Word of God has to say on the matters about which we are praying. There are certain things that the Bible declares to be the will of God for every Christian. Specific commands and promises are declarations of God's will for us. Holiness of life is God's will for us (I Thess. 4:3). So is the fulness of the Holy Spirit (Eph. 5:18). We can confidently pray for these things, and God will hear us. In other cases we will need to spend time with the Lord in His Word, being careful to submit our will to His. We must then ask Him to convince us of His will by the work of His Spirit applying the Word to our hearts. With that knowledge we can pray effectively.

Prayer is not a hit-or-miss exercise. Let us learn God's will and pray accordingly. Then will we obtain answers to our prayers.

—R. J. W.

**God can no more divest Himself of His
attribute of hearing prayer than of being.**
JOHN CALVIN

Balanced Service

Now the word of the Lord came unto Jonah the son of Amittai.
JONAH 1:1

Bible names are a very interesting study. Take, for example, the names of Jonah and Amittai. *Jonah* means "a dove," while *Amittai* means "my truth." Put together, these names show us what a child of God should be like: he should be a dove, like a child of truth.

The dove is a harmless bird (Matt. 10:16). It mourns (Isa. 38:14), and it flies away to be at rest (Psa. 55:6). The child of God should be harmless. He should not be involved in wicked practices. He should mourn over his own sins and the sins of others, and he should constantly be flying away into the arms of his Saviour to have sweet fellowship with Him. Of course, we can maintain a dovelike spirit only when we are filled with the Holy Spirit, who descended on Christ in the form of a dove at the Saviour's baptism.

But notice that Jonah is the son of Amittai—a son of truth. The Christian should be a child of truth. He must not seek to win people by flattery or deception. God requires truth of His children, and we can never succeed without the truth. After all, God's Word is truth, and how can we succeed without God's Word?

The tragedy today is that so many Christians are unbalanced: either they have the dovelike spirit and little or no truth, or else they are all truth with little or nothing of the spirit of the dove. In the first case they appear as soft-hearted compromisers; in the second, as stern "know-alls."

Get the balance right, and you have the secret of a life that will glorify God.

—G. F.

> The reprover should have a lion's stout
> heart, or he will not be faithful, and a lady's
> soft hand, or he is not like to be successful.
> GEORGE SWINNOCK

The Bottom Line

Fear God, and keep his commandments:
for this is the whole duty of man.

ECCLESIASTES 12:13

Knowing the bottom line is crucial in any contract or agreement. The bottom line gives the sum of the debt or obligation. After investigating God-given life, Solomon, the Preacher, brings us to the essence of man's obligation to God. The bottom line, the sum of our debt, is fearing and obeying our Lord. Not only should we be vitally interested in knowing our duty, we should be eager to give God whatever is due Him because He has done so much for us.

Fearing God means simply that we are constantly aware of Him. It is the heart of true piety and the proper motivation for doing God's will. Throughout Scripture, fearing God is linked to knowing God. We cannot know God as He reveals Himself in His Word without fearing Him.

There are two key elements to this fear that work together to give definition to Christian living. First, there is worship. As we recognize the beauty of His person and perfections, we must stand in awe and bow in reverence before Him. Not to worship the Lord is to confess ignorance of Him. Second, there is the dread of disobeying Him. This aspect is the bridge between our religion and our daily living. Whether like children, who fear the discipline of a loving father, or like a husband, who fears to mar his relationship with his wife, we should allow our awareness of the Lord to define everything that we do. Marring our relationship with Him ought to be a most dreaded thought. Such godly fear is the evidence of godly love and is possible only by God's grace.

> *'Twas grace that taught my heart to fear*
> *And grace my fears relieved;*
> *How precious did that grace appear*
> *The hour I first believed!*

—M. P. V. B.

None reverence the Lord more
than they who know Him best.
WILLIAM COWPER

Triumphant in Trials

My brethren, count it all joy when ye fall into divers temptations.
JAMES 1:2

God's people are not immune from trouble. Indeed, at many points in history the very fact that they were Christians assured them of special trials and tribulations. Whatever the cause and the course of their trials (for that is the meaning of *temptations* in our verse today), God's people are told to rejoice. That sounds strange until we realize that the divine purpose in our trials is entirely benign, and their effect is ultimately beneficial.

Trials come in various forms. Sickness, poverty, bereavement, persecution, and calamity are all trying afflictions. Our natural response would be to complain about them, but our natural response would be wrong. These trials all come from our Father's hand. He sends them to us to do us good, and we should rejoice under them.

We should rejoice when we are tried because testing shows the reality of our faith in Christ (I Pet. 1:7). It also is the Lord's means to purify us of our dross. It weans us from the world and drives us closer to the Lord. It brings us into a closer fellowship with Him who was the "man of sorrows" (Isa. 53:3). It allows us to prove the power of God to enable us to triumph over Satan when we are mentally and physically at our lowest ebb.

But *how* can we rejoice when we are hurting? Peter supplies the answer in I Peter 1:6: "Wherein ye greatly rejoice, though now . . . ye are in heaviness through manifold temptations." *Wherein* refers to the glorious truths of the gospel set forth in the preceding verses—election by the Father, sanctification by the Spirit, blood-cleansing by the Son, regeneration into a living hope, and an assured inheritance in heaven. When you are tried, think on these things. The joy they impart will cause you to triumph over any earthly trial or affliction. —A. C.

A dark hour makes Jesus bright.
ROBERT MURRAY MCCHEYNE

Show Me Your Company

He that walketh with wise men shall be wise:
but a companion of fools shall be destroyed.

PROVERBS 13:20

A saying of my maternal grandmother has come down to me and has often been repeated by me. There is little doubt that it is not original, but like many of Ulster's proverbs it is soundly Biblical. It runs, "Show me your company, and I will tell you who you are." Without question, you advertise your character in the behaviour, speech, and demeanour of your companions. You tar yourself with their brush.

The Christian has his own company. That company consists of those of "like precious faith" (II Pet. 1:1). Among them the Christian is at ease. Away from them he is vexed, as was Lot in the company of the Sodomites. Severed from them, he will return at the first possible opportunity. He will act as did Peter and John when they were released from prison in Acts 4:23: "They went to their own company." "East, west—home's best," proclaims the old saying. Home for the believer is amongst the redeemed.

Keeping the company of God's people is positively profitable. "He that walketh with wise men shall be wise." You become like those you befriend. Befriend the wise and you become wise. The psalmist said that a man who keeps the right company all the time is blessed—blessed with spiritual fruitfulness, universal prosperity, and a secure eternity (Psa. 1).

When we walk in someone's company, of necessity we must conform to that person. "Can two walk together, except they be agreed?" (Amos 3:3). Walk with the wise and you must keep his pace, follow his direction. You yield to his superintendence; you must become as he is.

The wisest of all companions is Christ. Holiness is advanced in our lives as we conform to Him. To be His disciple you must walk in His way. This is the simple meaning of that much misunderstood doctrine, sanctification. The companion of Christ is sanctified unto Him and so is made Christlike.

—I. F.

Keep such company as God keeps.
ANONYMOUS

340

True Nonconformity

Learn not the way of the heathen.

JEREMIAH 10:2

No command was more frequently given to the children of Israel than this. Moses and Joshua strongly impressed it on them as they began to take possession of Canaan. The prophets constantly called them back to the same standard. Yet no command was more disregarded. Even in the days of Moses there were flagrant violations. Israel made a golden calf and worshipped it, an imitation of Egyptian heathen religion. At Baal-peor the people fell into fornication and idolatry with the Midianites. Throughout the period of the Judges there were multiplied regressions into heathen religion and practice. In the end, it was learning the way of the heathen that led both Israel and Judah into captivity.

All this proves one thing very clearly: consistent separation unto the Lord is the heart of true holiness and yet is the most difficult thing for us to maintain. We are under strong and constant pressure to conform to the spirit of the age. We are bombarded by the heathen ideas and practices of the ungodly. The temptation is to try to come to terms with all this and not appear too extreme. That is fatal, as many a believer has found out.

Conformity to the world is killing the effectiveness of most churches because it is killing their holiness. The old saying, "I looked for the church and I found it in the world; I looked for the world and I found it in the church," is truer today than ever. Christians have learned the way of the heathen in their appearance, their actions, their entertainment, their families, and even their religion. The price they have to pay is enormous, for they lose their joy, their power, and very often their children—all sacrificed on the altar of conformity to the heathen.

"Be not conformed to this world" is the Lord's call to us (Rom. 12:2). Oh! for such a sight of Christ that we would be overcome with a desire to be like Him. The more we are like Christ, the less we will be like the heathen. This is true holiness.

—A. C.

Unless you are content with having God as your teacher you will necessarily go astray.
JOHN CALVIN

Imputed Righteousness
as a Breastplate

Stand therefore, . . . having on the breastplate of righteousness.
EPHESIANS 6:14

God gives to the believer the armour he needs to be victorious over the evil one. One piece of this armour is the breastplate that our Lord wore when He warred in His earthly ministry against Satan. The Scriptures record, "He put on righteousness as a breastplate, and an helmet of salvation upon his head" (Isa. 59:17). It is this righteousness that is imputed to the believer and that the believer must lay hold of each day.

In II Chronicles 12:9-10, Rehoboam the king made brass shields to replace Solomon's golden shields. In a similar fashion, many believers are trying to replace the imputed righteousness of Christ with their own man-made breastplate. Satan does not fear this inferior piece of armour, for confidence in one's own righteousness gives way to pride in the heart. In this pride, Satan finds a ready ally. In contrast, God's imputed righteousness humbles the heart. It is a constant reminder that the believer needs Christ in order to stand right before God. Luther called this righteousness an "alien" righteousness. That is, it originates not from within us, but from outside of us. It is found in Christ alone and is imputed, or reckoned, to the man who truly believes (Rom. 4:1-5; 10:1-4; Phil. 3:9).

When we by faith lay hold of this breastplate, a real righteousness springs up in our hearts. Putting on God's breastplate produces gratitude and love to the God who lovingly provided such protection. Just as we would not think of doing battle with the evil one apart from our shield or sword, so we must also daily lay hold of the heart of the gospel, which is God's righteousness. —M. W. A.

He justly suffered punishment due to our sins, and we justly receive the rewards due to His righteousness.
A. A. HODGE

A Fatal Flaw in a Faithful Man

*Gideon made an ephod . . . which thing
became a snare unto Gideon, and to his house.*

JUDGES 8:27

The intrepid conqueror of the Midianites fell into self-indulgence
(Judg. 8:30) and paved the way for national idolatry and apostasy. His failure should teach us that men achieve nothing great
for God by virtue of their own sterling character, but by the
gracious working of the Holy Spirit. We should certainly seek
to develop our character according to God's revealed will, but the
strongest character at best is weak. There is sin in the saintliest
of men. We need grace constantly, and this truth should keep us
constantly on our knees.

We should also learn not to think more highly of men than we
ought. We should render honour to whom it is due, but instead of
hero-worshipping the great men of church history we should rather
worship the One who wrought in them the greatness they achieved.
Doing so will help us to cope with the flaws in our heroes. All too
often the failure of someone we have set upon a pedestal discourages and destroys weak believers. No man is perfect. Our faith
does not stand in the wisdom or greatness of any man, but in the
power of God. When the best of His servants fail, the Lord Jesus
Christ is still perfect. He never fails; so let us fix our eyes on Him.

Gideon's failure should also make us examine ourselves. Past
victories are wonderful memories, but they are no excuse for
present unfaithfulness. We cannot live in the past. Another lesson
is clear: we cannot ape the world without wreaking havoc among
the very people we have the greatest interest in winning for Christ,
our own families. We must ever seek to ensure that we do not
distract men's gaze from Christ to our follies. The only way to do
this is to remain humbly obedient to God's Word and to stay in
constant fellowship with our Saviour.

—A. C.

Confidence in God and self-distrust are sure companions.
R. C. CHAPMAN

Quenching the Soul's Thirst

My soul thirsteth for thee, my flesh
longeth for thee in a dry and thirsty land.

PSALM 63:1

Physical thirst is intolerable. It will cause a man to do whatever is necessary to satisfy the intense desire for relief. A thirsty man is not satisfied with a sip of water; he drinks deeply. Spiritual thirst should be just as intolerable. If we thirst for God's presence, His love and His likeness, and seek to find satisfaction in Him, we will not be disappointed. "The Father seeketh such to worship him" (John 4:23). We should be willing to do whatever is necessary to satisfy our desire for God.

In the providence of God, we sometimes find ourselves in desolate and dry places. Rather than being occasions for disappointment and despair, these thirsty times should increase our yearning for the Lord's presence. It often takes the dry times to remind us of our need for Him. When David found himself in the wilderness, he determined to seek the Lord early. Seeking "early" speaks of David's diligence and persistence in searching for God. It was his all-consuming desire. He would not give up; he could not be satisfied until he experienced God's power and glory.

Significantly, he did not seek for a change of scenery. The wilderness was quite acceptable as long as God's presence was as real to him there as it was in the sanctuary. Too many times we seek the wrong things. We assume that if our circumstances change, we will be in blessing. If a change of circumstances can satisfy us, we are too easily satisfied. We must learn as David did that even the wilderness is a banquet hall if we find the Lord there. If we would quench our soul's thirst, let us drink deeply today of the water Christ supplies by His presence and grace.

—M. P. V. B.

> The pleasures of sense are puddle-water;
> spiritual delights are rock-water.
> MATTHEW HENRY

344

Crossing Jordan

How wilt thou do in the swelling of Jordan?

JEREMIAH 12:5

R. A. Torrey once said, "A refuge that only comforts you when you are well and strong, but will fail in that dread hour when you are face to face with death, God, and eternity, is absolutely valueless." That is the challenge Jeremiah sets before us with his question, "How wilt thou do in the swelling of Jordan?"

We must all cross the Jordan of death. It is no little stream that is easy to ford. It is a swollen, raging torrent over which only One can safely carry us. That One is the blessed Son of God, who through death delivered those who "through fear of death were all their lifetime subject to bondage" (Heb. 2:15). Christ gives a life that the grave cannot extinguish. "The sting of death is sin" (I Cor. 15:56), and Christ has put away all the sin of all His people by His blood atonement at Calvary. Thus no believer need fear the swelling of Jordan. Death is a conquered foe. Christ our Saviour has risen from the dead, and while He lives none of His people can ever perish. Death is but the gateway to glory for His saints.

Every unbeliever has cause to fear death. It is not just that it spells the end of life in this world with all its pleasures and opportunities. It is the first instalment of that second death that is eternal separation from God.

The question then is this: Are you a believer or an unbeliever? On the answer to that question depends the answer to today's text. If you are without Christ, you will not die well. You will be carried away in the raging current of the river of death. Every hope will be swept away. Every pleasure will be sunk in endless pain and misery, for the river of death for Christless souls issues into the lake of fire.

If, however, you have Christ as your Saviour, you will not have to cross Jordan alone. He will carry you safely to heaven. Do not waste your life worrying about dying. Your Saviour will not fail you. He will as surely bring you safely through death into heaven as Joshua led his people through Jordan on dry land into Canaan.

—A. C.

Let your hope of heaven master your fear of death.
WILLIAM GURNALL

Christ the Star and Sceptre

There shall come a Star out of Jacob,
and a Sceptre shall rise out of Israel.

NUMBERS 24:17

Christ is both this Star and this Sceptre. He is a Star out of *Jacob,* denoting His humiliation. He is a Sceptre out of *Israel,* indicating His exaltation, for He is the Prince of God. There was a star to signal His birth to the wise men, who then began to search for the One born King of the Jews, One with a royal sceptre. Once again, He is a Star, indicating His heavenly source, but at the same time He is a Sceptre, underlining His earthly supremacy. Christ came from glory to radiate light in a world of darkness and through His people. He is still "the light of the world" (John 8:12). He wields the sceptre of righteousness in His church and providentially controls all the affairs of this world as He works out His eternal purposes, for all power is His.

However, the ultimate fulfilment of these titles can only be at His second coming. A star shining in the nighttime is the emblem of hope, signalling the coming of day. Christ refers to Himself in Revelation 22:16 as "the bright and morning star." That star foretells that the sun is on its way to gladden the earth. Thus Christ would remind us that a better day is soon to dawn for the church. Right now we have the "sure word of prophecy" to which to take heed, "a light that shineth in a dark place, until the day dawn, and the day star arise" (II Pet. 1:19). Then He who is the Sceptre will come forth to dash in pieces all His and our enemies. In Numbers 24:19 the Holy Spirit states that Christ "shall have dominion, and shall destroy him that remaineth of the city," or who is the "hope" or "stay" of the city. This is the antichrist, the man of sin and son of perdition. He will be the false hope of Israel, but Christ the Star and Sceptre shall destroy him with the brightness of His coming and shall reign forever and forever.

—J. G.

Christ will come when He pleases, to show His sovereignty,
and will not let us know when, to teach us our duty.
MATTHEW HENRY

Unrecognized Royalty

Kings and priests unto God.

When the King of Kings walked this earth, He went unrecognized. It is little wonder then that the world utterly fails to perceive the real character and dignity of a Christian. However, there is no excuse for Christians themselves failing to see all that they have in Christ. Too many of us live under a constant cloud. We act as if we were helpless victims of our circumstances or impotent onlookers at the great drama of life. Are you like this? Are you limping through each day defeated and discouraged? Then learn what a high calling you really have as a Christian. When you truly know its extent, you will be able to live in the enjoyment of it.

Every Christian is a king unto God. He has a royal position, a royal prerogative, and a royal power. We are God's kings, and God's kings never abdicate. Our risen Redeemer has given us power over the world, the flesh, and the devil. By His own sovereign power He subdues our iniquities (Mic. 7:19) and empowers us to wield authority over lusts that once held us in bondage. He has set us free from every power of darkness. Why do we so often live as serfs instead of the sovereigns we really are?

We are not only kings, but priests. We have access to God. We come with an acceptable sacrifice, the Lamb of God whose blood has made a full atonement for us. Through Him we offer the sacrifice of praise and prayer. Not only does God accept these, but He accepts our persons as well. We are acceptable to God, welcome at His throne, and assured of an audience with Him every time we approach the mercy seat.

Let us then exert the spiritual influence proper to our calling. As kings, let us live in the world with all the spiritual authority of the throne we represent. As priests, let us centre our lives on the altar of Christ's blood atonement and learn to be mighty intercessors who know how to plead the merit of that blood in prevailing prayer. Wherever we go today, let us be aware of our royal dignity, even if the world is not.

—A. C.

God wants us to be victors, not victims; to grow, not grovel; to soar, not sink; to overcome, not to be overwhelmed.

W. A. Ward

A Mighty Fortress

The Lord of hosts is with us; the God of Jacob is our refuge.

PSALM 46:11

Luther said, "This is my psalm." His battle hymn, "A Mighty Fortress," took its cue from the robust tone of this psalm written in a time of crisis. That the exact crisis is not identified allows each of us to claim it for his own. Whether we face world, national, or personal crises, this psalm tells us that we can face them unafraid, because true security is in God.

We need not fear because God is our *help* (vv. 1-3). He is our refuge, a sure place of safety. He is our strength, a sure source of power. He is our abundant help, ready and sufficient. Although everything around us may fall apart, God never fails us.

We need not fear because God is our *comfort* (vv. 4-7). Knowing that "the glorious Lord will be unto us a place of broad rivers" (Isa. 33:21) is the greatest comfort possible in times of crisis. With the power of Jehovah of hosts and the grace of the God of Jacob in our midst, we have no reason for worry. Only as we rest in the reality of Immanuel can we face fearlessly and confidently the difficulties of life. "God with us" is the theme of inward joy, satisfaction, and consolation. What else matters if God never leaves or forsakes us?

We need not fear because God is our *deliverance* (vv. 8-11). Under the control of God, our trials are needful and serve a purpose. But faith looks to the outcome of peace. Sooner or later, "He maketh wars to cease." Between the crisis and the resolution, we must faithfully relax and acknowledge that He is Lord. Our peace will be in proportion to our sight of Him.

—M. P. V. B.

God will sooner empty heaven of angels
than leave a saint without defence.
C. H. SPURGEON

The Shedding of Blood

Without shedding of blood is no remission.

HEBREWS 9:22

One fact this text establishes is that the Saviour of sinners must shed His blood to provide them with pardon. The word *shedding* literally means "outpouring." Christ poured out His precious blood during the hours of His death agony, and He did so voluntarily. It was not a spilling of His blood in some accidental fashion, but a willing outpouring of it to make atonement for sin.

The Lord, in the days His flesh, often referred to the shedding of His blood. He spoke of giving His "life for the sheep" (John 10:11) and of laying down His "life a ransom for many" (Mark 10:45), terms which show the necessity of the shedding of blood. Since "the life of the flesh is in the blood" (Lev. 17:11), for the life to be given, the blood must be shed. That fact was typified innumerable times in the Old Testament Levitical economy. Thousands of sacrifices were offered in the tabernacle and temples of Israel, involving the shedding of an incalculable volume of blood. As the opening words of the text state, "Almost all things are by the law purged with blood." There was blood everywhere—on the altar, on the curtains, on the priest's garments, and on the mercy seat. What did this signify but that the Redeemer who would come to Zion would shed His blood in a voluntary fashion?

However, let us not miss the major thrust of the verse. The blood was shed to secure pardon for sin. Consequently, there is no other means of obtaining pardon but through that precious blood. Here is a text that destroys every "bloodless theology," every human effort to obtain forgiveness. At the same time, however, it brings hope to guilty sinners. It tells of a full satisfaction for sin. It indicates that your sins—innumerable, immeasurable, incalculable though they be—can all be pardoned. Have you received that pardon? If not, come and trust in the shed blood today.

—J. G.

The magnitude of the sacrifice which our sins
called forth manifests the supreme folly of
looking elsewhere for their forgiveness.
G. B. WILSON

The Middle Years

O Lord, revive thy work in the midst of the years.

HABAKKUK 3:2

The middle of anything is generally its weakest point, and middle years are years of particular danger. More and more, society has turned its attention to the problems people face in their middle years. The work of God faces its own peculiar difficulties in its middle years, and Habakkuk was led to pray that it might be revived at that time. The trouble with the middle years is that zeal tends to diminish while worldliness creeps in. Prosperity can lead to complacency, and God's people lose the vision of a world perishing in sin.

Habakkuk shows us that the work is still God's in the midst of the years. He prays, "Revive thy work in the midst of the years." Because the work is still God's, it demands the same level of faithfulness as at the beginning. Many people support the work when it is in its exciting initial stages and then lie back and become discouraged when it settles down.

What God's work needs in the middle years is revival. The word for "revive" is often translated *quicken* in the Old Testament. To quicken is to bring to life, and God can bring His work to life just when it seems to have lost its way and become powerless. No one could have anticipated the mighty revival that God sent to Europe in the sixteenth century. Men like Luther, Calvin, Knox, Zwingli, and Farel were raised up, and they led great multitudes to Christ.

In the midst of the years we stand in need of revival. Unless it comes, our strength will ooze from us, and we will be like Samson when shorn of his locks. All we can say to God is, "O Lord, revive thy work in the midst of the years."

—G. F.

There is no hope for true prayer and intercession for revival unless we realise that there is a need.

D. MARTYN LLOYD-JONES

Arguments for Holiness

But as he which hath called you is holy,
so be ye holy in all manner of conversation.

I PETER 1:15

The Holy Spirit presents a very strong case for the holiness of the believer in this verse. Let us not be afraid of the word *holiness*. It is a Scriptural word, though often misrepresented and misapplied. God wants His people to be a holy people. Peter argues first from the holiness of God Himself: "Be ye holy; for I am holy" (v. 16). Likeness to God is holiness. Conformity to the image of His Son is God's purpose of love for His people. How much of that likeness, that beauty of Christ, is seen in each of us? Are we indeed living epistles seen and read of all men?

The second motive for holiness that Peter brings to our attention is the happiness of the soul. Notice the word *wherefore* at the beginning of verse 13. It leads us back to the subject upon which the apostle had previously been discoursing—the happiness of the soul in anticipation of its glorious inheritance (vv. 3-5). Happiness and holiness are united. God is infinitely happy because He is infinitely holy. Likewise, a holy Christian is a happy Christian. The truth is that there can be no happiness hereafter unless we have holiness here (Heb. 12:14).

Finally, Peter focusses our attention on the hope of Christ's coming as a motive to holiness. "Seeing then that all these things shall be dissolved, what manner of persons ought ye to be in all holy conversation and godliness" (II Pet. 3:11). Let us labour through grace that we be not ashamed at His coming.

—R. J. B.

I often pray, "Lord, make me as
holy as a pardoned sinner can be."
ROBERT MURRAY MCCHEYNE

Endued to Stand

The Lord is with thee, thou mighty man of valour.

JUDGES 6:12

When the Lord called Gideon, He addressed him not as he was, but as he would be by the power of grace. Until this point, all we know of Gideon is that he threshed wheat to hide it from the Midianites. That was a lowly task, though it did take some courage to defy the power of Midian by withholding his wheat from them. But it was a small action of defiance, one that was necessitated by widespread need and hunger. There were no other heroic deeds to Gideon's name up to this time. He had taken no stand publicly against the prevailing Baal worship in Israel. He was virtually unknown, a most unlikely candidate for the position of national deliverer. But God made him a chosen vessel and guaranteed to give him the power to do His will.

Men may not perceive in us much sign of greatness. We may well be discouraged from undertaking some service for the Lord because we ourselves feel that we are very ordinary. Yet grace can make every weak Gideon into a "mighty man of valour." Our personal weakness, our lack of past experience, even our past failures are no valid reason to avoid doing the will of God now.

When the Lord calls, He will equip. Gideon was never sent forth to do a work for God without the gift of divine grace and power sufficient to enable him to do all the Lord called him to do. Who could have foreseen that the Lord would take a struggling monk in remote Germany to launch the Reformation? Who would have thought that He would use the untutored John Bunyan to give the world the greatest of Christian classics? Or who could possibly have dreamed that He would have employed four young rustics to bring about Ulster's great 1859 Revival? Who can tell what He will do through us if we but do His bidding?

—A. C.

The world has yet to see what God can do
with and for and through and in a man who
is fully and wholly consecrated to Him.
HENRY VARLEY

352

An Orderly Church

Let all things be done decently and in order.

I CORINTHIANS 14:40

Paul wrote his first Corinthian epistle to correct certain problems among the believers there. He addressed their spiritual *carnality* and *conceit*. In chapter 14 he reproves the *confusion* of their church services.

The first problem was with the *linguists*. Corinth was a melting pot of nationalities, a cosmopolitan city, a crossroads of many trade routes. Because of its diversity, many people were speaking publicly in the church in their own languages, which could not be understood by others in the congregation, and doing it while others were already speaking. The result was chaos and misunderstanding.

Then the *learned* added to the confusion, giving public expositions and overlapping one another in competing for the listeners' attention. Add to this the problem of the *ladies*, who sat separate from their husbands and who were shouting to their spouses for clarification on the different speakers' expositions.

The whole lot added up to bedlam in the Corinthian church, hence Paul's gracious appeal for order. He counselled that not more than three speakers with a foreign language should speak at a service, and always with an interpreter present for the benefit of those who did not understand that speech.

Similarly, the learned prophets should speak consecutively, and if the women had some questions, they were advised to ask their husbands at home. Paul closed the chapter with a strong appeal for discipline: "Let all things be done decently and in order."

This rule applies also to the individual Christian. He is not to live a disorderly, muddled life, as many seem to do. Jesus chose *disciples*. A disciple is simply a disciplined believer, one who is disciplined in daily Bible study, in frequent prayer, in attendance at the house of God, and in the practical duties of the Christian life. May God help us today to live in a disciplined manner, as disciples of Christ.

—F. McC.

Man's practices are the best indexes of his principles.
STEPHEN CHARNOCK

353

A Time To Weep

Oh that my head were waters, and mine eyes a fountain of tears.
JEREMIAH 9:1

Some tears are childish and petty. At times we weep in bitterness when we would do better to humbly accept the will of God. Such grief indicates our weakness and should be put away as useless and spiritually destructive.

There are, however, tears that are "the index of strength," to use Spurgeon's phrase. Tears of repentance are not signs of weakness. He who has never penitently wept before the Lord for his sin has seen neither the depths of his own heart nor the glory of God's holiness. Oh! that we could weep over our sins! Oh! that our God would remove our tolerance to sin and our insensitivity to the things of the Spirit! Oh! that He would so break our hearts that we may not only weep over sin and failure but with full purpose of soul repudiate them and overcome them!

Do we not need to weep over the slaughter that is taking place all around us? "The slain of the daughter of my people" are very numerous. Can Christians go on watching the spread of death and destruction by drugs, drunkenness, terrorism, and wanton violence without crying out to God from the depths of broken hearts? Have we become so inured to the sights and sounds of constant tragedy that we have forgotten how to weep?

If we should weep over slain bodies, how much more should we weep over slain souls? We live in the midst of a world that is like the valley of bones in Ezekiel's vision. Let us not look on men's outward appearance. Let us consider their souls. We dare not dismiss immortal souls from our thoughts because of their colour, or creed, or social status. Oh! for eyes to see the desperate need of Christless souls! May the Lord make us, like Jeremiah, mighty weepers over lost souls.

—A. C.

> If I weep for that body from whom the soul
> is departed, how much more should I weep
> for that soul from whom God hath departed.
> AUGUSTINE

Escape from Guilt

Have mercy upon me, O God.　　　　PSALM 51:1

Escaping the oppressive burden of guilt is one of the greatest problems we all face. As Christians we rejoice, knowing that because we are justified freely by God's grace on the merits of Jesus Christ, the guilt of our sin is gone and we stand before God legally righteous. Nothing can alter that acceptance and legal position. Yet in daily experience we sin, and the feeling of guilt over offending our Lord overwhelms us. That conviction by God's Spirit is good, but God does not want us to wallow in despair over our sin. He desires that we experience the joy of salvation. Psalm 51, David's prayer of confession, shows us the way to escape guilt.

Although David was conscious of the magnitude of his sin, he knew that God was ready to forgive. Rather than making some deal with God to work off his offence, he realized that forgiveness cannot be earned. That is the main lesson to learn. Too often when we feel the burden of our sin, we make certain vows to God that we will do this or that if He will just forgive us one more time. Pleas for forgiveness must appeal to God. David's asking for mercy indicates his awareness that forgiveness is a matter of grace. He could offer no argument from his own character; grace is divine favour based in God's character. Although no man can obligate God to be gracious, He has obligated Himself by covenant to be gracious to His people. When David appealed to the Lord's lovingkindness, he had the guarantee of forgiveness. David knew what we should know—that if we confess our sins, God is faithful to forgive. We escape from guilt by fleeing to God's grace, loyalty, and compassion.

—M. P. V. B.

Release! Signed in tears, sealed in blood!
The black ink of the indictment is written
all over with the red ink of the cross.
T. DeWitt Talmage

Unanswered Prayer

Ye ask, and receive not, because ye ask amiss.

JAMES 4:3

As believers in the Lord Jesus Christ, our greatest privilege on earth is fellowship with God. We have "boldness and access with confidence" (Eph. 3:12) through the merits of Christ. As we come into the presence of God in prayer, we have "exceeding great and precious promises" (II Pet. 1:4) that direct us how to pray and assure us that God's ears are open to our cry (Psa. 34:15). To obtain answers to our prayers from our heavenly Father should be as natural to us as it is for children to receive good things from their earthly fathers (Matt. 7:11).

But many of our prayers go unanswered. Why? God cannot deny His promise. He is faithful (II Tim. 2:13). So why do we suffer from powerlessness in prayer? James chapter 4 gives many of the answers.

The first reason for an absence of answers is an absence of real praying: "Ye have not, because ye ask not" (v. 2). Some people are so indefinite in their petitions to God that they would not recognize an answer if it came!

The second reason for unanswered prayers is sinful division among God's people. "Wars and fightings" (v. 1) among Christians who are supposed to gather with one accord to pray will always hinder prayer.

Another reason is a covetous, grasping, worldly spirit: "Ye lust, and have not: ye kill, and desire to have, and cannot obtain" (v. 2). Such people "ask amiss" (v. 3). God does not answer their selfish cries, for they would waste His benefits on carnal lusts. Those who are more interested in any worldly thing than they are in spiritual things cannot pray with power. Let us ponder our prayer lives today and clear away the things that cause our prayers to go unanswered.

—A. C.

There is nothing tells the truth about us as Christians so much as our prayer life.
D. Martyn Lloyd-Jones

When Little Is Better

*Better is little with the fear of the Lord
than great treasure and trouble therewith.*

PROVERBS 15:16

God has said that His thoughts are not our thoughts, nor His ways our ways (Isa. 55:8). Today's text demonstrates this truth. Nothing appears to be so contrary to the economic philosophy of the average man as does the opening statement of this verse. Man can never have enough. The nearest man can come in his thinking to this divine rule is "A little more is better."

Treasure is gained at great cost and maintained at even greater cost. Those who labour to obtain it must labour more to retain it. Thus they become the slave to their treasure. They serve it rather than it serving them.

As a little salt excites the taste buds and so heightens the enjoyment of our food, so the fear of the Lord enables a little of this world's goods to yield satisfaction and contentment. The fear of the Lord yields life and good days and ought therefore to be learned by all (Psa. 34:11-12).

The lust for great possessions in this life invariably yields great heartache. "They that will be rich fall into temptation and a snare, and into many foolish and hurtful lusts, which drown men in destruction and perdition. For the love of money is the root of all evil: which while some coveted after, they have erred from the faith, and pierced themselves through with many sorrows" (I Tim. 6:9-10). With their treasure they inherit great "trouble." The word that is used, *mehumah*, is a very strong word meaning "destruction," or "vexation" (Isa. 22:5).

Whatever measure of this world's goods providence has allotted to us, be sure of this: it is enough. "But godliness with contentment is great gain. For we brought nothing into this world, and it is certain we can carry nothing out. And having food and raiment let us be therewith content" (I Tim. 6:6-8). Why treasure that for which there is no use in heaven? —I. F.

**A crown of gold cannot cure the headache: no more
can honour or riches quiet and still the conscience.**
THOMAS BROOKS

357

Electing Love

As it is written, Jacob have I loved, but Esau have I hated.

ROMANS 9:13

See here sovereign mercy! We are not surprised that God left Esau to be an object of His wrath. We can understand why God, in the counsels of eternity, would pass over those who had sinned "in Adam" and leave them as objects of divine justice. But the thing that overwhelms the mind are those words, *Jacob have I loved.* Did not Jacob sin in Adam? Was not Jacob born in sin? Did not Jacob connive and deceive many a time in order to gain position or wealth? Why then did God set His affections on this man?

Paul answers, "That the purpose of God according to election might stand, not of works, but of him that calleth" (Rom. 9:11). So there was nothing in Jacob that drew forth God's love, not even some foreseen virtue or grace. The reason God loved Jacob is to be found in His own sovereign and eternal purpose. "The Lord did not set his love upon you," Moses told Israel, "nor choose you, because ye were more in number than any people . . . but because the Lord loved you" (Deut. 7:7, 8). The Lord says, in essence, "I chose to redeem you because I loved you, and I loved you because I loved you."

What a death blow this truth is to man's pride! How humbling it is to know just how unlovely we were in God's eyes! He saw sin's "wounds, and bruises, and putrifying sores" (Isa. 1:6) blackening our souls, certainly nothing to bring down His redeeming love. But simply because it pleased Him He declared, "I will love them freely" (Hos. 14:4). How this melts the heart of stone! When choosing His people, why did God not pass you by? Why did He not leave you to your sin, sorrow, and eternal destruction? The answer lies hidden with God. We do best to leave it there! But, thank God, He has loved us with an everlasting love! May we lay ourselves low before His throne today and offer up our praise, our love, and our service.

—J. W.

O, my brethren, be humbled under the sovereignty of God.
ROBERT MURRAY McCHEYNE

Ready for Battle

Hast thou given the horse strength?
hast thou clothed his neck with thunder?

JOB 39:19

These words form part of the Lord's description to Job of the war horse of bygone times. Note in passing that the children of Israel were not encouraged to retain many of these noble animals, as they were always associated with earthly power and might. God's ancient people were to turn from such and rest solely upon Him. As it was then, so it is today. Salvation is of the Lord, and power belongeth unto Him. Rest not in worldly works or deeds to justify. Only Christ can save and keep and deliver.

Nevertheless, the picture presented here in Job is of a magnificent animal, to be admired and honoured. The war horse was beautiful in appearance, attractive to the eye, of noble bearing, and possessing a lively intelligence. As it served its rider, so we who are redeemed should serve Christ. In ancient conflicts, one of the most imposing sights on earth was the cavalry lined up for the charge of war—the riders armed for battle, the standards fluttering in the breeze, and the horses bedecked with colour, heads plumed and hooves pawing the ground with impatience. These powerful beasts were not only instinctively aware of the atmosphere of battle and of the proximity of the foe, they were ready for the fray. In our Christian life we wrestle not against flesh and blood, but against principalities and powers. Our spiritual enemies are very near, and the battle lines are drawn. May we, like the war horse, be ready for the conflict, ever going forth in the strength of our King. Our spiritual warfare will end in glorious victory. In Revelation 19 we have the final mention of the war horse in Scripture. The Lord Jesus Christ's return is symbolized by John's vision of Him riding a white charger. Then will He be acknowledged by all as King of Kings and Lord of Lords. May we be there to share in His triumph.

—S. B. C.

It is impossible to be a true soldier
of Jesus Christ and not fight.
J. GRESHAM MACHEN

The Virgin Birth of Christ

Behold, a virgin shall conceive, and bear
a son, and shall call his name Immanuel.

ISAIAH 7:14

The incarnation of the Son of God was the mightiest miracle ever wrought on earth. No words can describe it. No mind but God's can comprehend the depths of the mystery of the union of God and man in two distinct natures and one person. It was a miracle of love, for it was our salvation. Athanasius, the great defender of orthodoxy against Arianism, said, "Christ became what we are that He might make us what He is." What wondrous love!

The incarnation was effected by the virgin birth. All the attempts to lessen the Bible truth that Jesus was born of a virgin have utterly failed. By the supernatural action of the Holy Spirit, the humanity of Jesus was made of the substance of the Virgin Mary. Our Lord had no biological father. His body was specially prepared by God (Heb. 10:5). Thus He did not inherit Adam's sin. He was sinless in His birth as well as in His life. He was as free from original sin as from actual transgression. But His humanity was a real humanity. Though without sin, He was not without feeling. The Lord Jesus was a real man who was tempted in all points as we are, apart from any lust from inbred sin, and is therefore able to help us when we are tempted.

The result of the incarnation is God with us, for that is the meaning of *Immanuel* (Matt. 1:23). He is with us as our Saviour and our Sustainer. He is with us as our Fellow and our Friend. He is with us now and forever. And because He is with us, we will surely go to be with Him.

—A. C.

The God who took a motherless woman out of the side of a man took a fatherless man out of the body of a woman.
MATTHEW HENRY

Redemption Revealed

He shall glorify me: for he shall receive
of mine, and shall shew it unto you.

JOHN 16:14

Christianity has the secret of all knowledge. The Spirit's work of bestowing spiritual enlightenment is imperative to an experimental knowledge of Christ. If a gold coin were buried in a particular spot in a field, what it was and where it was may be a mystery to you. But if the person who hid it should lead you to the spot and remove the topsoil, thereby showing the coin to you, it would no longer be a mystery. The mystery would have been revealed. Likewise the gospel is a revealed miracle to those whom the Spirit of God enlightens. His work is to remove the filth of the world from before your eyes and reveal Christ unto you.

This aspect of the gospel humbles the pride of the wise and gives hope to the simplest. "So then it is not of him that willeth, nor of him that runneth, but of God that sheweth mercy" (Rom. 9:16). If Christ is now the object of your faith, then praise Him for the sovereign operation of the blessed Spirit in your heart. Give praise that He has given you "the spirit of wisdom and revelation in the knowledge of him: the eyes of your understanding being enlightened" (Eph. 1:17, 18).

More can be done for the kingdom of God in one day if the Holy Spirit reveals Christ to darkened souls than a thousand preachers could accomplish in a lifetime without His operation. "It is the spirit that quickeneth; the flesh profiteth nothing" (John 6:63). Pray that the Holy Spirit will glorify Christ by revealing Him in all His saving power unto men who have been left sightless and hopeless in the sin of this world.

—I. G.

Though Christ merits grace *for us*, it
is the Holy Ghost that works it *in us*.
THOMAS WATSON

Excuses

The slothful man saith, There is a lion
without, I shall be slain in the streets.

PROVERBS 22:13

The making of idle excuses is the oldest, as it is the commonest, of sins. Adam was the first to take up the occupation. As the Puritan John Trapp quaintly put it, "Sin and shifting came into the world together." Few things are more often on human lips than excuses. Men continually excuse themselves from doing what they know in their hearts they ought to do.

Thomas Fuller rightly points out that "bad excuses are worse than none." How adept men are at creating such excuses! So it is here. The streets are not the haunt of wild beasts. It would be a very extraordinary thing indeed for them to be found there. It is in the darkness of the night, as the psalmist tells us, "wherein all the beasts of the forest do creep forth. The young lions roar after their prey, and seek their meat from God. The sun ariseth, they gather themselves together, and lay them down in their dens" (Psa. 104:20-22). This was only an excuse. Ah, child of God, what of our excuses? Has there been a "lion" in the way to the house of God—to the throne of grace—to the Scriptures of truth?

Beware of making excuses. They too easily become habitual. Tomorrow that duty you put off will be less thought of and still more easily let along. What a lack of honesty with ourselves, in the making of our excuses! As C. H. Spurgeon said, "You cannot quite extinguish your conscience, which is the candle of the Lord, and therefore you put it under the bushel of an excuse." Oh, let us examine our excuses in the searching light of the judgment seat of Christ. There no excuses will be heard; none will be attempted!

—M. P.

He that is good at making excuses
is seldom good at anything else.
BENJAMIN FRANKLIN

Grace More Abundant

He giveth more grace.

JAMES 4:6

God supplies the needs of His people "according to his riches in glory by Christ Jesus" (Phil. 4:19). The inexhaustible fulness of Christ is the measure of His giving to His people. Giving does not impoverish Him. Our needs do not stretch His resources. However much and however frequently He gives to us, He has always much more to give. His grace is greater than our need. God's grace is greater than our sin. It is more powerful than our depravity. Our sin brought us under condemnation, but God's grace is stronger and can keep us from falling (Jude 24). By grace, through faith in Christ, even the weakest Christian can overcome the dominion of inbred sin and live a holy life. And that same grace is quick to lift us up when we fall. Sin can never defeat grace in a Christian.

God's grace is greater than all our burdens and cares. He gives strength when we are weak. He draws alongside to help us when our trials would crush us. He directs us by His Word when we need wisdom. He reveals Himself to us in blessed fellowship when we seek His face and sustains us when earthly friends forsake us. He makes us happy in Christ whatever our prevailing circumstances. He whispers, "My grace is sufficient for thee" (II Cor. 12:9), and calms the storms that buffet our souls.

This all-sufficient grace will provide for us, protect us, strengthen us, and enable us to follow and serve Christ acceptably. It will carry us through every valley—even the valley of the shadow of death—and present us faultless at our Father's throne.

Rejoice, Christian! God's giving has only begun!

—A. C.

**God's grace is sufficient for us
anywhere His providence places us.**
ANONYMOUS

A Safe Retreat

I will be an enemy unto thine enemies.

EXODUS 23:22

"He hadn't an enemy in the world." I wonder how often these words have been said of some departed soul. I am sure we have memories of those who have been commended in this way, and yet one wonders how truthful such an epitaph can be. He is a foolish man who seeks enemies, but he is a most unusual man who does not have an enemy in the world.

Certainly the Christian has those determined to oppose him. When we are right with God, we shall have many enemies. All who hate Christ will hate us, but this is surely to our credit. It can be no surprise that those who have proved hostile to the Master of the household will be hostile also to His servants.

Enemies we will have, but let us be sure that our enemies hate us for the truth's sake. "If ye suffer for righteousness' sake, happy are ye" (I Pet. 3:14). We must take care that every enemy is inspired to act against us "for righteousness' sake" and not because of any sinful attitude or wicked action on our part. Let us also see to it that we cherish no spirit of hatred towards our avowed enemies. In their darkness and bitterness, they are to be pitied and prayed for.

There is encouragement for us in the Lord's promise to Israel. When our enemies are His enemies, He will deal with them. That is the best protection of all. We are not left to fend for ourselves. Our defence and our deliverance are in God's hand, and there is no greater comfort than that!

—T. N.

You will not get leave to steal quietly to heaven in Christ's company without a conflict and a cross.
SAMUEL RUTHERFORD

A False Compass

*There is a way which seemeth right unto a
man, but the end thereof are the ways of death.*

PROVERBS 14:12

Naaman said, "I thought," and thus indicated that he had come to
Elisha with a false impression of what was to take place. He had
a preconceived notion of what the prophet would do in order to
heal him of his leprosy. He was utterly wrong. So wrong was he
that he remained a leper while he persisted in his mistaken views.

The Bible refers to two "ways." One is in our verse, the "way
which seemeth right." The other is Christ, the Way, the Truth, and
the Life. The former ends in death. The latter ends in life.

Under the guidance of the compass of reason, man will always
follow the way of death. It cannot be otherwise. It is for this cause
that men from every nation and every age, when they depart from
the truth of God, always, but always, follow the same downward
path. Romans 1:21-32 plots the course of a bygone apostasy. Every
departure from God that man has entered upon since then follows
this same path. It is the only course that can be plotted when the
compass of what "seemeth right unto a man" is employed.

It is not that the gospel is contrary to reason. Rather, man's
thinking is perverted by sin. It seems right but is not. Instruments
used in precise measurements must constantly be aligned with a
standardized norm. Otherwise utter confusion would reign among
architects, draftsmen, and technicians.

The aligning of human reason with divine reason takes place
with the regeneration of the soul by the Spirit of God. The mind
is enlightened, the eyes of the soul are focussed, and man's
faulty reasoning is brought into alignment with God's Word.
Regenerate man follows the path that is right, the path of life,
which as a light "shineth more and more unto the perfect day"
of heaven's life and liberty.

—I. F.

No man can understand spiritual
mysteries by carnal reason.
THOMAS BROOKS

The Best Is Yet To Be!

O Lord God, thou hast begun to shew thy
servant thy greatness, and thy mighty hand.

DEUTERONOMY 3:24

Moses spoke these words as he approached the end of his life. They are just as appropriate for us as we come to the end of a year. Indeed, whether we are facing the end of a year or the end of a lifetime, the testimony of our heart is that the Lord has done great things for us—but they are only the beginning of His kindness to us.

We can look back with gratitude. The Lord has never failed us. In the year that is now ending He has proved His constant watch-care over us. His wonderful works on our behalf "are more than can be numbered" (Psa. 40:5). Every second of our lives He has surrounded us with blessings.

Best of all, He has shown us His greatness. He has revealed something of His own glory to us. What blessed times we have had in prayer and in the Word, when the Lord has granted to us glimpses of His greatness! Perhaps He has done this in the last year in bringing some of us into salvation, or in leading others of us into revival. Let us then praise Him for such grace.

But all the Lord has done for us is just a beginning. The best is yet to be. The year is dying, but our God is living. "The Lord shall increase you more and more" (Psa. 115:14) is His promise. Thus we are assured that, whatever next year holds, "the path of the just . . . shineth more and more unto the perfect day" (Prov. 4:18). That *perfect day* means "the ages to come" in which He will "shew the exceeding riches of his grace in his kindness toward us through Christ Jesus" (Eph. 2:7).

Ring out the old year with praise! Ring in the new with confidence! If we live, we shall see more of the Lord's greatness. If we die, we shall see its full glory.

—A. C.

The believer's future is as bright as the
promises of God and as secure as His throne.
ALEXANDER SIMPSON

Contributors

The following is a full list of the contributors to these devotional readings. Each of them is recognized at the end of each of his contributions by his initials.

M. W. A. Dr. Mark W. Allison
Greenville, S.C.

S. B. Rev. Stanley Barnes
Hillsborough, N.I.

M. P. V. B. Dr. Michael P. V. Barrett
Greenville, S.C.

R. J. B. Rev. R. J. Beggs
Ballymena, N.I.

A. C. Rev. Alan Cairns
Greenville, S.C.

S. B. C. Dr. S. B. Cooke
Armagh, N.I.

D. C. Rev. David Creane
Lurgan, N.I.

J. D. Dr. John Douglas
Lisburn, N.I.

G. F. Rev. Gordon Ferguson
Kilkeel, N.I.

D. F. Rev. David Fletcher
Calgary, Alberta

I. F. Rev. Ivan Foster
Kilskeery, N.I.

J. G. Rev. John Greer
New Town Square, Pa.

I. G. Rev. Ian Goligher
Cloverdale, B.C.

F. McC. Dr. Frank McClelland
Toronto, Ontario

T. N. Rev. Timothy Nelson
Rasharkin, N.I.

M. P. Rev. Michael Patrick
Port Lincoln, S. Australia

J. W. Rev. John Wagner
Orlando, Fla.

R. J. W. Rev. Randall J. Worland
Indianapolis, Ind.

Calendar of Daily Bible Readings

by Robert Murray McCheyne

JANUARY

	Gen.	Matt.	Ezra	Acts
1	Gen. 1	Matt. 1	Ezra 1	Acts 1
2	2	2	2	2
3	3	3	3	3
4	4	4	4	4
5	5	5	5	5
6	6	6	6	6
7	7	7	7	7
8	8	8	8	8
9	9-10	9	9	9
10	11	10	10	10
11	12	11	Neh. 1	11
12	13	12	2	12
13	14	13	3	13
14	15	14	4	14
15	16	15	5	15
16	17	16	6	16
17	18	17	7	17
18	19	18	8	18
19	20	19	9	19
20	21	20	10	20
21	22	21	11	21
22	23	22	12	22
23	24	23	13	23
24	25	24	Est. 1	24
25	26	25	2	25
26	27	26	3	26
27	28	27	4	27
28	29	28	5	28
29	30	Mark 1	6	Rom. 1
30	31	2	7	2
31	32	3	8	3

FEBRUARY

	Gen.	Mark	Est.	Rom.
1	Gen. 33	Mark 4	Est. 9-10	Rom. 4
2	34	5	Job 1	5
3	35-36	6	2	6
4	37	7	3	7
5	38	8	4	8
6	39	9	5	9
7	40	10	6	10
8	41	11	7	11
9	42	12	8	12
10	43	13	9	13
11	44	14	10	14
12	45	15	11	15
13	46	16	12	16
14	47	Luke 1:1-38	13	I Cor. 1
15	48	1:39-80	14	2
16	49	2	15	3
17	50	3	16-17	4
18	Ex. 1	4	18	5
19	2	5	19	6
20	3	6	20	7
21	4	7	21	8
22	5	8	22	9
23	6	9	23	10
24	7	10	24	11
25	8	11	25-26	12
26	9	12	27	13
27	10	13	28	14
28	11-12:21	14	29	15

MARCH					APRIL			
1	Ex.12:22-51	Luke15	Job 30	I Cor.16	1	Lev. 4	Psa. 1-2	Prov. 19	Col. 2
2	13	16	31	II Cor. 1	2	5	3-4	20	3
3	14	17	32	2	3	6	5-6	21	4
4	15	18	33	3	4	7	7-8	22	I Thes. 1
5	16	19	34	4	5	8	9	23	2
6	17	20	35	5	6	9	10	24	3
7	18	21	36	6	7	10	11-12	25	4
8	19	22	37	7	8	11-12	13-14	26	5
9	20	23	38	8	9	13	15-16	27	II Thes. 1
10	21	24	39	9	10	14	17	28	2
11	22	John 1	40	10	11	15	18	29	3
12	23	2	41	11	12	16	19	30	I Tim. 1
13	24	3	42	12	13	17	20-21	31	2
14	25	4	Prov. 1	13	14	18	22	Eccl. 1	3
15	26	5	2	Gal. 1	15	19	23-24	2	4
16	27	6	3	2	16	20	25	3	5
17	28	7	4	3	17	21	26-27	4	6
18	29	8	5	4	18	22	28-29	5	II Tim. 1
19	30	9	6	5	19	23	30	6	2
20	31	10	7	6	20	24	31	7	3
21	32	11	8	Eph. 1	21	25	32	8	4
22	33	12	9	2	22	26	33	9	Tit. 1
23	34	13	10	3	23	27	34	10	2
24	35	14	11	4	24	Num. 1	35	11	3
25	36	15	12	5	25	2	36	12	Philemon
26	37	16	13	6	26	3	37	Song 1	Heb. 1
27	38	17	14	Phil. 1	27	4	38	2	2
28	39	18	15	2	28	5	39	3	3
29	40	19	16	3	29	6	40-41	4	4
30	Lev. 1	20	17	4	30	7	42-43	5	5
31	2-3	21	18	Col. 1					

MAY					JUNE			
1	Num. 8	Psa. 44	Song 6	Heb. 6	1	Deut. 5	Psa. 88	Isa. 33	Rev. 3
2	9	45	7	7	2	6	89	34	4
3	10	46-47	8	8	3	7	90	35	5
4	11	48	Isa. 1	9	4	8	91	36	6
5	12-13	49	2	10	5	9	92-93	37	7
6	14	50	3-4	11	6	10	94	38	8
7	15	51	5	12	7	11	95-96	39	9
8	16	52-54	6	13	8	12	97-98	40	10
9	17-18	55	7	Jas. 1	9	13-14	99-101	41	11
10	19	56-57	8-9:7	2	10	15	102	42	12
11	20	58-59	9:8-10:4	3	11	16	103	43	13
12	21	60-61	10:5-34	4	12	17	104	44	14
13	22	62-63	11-12	5	13	18	105	45	15
14	23	64-65	13	I Pet. 1	14	19	106	46	16
15	24	66-67	14	2	15	20	107	47	17
16	25	68	15	3	16	21	108-109	48	18
17	26	69	16	4	17	22	110-111	49	19
18	27	70-71	17-18	5	18	23	112-113	50	20
19	28	72	19-20	II Pet. 1	19	24	114-115	51	21
20	29	73	21	2	20	25	116	52	22
21	30	74	22	3	21	26	117-118	53	Matt. 1
22	31	75-76	23	I Jn. 1	22	27-28:19	119:1-24	54	2
23	32	77	24	2	23	28:20-68	119:25-48	55	3
24	33	78:1-37	25	3	24	29	119:49-72	56	4
25	34	78:38-72	26	4	25	30	119:73-96	57	5
26	35	79	27	5	26	31	119:97-120	58	6
27	36	80	28	II John	27	32	119:121-144	59	7
28	Deut. 1	81-82	29	III John	28	33-34	119:145-176	60	8
29	2	83-84	30	Jude	29	Josh.1	120-122	61	9
30	3	85	31	Rev. 1	30	2	123-125	62	10
31	4	86-87	32	2					

	JULY					AUGUST			
1	Josh. 3	Psa.126-128	Isa. 63	Matt.11	1	Judg. 15	Acts 19	Jer. 28	Mark 14
2	4	129-131	64	12	2	16	20	29	15
3	5-6:5	132-134	65	13	3	17	21	30-31	16
4	6:6-27	135-136	66	14	4	18	22	32	Psa.1-2
5	7	137-138	Jer. 1	15	5	19	23	33	3-4
6	8	139	2	16	6	20	24	34	5-6
7	9	140-141	3	17	7	21	25	35	7-8
8	10	142-143	4	18	8	Ruth 1	26	36 & 45	9
9	11	144	5	19	9	2	27	37	10
10	12-13	145	6	20	10	3-4	28	38	11-12
11	14-15	146-147	7	21	11	I Sam. 1	Rom. 1	39	13-14
12	16-17	148	8	22	12	2	2	40	15-16
13	18-19	149-150	9	23	13	3	3	41	17
14	20-21	Acts 1	10	24	14	4	4	42	18
15	22	2	11	25	15	5-6	5	43	19
16	23	3	12	26	16	7-8	6	44	20-21
17	24	4	13	27	17	9	7	46	22
18	Judg. 1	5	14	28	18	10	8	47	23-24
19	2	6	15	Mark 1	19	11	9	48	25
20	3	7	16	2	20	12	10	49	26-27
21	4	8	17	3	21	13	11	50	28-29
22	5	9	18	4	22	14	12	51	30
23	6	10	19	5	23	15	13	52	31
24	7	11	20	6	24	16	14	Lam. 1	32
25	8	12	21	7	25	17	15	2	33
26	9	13	22	8	26	18	16	3	34
27	10-11:11	14	23	9	27	19	I Cor. 1	4	35
28	11:12-40	15	24	10	28	20	2	5	36
29	12	16	25	11	29	21-22	3	Ezek. 1	37
30	13	17	26	12	30	23	4	2	38
31	14	18	27	13	31	24	5	3	39

	SEPTEMBER					OCTOBER			
1	I Sam. 25	I Cor. 6	Ezek. 4	Psa.40-41	1	I Kgs. 3	Eph. 1	Ezek.34	Psa. 83-84
2	26	7	5	42-43	2	4-5	2	35	85
3	27	8	6	44	3	6	3	36	86
4	28	9	7	45	4	7	4	37	87-88
5	29-30	10	8	46-47	5	8	5	38	89
6	31	11	9	48	6	9	6	39	90
7	II Sam. 1	12	10	49	7	10	Phil. 1	40	91
8	2	13	11	50	8	11	2	41	92-93
9	3	14	12	51	9	12	3	42	94
10	4-5	15	13	52-54	10	13	4	43	95-96
11	6	16	14	55	11	14	Col. 1	44	97-98
12	7	II Cor. 1	15	56-57	12	15	2	45	99-101
13	8-9	2	16	58-59	13	16	3	46	102
14	10	3	17	60-61	14	17	4	47	103
15	11	4	18	62-63	15	18	I Thes. 1	48	104
16	12	5	19	64-65	16	19	2	Dan. 1	105
17	13	6	20	66-67	17	20	3	2	106
18	14	7	21	68	18	21	4	3	107
19	15	8	22	69	19	22	5	4	108-109
20	16	9	23	70-71	20	II Kgs. 1	II Thes. 1	5	110-111
21	17	10	24	72	21	2	2	6	112-113
22	18	11	25	73	22	3	3	7	114-115
23	19	12	26	74	23	4	I Tim. 1	8	116
24	20	13	27	75-76	24	5	2	9	117-118
25	21	Gal. 1	28	77	25	6	3	10	119:1-24
26	22	2	29	78:1-37	26	7	4	11	119:25-48
27	23	3	30	78:38-72	27	8	5	12	119:49-72
28	24	4	31	79	28	9	6	Hos. 1	119:73-96
29	I Kgs. 1	5	32	80	29	10	II Tim. 1	2	119:97-120
30	2	6	33	81-82	30	11-12	2	3-4	119:121-144
					31	13	3	5-6	119:145-176

1	II Kgs.14	II Tim. 4	Hos. 7	Psa.120-122
2	15	Tit. 1	8	123-125
3	16	2	9	126-128
4	17	3	10	129-131
5	18	Philemon	11	132-134
6	19	Heb. 1	12	135-136
7	20	2	13	137-138
8	21	3	14	139
9	22	4	Joel 1	140-141
10	23	5	2	142
11	24	6	3	143
12	25	7	Amos 1	144
13	I Chr.1-2	8	2	145
14	3-4	9	3	146-147
15	5-6	10	4	148-150
16	7-8	11	5	Luke1:1-38
17	9-10	12	6	1:39-80
18	11-12	13	7	2
19	13-14	Jas. 1	8	3
20	15	2	9	4
21	16	3	Obadiah	5
22	17	4	Jonah 1	6
23	18	5	2	7
24	19-20	I Pet. 1	3	8
25	21	2	4	9
26	22	3	Micah 1	10
27	23	4	2	11
28	24-25	5	3	12
29	26-27	II Pet. 1	4	13
30	28	2	5	14

1	I Chr. 29	II Pet. 3	Micah 6	Luke15
2	II Chr. 1	I Jn. 1	7	16
3	2	2	Nah. 1	17
4	3-4	3	2	18
5	5-6:11	4	3	19
6	6:12-42	5	Hab. 1	20
7	7	II John	2	21
8	8	III John	3	22
9	9	Jude	Zeph. 1	23
10	10	Rev. 1	2	24
11	11-12	2	3	John 1
12	13	3	Hag. 1	2
13	14-15	4	2	3
14	16	5	Zech. 1	4
15	17	6	2	5
16	18	7	3	6
17	19-20	8	4	7
18	21	9	5	8
19	22-23	10	6	9
20	24	11	7	10
21	25	12	8	11
22	26	13	9	12
23	27-28	14	10	13
24	29	15	11	14
25	30	16	12-13:1	15
26	31	17	13:2-9	16
27	32	18	14	17
28	33	19	Mal. 1	18
29	34	20	2	19
30	35	21	3	20
31	36	22	4	21